RIGHT TO EDUCATION, WORK, AND WELFARE IN ISLAM

Mohammad Hashim Kamali

RIGHT TO EDUCATION, WORK, AND WELFARE IN ISLAM

THE ISLAMIC TEXTS SOCIETY

First published 2010 by
THE ISLAMIC TEXTS SOCIETY
MILLER'S HOUSE
KINGS MILL LANE
GREAT SHELFORD
CAMBRIDGE CB22 5EN
UNITED KINGDOM
www.its.org.uk

British Library Cataloguing-in-Publication Data.
A catalogue record for this book is available from the British Library.

ISBN: 978 1930682 58 6 cloth
ISBN: 978 1930682 59 3 paper

Printed and bound in Poland by Books Factory Ltd, CUKROWA 22, 71-004 SZCZECIN.

The publishers make every effort to ensure their products are safe for the purpose
for which they are intended. For more information, check the publishers' website or
contact the publishers' EU representative: Authorised Rep Compliance Ltd., Ground
Floor, 71 Lower Baggot Street, Dublin, D02 P593, Ireland,
www.arccompliance.com.

Note on the "Fundamental Rights and Liberties in Islam" Series

The present volume is the sixth in a seven volume series on "Fundamental Rights and Liberties in Islam: Principles and Applications" by Mohammad Hashim Kamali. The final volume will be: *Freedom of Movement, Citizenship, and Accountability: An Islamic Perspective*.

The revised order in which the seven titles are now being arranged reflects their division under the two categories of General Part, and Special Themes. Whereas the three books, namely *The Dignity of Man*; *Freedom, Equality and Justice*; and *Equity and Fairness in Islam* constitute the general part, the remaining four titles address the special themes and topics of fundamental rights and liberties. The previously published titles in the series are as follows:

Volume 1: *The Dignity of Man: An Islamic Perspective* (2002);
Volume 2: *Freedom, Equality and Justice in Islam* (2002);
Volume 3: *Equity and Fairness in Islam* (2005); and
Volume 4: *Freedom of Expression in Islam* (1997).
Volume 5: *Right to Life, Security, Privacy and Ownership in Islam* (2008);

The reader may be interested to know that *Freedom of Expression in Islam* contains separate chapters on freedom of religion, freedom of association, and a chapter also on blasphemy and apostasy.

ABOUT THE AUTHOR

Mohammad Hashim Kamali is the Founding Chairman and CEO of the International Institute of Advanced Islamic Studies (IAIS) Malaysia. He studied in the UK from 1969 to 1976 and obtained an LLM and a PhD in Law from the University of London. He was Professor of Islamic Law and Jurisprudence at the International Islamic University Malaysia (1985–2004), and also Dean of the International Institute of Islamic Though and Civilisation (ISTAC) from 2004 to 2006. Dr Kamali was previously Assistant Professor at the Institute of Islamic Studies, McGill University in Canada; he was a Visiting Professor at the Capital University, Ohio, and also at the Institute for Advanced Study (Wissenschaftskolleg) of Berlin. He was a member of the Constitution Review Commission of Afghanistan (2003) and also served as a UN expert on constitutional reform in the Maldives (2004). He advised on the new constitution of Iraq (2004–2005) and is currently on the UN Alliance of Civilisations Global Experts panel. He now serves on the boards of 13 local and international academic journals. Kamali has addressed over 130 national and international conferences, and he has published 17 books and over 140 academic articles. His books *Principles of Islamic Jurisprudence*; *A Textbook of Hadith Studies*; *Freedom of Expression in Islam*; and *Shariʿah Law: An Introduction* have been adopted as textbooks at leading English-speaking universities worldwide.

Contents

Acknowledgements

An early segment of my research on this volume was carried out during my one year of Fellowship at the Institute for Advanced Study Berlin, better known as Wissenschaftskolleg zu Berlin in 2000–2001. I went to Berlin with unfinished work on a larger project: Fundamental rights and liberties in Islam: principles and applications, which I had started much earlier and full time concentration was what I needed at the time. This was precisely what the Kolleg provided and I would like to acknowledge the welcome and support I received for my proposed work. I was awarded a Gerd Baucellius Fellowship grant which enabled me to be a full participant of the Kolleg activities, not to mention its efficient inter-library service, during my stay in the pleasant Grunewald area of Berlin where the Kolleg itself is located.

Although ten months were not long enough in which to complete my research on the larger project, I was able nevertheless to make significant progress on the various themes of my project. I would like to acknowledge the co-operation and support of the then Rector of the Institute, Professor Dr. Wolf Lepenies, and his efficient Deputy, Herr Joachim Nettleback, the Head Librarian, Ms Gesine Bottomly, and Head of the computer unit, Herr Hans G. Lindenberg.

My research on the larger project had actually begun as of 1983 when I won a strategic research award from the Canada Council for Humanities and Social Sciences and concentrated then on completing my book, *Freedom of Expression in Islam*, published initially in Kuala Lumpur (1995) and later by the Islamic Texts Society (ITS) of Cambridge in 1997. As of this writing, I have published four books on the various themes of fundamental rights and liberties and am now relieved to have completed the remaining three volumes , including the volume at hand, on the particular themes of that exceedingly wide-ranging project. I would like to take this opportunity to acknowledge the financial assistance also of Canada Council that covered one year of my research on the project in 1984–85.

The remaining portions of the work on the larger project, and on the present volume, were carried out largely at the International Islamic University Malaysia where I have been employed ever since 1985. My long-term association with this University has availed me of continuity to focus on my writings side by side with teaching and administrative work. During the last two years (July 2004–June 2006) I assumed increased administrative duties as Dean of the International Institute of Islamic Thought and Civilisation (ISTAC) where I also had the good fortune of having the assistance of a highly accomplished P.A., Mrs. Salmah Ahmad, and also of my Research Assistant, Mr. Nirwan Syafrin, who is currently engaged in completing his Ph.D studies at ISTAC. I take this opportunity to thank them both for their valuable assistance and support.

Lastly I would like to acknowledge with gratitude the generous cooperation and support of Fatima Azzam, Director of the ITS in this and all the other compendium volumes of this seven volume series. Her involvement and initiative in the detailed preparation of these publications has been truly heartwarming and meaningful. The fine quality of the ITS publications, their careful attention to editing and design provided me with strong incentives to continue my fruitful engagement with Fatima and her colleagues ever since 1989.

International Institute of Advanced Islamic Studies
Malaysia
September 2010

Introduction

This book develops an Islamic perspective on three selected areas of rights and liberties. Selecting the three themes of education, work and welfare in one volume is reflective partly of their relevance and complementarity to one another. They tend to share some common features in that all the three are welfare-oriented themes and tend in many ways to complement one another. A person who acquires education, whether generally or at the more advanced levels of specialisation, is also likely to stand in a better position to enter the workforce and offer his services to the community. Education is often a necessary ingredient of professional work even more so now than in earlier times when the range and variety of specialised knowledge were relatively limited. Progress in education often leads to parallel progress in the labour market. The era of science and technology has generated an ever-increasing demand for greater advances on both the education sector and the labour market.

The right to welfare assistance, which is the subject of the last chapter of this book, is similarly related to developments in the education and availability of skilled labour force that enable the individual to contribute more effectively to the welfare capabilities of the society and state. A welfare assistance scheme is naturally enriched by the financial resources of individuals who earn enough not only to cater for their own needs but also pay taxes and contribute to welfare funds such as pension and insurance.

A perusal of the welfare commitments of state in Islam as elaborated in the following pages leaves little doubt as to Islam's profound concern to care for the poor, the elderly, sick and invalid. Yet this basic commitment of the state to welfare has remained altogether less developed in the positive laws of contemporary governments in Muslim societies. Muslim leaders and governments in recent times have hardly paid much attention to their welfare commitments, and have on the whole failed to make this a major component of their policies and programmes. Basic evidence in the Qur'ān and *Sunnah* that is reviewed in the following pages conveys a firm commitment of both the individual and government to the promotion of knowledge, engagement in productive work, and giving welfare assistance to those who need it.

Islam's emphasis on eradication of poverty is also manifested in the moral substance of its teachings and its laws. Our examination of the relevant principles of Islam in the following pages, especially in regard to rights and obligations that govern family relations, taxation and methods of redistribution all point to the centrality of its welfare commitment. Thus it is not an exaggeration to single out citizens' welfare as a *raison d'être* of the existence of government in Islam.

Our review of early historical developments in each of the three areas of concern in the present volume also exhibits the degree of prominence that the Pious Caliphs gave to the education and welfare needs of the people. The welfare goals of government were followed at times both of scarcity and affluence, but more so when availability of material enabled the government to allocate resources to education and assistance to the poor, the sick and the invalid, to child benefit and family support. The Prophet, peace be upon him, the Pious Caliphs and their successors in the subsequent periods promoted education and social assistance in a variety of ways which has altogether left an authoritative legacy and precedent—as we shall have occasion to discuss. Yet with few exceptions, the dynastic rulers of subsequent periods and the medieval caliphate that continued over many centuries under the Abbasids and Ottomans departed from the early precedent on welfare themes. This pattern of contrasting developments might have been influenced by medieval society values where dynastic regimes began to pay more attention to military conquest, warfare and building of palaces rather than the basic rights and welfare needs of their citizens. Nor is this pattern of development, one might add, unique to Islamic history, as the history of almost all nations of those times tends to exhibit similar tendencies, and it was only after the major revolutions of the 18th and subsequent centuries that the citizens' rights to freedom and equality, democracy and constitutional rule found a place on the list of basic commitments of states. But even then, it seems that the emphasis was initially on personal rights of the individuals of concern mainly to equality and the rule of law and protection against oppressive rule that topped the list—rather than the citizen's welfare as such.

A significant advancement of the idea of the welfare state in Europe really features in the post WWII period. Yet by this time European colonialism had subjugated and colonised much of the Muslim World in the Middle East, Asia and Africa. Colonialism marked a persistent, one might say merciless, exploitation of the poorer sections of humanity and this was not the time that Muslim countries could pay much attention to constitutional governance, basic rights and welfare needs of their citizens. It was also during these times when unprecedented wealth poured in from the colonies that enhanced Europe's capabilities to advance its welfare state programmes—aided, of course, by the industrial revolution and its wealth generation potentials. Then the struggle for independence through both peaceful means and warfare engaged the Muslim nations for several decades to come, which naturally sapped their vitality and resources. Nationalist agendas of mobilising the people against colonial powers became a major preoccupation of the subjugated nations that could consequently not address themselves to their welfare commitments. This pattern of the inability of the have-nots continues to this day as the vast majority of them still remain unable to take the idea of welfare state, education and employment to significant heights. Major progress on citizen welfare programmes is largely a question of affordability and means. These continue to be limited in most present day Muslim countries, and indeed are in short supply for the vast majority of Third World countries at the dawn of 21st century.

All statistical evidence we have seen in recent decades tends to confirm the grim reality that both absolute poverty and the gap between the poor and rich nations have increased at a rapid pace. This naturally does not bode well for the basic rights and welfare prospects of the developing nations, including the vast majority of Muslim nations. The scale of tension and discontent over disparities in wealth and international trade regulations, and the most recent turn for the worse over international terrorism, do not make those prospects look any better for the foreseeable future.

Yet it is essential nevertheless to focus on what in the final analysis is of great importance for people's wellbeing in the Muslim world, areas of concern where law and government and advocacy of basic rights have remained underdeveloped and where much uncertainty has prevailed as a result of persistent neglect of the basic principles of Islam. There is also much misinformation about Islam and its basic humanitarian principles that enhance humanity's common objectives to improve the people's rights wherever they may be.

Education and pursuit of knowledge, being the subject of the first Chapter in this volume is both a right and also a choice from the Islamic perspective. It is a right of all school age children to be provided with basic education, especially with reference to the fundamentals of Islam, and there is a corresponding obligation, as our analysis will show, on the part of the family and the state, to provide and facilitate children's education. Yet it will be noted at the outset that our discussion of education from the Islamic perspective is not strictly confined to a religious or a juristic framework of seeing education strictly as a right or a liberty, but goes beyond this framework. To some extent, this is suggested by the nature and scope of our subjects: knowledge (*'ilm*) and education (*ta'lim*) in Islam, or in any major world tradition for that matter, extend far beyond the scope of juristic questions, as knowledge as such cannot be easily reduced to addressing contemporary issues of concern, to a juristic framework alone. The scope of our discussion thus stretches to questions over the persistent bifurcation of education, in most Muslim countries, into the two streams of religious knowledge and scientific knowledge. It is noted in this regard that the discourse of the *'ulamā'* and educationists in the present day Muslim countries is not focused on rights and liberties as such. And then the question of compatibility or otherwise of religion and science inevitably brings us face to face with the prevailing methods and programmes of the school and university education in the Muslim world. We shall also review the attempted reforms in Muslim countries with a view to bring harmony between the Islamic and western perspectives on education. We will note that the western methods of public education have been widely adopted and utilised almost everywhere in the Muslim world. The challenges that Muslim countries are faced with in this area tend to go beyond the juristic framework of rights and liberties. An effort has been made, nevertheless, to explore the juristic aspects of education as a basic right, or a liberty and the extent of the state and community's responsibilities as the case may be. The wider approach to the study of education we have taken is also suggested by our readings of the source evidence in the Qur'ān and *Sunnah* as well as the more philosophical issues of concern to our understanding of the subject in its contemporary context.

Early developments in Islamic education are distinguished by a twin emphasis on religion, due mainly to the emphatic language of the Qur'ān on *'ilm*, and the other is the mosque as a place both of worship and learning. The first of these also implied a degree of emphasis on the learning of Arabic as the lingua franca of Islamic education, and the other suggested a prominent role for the religious leaders and *ʿulamāʾ*. Both of these influences endorsed, in turn, the prominence of religious education, the knowledge of Islamic laws and values. The Qurʾān and Arabic have remained influential ever since and the concern to retain them as the basic groundings of education is manifested in our discussion of the classification of sciences by the *ʿulamāʾ* as we shall later elaborate. The religious underpinnings of *ʿilm* can also be seen in the *ʿulamāʾ's* attempt to evaluate acquisition of knowledge on the scale of *wājib, mandūb* and *mubāh* (obligatory, recommendable, permissible) and so forth, which we have covered in some details below.

Institutionalisation of education in modern schools and universities signified a certain shift away from the earlier pattern of the mosque-centred education although many of the larger institutions of learning in the Muslim world continued to combine the mosque as a place of worship, sermons, early literacy and education. This also helped the institutions of learning to maintain a certain level of contact and in-volvement with the local communities. The mosque remained in the meantime an important venue of literacy and religious education for Muslim children in the village-based communities. The charitable en-dowment (*waqf*) has historically played a significant role in institution-alised education. It is a pattern of development which endorsed the religious leanings of Islamic education, as we shall presently elaborate on.

Westernisation of public education in the Muslim world during the colonial period brought reformist ideas of the secular west, especially of its post-Enlightenment period, into a basically tradition-bound and theocentric educational system and the trend continued well into the 20th century. The basic model of a western style school remains intact in many Muslim countries to this day. A persistent duality in education between the traditional methods of Islamic education and the more secular patterns of the west entrenched itself and efforts to integrate the two streams into a unified and harmonious whole have showed but only limited success. This led to the development among Muslim educationists of a critical view of western education and prompted them to address problematics of the uneasy blend of the two methods. In almost every Muslim country, attempts were made at introducing piecemeal reforms into an otherwise westernised models of school and university education. The purpose was to revise both the methods and curricular contents of public education in the wake of a general dissatisfaction that wholesale importation of western methods had the overall effect of alienation of the Islamic heritage and values.

The Islamic revivalism of the latter part of 20th century prompted Muslim educationists to review and evaluate their teaching methods at various levels and organised a series of international conferences to that effect. One of the outcomes of these efforts was the emergence of Islamic Universities that were intended to harmonise and amalgamate the best methods of education, both Islamic and western, into integrated formulas and also to use English and Arabic as their principal mediums of instruction. It seems that these efforts are yielding some results, yet it may still be too early for these limited reforms to overcome the long-standing problem of integration of traditional and modern institutionalised education. When we compare, for example, a *madrasah* with a modern school, one is still struck by the differentials in the basic philosophy and outlook of the two systems. Efforts to reduce the differences are, however, continuing at varying levels of intensity and scope in many Muslim countries.

On the one hand, there is the concern to integrate the best of traditional values and methods in public education. On the other hand, there is the desire to achieve parallel progress in the scientific components of education. Since the modern scientific knowledge owes much to Western academia, western university textbooks in science disciplines and certain areas of social sciences still feature prominently in the course coverage of all universities, including the more conservative Islamic ones. But the basic sense of unease in combining Western scientific curriculum with traditional Islamic texts is not expected to be easily overcome.

This also brings us face to face with the debate over religion and science, secularity and tradition. Questions arise whether the basically theocentric Islamic education that emphasises integration of revealed knowledge with human sciences is not fully compatible with the secularist premises of modern science. This would further explain our attempt below to review a cross-section of Muslim opinion on the compatibility or otherwise of religion and science. For there is a view, which we have explored in some detail, that Islam is for the most part accommodative of scientific knowledge.

Work (*ʿamal*) being the subject of chapter two of this volume is also an engaging theme, and somewhat like education, is a multi-faceted subject that is by nature not confined to a juristic context and debate. Apart from the various definitions that are available for work, as are reviewed in the following pages, one of the issues addressed is also to draw a functional distinction respectively between the religious and economic dimensions of work in Islam. A perusal of the Qur'ān and *Sunnah* on this subject that is attempted at the outset tends to underscore the religious connotations of work, even though the Qur'ān also refers on many occasions to work as an agent of productivity and wealth. A typical Qur'ānic reference to *ʿamal* occurs in combination with the word *ṣāliḥāt*, that is, upright works often associated with piety and *ʿibādah*. Yet a closer examination of the source evidence shows that upright work need not be confined to the religious context. We have explained that the Qur'ānic phraseology and reference to the subject are indicative of a broader perspective on work. This aspect of Islam's viewpoint is also manifested in the *ḥadīth* wherein all good work, be it actual or verbal, manual or skilled, professional work, intellectual exertion, indeed all beneficial work tends to carry some spiritual merit and reward, and could therefore be known as *ʿamal ṣāliḥ*. This was also a part of Islam's effort to elevate the public image of work amidst the somewhat derogatory connotations that medieval Arab society attached to manual as well as certain other varieties of labour. A robust attitude to work that is taken in the Qur'ān and *Sunnah* marked a departure in many ways from the customary dimensions of manual labour that was assigned mainly to the slaves. Work in Islam is also shown as an extension of the personality and self-image of a Muslim and a source of his dignity in the eyes of God the Most High. This attitude-building effort is a significant dimension of our reading of the textual data of Islam on this subject.

Somewhat like education, Muslims scholars have attempted to evaluate work on the five-point scale of values ranging from work that is obligatory to that which is forbidden and *ḥarām*. The in-between categories of recommendable, neutral and reprehensible, which tend to occupy a much wider range, both within and outside religion, is once again reflective of the religious groundings and implications of all work in Islam. Our review of the juristic discourse of the *fuqahā* in an historical context also conveys a civilisational perspective on work that is value-oriented and helps develop a sense of goal and purpose on the choice of work. The customary outlook on work is not only often manifested in the attitude of individuals and societies but also in the juristic evaluation of work. The attitude of the Arab society and culture seem to be reflected, for example, in the parts of our discussion that compare the merits and demerits of trading activity with agricultural work, and of both of these, in turn, with the work of a learned scholar and judge. Although references to the medical profession, astronomy and mathematics occur from time to time, references to science and technology tend to occur in the more recent writings of Muslim jurists and commentators. Modern discourse on work-related themes thus tends to highlight the more objective aspects of the source evidence on *'amal*. All work that is of benefit to humanity, including work outside the sphere of religion, is thus subsumed under meritorious work that partakes in the Qur'ānic conception of *'amal ṣāliḥ*, which may well constitute a *farḍ kifā'ī* (a collective obligation), praiseworthy or recommendable work (*mandūb*), and even work that may form a personal obligation (*farḍ 'ayn*) for a Muslim jurist and man of science.

In a section that discusses Islamic work ethics below, we also examine the source guidelines on trustworthiness (*amānah*) and commitment to what is conveyed in a number of *ḥadīth*s to that effect. Work so undertaken should be done well and should aspire to perfection. The employer and employee are both expected to be fair to one another, and both are, in turn, advised to avoid promoting self-interest at the expense of the common good of society. The kind of trade union practices that put the community in hardship in order to promote partisan interests is not encouraged and may even be banned in extreme situations. The employer and government are strongly advised to promote a fair work regime that is observant not only of the best values of Islam, but also of the approved custom of society, and that is conducive to the smooth flow of market activities.

Considerations of honesty and fairness that constitute an integral part of the Islamic ethos must be manifested in the regulatory regime of the market place, normal flow of supply and demand, and a watchful eye on wages and commodity prices. What is a fair wage and a fair market price are the questions that feature in the writings of Muslim scholars of both earlier and modern times as we shall later elaborate. The market inspector (*muḥtasib*), or one who is entrusted with his duties, is expected to ensure that the work place and the market are not exposed to distortion and deviation of the kind that violate normal trade and considerations of fairness. Yet both the government, and the *muḥtasib* are advised not to interfere in the normal flow of supply and demand, and also to avoid price control measures, as far as possible, but to intervene only to suppress profiteering and monopolistic practices that are deemed prejudicial and oppressive.

The question of fair wages has been raised and addressed in general terms in the basic evidence of *ḥadīth* when it specifies and enumerates that the workers' pay must be sufficient to cover his needs and those of his immediate dependants for food, clothes, shelter, transport and even marriage expenses, but adds the proviso that excessive demands which go beyond these legitimate needs partake in oppression. Evidence of this kind has enabled writers on modern Islamic economics to draw certain conclusions and raise the idea, for example, of the acceptability or otherwise of minimum wages from the Islamic perspective.

Our examination of the evidence in the Qur'ān and *Sunnah* and the *fiqh* rules also points to the conclusion that the state is under an obligation to provide employment opportunities for those who are capable and willing to work. This obligation also creates a corresponding right for the workers to be availed of the opportunity to work. Muslim jurists have drawn the conclusion that it is a personal obligation of able-bodied individuals to support themselves and their dependants, through lawful work. In the event they refuse to exert themselves, they lose their right to welfare assistance and may be pressurised to undertake suitable work. The obligation (*wājib*) of a fit person to support himself and his dependants through lawful work converts to a *mandūb* (recommendable) for able-bodied individuals who may have enough by which he and his family can survive, but it is still desirable for them to be occupied with productive work. In the case of skilled but unemployed individuals, the state bears a duty to provide them with the basic tools of trade to enable them to practise their line of work. Sustained professional work is highly recommended in Islam and often commands a spiritual ranking above the level of supererogatory *ʿibādah*.

The *fiqh* discourse pertaining to liability for loss, as reviewed in the following pages, examines aspects of negligence and its consequences to work-related accidents. In the event of proven negligence the worker may be faced with its consequences which may affect his entitlement to pay. Work that is abandoned prior to completion is governed by the rules of contract and the extent of unforeseen developments that might have hindered normal progress. A worker who signs a contract to dig a water well, for example, but hits on hard rock below the surface may be unable to accomplish the task, in which case he will be paid for the amount of work done regardless of completion or consequences to the employer. Unforeseen developments of this kind are partially governed by the rules of equity and fairness (*istiḥsān*). However unfinished work by a contractor who is proven to have been negligent or had an element of choice in the matter is often judged by the extent of its utility and benefit to the employer, which may entitle the worker to payment for the amount of work done. Most of the work-related disputes we have discussed in the following pages are covered under the *fiqh* rules pertaining to lease and hire (*ijārah*) and other relevant provisions of the law of contract.

Some of the rules of *fiqh* pertaining to contract may relate only in a general way to the now highly technical types of industrial works where determining the causes of failure to fulfil a contract may relate to a series of complex causes and factors, including faulty design, for example, that even the worker may not have known. There may be a range of factors that bear only a remote relationship to an *ijārah* contract. A fair regime of statutory law on labour relations that may address modern industrial and work-related disputes in a better way would on the whole be acceptable to the *Sharīʿah* as this area, being a part of civil transactions (*muʿamalāt*), is governed by rational consideration, laws and policies that serve the cause of justice and facilitate fair and reasonable methods of resolution of labour disputes.

There is evidence in *Sharīʿah* on workers' entitlement to a fair work regime and leisure that may be specified and articulated by reference to the nature and attributes of the work involved and also by reference to prevailing custom. The *Sharīʿah* only provides what may be seen as basic guidelines to the effect that the creative energy of workers must not be exhausted by excessive hours and difficult demands. A work regime that is supportive of the long-term prospects of productive work is thus within the contemplation of the guidelines that are reviewed in the following pages.

A section of our discussion on work also addresses the question of permissibility of workers' association and whether creating workers' unions may be seen as a complimentary aspect of a fair work regime. The *fiqh* evidence on this is not elaborate and answers to some basic questions in this regard are determined by reference to the utility or otherwise of workers' association to promotion of justice in the work place and whether it would be likely to enable the workers in various lines of industry and trade to have a say in the welfare aspects of their work. On these basic questions the *fiqh* discourse available is on the whole supportive of the workers right to association provided that they do not seek to jeopardise the common good nor inflict hardship on the community in which they operate. It may be added in this connection though that the rights of workers are not always expected to give way to the considerations of *maṣlaḥah*, and the common good of the community. The normal *Sharīʿah* guideline in such situations would be to reconcile the respective rights and interests of the workers and those of the larger community and encourage some adjustment on both sides. Only when the harm of a compromise approach outweighs its possible benefits, is a lesser harm tolerated in order to prevent a greater one, on whichever side such a solution may prove advantageous.

The last section of our discussion on work looks into the role and responsibility of the government to ensure a fair work regime that contemplates considerations of justice and *maṣlaḥah* for the workers and the community at large. Our reading of the general guidelines of *Sharīʿah* in this regard tends to assign a fairly active role to the government that is enhanced by a structure of obligations to ensure that it is not only an impartial bystander and referee but a proactive and, in many cases, an active partner in industry and trade. The state is expected to invest in beneficial industries and take policy measures to create employment opportunities. The government role and activity in this regard is not only regulated by the legal guidelines of *Sharīʿah* but also by extra-*Sharīʿah* considerations that may partake in *Sharīʿah*-oriented policy (*siyāsah sharʿiyyah*). The state is under a *Sharīʿah* obligation to fight poverty and oppression, ensure the availability of basic provisions and services, and take all appropriate measures to meet these objectives through supportive policies or active involvement in market activities.

It is generally understood that the state should encourage individual initiative in a market economy that is propelled by the creative energies of entrepreneurs, workers, partnerships and companies that allow and observe the natural flow of supply and demand and the state intervenes only when this is deemed to advance a *maṣlaḥah* (benefit) or prevent a real or perceived harm. The entire subject tends to be governed by rational policies and measures that fall under *siyāsah sharʿiyyah*. Even the regulated aspects of the *Sharīʿah* in this area partake on the whole in civil transactions (*muʿamalat*) on which the *Sharīʿah* itself maintains a fairly liberal regime of rules that are designed to give a wide scope for individual initiative. The *fiqh* rules support on the whole the people's freedom to choose their professions and play a role they determine for themselves in business activities and work. Only a set of basic prohibitions must be observed by both the individuals and governments to prevent usury, gambling, trading in unlawful substances, profiteering and unlawful occupations.

Beyond this somewhat limited range of prohibitions the basic position and guideline of *Sharīʿah* is one of permissibility (*ibāhah*) which is an integral part of the civil liberty of the individual that must be protected and observed by all parties concerned.

The last chapter of the present volume addresses welfare and the social support *(al-takaful al-ijtimāʿī)* aspects of the *Sharīʿah*, and it begins, as in the previous chapters, with a review of the source evidence in the Qur'ān and *Sunnah*. Our perusal of Islam's commitment to assisting the poor and the invalid, the orphans and the travellers and those afflicted by calamity and disease and even those who suffer from the burden of debt they cannot afford to pay shows the *Sharīʿah* on the whole to be unequivocally welfare-oriented and supportive. Our examination of the *fiqh* rules on other aspects of support within the family, among neighbours, and the community at large also endorses the assertive character of the textual guidelines on welfare.

The family support system is manifested through the regime of obligatory maintenance (*nafaqāt*) for close relatives, both male and female, and the rules that govern the *nafaqāt* are normally enforceable in the courts of justice. The laws of inheritance and bequest which are also legally enforceable similarly operate among relatives and tend to ensure a welfare-oriented system of redistribution within the family. The obligatory aspects of welfare and social support in the larger community are in turn manifested in the levy of specified portions of *zakāh* on personal wealth. *Zakāh* is a tax specifically intended to assist the poor and the indigent. The same may be said of the required charities of ʿ*Īd al-fiṭr* and ʿ*Īd al-aḍhā*, the two religious occasions in the Islamic calendar, one of which marks the end of the fasting month of Ramaḍān, and the other that of the *hajj* pilgrimage. Both the fast of Ramaḍān and the *hajj* are the proclaimed pillars of Islam and religious duties of all Muslims. Whereas the *zakāh* tax is levied on the yield of profitable assets, as well as the capital of certain other assets that are kept for one whole year, the *fiṭr* and *aḍhā* charities resemble a poll-tax which is levied on everyone, including women and children. They are deductible out of any assets the child might own or else the parents and guardians would have to pay on behalf of their minor wards. The *Sharīʿah* has thus envisaged a range of both obligatory and optional taxes and charities that are altogether fairly substantial and clearly indicative of Islam's commitment to a welfare programme.

Early historical developments, especially under the Pious Caliphs and some Umayyad leaders, confirm the strong welfare orientations of Islamic government to the extent that the state saw itself as an agent of redistribution and a bulwark of support to the poor. The public treasury (*bayt al-māl*), as a prominent institution of government, played a key role in its capacity as a collector and distributor of wealth in the community. A principle of distribution the *bayt al-māl* applied across the board was that taxes and charities collected were to be expended among the deserving parties in the same locality. Hence revenues collected from one locality or province were not to be transferred to another unless it was for some special reason to justify the transfer. The government saw itself, as understood from the statements of early caliphs such as ʿUmar I and ʿUmar II etc., as a custodian and trustee of the nation's wealth, an attitude which they exhibited in their personal dedication and piety to the extent of self-abnegation and a modest life style—lest they fell short of honouring the people's trust. Those pious leaders made a lasting impact through personal example which set a strong welfare-oriented precedent that reverberates to this day. Some pious caliphs went so far as to donate all their personal wealth to charitable causes and became personally involved in welfare activities. Ambitious and opulent lifestyle of rulers in the much longer periods of the Abbasids and Ottomans tended on the whole to follow the Sassanian imperial practices where commitment to service and helping the people was no longer apparent in their behaviour patterns. Self-styled individuals began to amass personal and family wealth of the kind that found no valid precedent in Islam and were rather seen as a reversal of the early precedent and arbitrary departures that hardly inspired public confidence and support.

Signs of departure from the early precedent of modesty in personal and leadership style toward the Persian ceremonious methods had emerged even earlier during the time of the Companions. We note at this juncture the strong views of a leading Companion, Abū Dharr al-Ghaffārī, who publicly protested against self-seeking governors and military commanders that had amassed extensive wealth during their period in offices. This was during the reign of the third Caliph ʿUthmān, barely four decades after the advent of Islam. Abū Dharr was of the view that in principle, government employees were entitled to salaries that were adequate for their personal needs, and demanded that deviant governors should be taken to task and their wealth confiscated and transferred to the public treasury. Abū Dharr voiced these views at a sensitive time when early signs of factionalism and rift threatened the unity of the nascent Muslim community. His views were consequently not well-received by the caliph and the powerful governor (of Sham), Muʿāwiyah at the time. The basic premises of Abū Dharr's views, which he duly supported by his readings of the Qur'ān and *Sunnah*, were sound nevertheless and could hardly be dismissed for violation of the basic teachings of Islam. Abū Dharr's views could, on the contrary be seen to have been reflected in the precedent of ʿUmar I who confiscated personal wealth of many of the leading government figures at the time, so much so that ʿUmar's precedent became the basis later of an institutional development, as we have elsewhere elaborated during the benign Abbasid ruler al-Mahdī in the third century *hijrah*. A separate department of government, namely of *Dīwān al-Musadirīn* (department of confiscated assets) was set up for the very purpose of the transfer of those assets to the *bayt al-māl*.

The range of obligatory levies that are designed to help the poor also include the expiations (*kaffārāt*) which are imposed either as principals or as supplementary penalties for certain religious violations and crime. A number of such expiations are thus attached to offences such as unintentional homicide, the deliberate breaking of fast in Ramaḍān, the breach of a solemn oath, and certain other violations. The *kaffārāt* often consist of optional and self-imposed penalties whereby the violator is typically given the choice to either free a slave (when this was possible) or provide food for a number of poor individuals, or else to observe a specified number of days of fasting. The first of these three options aimed at the termination of slavery when slavery still existed. Later when the practice diminished (and nowadays that slavery has come to an end), either of the remaining two options were practised. Since the release of a slave is to give someone the gift of freedom, and its merit according to the Qur'ān resembles giving someone his life back, a possible substitute nowadays to releasing a slave may be to help someone seriously ill who may be unable to bear the high cost of surgery or medication. A suitable mode of payment for a *kaffarah* of that kind can in other words be worked out. The point here is that *kaffārāt* are an obligatory levy and a proper management thereof can advance further the welfare commitment of the Islamic community and state.

The *Sharīʿah* also provides for other varieties of obligatory levies, such as tax on mines and treasure troves (*al-rikāz*), tax on unclaimed assets (*al-ḍawāʾiʿ*), and also charitable endowments (*awqāf*). This last variety is basically a voluntary charity that entails a binding element. The actual placement or dedication of landed property, and some varieties even of moveable goods such as books and tools, into *waqf* is basically optional, but once a *waqf* deed has been validly concluded, the property of that *waqf* transfers theoretically to the ownership of

God the Most High—hence a *waqf* once lawfully concluded becomes permanent and irreversible.

Waqf has historically been a major source of welfare support and advanced various causes and objectives, including assistance to the mosques, establishments of schools and *madrasahs*, hospitals, assistance to the poor and student stipends. Since the *waqf* endowment is permanent, it has historically remained a cumulative asset of ever-increasing size. Problems of mal-administration and improper usage of *waqf* properties have, however, also been cumulative and long-standing. Muslim communities and governments are now paying attention to the reform of *waqf* administration, and if these efforts bear fruit, the *waqf* sector can substantially advance the welfare objectives of Islam.

As a last resort, in the event when the Muslim government is unable to fulfil its basic commitments in respect of defence, administration of justice and assistance to the poor, then the *Sharī'ah* authorises the government to impose additional taxes on the wealthy in order to meet the basic needs of the community.

Finally, the Qur'ān and *Sunnah* speak profusely of the value of voluntary and supererogatory charity (*ṣadaqat al-tatawwu'*) beyond the scope of its obligatory provisions. Pious and well-meaning Muslims have often acted in various ways to assist charitable causes almost everywhere through giving generously to support the mosque activities, helping orphanages, hospitals and libraries and through direct donation to the poor without limitations of quantity and time.

CHAPTER ONE

Right to Education (*Ḥaqq al-Taʿlīm*) and an Islamic Educational Agenda

I. Chapter Summary

This chapter begins with a review of the Qur'ānic verses and *ḥadīth* which characterise Islam's attitude to education and learning, and constitute the basis of a right to education (*ḥaqq al-taʿlīm*). Apart from the affirmative advice and incentive to learning that the Qur'ān and *Sunnah* provide, they advocate a holistic view of knowledge, which tends to rise above the religious and secular dichotomy of knowledge that has appeared and persisted in the writings of Muslim scholars of subsequent periods. Since the ability to read and comprehend the Qur'ān is in many ways the starting point of Islamic learning, Islam's perspective on knowledge also tends to be Qur'ān-centred and a rich legacy of Qur'ānic sciences feature prominently in the epistemology of Islam. An overview of the Qur'ān and *Sunnah* in the following pages also leads us to a brief review of Qur'ān's perspective on science. Moreover since the Qur'ān is primarily a book of religion, religious sciences naturally tended to dominate Islam's outlook on knowledge. But there was a notable change in this perception in the writings, for example, of Ibn Sīnā, al-Ghazālī, al-Shāṭibī and Ibn Khaldūn who advocated a holistic view of knowledge and marked a departure from the dichotomy that had hitherto dominated the scene. This is the subject of section three of this chapter, which also probes into what the *ʿulamā'* and scholars were inclined to include into, or exclude from, the educational agenda of Islam. What are the major classifications, contents and priorities of an Islamic educational programme is also among the questions that are addressed in this section. A certain revision of the Islamic education programme, which has become the subject of International conferences in recent decades, has also been addressed in this section. Section four addresses children's education and reviews juristic writings on the role and responsibility of parents, teachers, the community and the state toward the education of children. This section also reviews issues over child discipline, student-teacher relationship, issues over female education, as well as some of the conclusions of the International conferences on Muslim education that were held on the subject. The next section raises the question as to whether or not Islam recognises a basic right to education. This is followed, in section six, by a review of the history of institutional developments in education in the Muslim lands. The discussion here explores the roles of the mosque and *madrasah* in the provision of free education. There is also some discussion of the diversification of curricula from the strictly religious into such other fields as medicine, arts, and sciences. Section seven is devoted to a discussion of the scope and substance of academic freedom in Islam, and the last section addresses the issue whether a basic harmony can be claimed between Islam and modern science. Academic freedom is discussed in conjunction with *ra'y* and *ijtihād* and the discussion on science evaluates the argument over a basic harmony, or lack of it, between the scientific method of enquiry, rationality and secularism, on the one hand, and the Islamic outlook on knowledge on the other.

A brief note may be added here to say that the subject I address in the following pages is not only concerned with education as a basic right but also with the Islamic orientation of that education. This brings us face to face with the Islamic theory of knowledge and its compatibility or otherwise with modern scientific methods that now seem to dominate institutional education in the Muslim countries. The last section of this study on Islam and science raises the question of conflict and harmony between them. The discussion in this section is not strictly confined to a juridical framework but tends to provide a general view of an Islamic Education programme for the future generations of Muslims.

II. A Glance at the Qur'ān and *Sunnah*

Islam's outlook on knowledge is dominated by the principle of divine unity (*tawḥīd*), which Muslim thinkers have believed and understood as a most pervasive feature of Islamic epistemology. An understanding of *tawḥīd* and the knowledge of God from that perspective necessarily extends to the knowledge of all of God's creation. Belief in the Oneness of God (*tawḥīd*), in this way gives rise to the idea of the basic unity of all knowledge. The revelation of the Qur'ān began with a single command: اقرأ باسم ربك الذي خلق 'Read in the name of thy Lord' (96:1), which is understood to mean that acquisition of all knowledge should be founded on a basic acknowledgment and recognition of the existence of God. According to the Islamic epistemology, God is the source and fount of all knowledge; man's knowledge, whether corporeal or spiritual, is possible because God has given him the necessary faculties of knowledge. Muslim philosophers and scientists have held as a result that in the act of thinking and knowing, human intellect is illuminated by the Divine Intellect. Knowledge thus acquires a spiritual dimension in Islam and becomes a means to salvation of the soul and attainment of felicity in this life and the hereafter.

The Qur'ān speaks effusively of the dignity of man and of man's superiority over the rest of God's creation. For God has bestowed on man the faculty of reason. But reason develops and flourishes through knowledge, which becomes, in turn a central theme of the teachings of the Qur'ān. The fact that the revelation of Qur'ān began with a sura on knowledge, addressed to the Prophet Muḥammad to 'read in the name of thy Lord the Most Bountiful, He who taught (the use of) the pen and taught man that which he knew not.' (96:3–5)

اقرأ وربك الأكرم الذي علّم بالقلم علّم الإنسان مالم يعلم

The sacred character of knowledge is here indicated by the fact that God refers to Himself as the first teacher. Many verses in the Qur'ān that were to follow affirmed the sacred dimension of knowledge, one of God's illustrious names being the 'All-Knowing' (*al-ʿalīm*). The Qur'ān has advanced the cause of learning such that it is 'considered by all Muslims to be the quintessential sum of all knowledge, both human and divine.'[1] There is another sura in the Qur'ān, bearing the title '*al-Qalam*' (the pen) which begins with the phrase '*Nūn*, by the pen, and by the (record) of what (men) write with it.' (68:1)

ن والقلم ومايسطرون

In yet another sura attention is focused on the 'written book' as the chapter opens with these words:

والطور وكتاب مسطور في رقّ منشور

'By the Mount (of Revelation), and the book written on unfolded scroll.' (52:1–2)

The pen and what can flow from it, the paper and the book, the three elemental tools of knowledge have thus been taken as objects of solemn oath. Commentators have also noted that the letter '*Nūn*' here might mean an ink-holder.[2] In another chapter of the Qur'ān, entitled '*al-Raḥmān*' (the Most Merciful), the text identifies God's act of the creation of man, bestowing on him the ability to learn, and then teaching him the Qur'ān as the most salient of God's favours on mankind.[3] Furthermore the Qur'ān describes the mission of the Prophet Muḥammad as being to 'Rehearse to the people of God's signs (in order) to purify them, and to teach them the Book and the wisdom...' (62:2)

يتلوا عليهم آياته ويزكيهم ويعلّمهم الكتاب والحكمة

Knowledge is evidently viewed as an instrument of faith (*īmān*) and a torchlight in the quest for spiritual refinement. Whenever the Qur'ān refers to darkness and light (*al-ẓulumāt wa'l-nūr*) they signify ignorance and knowledge respectively. In several places the text declares its own purpose as being to show the way from darkness into the light (2:257; 5:16; 14:1). And then the '*ulamā*' are singled out as the most God-fearing of all of God's servants: 'Only those of His servants who possess knowledge fear God most.' (35:28)

إنما يخشى الله من عباده العلماء

Knowledge is envisaged as a means of attaining spiritual purity and *taqwā*, mainly because knowledge distinguishes the true and false in matters of belief, and right and wrong, recommendable and reprehensible, in matters of practical conduct. In another passage God Most High has mentioned the learned next to the angels in the matter of faith:

شهد الله أنه لا إله إلا هو والملائكة وأولوا العلم قائما بالقسط

God (Himself) is witness that there is no God save Him. The angels and the men of learning too are witnesses, maintaining His creation in justice… (3:18)

In numerous other places, the Qur'ān ranks with distinction 'those who have faith and knowledge' (58:11) and poses a rhetorical question: 'Are they equal, those who know and those who know not?' (39:9)

قل هل يستوي الذين يعلمون والذين لايعلمون

Some of God's messages are only understood by the learned as according to another Qur'ānic verse:

وتلك الأمثال نضربها للناس ومايعقلها إلا العالمون

And We cite these examples to the people, but only the learned are the ones who understand them. (29:43)

Knowledge is seen as a perpetual quest that knows no bounds and no one, it seems, can ever attain it to absolute perfection. This is clear from the affirmation:

وفوق كلّ ذي علم عليم

Above everyone endowed with knowledge there is one, the All-Knowing. (12:76)

This is also conveyed in a verse to the Prophet Muḥammad to 'Say! O my Lord, increase my knowledge.' (20:114)

قل ربي زدني علما

The vision that knowledge knows no boundary is again depicted in a verse addressing the people in such terms that 'of knowledge, only a little has been communicated to you.' (17:85)

وما أوتيتم من العلم إلا قليلا

The twofold message here not only signifies the limitations of human beings, but also engages them in a continuous quest for knowledge. The last three passages quoted are evidently not confined to the knowledge of religion. The point here may be generalised so as to say that the Qur'ānic references to knowledge are as much to religious knowledge as they are to scientific and rational knowledge of world affairs. This is also confirmed by the numerous references one finds in the Qur'ān to rational enquiry and observation, to the physical world around us, the earth and its hidden resources, and what it can nurture of flora and fauna, the mountains and the seas (6:97, 99) plus the affirmation that they are all created for the benefit of man (2:164). Passages such as قل انظروا ما في السموات والأرض 'Say, and look into what is there in the heavens and the earth' (10:101); and قل سيروا في الأرض فانظروا كيف بدأ الخلق 'Say, travel in the earth and see how God originated the creation' (29:20) are not confined to spirituality and religion. The invitation in these and similar other passages is 'to rational thought in all its possible varieties,' from the purely intellectual, to the data obtained by the senses and by the intellect to spiritual and religious matters.[4]

When God Most High addresses the people in such terms as

أو لم ينظروا في ملكوت السموات والأرض وما خلق الله من شيئ

'Have they not considered the dominion of the heavens and the earth and what things God has created?' (7:185), the appeal is to rationality and experimental knowledge. It is observation through the senses and rational conclusion that the text has envisaged. Pursuit of knowledge, be it religious knowledge, scientific knowledge or knowledge of service to humanity, falls under the one and same conception of knowledge in the Qur'ān. Beneficial knowledge may be understood as knowledge which advances the goals and purposes of Islam on such matters as protection of life, faith, intellect, property and family, known as the five essentials (*al-ḍaruriyyāt al-khamsah*) in their broadest sense. This virtually subsumes all spheres of knowledge including religion, law, philosophy, medicine, architecture, mathematics, etc., excepting such things as sorcery, black magic and knowledge that is destructive and fails the test of benefit to mankind.

The Qur'ān also maintains an open outlook on knowledge, which is open and receptive toward acceptance and acquisition of knowledge from any source. This is the purport of the verse which directs the Muslims to 'ask those who know if you know not yourselves.' (16:43)

فاسئلوا أهل الذكر إن كنتم لا تعلمون

Reports indicate that this verse was revealed concerning the Jews and Christians. The Muslims were consequently encouraged to seek their advice on matters over which they were more knowledgeable. The learned have, on the other hand, a responsibility to educate others. This is the purport of a verse in which it is provided 'If a contingent from every expedition remained behind, they could devote themselves to studies in religion and admonish their people.' (9:122)

فلولا نفر من كلّ فرقة منهم طائفة ليتفقهوا في الدين

ولينذروا قومهم

The text here stresses the importance of education even at the time of military mobilisation, let alone during peacetime. Warfare is not an excuse to halt education and knowledge of religion. The head of the family is responsible for the education of the family members. This is the purport of the instruction to the believers to 'protect yourselves and your families against the (torment of) fire.' (66:6)

قوا أنفسكم وأهليكم نارا

The fourth caliph 'Alī is reported to have commented that it means, 'you should educate your family.' According to a *ḥadīth* al-Bukhārī has recorded, a delegation of 'Abd al-Qays tribe visited the Prophet who instructed them on two things: to be diligent in religion, and the acquisition of knowledge. The Prophet asked them to 'go back to your families and educate them.'[5] This *ḥadīth* also signifies perhaps that diligence in religion and education are not the same.

The Prophet is also reported to have said that 'wisdom (*al-ḥikmah*) is the lost treasure of a Muslim and he is entitled to take it wherever he finds it'.[6]

الحكمة ضالّة المؤمن فحيث وجدها فهو أحق بها

One also reads in another *ḥadīth* in the broadest of terms the message that 'people are of two types: they are either the learned or the learners, and no good will come out of those who do not belong to either.'[7]

الناس رجلان، عالم ومتعلم ولا خير في سواهما

It is of interest to note in this connection that al-Bukhārī begins his renowned work on *ḥadīth* with a chapter on belief (*īmān*), which is followed by chapter two on 'the superiority of knowledge—*faḍl al-ʿilm*.' Chapter two also begins with a commentary on the Qurʾānic verse, earlier quoted, that 'God will elevate in ranks those of you who believe and who have been granted knowledge.' (58:16)

يرفع الله الذين آمنوا منكم والذين أوتوا العلم درجات

Further on the superiority of *ʿilm* and *ʿulamāʾ*, ʿAbd Allāh b. ʿUmar reported the following:

مرّ رسول الله صلى الله عليه وسلم بمجلسين في مسجده
فقال: كلاهما خير، وأحدهما أفضل من آخر. أما هؤلاء
فيدعون الله ويرغبون الله، فان شاء اعلاهم وان شاء
منحهم، وأما هؤلاء يتعلمون الفقه والعلم ويعلمون الجاهل
فلهم فضل وانما بعثت معلما ثم جلس بينهم

The Prophet, peace be on him, passed by two separate gatherings in his mosque (in Medina) and then said 'Both are good, but one of them is superior to the other. As for the first, they are engaged in prayer and invitation to the way of God. If God is pleased, He will grant them what they want, but He may also not grant them that. As for the second group, they disseminate knowledge and educate the ignorant; they are superior. For I myself have not been sent but to be a teacher'. Then he sat with this group.[8]

The Prophet is also reported to have said:

العلماء مصابيح الأرض وخلفاء الأنبياء

Those who possess knowledge are lights of the earth and successors of the prophets.[9]

There is no rank above that of the Prophet and the learned have been honoured to carry the mantle of prophethood. Since all the prophets were teachers who educated their people, and prophethood came to an end with the demise of the Prophet Muḥammad, his role as an agent and propagator of learning is to be carried over by the learned members of his community. Successorship (*warāthah*) here is also indicative of permanency, a role in other words, that no one may take away from the learned.

According to another renowned *ḥadīth*:

$$ طلب العلم فريضة على كل مسلم $$

Pursuit of *ʿilm* is an obligation of every Muslim.[10]

Another version of the same *ḥadīth* adds the words 'wa muslimatin' (and Muslim woman) thus making pursuit of knowledge a common obligation of the believers, men and women alike.[11] Some commentators have noted that this addition is a mere elaboration as the phrase 'every Muslim' includes women. While quoting this *ḥadīth*, al-Ghazālī (d. 505/1111) wrote that some *ʿulamā'* have considered the reference here to be to the knowledge of *ḥalāl* and *ḥarām*. To substantiate this, another *ḥadīth* is quoted, on the authority of ʿAbd Allāh b. Masʿūd, which provides 'to earn a lawful living is an obligation of every Muslim.'[12]

Al-Ghazālī then adds that the two *ḥadīth*s basically convey the same message.[13] In drawing this parallel between knowledge and work for a living al-Ghazālī evidently conveyed a basic preoccupation of Islamic knowledge with the issues of life and work so much so that they were inseparable.

The Prophet took a decidedly affirmative stance on the dissemination of knowledge when he said:

$$ لا ينبغي لأحد عنده شيئ من العلم أن يضيّع نفسه $$

It is not becoming of a person gifted with knowledge to ruin himself (by abstaining from teaching it to others).[14]

People were encouraged, according to another *ḥadīth*, to 'disseminate knowledge by teaching it to others. For knowledge does not vanish unless its bearer keeps it secretly to himself.'[15]

Those who attended the sermons of the Prophet were instructed to convey the basic message of his teachings to others who were unable to attend. Women were also encouraged to advance their knowledge of Islam and to this effect the Prophet responded positively to a request made by women of Medina 'to fix a day for us as the men were taking all of your time.' On (hearing) this he promised them one day in which to meet them and teach them.[16]

The Prophet has expressed the concern, in another *ḥadīth*, that a time may come when ignorant people pose themselves in the garb of the learned; people begin to ask them questions that they answer even though they do not possess the necessary knowledge. This is where dissemination of knowledge will suffer as both the teacher and the taught would have been misguided.[17]

A spiritual incentive to the faithful is provided in another *ḥadīth* which is as follows:

إذا مات الإنسان انقطع عمله إلا من ثلاث: صدقة

جارية، أو علم ينتفع به أو ولد صالح يدعوا له

When a son of Adam dies, his deeds discontinue except in three cases: continuous charity, knowledge which the people find beneficial, and upright offspring that prays for him.[18]

The message is also conveyed in another *ḥadīth* to the effect:

طلب العلم كان كفارة لما مضى

Pursuit of knowledge acts as an expiation (*kaffārah*) to what has taken place (of sins) preceding it.[19]

The Prophet encouraged the learned among his Companions to educate others and sent some of them to the outlying regions such as the Yemen, Sham and Basra for that purpose.[20]

Following the battle of Badr, a number of war prisoners were offered release in exchange for ransom and when some of them expressed their inability to pay it, they were asked to teach the Muslim children basic literacy. Each of them was assigned ten children to educate as a substitute for ransom. Zayd b. Thābit, the renowned Companion who later became the Prophet's secretary and played a major role in the writing of the Qur'ān, was among those who was taught by the prisoners of Badr.[21] Later when the Persian territories were conquered, there were in Hirah numerous individuals who could write, and a group of them were consequently invited to Medina and assigned teaching duties. The Prophet also encouraged some of his Companions to learn foreign languages as there was a need for it. Zayd b. Thābit thus went on record to say that the Prophet assigned him the task of learning Assyrian language, which he consequently did. We learn further that the Prophet validated the teaching and memorisation of Qur'ān as a substitute to dower (*mahr*) in a contract of marriage, which the prospective husband might give to his wife.[22]

The caliph ʿAlī (d. 40/661) is reported to have spoken of the superiority of knowledge over wealth in that knowledge is not diminished by use whereas wealth is; knowledge safeguards its bearer whereas wealth needs to be safeguarded; knowledge accompanies its bearer at all times whereas wealth does not; knowledge begets spiritual distinction of the order that wealth can hardly achieve.[23]

The caliph ʿUmar b. ʿAbd al-ʿAzīz (d. 101/720) has been quoted to have said that 'one who acts without knowledge is more likely to cause mischief rather than benefit.' Ḥasan al-Baṣrī has spoken, in a similar vein, on the doubtful benefit of action that is not founded on knowledge and resembled a person who acts without having knowledge to a traveller on the wrong route who may cause himself harm rather than benefit. 'So seek *ʿilm* that is not harmed by devotion to worship, and seek worship that is not harmed by pursuit of *ʿilm*.' For history is reminiscent of people who engrossed themselves in worship and abandoned *ʿilm* until they unleashed their swords on the *ummah* of Muḥammad, peace be on him. If they had pursued knowledge, they would not have fallen into that predicament (the reference seems to be to the Kharijites).[24]

The renowned Shāfiʿī jurist, ʿIzz al-Dīn ʿAbd al-Salām al-Sulamī (d. 660/1262) depicted the much-cherished attitude of enlightened Muslims in his statement that 'the wealth of knowledge and education of people is better and immensely more satisfying than property and power'.[25]

The Qur'ānic vision of knowledge may also be characterised as knowledge that is founded on understanding (*al-fahm*) and insight (*al-tafaqquh*). This is understood from the numerous references in the text which encourage rational observation, thought and reflection on the observable world and the universe beyond. It is knowledge that is espoused with insight that the Qur'ān has visualised in its expression *al-tafaqquh fi'l-dīn*, that is, understanding the religion. This signifies a rational and inquisitive approach to the religion itself. Religion (*al-dīn*) in other words, recommends analytical knowledge and understanding, rather than a purely dogmatic approach. Thus it is declared in a verse, as may be quoted again: 'if some individuals from every multitude would devote themselves to the study of religion (*li-yatafaqqahū fi'l-dīn*) and admonish their people...' (9:122)

فلولا نفر من كلّ فرقة منهم طائفة ليتفقهوا في الدين ولينذروا قومهم

The distinction between these two aspects of knowledge is reflected in the juristic terminology of *'ilm al-dirāyah* and *'ilm al-riwāyah*, that is rational knowledge and transmitted knowledge respectively. The former is true and substantive knowledge that is based on *tafaqquh* that takes priority over the latter. Whereas *'ilm al-riwāyah* relies mainly on transmission, memory and retention, *'ilm al-dirāyah* is founded in cognition, understanding and analysis.

The learned among the first three generations of Muslims, namely the Companions of the Prophet and the succeeding two generations are venerated for their distinctive contributions to Islam largely because of their prominence on the level of understanding and *tafaqquh*. Their mantle was taken over and carried by the *'ulamā'* who laid down the foundations of the schools of theology and law. The era of imitation and *taqlīd* during the subsequent periods produced scholars in the category of *al-ḥuffāẓ*, that is, retainers and memorisers who went down on the scale of originality and independent thought. The main difference between a *muqallid* (imitator) and an independent thinker (*mujtahid*) relates basically to understanding, originality and independence.

Qaraḍāwī has reflected on the current realities of public education in Muslim countries and made the comment that 'the system relies on memorisation and cramming more than it does on comprehension and analysis. A typical weakness of this method is that the memoriser forgets as soon as the exams are over. But if what is learned is founded on understanding and comprehension its substance will remain in the mind and will not be prone to oblivion so fast.'[26] But the issue that we raise here is well entrenched and originates in the overall emphasis that almost every educationist and *faqīh* of earlier times have placed on the textual study of the Qur'ān calling attention to its words and sentences often at the expense of its comprehension. The basic approach to Qur'ān studies thus emphasised correct pronunciation and memorisation, which was to a large extent also true of the study of *hadīth*. This memory and repetition-based system of learning was particularly pronounced in the context of child education although it was not confined to this framework as other and more advanced levels of Islamic scholarship also bore the same influence.[27]

A somewhat parallel analysis to that of *ʿilm* and *tafaqquh* has been advanced by al-Ghazālī in his discussion of the two sources of learning that Muslim scholarship has recognised. One of these was through human teaching (*al-taʿallum al-insānī*) and the other through divine teaching (*al-taʿlīm al-rabbānī*). The former is externally transmitted from teacher to student, whereas the latter is conveyed by the Universal Intellect which is superior, more intense and more effective than any human teacher can accomplish. This knowledge is internally acquired either through revelation (*wahy*) which is a prerogative of the Prophets, or it is acquired through meditation and reflection. Al-Ghazālī subscribes to the view that the essence of all knowledge is centred in the inner self of the human person in much the same way as growth potential that is vested in the soil and seed, and it is through teaching that the individual's potential is developed. These two aspects of knowledge, that is, the external and the internal, are complementary to one another. This is because no one can possibly teach, or learn from any teacher, all the sciences, some of which are learned through teaching but the rest is inferred by the reflective thought of the individual. It is therefore important that the avenues of learning remain open both through teaching and through inner reflection and illumination.[28] This is another way of saying that knowledge is acquired either through the senses or through inner reflection, analogy and conjecture. Al-Ghazālī's view on this tended to correspond to those of Ibn Sīnā, but which differed, at least partially, from those of the Brethren of Purity (*ikhwān al-ṣafā*). All knowledge, according to the *ikhwān al-ṣafā*, is acquired through the senses and nothing of it inheres in human nature. Knowledge that is developed through meditation and thought also originates in the senses. The same analysis is extended to the axiomatic knowledge of postulates that essentially consists of images that are derived and confirmed through the senses. In support of this theory *ikhwān al-ṣafā* have cited the Qur'ānic verses which declare that 'God brought you out of the wombs of your mothers while you knew nothing.' (16:78)

والله أخرجكم من بطون أمهاتكم لا تعلمون شيئا

All knowledge is therefore acquired knowledge, a view which may perhaps strike a closer note with some of the modern theories on the subject.[29]

Muhammad Iqbal (d. 1937) has convincingly argued that Greek philosophy had broadened the outlook of Muslim thinkers but it also 'obscured their vision of the Qur'ān.' Socrates focused his attention on the human world alone paying little attention to the natural world that surrounded the human existence. Socrates's disciple, Plato despised sense-perception which in his view yielded mere opinion and no real knowledge. How unlike the Qur'ān which sees the humble bee a recipient of Divine inspiration and constantly calls upon the reader to observe the natural world around him. The Qur'ān regards 'hearing' and 'sight' as the most valuable Divine gifts and declare them to be accountable to God for their activity in this world. This is what the earlier Muslim students of the Qur'ān completely missed under the spell of classical speculation. They read the Qur'ān in the light of Greek thought. It took them over 200 years to perceive that the spirit of the Qur'ān was essentially anti-classical and the result of this perception was 'an intellectual revolt, the full significance of which has not been realised even up to the present day.'[30]

The Qur'ān recognises intuition as organically related to thought and together with it constitutes a source of knowledge.[31] Two other sources of knowledge that the Qur'ān has recognised are nature and history; and it is in tapping these sources of knowledge that the spirit of Islam is seen at its best. The Qur'ān sees the signs of Ultimate Reality in the sun, the moon, the lightening out of shadows, the alternation of day and night, variety of human colours and tongues, the alternation of the days of success and its reverse among peoples— in fact the whole of nature as revealed to the sense-perception of man. And the Muslim's duty is to reflect on these signs and not to pass by them 'as if he is deaf and blind,' for he 'who does not see these signs in this life will remain blind to the realities of the life to come.' (25:73) This appeal to the concrete, combined with the slow realisation that according to Qur'ān, the universe is dynamic, eventually brought Muslim thinkers into conflict with Greek thought which, in the beginning of their intellectual career, they had studied with so much enthusiasm. They attempted to understand the Qur'ān in the light of Greek logic. In view of the concrete spirit of the Qur'ān and the speculative nature of Greek philosophy which enjoyed theory and was neglectful of fact, this attempt was doomed to failure. And it is what follows their failure that brings out the real spirit of the culture of Islam.[32]

III. Classification of Sciences from an Islamic Perspective

This section is concerned with an identification of the main contours of Islamic sciences and a rough order of priority that the 'ulamā' have suggested in favour of certain types of learning. One of the central concerns here has been the basic unity of all knowledge, which has profoundly influenced the development of Islamic sciences. The various branches of knowledge in Islam have thus come to be regarded as so many branches of a single tree, which grows and sends leaves and fruit in conformity with its natural capacity and endowment. Just as a branch does not continue to grow indefinitely, nor does science. None of its branches may be extended and pursued beyond certain limits, for any disregard of such natural limitations is likely to disturb and destroy the harmony and proportion of things and ultimately prove to be a useless activity. A branch that continues to grow in disproportion to the tree itself is likely to destroy the harmony of the tree as a whole. The attempt to classify knowledge in certain inter-related categories is a means by which the scholars have sought to preserve the balance and unity of the sciences.[33]

The Islamic agenda of education tends to focus on the relative merits of the various branches of knowledge by posing the question, which the 'ulamā' have often raised as to what is obligatory knowledge (al-ʿilm al-mafrūḍ) as opposed to that which is optional (al-ʿilm al-mubāḥ). In al-Ghazālī's writing, the discussion begins with the citation of the ḥadīth, quoted above, which declares that 'pursuit of knowledge is an obligation to every Muslim.' Different responses have been given as to how this ḥadīth is to be understood. The underlying assumption of this discourse has been that not everyone could be expected to acquire all knowledge; some sort of specification was therefore necessary if the ḥadīth were to be correctly understood. The 'ulamā' of kalam (theology) considered theology as obligatory knowledge since it is concerned with the dogma of Islam, knowledge of God and His attributes and the essence of *tawḥīd*. The *fuqahā'* have, on the other hand, considered knowledge of *fiqh* a matter of priority as it conveys knowledge of the *ḥalāl* and the *ḥarām* in social relations and commerce and rules that regulate the practical conduct of Muslims in their daily lives. Others have said that knowledge of *tafsīr* and *ḥadīth*, which are the source disciplines and gateway to all other disciplines must be given priority over all other branches of learning. The Sufis have added their voice to say that since *taṣawwuf* (mysticism) is concerned with the essence of spirituality and sincerity in devotion as well as the inner knowledge of the self, it should be given precedence over the other branches of knowledge. Al-Ghazālī has also quoted, in this connection, Abū Ṭālib al-Makkī to the effect that the knowledge that is meant in the *ḥadīth* under review is one that concerns Islam itself; it is the knowledge of the pillars and foundations of Islam as specified in another *ḥadīth* to the effect that 'Islam has been founded on five pillars… (*buniya al-Islāmu ʿalā khams*).' Al-Ghazālī elaborates that the knowledge that is meant in the *ḥadīth* under review is knowledge that can constitute the subject of responsibility (*taklīf*) for a competent person. This is knowledge of the practical teachings of the religion that consists of belief (*iʿtiqād*), action (*fiʿl*) and abandonment (*tark*). This would preclude knowledge of spiritual discovery and inner illumination (*mukāshafah*) which has no direct bearing on the practicalities of life. Knowledge in the *ḥadīth* before us thus means basic and practical knowledge of Islam that is of common application to the lives and daily experiences of Muslims.[34]

As an extension of the same analysis, it is added that the *ḥadīth* under review makes obligatory the knowledge of *ḥalāl* and *ḥarām*, and it is therefore the knowledge of *fiqh* that is meant. The protagonists of this view have supported their position by citing another *ḥadīth* in which a derivative of the word '*fiqh*' has been used. The *ḥadīth* quoted here provides: 'When God favours a person, He enables him to become learned in religion.'[35]

من يرد الله به خيرا يفقّهه في الدين

Yet one might hasten to add that the point made here is less than accurate as the word '*yufaqihhu*' in the *ḥadīth* is used literally, that is, it does not refer to *fiqh* in the sense of a particular discipline. Neither of the two *ḥadīth*s therefore provide authority in favour of a particular branch of knowledge that the Prophet might be said to have exclusively meant. To this it may be added that the word ʿilm in virtually all of the Qurʾānic verses, and also in most ḥadīths, including the one under review, occurs in its absolute and unqualified sense. To try to specify or qualify it in favour of fiqh or any other discipline is therefore unwarranted.[36]

It will also be noted, that much of the particularist discourse in favour or against a certain branch of knowledge is inconclusive and tends to be premised on unnecessary compartmentalisations and dichotomies. The attempt to specify the general message of the ḥadīth is also questionable in a basic sense. The general message and purport of the ḥadīth may be said to be clear enough, and it is, as such, in no need of specification. Al-Ghazālī recounts the various responses given to the ḥadīth but he himself is inclined to support the general message and purport of the ḥadīth, which is really concerned, not so much with the details and branches of knowledge as it is with a basic message on its value. Al-Shāṭibī (d. 790/1388) has also upheld an essentially unitarian and holistic view of ʿilm, as will presently be discussed.

Ibn Ḥazm (d. 456/1064) has elaborated that the search for knowledge is either a personal obligation (farḍ ʿayn) or it is a collective duty (farḍ kifāyah). The former includes knowledge of the rules of Sharīʿah on devotional matters such as ablution, prayer, zakāh, fasting, and the ḥajj. It is a personal obligation of every competent Muslim, man and woman, to acquire sufficient knowledge of these as well as the ḥalāl and ḥarām in food, clothing and drinks, and the limits, of course, of proper behaviour in speech and action in society and with members of the opposite sex. He or she must also know the rules, for instance, pertaining to the payment of zakāh, the quorum of zakāh and situations where one may not have to pay it. To acquire knowledge of what is a personal obligation is also obligatory to the extent as to facilitate its proper implementation. To impart such knowledge through teaching also partakes in the same value as applies to its acquisition in the first place.

People who occupy themselves with trades and professions must likewise learn the rules of Sharīʿah that apply to their line of business, especially the ḥalāl and ḥarām in commercial transactions. The army commanders must know the rules and aḥkām of jihād, and governors and judges must be knowledgeable of the rules of Sharīʿah relating to adjudication, trial procedures and the prescribed (ḥudūd) punishments. Every Muslim must obtain the necessary degree of knowledge that relates to his or her situation and every Muslim must acquire knowledge of the basics by the time he or she attains the age of majority, or in the case of non-Muslims, when he or she converts to Islam. It is not necessary on the other hand, for a dumb or a blind person to know what is or is not permissible to speak or to see respectively. There is thus a situational aspect to the duty under review and the question as to when a collective duty is no longer a duty in regard to some persons, but it becomes an emphatic duty in regard to others. A general knowledge of the prohibition of *ribā* (usury) is sufficient, for example, for Muslim traders, but it becomes an emphatic duty if the trader in question operates in a market where *ribā* is widely practised so that he can avoid it. It would naturally be difficult to refrain from something unless one knows its nature, signs, causes and ways of prevention etc. It is a collective obligation of the society at large to maintain and facilitate the knowledge of *Sharī'ah*, and it is recommendable (*mandūb*) for all to pursue their basic knowledge to higher stages of attainment.[37] Pursuit of knowledge in general, that is, outside the *Sharī'ah* disciplines, is also recommendable for the individual, but it is a collective obligation of the community as a whole.[38]

Ibn Ḥazm's approach is somewhat different from that of al-Shāṭibī in that Ibn Ḥazm tends to comply with the conventional dichotomy of religious and secular sciences whereas al-Shāṭibī tends to depart from it. Al-Shāṭibī's vision of 'Sharī'ah knowledge' sets aside the conventional dichotomy of *'ilm* and by doing so, he strikes a closer note with the *maqāṣid* of *Sharī'ah*. We shall have occasion to elaborate on whether al-Shāṭibī's integrationist approach has a wider base of support in the works of *'ulamā'* like al-Ghazālī, Ibn 'Ābidīn as well as the more recent writings of commentators on the subject.

Al-Shāṭibī has held the view that knowledge (*'ilm*) which Islam has made obligatory is all 'Sharī'ah knowledge.' This includes knowledge which is instrumental to worshipping God Most High and protecting the objectives (*maqāṣid*) of *Sharī'ah* in the spheres of essential and complementary interests (*ḍaruriyyāt wa ḥājiyyāt*) as well as unregulated interests (*al-maṣāliḥ al-mursalah*) that are indispensable for the good management of man's affairs both in this world and the hereafter. To be engaged in this pursuit and the effort that it takes to secure these interests partakes, according to al-Shāṭibī, in the wider meaning of worship (*ta'abbud*) in Islam. Based on this analysis, al-Shāṭibī concludes that 'all the sciences which contemplate protection of the *maqāṣid* of *Sharī'ah*, such as physics, geometry and medicine, acquire the value (*ḥukm*) of the religious sciences such as Qur'ānic exegesis, *Ḥadīth*, and *fiqh* provided that they secure the people's interests (*maṣāliḥ al-nās*) and do not lead to their destruction and prejudice.'[39]

'*Sharīʿah* knowledge' for al-Ghazālī consists of knowledge which is based in divine revelation addressed primarily to the Prophets and stands in a separate category to rational sciences. *Sharīʿah* knowledge is transmitted knowledge which is neither the product of human experience nor of the exercise of intellectual faculty and reason. *Sharīʿah* knowledge is all praiseworthy (*maḥmūdah kullihā*) but since a clear-cut division between *Sharīʿah* and rational sciences is not feasible, non-*Sharīʿah* knowledge may be joined to, and even confused with, *Sharīʿah* knowledge. Then it is possible to divide the *sharʿī* knowledge into the two types of praiseworthy and reprehensible (*maḥmūdah, wa madhmūmah*). Knowledge of the Qur'ān, *Sunnah* and consensus (*ijmāʿ*) as well as the precedent of Companions (*athar al-ṣaḥābah*) tops the list of Ghazālī's *Sharīʿah* knowledge, but then such areas of the hermeneutics (*tafsīr*) of Qur'ān as may consist of superfluous and unwarranted elaboration would fall under the reprehensible category. This analysis can also be extended to the *Sunnah* and *ijmāʿ*.

A four-tier classification of *Sharīʿah* knowledge that al-Ghazālī has provided consists of the roots, the branches, preliminaries, and the supplements (*uṣūl, furūʿ, muqaddimāt, wa mutammimāt*). Knowledge of the branches (i.e. *furūʿ*) is derivative knowledge as it is derived from the sources, or *uṣūl*, not in what is conveyed by their words, but in what is derived by implication and rational extension of their application. This derivative body of knowledge may in turn relate to the benefit of this world, or that of the next. The former falls under *fiqh*, and the latter under morality and spiritual refinement.

The class of knowledge which is designated as *muqaddimāt*, or preliminaries, consists of auxiliary disciplines which facilitate better understanding of the first two classes, such as language and grammar, which are not *Sharīʿah* sciences per se but are instrumental in advancing the *Sharīʿah* knowledge. And lastly the supplements, or *mutammimāt*, in every branch of knowledge enrich and develop the discipline in question. The rules of interpretation in relationship to the Qur'ān, and chronology of *ḥadīth* transmitters (*asmāʾ al-rijāl*) in relationship to the *Sunnah* consist of supplementary knowledge. Having expounded his four-tiered classification of *Sharīʿah* knowledge, al-Ghazālī writes once again that 'these are all praiseworthy, indeed all partake in collective obligations.'[40]

Promotion and pursuit of the sciences that are essential to life, such as medicine, partake in *farḍ kifā'ī* and become, according to al-Ghazālī, a collective obligation of the community and its government. This category of sciences also includes mathematics which is necessary in the management of commercial transactions, distribution of inheritance, and such other areas of knowledge as industries, agriculture, political science and so forth. Absence of facilities to secure and promote these will hasten the weakness and eventual destruction of cities and people, which is not permissible. If some people in every city attend to them, the duty is fulfilled; but a total neglect of them is not permissible.[41] To acquire specialised and in–depth knowledge of these basic disciplines is praiseworthy (*faḍīlah*) and recommendable, but not obligatory.

The basic strength of this holistic approach to knowledge may be said to be its attempt to give priority to useful knowledge (*al-ʿilm al-nāfiʿ*), as opposed to pernicious knowledge (*al-ʿilm al-madhmūm*). This latter category refers to reprehensible knowledge of such things as sorcery, heretical doctrines, freewill and predestination, and issues relating to the exalted self of God Most High. We may add, however, that if acquisition of knowledge in these disapproved areas is deemed necessary in order to wage an effective campaign against them, then this would again fall under the general heading of beneficial knowledge.

Beneficial knowledge is that which is purposeful and the time and effort that is taken to gain it are worthwhile making, as it would otherwise mean engaging oneself in futile pursuits. Al-Ghazālī illustrates this by saying that it would not be useful, indeed it would be reprehensible, for a student to spend an enormous amount of time on delving into the minute details of a branch of learning prior to looking into its main headings and principles, ignoring the obvious and searching for the hidden and remote pieces of information. It thus appears that Ghazālī applies the dual classification of knowledge into praiseworthy and reprehensible not just to the subject matter of what is learnt but also to the approach taken towards learning. Thus if a student takes a wrong and futile approach towards an approved discipline of learning, that exercise would be reprehensible in regard to that particular student.[42]

And lastly al-Ghazālī classified the distortion of the correct principles of an otherwise approved area of knowledge as reprehensible. Here he gives as an example the story that 'the *qāḍī* Abū Yūsuf used to make a gift of his property to his wife at the end of the year which she would make a gift of it in reverse later so as to evade the *zakāh*.

When this was reported to Abū Ḥanīfah, May God bless him, he said that this was his (Abū Yūsuf's) *fiqh*.' This was the sort of worldly *fiqh*, al-Ghazālī added, whose harm in the Hereafter 'is greater than all heinous offences, and it is none other than harmful knowledge (*al-ʿilm al-ḍār*).'[43]

Al-Ghazālī has also spoken at length against the deviations he observed, even in his days, in the writings of the *fuqahā'* and theologians (*mutakallimūn*) from the path of the Companions and the learned Imams. Instead of emphasising clarity and directness, the writings of many of these scholars and jurists are burdened with sophistry, length and complexity of the sort that fail to achieve a good purpose. Many of the *fuqahā'* had abandoned the style and leadership of ʿUmar b. al-Khaṭṭāb to legal issues and immersed themselves in argumentations that enhance rather than clarify doubt. This is tantamount to losing sight of the very purpose of *fiqh* as a problem solving discipline that should ease the people's difficulties rather than facing them with new problems in understanding the discourse of the *fuqahā'*.[44]

The preference that is given to the promotion of beneficial knowledge finds support in the Qur'ān and *Sunnah*. References are thus found in the Qur'ān which speak in praise of those 'who turn away from indulgence in futility.' (23:3)

$$والذين هم عن اللغو معرضون$$

In another place, resistance is recommended to the enticement of the misguided: '…when they are addressed by the foolish, they merely answer: peace.' (25:63)

$$وإذا خاطبهم الجاهلون قالوا سلاما$$

The following supplication of the Prophet provides clear evidence on the importance of beneficial knowledge:

$$اللهم انفعني بما علمتني وعلمني ماينفعني وزدني علما$$
$$الحمد لله على كل حال وأعوذ بالله من عذاب النار$$

O My Lord! Help me benefit from what you have taught me, and teach me what is beneficial to me, and (help me) increase my knowledge. Praise be to God in all conditions, and I seek refuge to God from the torment of fire.[45]

The Prophet has also related the benefit of knowledge to its quality of pragmatism, as in the following *ḥadīth*:

تعلّموا ما شئتم فلن ينفعكم الله حتى تعملوا بما تعلمون

Learn whatever (branch of knowledge) you wish to learn but (beware that) God will not make it beneficial unless you act on what you have learned.[46]

Another version of this *ḥadīth* has been recorded as follows:

تعلّموا من العلم ما شئتم فوالله لا تؤجروا بجمع العلم حتى تعملوا

Learn of knowledge what you wish. By God you will not be rewarded by gathering knowledge unless you espouse it with action.[47]

A second classification of *fard kifāyah* knowledge that features in al-Ghazālī's writing is the division of knowledge into the juridical and non-juridical varieties (*ʿulūm sharʿiyyah, ʿulūm ghayr sharʿiyyah*). The former included jurisprudence, ethics and Arabic language, whereas the latter comprised medicine, mathematics and philosophy etc. These classifications apparently constituted the basic framework of educational planning in *madrasahs* until Ibn Khaldūn (d. 808/1406) replaced and subsumed them under his proposed classification of transmitted (*naqliyyah*) and rational (*ʿaqliyyah*) sciences. The *naqliyyah* category included the Qur'ān, *ḥadīth*, theology, Sufism, and linguistic sciences, whereas the *ʿaqliyyah* included medicine, agriculture, metaphysics, alchemy and astrology etc.[48]

Political domination of the Muslim world by European powers during the 18th and 19th centuries led to the introduction of Western liberal education in place of the *ʿaqliyyah* sciences, and a simultaneous downgrading of the *naqliyyah* sciences by assigning them only a limited role in public education. Only one of the many such subjects, namely theology, was, for example to be taught at government schools. Whereas previously it was possible for a student to take a balance of the *ʿaqliyyah* and *naqliyyah* sciences together, the revised school curricula not only made this unfeasible but also set in place a pattern of duality between religious and secular education. This development made a holistic approach to education unfeasible, and the duality has persisted ever since.[49]

'It is a mistake,' writes Muḥammad al-Ghazālī (d. 1993) 'to think that praiseworthy knowledge (al-ʿilm al-maḥmūd) is confined to the study of *fiqh*, *tafsīr* and the like, and that what lies beyond is merely supererogatory that may be abandoned as one pleases.' Al-Ghazālī added that 'this is a great error;' for the knowledge of life and creation (al-kawn wa'l-ḥayā) is no less significant than purely religious knowledge, and the two are, in any case, complementary. It is also a regrettable consequence of a basic confusion and shallowness of thought to confine scientific knowledge only to rational and empirical knowledge. For it is unwarranted and incompatible with Islam's holistic vision of ʿilm.[50]

Knowledge in all of its varieties and branches has been further classified into the three evaluative categories of high, average and low (aʿlā, mutawassiṭ, asfal). This classification may be said to be neither new nor peculiarly Islamic as it has also been held by the followers of other religious traditions.

Knowledge of the first and highest category is embodied in religious knowledge which is taken only from God Most High through His Prophets and Messengers. No one else has the authority to create this variety of knowledge. God being the source and author of religion elevates religious knowledge above all of its other branches.

The lower type of knowledge is that which involves practical physical training and development of applied skills and manual labour, such as horse riding, tailoring, manufacture and handicraft etc. The average variety of knowledge in this classification refers to temporal knowledge, in contradistinction to religious knowledge, which comprises such branches of learning as medicine, architecture and mathematics etc.[51]

There seems to be a certain discord between this and Abū Ḥāmid al-Ghazālī's classification into the two categories of ʿaynī and kifāʾī as discussed earlier. This is because all useful knowledge of worldly affairs falls according to Ghazālī under the broad heading of *farḍ kifāʾī* (collective obligation) which is a religious classification and cuts therefore across the division between religious and temporal knowledge.

The government bears an obligation especially in respect of individuals and families who cannot pay for their own education. This is because preservation of human intellect (ʿaql) and its promotion is one of the essential values (al-maṣlaḥah al-ḍarūriyyah) of Islam. Intellect can only be developed with the promotion of knowledge and combat against ignorance and decay. To promote knowledge and help all those who are capable to acquire it is therefore a matter of priority in an Islamic polity. Since the promotion of intellect is a basic obligation under the *Sharī'ah*, the means that are necessary for its attainment also partake in that obligation. This is the purport of a legal maxim of *fiqh* which provides: 'what is necessary for the accomplishment of a *wājib* is also a *wājib.*' The *Sharī'ah* obligation that is referred to here comprises all essential knowledge within and outside of the sphere of religious sciences. This would include not only knowledge that promotes the essential benefits (*maṣāliḥ*) but also of supportive sciences that are utilised in the provision of amenities, eradication of poverty, and economic development.

Islamic educational reform has been the subject of four international conferences between 1977 and 1982, and I summarise here the salient conclusions of their deliberations in so far as they relate to our discussion of an Islamic education programme in schools and universities.

The first World Conference on Muslim Education held in Makkah in 1977 reasserted the unitarian Islamic view of knowledge and held that education should aim at a balanced growth of the total personality of the individual and cater for his or her growth 'in all its aspects, spiritual, intellectual, imaginative, physical, scientific, and linguistic, both individually and collectively and motivate all these aspects towards goodness and perfection.'[52]

In order to facilitate implementation of this holistic approach to education, the 1977 Conference suggested that educational curricula should be designed on the basis of a new classification of knowledge into the two categories of 'revealed' and 'acquired' knowledge. Divine revelation, as is contained in the Qur'ān and *Sunnah*, teaches that man cannot by himself be rightly guided without the aid of a stable and unchangeable scheme of values. Acquired knowledge on the other hand is a product of human intellect that is in constant interaction with the physical universe on the levels of observation, contemplation, experimentation and application. 'Acquired' knowledge is, as such, susceptible of quantitative and qualitative growth and multiplication, variation and cross-cultural borrowing, and there is no objection to all of this provided that consistency with the *Sharī'ah* as 'the source of value is maintained.'

The report adds that 'there must be a core knowledge drawn from both of these, with major emphasis on the first, especially on the *Sharī'ah* which must be made obligatory on all Muslims at all levels of the educational system 'from the highest to the lowest graduated to conform to the standards of each level.' One other subject that is included under 'General Recommendation' is compulsory teaching of Arabic as a part of the core curriculum. 'These two alone (i.e. *Sharīʿah* and Arabic) can sustain Islamic civilisation and preserve the identity of the Muslims.'[53]

In its part on university curricula in the area of revealed knowledge, the 1977 Conference provided that such curricula must include the study of *Sharīʿah* 'with all its related branches... as core courses in the faculties of law together with comparative studies between *Sharīʿah* and secular laws when the need arises.' Teaching in the *Sharīʿah* subjects should be conducted as 'an effective instrument in serving the interests of the people and meeting the needs of the community.'

The Conference noted that the knowledge of Arabic was 'extremely poor in Arab and Islamic countries alike' and recommended that Arabic language with all of its branches should be made a compulsory subject 'in all Muslim countries of the modern world.'

In the sphere of acquired knowledge a range of subjects have been recommended, and the list begins with literature and literary criticism, Islamic arts, and social sciences. In this connection, it is suggested that 'Western social sciences be replaced by a newly revised set of social sciences whose principles are not only not contradictory to Islam but are drawn from the principles to be found in the Qur'ān and *Sunnah*.'[54]

With reference to natural sciences, it was recommended that educational curricula in the Muslim world should at all stages include the study of the history of sciences and the role of Muslim scientists and scholars in their development. The causes of the development of sciences during the heydays of Islam and their subsequent decline should be carefully investigated. Courses that are offered on natural and applied sciences should be reformulated 'in such a manner as to link them with faith, intensify the religious outlook of the learner so as to make them appreciative of the greatness of the Creator and His miraculous creativity, as Allāh says in the Holy Qur'ān 'only those who know fear Allāh.' The artificial gap between the *Sharīʿah* sciences on the one hand, and the physical and non-physical sciences on the other must also be removed. The report goes on to add that the gap in question has resulted 'from our failure to adopt Islamic methodology in teaching those subjects separately from religion.'

The 1977 Conference urged that the curricula and prescribed textbooks of these sciences 'be purged of ideas and attitudes which directly conflict with Islamic faith.'[55] The Conference also recommended that university students of pure and applied sciences should be able to have some knowledge of the *Sharīʿah* sciences. This point was taken up further in the Second World Conference on Muslim Education of Islamabad 1980 which recommended that the curricula structure in these courses should be divided into technical and *Sharīʿah* streams, and that the *Sharīʿah* stream should be allocated about one-fifth or twenty percent of the time of the total of courses required for graduation.[56]

The 1981 Third World Conference on Muslim Education in Dhaka stressed on the provision of suitable textbooks but noted that this cannot be effectively done unless the Muslim countries take concrete steps to adopt a common curriculum. This is necessary in order to develop uniformity among Muslim countries and also to gradually eliminate the conflict between the traditional and modern systems.[57]

On a more philosophical note, the Dhaka Conference called attention to the Islamic concept of Man as the vicegerent of God, which implies that Man's intellectual and spiritual growth is potentially limitless, since knowledge is the source of this growth, Islam does not put a barrier to the acquisition of knowledge. Islam also seeks a total and balanced development of Man in the context of his relationship with God and nature. Thus a hierarchy of knowledge is established according to which spiritual knowledge has the highest priority. Spiritual knowledge is manifested in a code of morality and ethics that consists of intellectual and physical disciplines.[58]

Writing in 1982 Ashraf noted that these conference resolutions have not been implemented by the Muslim countries. 'No one has tried to implement them,' despite the assent and participation of member countries. Two factors have been noted to explain this, one of which is a persistent confusion over the philosophy of liberal or general education that Muslim countries have borrowed from the West and have attempted to mix up with Islam. The second factor, which is tied up with the first is ambiguity over methodology, classification and curricula; added to these is the problem over the shortage of suitable textbooks.[59] A change of attitude in favour of the proposed reforms was needed but it has not materialised. Instead of altering the post-colonial pattern and trying to produce an Islamic agenda and approach, the authorities in Muslim countries considered it easiest to make superficial changes or simply take a *laissez faire* attitude to the Western secular system of education and seem to have fallen short of making the necessary adjustment. The result of this attitude is continued duality in the educational system and a persistent divide between the religious and secular models of education that seem to be resistant to integration.

IV. Education of Children

Notwithstanding the fact that the Qur'ān and *Sunnah* do not specifically address child education, the general guidelines they provide on education would seem to apply equally to children. The parents have a duty to teach their children the basic principles of Islam that guide them in their daily lives in the performance of ritual prayer, the lawful and unlawful varieties of food, social etiquettes and so forth. It is a responsibility of the parents to enable their young to read and write and also to inculcate into them the moral virtues of decorum, compassion and respectful behaviour toward others. The *Sunnah* also provides evidence to the effect that children must not be preoccupied with the practicalities of life so much so as to prevent them from learning. 'Abd Allāh b. 'Umar has thus reported that when he was fourteen years of age he volunteered to partake in *jihād*, but the Prophet did not permit him because of his tender age. Later at the age of fifteen he volunteered again and this time he was allowed to participate in the battle of Tabūk. When this *ḥadīth* was later recounted by one Nāfi' to the Umayyad caliph 'Umar b. 'Abd al-'Azīz, he decided there and then that fifteen should be the age of majority, a ruling which has been upheld ever since.[60]

Child education is a particular theme which many prominent 'ulamā' have addressed in their general treatment of 'ilm, its priorities and objectives, and what is presented here is a summary of the views of al-Qābisī, al-Ghazālī and Ibn Khaldūn among others.

The fourth century scholar, Abu'l Ḥasan 'Alī b. Muḥammad al-Qābisī (d. 403/1012) wrote that educating the children is an obligation under the *Sharī'ah*. Every child, whether male or female, has a right to education and it is a duty primarily of the father to provide him or her with the education of the essentials of Islam, including the rules of 'ibādāt.[61] The father is also under an obligation to teach his child the Qur'ān as the ability to read the Qur'ān and memorise a portion of it is required in *ṣalāh*. If he is unable to do so, he should hire someone to do it. In the event where the parents cannot afford to pay for the essential education of their children, the close relatives are under an obligation to help with their education.

Al-Qābisī continued that everyone who wishes to advance a good cause is encouraged, especially the learned members of the community, to teach others in the true spirit of *ḥisbah*, that is, enjoining good and preventing evil. The state is also under a similar duty to provide education for children and must pay the teacher, if need be, out of the funds of *bayt al-māl*. Al-Qābisī expressed surprise as to why the earlier *ʿulamāʾ* and leaders had remained somewhat non-committal over this issue, for it is no less important than the appointment of muezzin and prayer leader in the mosque. But then he added that this was probably due to a desire on the part of the *ʿulamāʾ* not to impinge on the parents' freedom of choice in respect of the education of their children. Al-Qābisī added that even when the state provides the funds for children's education, the Imam should not compel the parents who do not wish to send their children to school, but should admonish and persuade them to do so. The state may, however, ask the parents to contribute a specified sum for this purpose, for if the matter is left to voluntary contribution, children may not have the opportunity to be educated in the Qurʾān, and ignorance will prevail. In short, al-Qābisī has come close to the idea of universal and compulsory education for children, and he included female children, as education in the essentials of Islam and ability to read the Qurʾān was equally necessary for all children regardless of gender. The primary objective of education for al-Qābisī was, however, a religious one, dominated by literacy in the Qurʾān and knowledge of religious duties.[62]

In the early days of Islam, education used to be free, especially the mosque education, as it was regarded as an act of religious devotion and no fee was charged for it. That situation soon changed and education began to be either centred in schools or conducted by private teachers on a fee-paying basis. The question then arose whether education was an obligation, and if so, whose obligation it was, and what sort of education was to be given priority for children.[63] Many of these questions did not receive a categorical answer from the early educationists and jurists. They did not directly address the subject of education of children nor did they categorically address the question whether it was an obligation of the community and state to educate them. This may be explained by reference to the fact that except for some verses concerning the protection of orphans, the Qurʾān did not provide specific guidelines on child education.[64] This can also be said of the *Sunnah* which contained general directives on the superiority of knowledge and the merits of its dissemination for everyone but did not specifically address the subject of child education. There was also nothing in the precedent of Companions to suggest that the people were under an obligation to send their children to school. This absence of information in the early sources is not surprising given the fact there were no schools at the time and the matter was left to the effort and initiative of individuals to send their children to the mosque or hire private tutors for the purpose.

Al-Qābisī addressed the issue for the first time and drew the conclusion, as already noted, that education of all children, especially in so far as to enabling them to read the Qur'ān, was a religious obligation. It seems that Imam Mālik had earlier been asked by one of his disciples, Ibn Wahab, as to whether pursuit of learning was obligatory (*wājib*) to which the Imam had briefly replied that it was not so on all the people, without making any further comment on child education.[65] Al-Qābisī would thus appear to have been the first to address this issue. Al-Qābisī's affirmative views on compulsory child education was subsequently maintained by the *ʿulamā'* and jurists, including Ibn Rushd, al-Ghazālī, Tāsh Kubrazada (d. 969/1585— author of *Miftāḥ al-Saʿādah*) and others who considered it a *farḍ kifā'ī* and a duty therefore of the parents and the community at large to provide basic education for their children.

Al-Ahwānī observed that early commentators have responded to the question of education in consonance with the prevailing conditions of their time. The idea of universal compulsory education as a basic function of the state, especially for children, up to a certain age, is relatively recent which emerged with the constitutionalist movement and its attendant clauses on basic rights of the individual. As a result of new legislation on the subject child education is now widely regarded to be an obligation of the community and state as well as parents and guardians, who can even be prosecuted, in some countries at least, in the event they obstruct the education of their children. Compulsory child education thus began in the nineteenth century followed by major developments in the twentieth-century. Even al-Qābisī's views on child education fell short of making its obstruction liable to prosecution. In response to a question, for example, whether the Imam can compel a parent to send his son to school, Qābisī replied that the Imam might not compel but should advise and admonish the parent.[66] Al-Qābisī did not address the prospect of a legal action and prosecution presumably because issues pertaining to prosecution and punishment involved juridical judgement and *ijtihād*, which was perhaps difficult to advance, particularly in the absence of a precedent in the sources or general consensus (*ijmāʿ*) on the subject.

Al-Qābisī's view of child education did not draw a distinction between boys and girls in respect of the Qur'ān studies which was the focus of early education. Boys and girls were both encouraged to study at schools or mosques outside their homes at the early stages of education. Al-Qābisī encouraged segregation for older girls so that they were not distracted. He did not, however, recommend teaching of non-religious subjects such as poetry and orthography for girls.[67] Restrictive views of this kind on female education had been advanced even before al-Qābisī. The renowned Mālikī jurist, Saḥnūn al-Tanūkhī, and also al-Jāḥiz went on record, for example, to advise that girls should not be taught orthography, nor be exposed to reading of poetry. They should focus instead on reading the Qur'ān. The view thus gained ground that girls should not go to schools with boys for fear of promiscuity and corruption and that girls approaching puberty should be taught at home.[68]

Al-Qābisī's approach to the discipline and punishment of children is an extension of his general views on punishment. Human beings are prone to error, temptation and evil throughout the different stages of their lives. Islam permits punishment of evil conduct in various forms, whether the perpetrator is a man or woman, young or old, anyone can be the subject of punishment when his or her conduct calls for it. In this way al-Qābisī subjects everyone to the possibility of punishment, but then he adds that Islam is equally emphatic on leniency and compassion, which often achieve reformation as well as excellence and beauty. This is allowed with regard to adults, even criminals, and is highly recommended with regard to children. But he adds that there is a limit to forgiveness and leniency in which case punishing a child may become necessary. Misconduct in children should be met with firmness that is moderated by leniency especially by the teacher. For the teacher to a pupil is like his father who should not punish the child in a way that leaves resentment. The best approach to discipline is to communicate with the child, with kindness and concern, in an effort to identify the causes of the issue and try to appeal to the child's understanding, 'for the child, despite his immaturity is a human being that is distinguished from an animal by the gift of reason and understanding and by his ability to know the causes of things, even if his level of understanding may be far from maturity and perfection.'[69] Punishment of unruly behaviour is in principle allowed, if verbal advice and reprimand fail to be effective, but beating the child for misconduct should be limited to three strokes. The teacher should not do this in a state of anger so as to avoid mixing discipline with punishment and revenge.[70] But it is advisable that the teacher himself administers the punishment and that he does not delegate this to another child unless this latter has already completed his course of study in the Qur'ān and has become fully conversant in it. When this is the case and the child has graduated and is no longer a student, the task may be delegated to him.[71]

Al-Qābisī is not the first to speak on physical punishment as many scholars and jurists before him have in principle allowed physical punishment of children by their parents and teachers. The ruling here takes its origin in the *hadīth* which instructs the parents to encourage their children at the age of seven to do the ritual prayer (*salāh*) and to beat them, if necessary, when they neglect it at the age of ten. From this the conclusion is drawn that beating a child below the age of ten is not allowed due to tenderness of age and absence of legal responsibility. But then the jurists have by analogy extended the purport of the *hadīth* from parents to teachers, so as to validate physical punishment of children by their teachers for neglectful behaviour in learning.[72]

Muslim jurists have generally held that beating is permitted only when advice and admonition fail, but when it is deemed necessary, it must be disciplinary rather than punitive in purpose. Beating the child must also be restricted to specific instances of mischief. The permitted disciplinary beating is up to three strokes, which may be extended to ten strokes, preferably with the permission of the parents or guardians and in respect of older children who are approaching the age of majority. The teacher himself, and no one else, should administer the strokes and the teacher may not ask another child to represent him in this. And lastly a safer part of the body, such as the feet, should be aimed at and the child may not be struck on the head or face.[73]

In his treatise entitled '*Adab al-Muʿallimīn*' Ibn Saḥnūn, the son of the renowned Mālikī jurist, Saḥnūn al-Tanūkhī (d. 240/854) to whom al-Qābisī has referred, begins his section on discipline (*al-adab*) with reference to a *hadīth* from one Yūsuf b. Muḥammad who said that he was sitting with Saʿd al-Khaffāf when the latter's son came weeping, and when his father asked him about it, the child said that his teacher beat him. His father then said 'by God I say this today what ʿIkrimah narrated to me from Ibn ʿAbbās that the Prophet, peace be on him, said 'Among the wrongdoers of my *ummah* are those who teach their children, while they are least compassionate on the orphans and most severe on the poor.'[74]

Ibn Saḥnūn commented that this *hadīth* singled out teachers who beat the children when they become angry and punitive, not because of punishment that is inflicted for the benefit of children. When the purpose is to realise the child's benefit, beating is not forbidden, but it should not exceed three strokes. Anything more than this should be with the permission of the father especially when the child causes hurt to someone else or to another child, and when a group of them join together in mischief. But all of this should be kept within the limits of moderation. The teacher may discipline the child up to three strokes for laziness and neglect in learning the Qur'ān, but no disciplinary punishment may exceed ten strokes. The teacher may not delegate any of this to another child nor to any of his associates.[75] Ibn Saḥnūn adds that what he wrote on this subject was not by way of issuing a juridical judgement but as an advice which he had on occasion discussed with other colleagues with which they were in agreement.[76]

Ibn Sīnā (d. 1037 AD) held similar views on child's discipline to that of Qābisī both of whom spoke for a persuasive approach to child discipline that blended encouragement with warning and praise with reprimand whenever appropriate. But when all persuasive methods fail, then recourse may be had to physical punishment that is preceded by a stern warning. But Ibn Sīnā seems an exception by holding a somewhat unusual opinion on child discipline: When the need arises to punish the child, the teacher may punish but let him make the first punishment painful so that it acts as a deterrent and generates sufficient fear to prevent repetition. If the initial punishment is light and not painful, the child may not have much fear of its possible repetition.[77]

Al-Ghazālī's advice to parents and teachers is to restrain their severity and anger and not to rebuke the children too frequently as this is likely to damage their ability to respond to gentle advice and normal communication.[78] But disciplinary punishment may be called for when gentler methods do not prove effective, in which case the child may be punished. The basic purpose and rationale of punishment, according to al-Ghazālī, is to deter repetition and create fear through infliction of some pain. To quote al-Ghazālī 'the best advice concerning the animals is not to make the whip totally absent, and the same may be said concerning the child, but this should not mean that going to excess in punishment is recommended.'[79]

Ibn Khaldūn (d. 808/1406) drew attention to the harm that severity causes to a child. Parents and teachers are advised to be lenient as anger and severity suppresses the child 'and robs him of the joy of childhood, inclining him instead to laziness and recourse to making excuses and lying.' This sort of behaviour is caused by the fear of anger and punishment. It is therefore advisable for the parent and teacher not to be tyrannical in disciplining the child. The teacher may admonish and discipline the child but only through persuasive and lenient methods. However when beating is deemed necessary it may be resorted to 'but the teacher of young children may not exceed three strokes.'[80]

Shams al-Dīn al-Anbānī, a late 19th century Rector of Azhar, drew attention to the importance of commendation in the teaching of children. When a child exhibits 'excellence in behaviour or does something praiseworthy it is important for the teacher to acknowledge it. The child should be allowed to take pleasure in his success and it is good if he receives praise from the people.' Should there be an odd occasion of recalcitrance on the part of the child, it should preferably be ignored and should not be declared. For declaring it in such circumstances may reduce his inhibition for repeating it. A second instance of unruly conduct may be reprimanded in private and the child should be told that repetition on his part will be made known to his peers, but blaming the child should not be done frequently as each instance of blame tends to reduce the weight of that exercise for the next time. When he relapses in misconduct again he should be rebuked in an appropriate proportion (*bi-mā yalīq min tawbikhihi*).[81] It thus appears that al-Anbānī has not considered physical punishment of a child of tender age a suitable option.

Both Qābisī and Ibn Saḥnūn advised that children should be given time for relaxation and their education regime should not be strict nor continuous so as to cause them dullness and fatigue. Qābisī advised a weekend break of one and a half days that included Thursday afternoon and Friday. The school day that Qābisī envisaged comprised both morning and afternoon sessions. The morning session was to be devoted to Qur'ān studies and the afternoon to Arabic language, poetry, mathematics and so forth. Children should also have vacation of up to three or even five days for each of the two ʿĪd festivals and other customary holidays.[82]

Al-Ghazālī similarly advised parents and teachers not to overwhelm the children with education so that they are deprived of time and opportunity to play pleasant games which relax them and relieve them of the fatigue of schooling. To deprive a child of play 'and perpetually suppress him with learning causes dullness of intellect and suffocation (*irhāq*). The result of such over-exertion is often seen in the child's recourse to excuses and stratagems to find an exit out of his predicament.'[83] Al-Ghazālī added, however, that children should be taught to be courteous; their parents should not indulge them in 'luxury and comfort, nor in wearing expensive clothes as this will have an adverse effect on their character'.[84]

In a section of his *Iḥyā'*, devoted to proper conduct of student and teacher (*adab al-mutaʿallim wa'l-muʿallim*), al-Ghazālī is evidently concerned with juvenile and adult education and has much to say by way of moral advice which he enumerates, nevertheless, into a list of duties of the student and teacher respectively. The ten duties of students that are discussed may be summarised as follows:

(1) The student must purify his inner self and show this by renouncing immorality and turpitude in his thought and conduct. For knowledge is tantamount to the worship of God and it should be seen as an experience in self-purification of such things as arrogance, anger, caprice and envy. For the light of *ʿilm* does not enter a heart that is filled with such abominations.[85]

(2) The student should reduce his preoccupation with worldly affairs and avoid excessive involvement even with friends and associates so that he can pay full attention to learning.

(3) The student should inculcate in himself humility toward his teacher and the subject he studies, and avoid high-handed behaviour and intellectual arrogance.

(4) The student should not try to delve into disputed matters and issues, be it in the religious or temporal sciences, but should first acquire a firm grasp of the basic data that his teacher has imparted, and only then may he engage himself in disputed matters.

(5) The student should seek knowledge in proportion to his standing. If he is a beginner, his engagement is different to the one who seeks to acquire mastery of the subject.

(6) A gradual approach to learning is advisable. One should not throw oneself into the depth of a certain discipline and seek all and sundry at once. One should instead be selective and purposeful.

(7) What is preliminary to a subject should be covered first as this paves the way to regular progress toward the more advanced stages of learning.

(8) The student should view branches of knowledge in the light of their objectives and consequences. To compare religious knowledge with the knowledge of medicine, for example, the former is focused 'on the hereafter which is permanent, whereas the fruit of the latter is confined to this life. Hence the superiority of the former.'[86]

(9) Pursuit of knowledge should aim at seeking closeness to God Most High and not be focused on acquisition of worldly gain.

(10) It is important for the student to know the relevance of sciences to his own purpose and then to give priority to what is more important to him over that which is more remote.[87]

Al-Ghazālī also expounds the proper conduct of teachers in seven points:

a) The teacher should be kind to his students and consider himself in the position of a parent, except that the parent looks after the worldly needs of his child whereas the teacher combines the concerns of this world with those of the next.

b) The teacher should follow the example of the Prophet who taught his followers not for the sake of worldly gain but for the sake of gaining the pleasure of God.[88]

c) The teacher should not spare his sincere advice (*naṣīhah*) to alert the student of the spiritual superiority of *ʿilm* and how it can be utilised to gain purity of thought and conduct.

d) It is the teacher's duty to admonish the student and speak to him with firmness when the student becomes unruly, but this should be done from a position of kindness and compassion, and not from a punitive stance. All of this should be in the open and no hidden thoughts should burden the student that may impede his progress.

e) The teacher must not speak ill of other branches of knowledge which he may not like himself. The language teacher, for example, should not denounce *fiqh* or *ḥadīth* and vice versa. This should strictly be avoided.

f) The teacher should act on his own advice and his words should not be contrary to his deeds.

g) The teacher should not overburden the student and try instead to address him in proportion to his capacity. Even the Prophets have seen it an important part of their mission not to address their people in a language that would be above their people's level of understanding and experience.[89]

Al-Ahwānī has considered most of al-Ghazālī's views on education to be in conformity with the advice of modern experts on behavioural disciplines, and confirms that their priorities are in the right order. Ahwānī has nevertheless expressed reservation over two points, one general and one more specific. Ahwānī's general critique is addressed to al-Ghazālī's somewhat sufi-oriented approach to education which tends to be overbearing and puritanical. More specifically, Ahwānī is critical of Ghazālī's view that the teacher of religion should not charge a fee for it and do it in order to gain spiritual merit.[90] One might add to this briefly that some of al-Ghazālī's ten-points list of advice to students tend to be over-lapping and repetitive.

Graduality in learning, which is what al-Ghazālī has advised, also finds support in the *Sunnah*, especially in the following *ḥadīth* al-Bukhārī has recorded in this connection:

الرباني الذي يربّي الناس بصغار العلم قبل كباره

A good teacher is one who teaches the people simple and minor subjects before engaging them in bigger and more difficult ones.[91]

Al-Ghazālī's advice to the teacher to avoid over-imposition on his students, also finds support in the *Sunnah*. Thus it is reported by ʿAbd Allāh b. Masʿūd that the Prophet 'used to take care of us and selected a suitable time for his preaching and lectures so as to avoid causing us aversion. He also abstained from addressing us too frequently.'[92]

One of the students of ʿAbd Allāh b. Masʿūd, Abi Wā'il, also reported that Ibn Masʿūd used to teach his students every Thursday. Then 'a man' said to Ibn Masʿūd that 'I wish if you could teach us every day,' to which Ibn Masʿūd replied that 'the only thing which prevents me from doing so is that I hate to bore you with my teaching. I deliver a sermon to you at a suitable time just as the Prophet, peace be on him, used to do with us, for fear of over imposing on us.'[93]

In his chapter on knowledge, al-Bukhārī has also quoted the *ḥadīth* in which the Prophet instructed two of his Companions, Muʿādh b. Jabal and Abū Mūsā al-Ashʿarī, when they were leaving, as judges and teachers for the Yemen in the following terms:

يسروا ولا تعسروا وبشروا ولا تنفروا

Make matters easy (for the people), not difficult, and give good news and repel not (the people) with bad news.[94]

Al-Ghazālī opened up the horizon of education by holding the view that the affairs of religion are closely related to worldly affairs and that good management of religion cannot be attained without parallel progress in worldly matters. This is because this world is a preliminary to the next and the way we manage our worldly affairs is instrumental to failure and success in the hereafter. Essential education is therefore not confined to the religious sciences but must include such other branches of knowledge as industry and science, next to the sciences of religion.[95] Al-Ghazālī then attempted to divide knowledge into the two categories of knowledge that constitute an emphatic obligation (*farḍ 'ayn*) which includes knowledge of the essentials of belief, commands and prohibitions, and knowledge that constitutes a collective obligation (*farḍ kifā'ī*) of the community such as mathematics and medicine.[96] It is not only the acquisition of knowledge that is a collective obligation but also its propagation by the learned that falls under *farḍ kifā'ī*. Thus it is a requirement that 'there be in every mosque and every district of the city a *faqīh* that teaches the people their religion.' Should there be a shortage of learned men of *fiqh*, 'it is the duty of the *faqīh* in villages to go to the neighbouring villages and teach the basics of religion to the people.'[97] Al-Ghazālī thus favoured a mixed but unified approach to education, by bringing temporal knowledge within the ambit of *farḍ kifāyah*, and yet maintaining a basically religious approach to *'ilm*. The basic perception and scheme of all knowledge to both al-Qābisī and al-Ghazālī remained to be focused on religion. Whereas Qābisī added syntax and writing next to a basic grounding in the Qur'ān, al-Ghazālī expanded this sphere to such other subjects as mathematics, architecture and medicine next to the knowledge of the Qur'ān. These additions were deemed necessary for good management of the affairs of this world.

Ibn Khaldūn (d. 808/1406) is basically in agreement with al-Ghazālī's exposition of the Islamic objectives of education, which is, first and foremost, the knowledge of God (*ma'rifat Allāh*) and knowledge of that which shows us how to worship and obey Him, but also to attain a degree of intellectual acumen and awareness that enables man to manage his religion and worldly affairs, and ultimately to be a useful agent in the advancement of civilisation. To attain this degree of intellectual ability will therefore depend on knowledge of various disciplines, as well as on man's state of progress in different stages. On a more practical note, however, Ibn Khaldūn has observed that basic literacy and the ability to write is indispensable to all learning. Although he noted that the Qur'ān was not an easy subject with which to start Islamic education, yet he did not actually recommend to change the entrenched pattern and maintained it is a matter of priority to enable the children to read the Qur'ān, which constituted the fount and foundation of Islamic knowledge.[98]

In a chapter entitled 'the Instruction of Children and the Different Methods Employed in the Muslim Cities,' Ibn Khaldūn pointed out that giving the children a grounding in the Qur'ān symbolised the Islamic education of his time. The reason for this he explained was that early childhood teaching takes root more deeply and forms the foundation of all subsequent knowledge. Ibn Khaldūn then describes the Maghrebi, Spanish and African methods of child education as follows.

The Maghrebi Method is to restrict the education of children to instruction in the Qur'ān, its orthography and discourse among Qur'ān experts. The Maghrebis do not bring any other subject to their classes, such as traditions, jurisprudence or Arabic philology until the pupil is skilled in the Qur'ān. This is the method the urban population in the Maghreb and the mature Berber Qur'ān teachers followed in educating their children up to the age of manhood. Consequently the Maghrebis know the orthography of the Qur'ān, and know it by heart, better than all other Muslims.

The Spanish method is to instruct the children in reading and writing first. Although they still made the Qur'ān the basis of their instruction, the Spaniards did not confine children's education exclusively to the Qur'ān. They also brought subjects such as poetry and composition and gave their children a good knowledge of Arabic and handwriting. They did not stress the teaching of the Qur'ān more than other subjects, and tended in fact to emphasise handwriting until the child reached manhood.

The people of Ifriqiyyah (North Africa) according to Ibn Khaldūn, combined the instruction of Qur'ān to their children usually with the teaching of *ḥadīth*. They also included instruction in basic scientific norms and emphasised handwriting. Their methods of child education were generally closer to that of the Spanish than to the Maghrebi, due probably to geographical proximity and scholarly exchanges.

Ibn Khaldūn added that 'the people of the East too applied a mixed curriculum in the education of children. The fact that the people of Ifriqiyyah and the Maghreb restricted themselves to the Qur'ān makes them altogether incapable of mastering the linguistic habit.' For as a rule no scholarly habit can originate from the Qur'ān because 'no human being can produce anything like it.' Consequently the person who knows the Qur'ān does not acquire the habit of the Arabic language. This situation is not quite so pronounced among the people of Ifriqiyyah as among the Maghrebis due to the fact that the former combined instruction in the Qur'ān with the teaching of scientific norms.[99]

Child education was one of the main subjects of deliberations in each of the four international conferences on Muslim education that were held between 1977 and 1982. The First World Conference on Muslim Education was held in Makkah, Saudi Arabia in 1977. Some of the main points of the proceedings of these conferences may be summarised in the following paragraphs.

Section (3) of the 1977 Conference recommendations on 'Curricula and Syllabi' is concerned mainly with child education and draws attention to the study of the Qur'ān as 'the basic step in the formation of a Muslim's faith, his ethics, ideas and concepts.' It is observed that students nowadays are often 'completely unable to recite properly one single sura of the Qur'ān or memorise or read it.' The recitation and memorisation of Qur'ān should therefore be made 'obligatory from the elementary stage of education onwards with gradually increasing emphasis on interpretation and understanding at later stages.' By the time the student completes his secondary school, he will have 'memorised at least some parts of the Qur'ān and understood their general meaning. More and more Qur'ān schools should be established for boys and girls alike throughout the Muslim world. At the same time, the study and understanding of the *ḥadīth* should be emphasised at all stages.[100]

Child education was also the focus of attention in the Second World Conference on Muslim Education of Islamabad 1980. Beginning with the postulate that children assimilate very quickly and imitate what they see, hear and feel, the conference provides in one of its resolutions that 'it is necessary to teach them both through examples and through practice the fundamentals of Islam. . . (so that they) grow up as Muslim children.' Instructional programmes for children should be concrete and practical and 'the institutional environment should reflect the Islamic ideals, and healthy group activities should be guided by the exemplary conduct of teachers. The teaching of the Qur'ān, reading and reciting (*qirā'ah*), memorisation (*ḥifẓ*) and learning the meaning of selected suras in the national language should be a basic part of early schooling. This should be supplemented by reading and writing the national language, elementary lessons in Arabic and mathematics.[101]

Primary education for children should include theology (*dīniyāt*) on the basics of Islamic dogma and *fiqh*. Other subjects to be taught are the early Islamic history, narratives and poems, geography, mathematics, Arabic and elementary natural science. A similar range of follow-up courses is suggested for secondary education.[102]

The Third World Conference on Islamic Education of Dhaka 1981 contained two basic recommendations on early education for children, one of which was to introduce Islamic culture and civilisation as a basic subject 'at all stages of education—elementary, secondary and university stages.' The conference made detailed proposals on curricula and textbooks to facilitate its stated purpose. The Dhaka Conference basically elaborated a similar proposal that had earlier been made by the 1977 Conference of Makkah. On a broader note, the conference observed that 'a child can become religious or secularist because of the literature he is taught from childhood, from the nursery stage to college level.' The selection and preparation of lessons should therefore be undertaken in such a manner that up to the early secondary stage, Muslim life and culture and 'all the major ethical values of Islam are instilled into the hearts and souls of children.'[103] Furthermore, basic science teaching at the primary level should stimulate 'the elements of awe and wonder in God's creation. . . and arouse curiosity in young minds to know about the unknown.'[104]

The Fourth World Conference on Islamic Education of Jakarta 1982 further noted concerning primary education that its teaching methodology should be so formulated that the teaching of Islam is value oriented: Instead of it becoming a dogmatic imposition of certain rules, it should be 'more a method of instilling into the child basic primary values of life' which he can understand at his age. Children should also be made conscientious of their relationship with the rest of the Muslim world and the *ummah*.[105]

V. Is There a Right to Education in Islam?

In response to the question whether education is a basic freedom, a right or an obligation, it may be said that the quest for education, especially when one speaks of adult and university education, manifests one of the basic liberties to begin with, since a competent individual must basically have the choice whether or not to seek education. It is also a right of the individual to choose the kind of education that is important and relevant to his concerns. But a consensus has emerged, which has found expression not only in the 1948 Universal Declaration of Human Rights (Art. 26) but also in the writings of educationists and scholars that all individuals, especially the children, have a right to free education up to a certain level, and that the state is under a corresponding duty to provide it on a non-discriminatory and universal basis. The UDHR also recognises the right of the parents to choose the type of education they wish to have for their children (Art 18). It thus appears that the UDHR identifies education as a basic right, and it is in any case more consequential to speak of education as a right than a mere liberty that may be a concern mainly of individual choice. The message that education is not a matter only of concern to individual liberty but it is a collective obligation and concern of the community, the parents and the state is echoed in the UDHR and finds even a more forceful expression in the Qur'ān and *Sunnah*.

To say that education is a right of every Muslim can be deduced from the very first verse with which the Qur'ānic revelation began and addressed the Prophet and therefore his community to 'read in the name of thy Lord Who created you...read in the name of the Lord your Cherisher Who taught man by the pen what man did not know.' (96:1–5)

اقرأ باسم ربك الذي خلق. . . اقرأ وربك الأكرم الذي علّم بالقلم علّم الإنسان ما لم يعلم

The Qur'ān (lit. a reader) derived its name from the contents of this verse wherein the message is clearly conveyed that reading, writing and pursuit of knowledge occupied a central position in the Muslim faith. The Prophet himself took education of his people as his personal responsibility by giving frequent sermons to both men and women so much so that he made himself a reference point to answering questions put to him by his Companions. Some of these questions were also addressed by the Qur'ān. The Prophet employed women teachers to teach basic literacy, as well as intermediate education, to his wives, and also employed teachers to teach basic literacy to Muslim children. It is most likely that he did so in his Prophetic capacity which would confirm that education is both a right and an obligation of every Muslim, but if some of what he did was in his capacity as head of state, then that would further support the conclusion that education is one of the basic functions of state in Islam.

Since Islam obligates the learned to disseminate knowledge by teaching it to others, and obligates the ignorant to acquire knowledge, the picture that emerges is one of universal education in that every individual must have some level of involvement in education. The emphatic tone of the Qur'ānic references, and those of the *Sunnah*, on knowledge have led many commentators to the conclusion that the Islamic polity is under an obligation to provide free universal education to the extent of its capability for all citizens, especially the young, and it is, consequently, a corresponding right of every citizen vis-à-vis the state to be provided with basic education.[106] The 'ulamā' of *fiqh* have basically conveyed the same message when they spoke that pursuit of knowledge is a collective obligation of the community as a whole, which, in turn, falls upon the state in its capacity as representative (*wakīl*) of the community. Ibn ʿĀbidīn (d. 1820) has stated that 'the collective obligation of the community relating to ʿ*ilm* comprises every branch of ʿ*ilm* which is necessary for the maintenance of its worldly affairs (*qiwām umūr al-dunyā*).' This is because maintenance of religion depends on good management of worldly affairs and the two are thus closely related to one another.[107] In the writings of Muslim jurists this duty is more emphatic in certain areas, such as the essentials of religion, and less so in regard to certain other branches of knowledge, which may be outside this sphere but which promote the objectives and *maqāṣid* of *Sharīʿah*. It is generally recommendable (*mandūb*) for the individual, and *farḍ kifāʾī* on the community as a whole, to promote and disseminate beneficial knowledge (*al-ʿilm al-nāfiʿ*) outside the sphere of essential religious sciences.[108] Fuʾād Aḥmad's observation portrays this *fiqhī* perspective when he writes: 'since the pursuit of knowledge is either an emphatic obligation (*wājib ʿaynī*), or a collective obligation (*wājib kifāʾī*), or it is recommendable (*mandūb*) from the viewpoint of *Sharīʿah*, depending on the type of knowledge, the Islamic polity is under an obligation to facilitate the fulfillment of this *wājib*, or *mandūb*, as the case may be, and exert itself to the utmost of its capabilities to that end.'[109]

Knowledge of certain subjects such as the performing arts, theatre and journalism etc., may fall under the category of permissible (*mubāḥ*) but even these may be elevated to the category of *mandūb* if teaching or studying them is espoused with the intention of gaining the pleasure of God and rendering service to the people. Sibāʿī and Shīshānī have similarly observed that Islam makes acquisition of knowledge into an obligation on all Muslims, men and women; it becomes a duty of the state therefore to facilitate public education as an essential service. But even so, the state should by no means be seen as the only actor in this regard. The obligation that is conveyed in the *ḥadīth* is also addressed to the parents, spouses and relatives, even neighbours, to play a direct or indirect role in the education of their dependants and other children they might be in a position to help.[110] The responsibility is naturally addressed to the learned who are instrumental to the dissemination of knowledge. The caliph ʿAlī went on record to underscore this in one of his statements: 'on the Day of Judgement the ignorant will not be asked as to their failure to acquire knowledge until the learned have been faced with the question as to why did they not make it available in the first place.'[111] It is also reported that the Prophet once addressed and told ʿAlī b. Abī Ṭālib in such words 'When you give even a single person correct guidance, by God that this is better for you than having flocks of red camels.'[112]

It is further reported that when the Prophet learned that the Ashʿariyyīn, a group of learned individuals at the time, had neighbours who were illiterate, he criticised them for their neglect to teach their neighbours basic literacy. Upon hearing this, the Ashʿariyyīn came to the Prophet and received from him the advice that within one year, they should teach their neighbours basic literacy and absolve themselves of the responsibility they would have otherwise not fulfilled. The Ashʿariyyīn who themselves asked for a year of respite, undertook the responsibility, and the Prophet was pleased with their response.[113]

In response to the question as to which of the two types of knowledge, namely knowledge that partakes in *farḍ ʿayn*, or that which falls under *farḍ kifāʾī*—is preferable to acquire, the majority has given priority to the former. But there is a minority opinion which maintains that the latter type of knowledge should be sought first and be given priority over the former. This is because advancement of knowledge of the latter variety is beneficial to the larger number and exonerates the whole of the community from falling into sin, whereas acquiring knowledge of the former variety only discharges the personal duty of a single individual.[114] The essence of the state's responsibility to discharge the *farḍ kifāʾī* here is to ensure not only the availability of basic education but also to ensure that it is adequate. When there is a need for example, for one hundred teachers to impart basic literacy to the population and there are only fifty of them available, the community and state would have fallen short of fulfilling their collective duty under the *Sharīʿah*.[115]

Al-Nabhānī has reached the conclusion that it is obligatory on the state (*farḍ ʿalā al-dawla*) to provide every individual, male and female, with free education at the primary and secondary levels of schooling which are deemed necessary in order to meet the demands of contemporary life. The state is also under a duty to facilitate higher education on an objective basis to the best of its capabilities. Al-Nabhānī characterises as 'essential education' the learning of disciplines that secure the basic interests of the people (*al-maṣāliḥ al-asāsiyyah*) and prevent them against prejudice and harm. The state is under a duty in *Sharī'ah* to secure the basic interests of the people and this includes essential education.[116] Al-Nabhānī's analysis is in line with that of al-Shāṭibī and Ibn ʿĀbidīn in that it departs from the conventional bifurcation of sciences into religious and secular, and takes instead the essential *maṣlaḥah* as its basic criterion by which to evaluate the responsibility of the state and the priorities of its educational programme.

Among modern Muslim Scholars, Maḥmaṣṣānī has observed that 'education from the *Sharī'ah* viewpoint is not only a privilege, a right or liberty, but it is an obligation that is clearly conveyed in the Prophetic directive to 'seek knowledge even if it be in China,' and that 'pursuit of *'ilm* is an obligation of every Muslim.'[117] According to yet another observer, 'Islam recognises education as a natural right of every individual.'[118] Al-Sibāʿī, Ahwānī, Muṣaylihī and ʿAfīfī have similarly held that everyone has a right to education in Islam and that includes men, women, rich and poor, ruler and ruled, rural dwellers and urban people all alike without any discrimination or preference.[119] These conclusions tie up well with some of the rulings of *fiqh*, which include the following:

a) The adult son is entitled to leave home in pursuit of the required knowledge (*al-'ilm al-mafrūḍ*) even without the permission of his parents, just as he is entitled to leave in pursuit of the required *jihād* (*al-jihād al-mafrūḍ*), provided that he does not expose himself to starvation and imminent danger.

b) The wife is entitled to leave her marital home without the permission of her husband, and even when he disagrees, in pursuit of knowledge that the Lawgiver has made obligatory on all.

c) It is a duty of the affluent father to support his son during his studies even if the latter might be capable of earning a living.

d) Books are counted among the essential goods, side by side with such other things as food, shelter, and clothing, and they are not therefore liable to the obligatory *zakāh*. On a similar note, a person who is otherwise entitled to be a recipient of *zakāh*, but owns large quantities of books, regardless of their quantity or price, his entitlement to *zakāh* is not affected. By the same token, he is not liable to the payment of the required charity of *al-fiṭr* (*ṣadaqat al-fiṭr*) if he has no assets other than his books.

e) A learned person who owns books but no other assets is similarly not required to sell them in order to go to the *ḥajj*.

f) When a learned man is unable to pay his debts and is consequently declared bankrupt, he is still entitled to retain his books.

Al-Ghazālī, who wrote the above, added that the learned man who owns books uses them in due fulfilment of a collective duty (*farḍ kifā'ī*) and is therefore exonerated from the said liabilities.[120] Ibn ʿĀbidīn confirmed these rulings and wrote that 'scholarly works that are owned by an *ʿālim* are counted as basic necessities, as without them the *ʿulamā'* will be incapacitated and exposed to destruction (*al-halāk*).'[121]

Being in charge of the affairs of the community the government in an Islamic polity is naturally entitled to supervise public education in the institutions of learning, *madrasah*s and universities. A sense of leadership and direction is also necessary to ensure the availability of a right mix of essential and beneficial education as well as to prevent the spread of inimical and reprehensible knowledge (*al-ʿilm al-madhmūm*) that violates the dictates of *Sharīʿah* and sound reason.[122] With regard to female education, it will be noted that almost all the directives of the Qur'ān and *Sunnah* on education are conveyed in the form of general (*ʿām*) provisions that apply equally to men and women. There is no text in either of these sources that makes an exception for females or which discriminate in favour of the male sex. All the passages that have been quoted from the Qur'ān are in the nature of *ʿām* provisions, and so are the *ḥadīth*s. When the *ḥadīth* declares that pursuit of *ʿilm* is an obligation of all Muslims, that is a *ʿām* provision. Similarly the guidelines and directives that are concerned with the education of one's family are not gender biased.[123]

To educate one's family naturally included both boys and girls. More specially, we note that one of the renowned figures among women during the time of the Prophet, Shifā al-ʿAdawiyyah had taught literacy to women before Islam. Included among her students were Ḥafṣah, the daughter of ʿUmar b. al-Khaṭṭāb. Later when the Prophet married Ḥafṣah, he employed Shifā to continue educating Ḥafṣah in order to advance her writing ability. It was the same Ḥafṣah who became the keeper of the original text of the Qur'ān, which remained in her custody for many years. Following the battle of Yamāmah when many Qur'ān memorisers had died, the Caliph Abū Bakr made the suggestion to compile the Qur'ān in a single volume. He consulted ʿUmar b. al-Khaṭṭāb on this and after some hesitation by the latter, the agreement was reached nevertheless to compile the Qur'ān and they obtained the entire collection from Lady Ḥafṣah. Zayd b. Thābit who had written most of the text was then asked to work on its compilation in a single volume. This episode provides practical implementation of the normative guidelines of the sources on the merit of education for men and women alike. It is well-known also that women during the Prophet's time did not suffer the sort of disabilities that were later visited upon them by customary developments in Muslim societies. To illustrate the substance of this analysis, one may refer to a *ḥadīth* that consists of a general statement addressed to men, women, young and old without any distinction. The Prophet thus said '. . . Anyone who treaded on the path of seeking knowledge, God will make easy for him the way to Paradise.'[124]

ومن سلك طريقا يطلب به علما سهّل الله له طريقا إلى الجنة

In another *ḥadīth* it is reported that the women of Medina complained to the Prophet as follows:

قال النساء للنبي صلى الله عليه وسلم : غلبنا عليك الرجال
فاجعل لنا يوما من نفسك فوعدهن يوما لقيهن فيه
فوعظهن وأمرهن

Men have dominated us in respect of your time. Will you assign a day for us so that we can meet with you and receive your teaching? The Prophet then assigned a day for them for the purpose.[125]

To be reserved and introspective and have a sense of modesty (*al-ḥayā*) is generally recommended as an aspect of character, but not in one's quest for knowledge, especially when it concerns women. Al-Bukhārī has in this connection quoted two prominent Companions, Mujāhid and ʿĀ'ishah, in a *ḥadīth* bearing the title '*al-Ḥayā' fi'l-ʿIlm*' (to be shy concerning knowledge) which is as follows: Mujāhid said 'Knowledge is not attained by one who is very shy or high-handed and arrogant. And ʿĀ'ishah said 'How excellent the women of the Anṣār are; they do not feel shy while learning religious knowledge'.[126]

قالت عائشة : نعم النساء نساء الأنصار لم يمنعهن الحياء أن
يتفقهن في الدين

In conclusion, it may be said that women have an equal right to education and no discrimination is envisaged in the pursuit of *'ilm* for either of the sexes. If there were historical and customary developments that led to segregation and veiling and had a derogatory effect on women's status and also their education, it did not originate in the source evidence on the subject of *'ilm*. Rather it was a part of a more general problem of a discriminatory pattern of customary developments that women suffered, not only in respect of education, but also in regard to other rights as well.

VI. Institutionalisation of Learning

Institutionalised free education in Islam takes its historical origin in the mosque where the leading *'ulamā'* addressed the public in Friday sermons and other occasions when they imparted knowledge of religion and also addressed community issues from the pulpit. The mosque was open to everyone and there was no ceremony or payment of any fee. The mosque began to serve as a school as early as the reign of the second Caliph *'Umar*, who appointed Qur'ān readers to the mosques of such cities as Kufa, Basra and Damascus for the purpose of reciting the Qur'ān and *ḥadīth*. Gradually, instruction in Arabic grammar and literature were incorporated into this rudimentary system of education. Out of this early instruction in language and religion, there grew the popular elementary school (*maktab*) which was designed to acquaint the young with reading and writing and more specifically, with the principles of religion. Both boys and girls were given instruction in the mosque, but also sometimes in private houses. The *maktab*, which still survives in many parts of the Islamic world, served as an institution of basic and preparatory education for more advanced learning. Whether given in formal sessions held at the mosque, or through private tutoring held at the houses of the wealthy, the *maktab* education shaped the student attitude of respect both for learning and the learned.[127]

The mosque circles (*ḥalaqah*, or *majlis*) were led by leading scholars who instituted study groups and taught a select number of students in religious sciences, *ḥadīth*, law, grammar, logic etc., on a regular basis. These circles centred on a particular person (called *Shaykh*, *ḥakīm* or *ustādh*) and provided a platform for preaching, disputation and solicitation of legal opinion. Once again this service was given free of charge, and the main purpose was dissemination of knowledge and gaining the pleasure of God Most High. Poor and rich took part without discrimination and the local population supported the effort through charitable donations (*awqāf*) and patronage. The mosque-centred activities continued even after the formation of the colleges (*madrasahs*) although in a peripheral manner. It was in the earlier part of the fifth/eleventh century that colleges witnessed important development under the Seljuq Vizier, Niẓām al-Mulk, whose name is associated with the development of this institution.[128]

The colleges or *madrasahs* were opened usually adjacent to the mosque. Not all had separate quarters. Some colleges consisted of circles in a particular mosque. The separation of mosque and *madrasah* was with the purpose of protecting the serene environment of the mosque that was to remain a place of worship away from the hustle and bustle of child and adult education. The college curricula and activities were to some extent guided by the type of endowment deed on which they were based, and they were devoted to teaching religious subjects and *fiqh* of one or more of the leading schools. The person who endowed a college normally stipulated for food, clothing and allowance of students in addition to its academic matters.[129]

The mosque-based *maktab* and *ḥalaqah* remained the main institutions of learning until the fourth/tenth century. In 395/1005, the Fatimid caliph al Ḥakim constructed the *Dār al-ʿIlm* (House of Knowledge) in Cairo where mathematics and physics were taught and had a vast library which by some accounts had one million books. But it is interesting to note that philosophy, natural and mathematical sciences were taught in the *Bayt al-Ḥikmah* (House of Wisdom) constructed in Baghdad by the caliph al-Ma'mūn around 200/815, to which a library and an observatory were joined. This early development of interest in the sciences was prompted by the new challenges that the Muslim community had faced not only from Greek philosophy, but also from Jewish and Christian theologians and philosophers that lived in places such as Damascus and Baghdad. For Muslim scholars 'were unable to defend the principles of faith through logical arguments, as could other religious groups. . .'[130]

Then came the stage of inauguration of state-sponsored *madrasah* in the capital cities and towns which enjoyed direct support from the state funds and also charitable donations and grants by local population and benefactors from other places. As institutions of higher learning the *madrasahs* saw the climax of their development in the latter part of the fifth/eleventh century, when the Seljuq vizier, Niẓām al-Mulk, established a chain of colleges in Baghdad and other cities culminating in the great Niẓāmiyyah of Baghdad which was founded in 459/1067.[131] The institutional format and diversity of subjects that were studied in this, the Bayhaqiyyah of Nīshāpūr, the Madrasah al-ʿUmariyyah of Damascus and the Ruwaḥiyyah of Aleppo included in their curricula the all-important propedeutics, *hadīth* and the Qur'ān. Some only specialised in certain subjects, such as the Qur'ān, *hadīth* and *fiqh*. There were some curricular differences also between the Sunnī and Shiʿī *madāris*. The Sunni schools were in general more inclined toward the study of law and theology, whereas the Shiʿa taught more of the natural sciences and mathematics. Logic was always a part of the programme of the al-Azhar University, and Islamic philosophy was taught in the Qarawiyīn in Fez, Morocco.[132] Regardless of some curricular differences that had notably existed between the Sunnī and Shiʿī *madrasahs*, the general academic atmosphere in them did not differ much.

Transmission of knowledge in these institutions has always had a personal aspect in that the student primarily sought a particular master rather than an institution. The student revered his teacher, even in personal matters not connected with his formal studies. The atmosphere at these schools has been very relaxed and informal without there being any great academic and financial pressure upon the student. Nor has there been a strong incentive to obtain a diploma or certificate. Religious education remained free and the *madrasah* included residential facilities for students and provided specialised and advanced courses of learning in various disciplines.[133] Some of the *madrasahs* specialised in skills such as surgery and pharmaceuticals, and also offered specialised courses on mathematics and chemistry, in addition to the study of *fiqh* either generally, or according to a particular school thereof. The Manṣūriyyah of Cairo, ʿAdudī of Baghdad, and the Nūrī of Damascus specialised in medicine, and some of them were also teaching hospitals.

The institution of *waqf*, or charitable endowment, parental support and patronage by pious individuals also played a notable role in the continuity of the sources of income for these institutions. Scholastic centres in certain particular cities and regions became well known for their rationalist leanings and association with the *Ahl al-Ra'y*, and those in the Hijaz became known for their pro-*hadīth* orientation and specialisation in *hadīth* sciences. Some *madrasahs* in the Iraqi cities of Kufa and Basra also specialised in Arabic language and syntax. The first college in Damascus was opened in 491/1097 and in Cairo not long after. By the middle of Mamluk era in the tenth/16th Century there were seventy-three colleges in Cairo and more than a hundred in Damascus. The Maghreb and Spain were by contrast poorly endowed and lagged behind the pace of development in Syria and Egypt.[134]

The *madrasahs* remained the core of the higher educational system and they were in many ways connected with the schools of law. This is perhaps indicated in their academic programmes and ranks. The term *faqīh* in those days simply meant an advanced student. *Mudarris* (professor), also generally termed as *ʿālim* (pl. *ʿulamāʾ*), *shaykh* (master) and *mujtahid* were the academic ranks many of which had a *Sharīʿah* based connotation. The *mujtahid* signified the highest rank in scholarly achievements in the *madāris* (pl. of *madrasah*). The establishment of *madāris* on the whole signified professionalisation of scholarship under the state patronage. Educational establishments were basically controlled by those who instituted the endowment (*awqāf*) for their maintenance and these were usually the ruling classes, men of the sword and men of the pen. State control and patronage was more pronounced in the legal education and the judiciary. Teaching in non-traditional sciences does not on the other hand, reveal official control of the same scale.[135]

A typical treatise on education, such as the *Taʿlim al-Mutaʿallim* of Burhān al Dīn al-Zarnūjī, a Khurasani who died sometime between 591/1194 and 640/1242, consisted of sections on proper conduct which exhorted the student, by example and *hadīth*, to be serious, pious and perseverant, and gave details of etiquette to be followed in dealing with peers and superiors. Such were the matters deemed to constitute the conditions of learning, which the author said his contemporaries did not properly observe. The veneration of teachers was axiomatic to the point that the teacher was almost to be sanctified.[136]

There was considerable mobility and travelling in pursuit of scholarship and a certain attitude began to be entrenched among seekers of knowledge that erudition and competence often necessitated travelling and residence in one or more of these well-known centres of learning. Travelling, or *rihlah*, was without formal restrictions and scholars were well received and were given help to enable them to concentrate on their scholarly pursuits.

All of this drew incentive and stimulus from the teachings of the Qurʾān and *Sunnah*. Muslim individuals and teachers showed dedication and excellence in their achievements, which helped to nurture a healthy respect for knowledge among the populace. Islamic civilisation acquired fame for being a knowledge-based civilisation wherein no other class of people carried greater influence with the community than the *ʿulamāʾ*. Political leaders and rulers often sought legitimacy from the teachings of Islam and endorsement of *ʿulamāʾ*. It came thus naturally to Ibn Khaldūn to write that 'knowledge and education is a natural requirement of human development. Civilisation flourishes with the burgeoning of sciences and culture attains its regularity and perfection through knowledge.'[137]

VII. Academic Freedom

The basic impulse of Qurʾānic teachings on rational enquiry and knowledge is, on the whole, affirmative on academic freedom. If one were to single out an aspect of the Qurʾān, it would be its advocacy of intellectual freedom as a dimension of the dignity of the human person and its commitment also to the dissemination of knowledge. Islam's view of academic freedom is within a given set of values, which are to promote God-consciousness (*taqwā*) and human welfare (*maṣlahah*). The basic interests of Islam can be seen within the framework of the goals and objectives of *Sharīʿah* (*maqāṣid al-Sharīʿah*) which exhibit a prior commitment to the protection and advancement of human life, basic principle of the faith, good management of property, advancement of human intellect and protection of the family. Knowledge is beneficial when these goals are pursued, in which case its advancement and dissemination are not only free but are positively encouraged. Anyone who is engaged in this pursuit is deemed to be involved, in the meantime, in service and devotion to God (*ʿibādah*), and service to humanity whose freedom in these pursuits is basically unhindered.

The Qurʾān and *Sunnah* have spoken profusely in praise of the learned and their superiority because of their commitment to a superior cause. Indeed the first and foremost of all messages that the Qurʾān conveyed was to ask the people to read, and learn how to write by the pen. This commitment to the pursuit of knowledge was seen as a favour of God to mankind 'Who taught man what Man did not know' (96:5) علّم الإنسان ما لم يعلم . God named His illustrious Book as a Reader—Qurʾān (from the root word *qaraʾa*— to read). When the Prophet was asked to 'Say! O My Lord increase me in knowledge' (20:114), وقل رب زدني علما the message was one of uninhibited freedom in the quest for knowledge. It was indeed a language, not just of permissibility or freedom, but also of full approval and support. To acquire knowledge became a collective obligation (*farḍ kifā'ī*) and the subject of a command in the Qur'ān asking the people to 'look into what is in the heavens and the earth' (10:101). All of this, one might even say, makes the question over the existence of academic freedom in Islam almost redundant. Only when knowledge is distracted from its constructive course to what may be seen as prejudicial to the basic values that Islam advocates, then the question of restriction on academic freedom and education becomes relevant. Islam would in this way discourage propagation of heresy and misguidance that interferes with its basic dogma and values. Dissemination of corrupt and misleading ideas and doctrines that are prejudicial to human welfare will also be deemed suspect, and may even amount to an offence and the subject therefore of a legal action. This naturally means that there is no absolute freedom and people are therefore not free to attack the moral fabric of society and cause commotion and mischief in the name of academic freedom.

Academic freedom and freedom to express an opinion is manifested in the Sharī'ah doctrine of *ijtihād* which entitles qualified scholars, judges and jurists to deduce the ruling of new and unprecedented issues by recourse to interpretation and independent reasoning. Should there be a clear text which applies to the issue concerned, there should be no need for *ijtihād* and therefore little freedom that one can speak of. But if the text only provides a partial guidance which may either be too general or too specific to deliver the needed solution, the scholar and *mujtahid* have greater flexibility and scope to exercise considered judgement in their quest for a desired solution. In the event where the text only provides a partial guidance, *ijtihād* is likely to consist of interpretation that clarifies the relevance of the text to the issue concerned. In the more likely event, however, where the text does not cover the new issue, the researcher may resort to independent reasoning and exercise *ijtihād* based on his best opinion and judgment.

Ijtihād (lit. exertion) is a broad concept that applies to almost all areas of academic enquiry and research, and the scope of its application need not be confined to legal matters. Notwithstanding the historical tendency which saw *ijtihād* as a juristic concept and a preserve therefore of the jurist, *ijtihād* essentially consists of enquiry and research that is informed by the relevant data of the Qur'ān and *Sunnah*. *Ijtihād* as such can be exercised in *Sharī'ah* as well as such other fields of scholarship as economics, medical and biological research, political science, environmental studies, and indeed all areas of research which involve the exercise of opinion and judgement.

Notwithstanding the wide scope that the theory of *ijtihād* allows for rational enquiry into the source evidence of Islam, there are some limitations on this exercise. The science of the sources of *Sharīʿah* (*uṣūl al-fiqh*) expounds the limitations of *ijtihād* and the various modes and formulas in which *ijtihād* can operate. *Ijtihād* may thus consist of analogical reasoning (*qiyās*), juristic preference (*istiḥsān*), considerations of public interest (*maṣlaḥah*) and so forth.[138] A basic limitation that occurs in almost all of these various *ijtihād*-based doctrines is that the result of *ijtihād* may not contradict a clear injunction of the Qur'ān or the authentic *Sunnah*. As a basic postulate of *uṣūl al-fiqh*, the Qur'ān, being the embodiment of divine revelation, commands a higher authority than human reason (*ʿaql*). If the clear text imposes a prohibition, for example, that usury (*ribā*) is forbidden, or it is forbidden for a Muslim to engage in illicit sexual intercourse etc., these are taken on face value and there is basically no academic freedom to engage in a rational analysis to the contrary. In the event where the Qur'ān itself leaves room for interpretation and rational analysis, which is more often the case rather than not, then the Qur'ān remains open to reasoning and provides scope for academic freedom.

The text of the Qur'ān or *ḥadīth* is either decisive (*qaṭʿī*) or speculative (*ẓannī*); only the latter is said to be open to interpretation, but not the former. Thus according to a legal maxim of *fiqh*, 'there is no *ijtihād* in the presence of a definitive text'—*lā ijtihād maʿ wujūd al-naṣṣ*.' Notwithstanding the presence of this and similar other epithetic declarations on the subject, my own familiarity with Islamic jurisprudence tells me that things are seldom as black and white as these declarations tend to suggest. I have often found that even in cases where a clear text (*naṣṣ*) might exist, there is room for rational enquiry and *ijtihād* that either elaborates and explains the text, explores best methods of its application, or indeed brings to light some aspect of its understanding which may not have been known before. I do not propose to enter into details, but one general example that comes to mind is the prescribed penalties, known as *ḥudūd*, which are determined by the text and are often seen as typical examples where the scope of *ijtihād* concerning them is minimal. My own enquiry into this subject indicates that there is a fairly wide scope for *ijtihād* if the *ḥudūd* were to be meaningfully understood and applied. To take a dogmatic approach to the *ḥudūd* and close the door to rational analysis and enquiry concerning them, and worst still, to apply them in a dry mechanical fashion, would be self-defeating and would be likely to fall short of serving the Qur'ānic ideals of justice. This is why I have concluded that the *ḥudūd* are open to *ijtihād*, due mainly to the changed conditions of society.[139] A gap has often developed between the text and the living conditions of people which affect the basic rationale and *ʿillah* of that text. The gap needs to be bridged first. I venture to speculate that a similar perspective can be advanced with regard to many other issues that are addressed in the context of a totally different set of conditions that contemporary society may have experienced concerning them.

Scientific research is normally guided by its own objectives, one of which is the quest to understand and discover the unknown mysteries of the observable world. Science as such, or a major part of it at least, may be seen as a part of knowledge (*ʿilm*) that finds much encouragement in the Qur'ān and *Sunnah*. It is doubtful, however, whether modern scientific research can all of it be seen in this light. Be that as it may, science by itself cannot determine values in relationship to many questions which affect human life and welfare. Advanced research in genetic engineering, or questions over permissibility of human cloning, for example, are guided by their own scientific objectives, but the efficacy or otherwise of the results that are obtained cannot be determined on grounds of science alone. On instances such as this, value-oriented *ijtihād* by government and community leaders has a role to play in order to determine an appropriate framework for the application of science to human life, society, and environment. In the case of human cloning, for example, only a one-parent child is brought into the world and the question naturally arises over the efficacy of such a prospect. Thus it may be said that the unprecedented pace of progress in science and technology has also created a wider role for creative thinking and *ijtihād*. The researcher may be guided, not always by the technical data of jurisprudence, although this can provide valuable help, but by the goals and purposes of Islam, that is, the *maqāṣid al-sharīʿah*, which seek to promote human values and welfare in a way that can be more readily related to science, and play a supportive role to beneficial scientific research. Scientific research should therefore operate within the valid perimeters of the *maqāṣid al-sharīʿah* which seek to promote essential human values. Academic freedom and scientific research should be used to advance these objectives, and not otherwise.

The theory of *ijtihād* is explicit on the inviolability of its result and demands respect for the freedom of the person who conducts *ijtihād*. The qualified scholar (*mujtahid*) accordingly enjoys total liberty in the conduct of his enquiry and determination of its results. The essence of this freedom is conveyed in the Qur'ān which encourages recourse to rational enquiry and judgement by everyone who is capable of making a contribution to the cause of knowledge. To quote but two short verses from the Qur'ān:

كذلك يبين الله لكم الآيات لعلكم تتفكرون

God thus expounds for you the signs that you may think (2:266).

أو لم ينظروا في ملكوت السموات والأرض وما خلق الله من شيئ

Do you not look into the dominions of the heavens and the earth and what things God has created? (7:185).

Abū Zahrah has rightly observed that the rational enquiry which the Qur'ān has encouraged 'would not be possible to realise without the freedom to express one's thought, opinion and judgement.'[140] Wāfi has similarly noted that the Qur'ān provides incentive to enquiry and investigation 'without advocating any particular scientific theory or restrictive conditions other than the enquiry itself, granting in the meantime the individual complete freedom to draw conclusions from his observation.'[141]

Every person who is capable of research and inquiry into the source, be it man or woman, ruler and ruled, or those who occupy government positions—all are equally entitled to conduct *ijtihād*, just as they are all liable to making errors. No one is immune to error except the Prophet in respect only of what he received through revelation. But even the Prophet was not immune to error in respect of what originated in his own *ijtihād*. This can also be said in regard to interpretation of the text in which no one has a prerogative and everyone qualified is entitled to advance an interpretation. There is no requirement in Islam for anyone to follow the views of any individual or *madhhab*. The leading imams of the *madhāhib*, and the leading Companions before them have all warned others not to consider themselves bound by their opinion but to refer to the source on which they had relied themselves. Everyone is encouraged to look into the rationale of the *ahkām* and the balance of evidence on which they are founded.[142]

An aspect of academic freedom that became the focus of attention in the early history of Islamic scholarship is *hurriyat al-ra'y*, that is, freedom to express an opinion. *Ra'y* is defined as an opinion on a matter which has not been regulated by the Qur'ān and *Sunnah*. In the usage of the Arabs, *ra'y* applies to things which are not seen but are known through reason, intuitive judgement or the light of one's heart. Matters which are regulated by definitive factual or rational knowledge, and matters on which all signs are bound to concur are thus precluded from the scope of *ra'y*. *Ra'y*, opinion and judgement can, in other words, proceed with regard to matters which are open to opinion, and not on factual matters that provide no scope for it at all.[143]

The early juristic discourse in the two camps of *Ahl al-Ra'y* (partisans of opinion) and *Ahl al-Ḥadīth* (partisans of *ḥadīth*) revolved around the question as to whether a framework should be devised for the valid exercise of *ra'y*, and the result of that was a prolonged engagement in the development of a set of methodological guidelines and doctrines that regulated the exercise of *ra'y*, which then constituted the subject of a separate discipline, namely the *uṣūl al-fiqh*. The basic purpose of *uṣūl al-fiqh* is to regulate *ra'y* and *ijtihād* especially in religious and juridical matters, and by doing so it also provides a set of criteria by which to ascertain the valid exercise of academic freedom in these areas.[144]

The caliph and *muftī* are not immune to error and what they say of their own personal opinion does not bind anyone. They are all entitled to give good and sincere advice to others by way of encouragement and guidance. They can only issue enforceable decisions within the basic framework of the *aḥkām*. The main task of a *muftī* is to give *fatwā* (legal opinion) which either explains the existing law or advances a fresh interpretation. Only the law itself and not the personal opinion or *ijtihād* of *muftī* can have a binding force. There is no recognition in *Sharīʿah* of titles and official posts such as *Shaykh al-Islām*, Grand Muftī and the like who can issue a binding decision in their own right or issue judgment on *ḥalāl* and *ḥarām* without evidence. The *Sharīʿah* naturally entitles the judge and the imam to issue binding orders in accordance with correct principles and procedures, but that is a separate matter which has no direct bearing on academic and personal freedom of individuals and scholars.[145]

The Qur'ān and *Sunnah* also support recourse to consultation (*shūrā*) in public affairs (cf., 3:159; 42:38). *Shūrā* essentially consists of the personal opinion of one who gives a counsel and it would not be worth its name if the latter did not enjoy the freedom to give it. The Qur'ān also validates *ḥisbah*, that is, promotion of good and prevention of evil (*amr bi'l-maʿrūf wa nahy ʿan al-munkar*). *Ḥisbah* entitles the individuals, including laymen and specialists, to promote a good cause or to avert a bad one through such ways and means as they have at their disposal, be it in words or through action, provided that the person who attempts it knows that the good cause he or she is pursuing does not in the meantime cause a harm greater than the benefit it can secure. There is much detail in the *ḥadīth* and juristic manuals on *ḥisbah*, but what needs to be stressed here is that *ḥisbah*, as well as its allied (also Qur'ānic) concept of *naṣīḥah*, that is, giving sincere advice to someone that might help him to see a weakness in his conduct or an error that had escaped him—both take for granted the freedom to speak out and act according to one's convictions. But unlike *ḥisbah* which is confined to situations and incidents that a person witnesses by direct observation, *naṣīḥah* is not so restricted and can be given at any time and to anyone, including one's friends and associates as well as to government leaders and the media. The subject of *naṣīḥah* may also be personal relations, public affairs or academic advice. Here too, the basic idea of *naṣīḥah* takes for granted the freedom of its donor to give an advice provided that it is sincere, courteous and constructive.[146]

The administrative and organisational structure of al-Azhar has been reformed and modernised on several occasions in the twentieth century, which has meant that it currently operates on par with other universities in Egypt, although it is still widely regarded as the most respectable institution of Islamic learning. Its academic reputation and credentials are in many ways due to its long history of operation as an institution of traditional Islamic scholarship. I now take a brief look at academic freedom in Al-Azhar University of Egypt.

Al-Azhar was restructured and modernised under the Egyptian law (no. 103) of 1961 which not only opened the university's doors to female students but also added faculties of medicine, architecture, management and administration etc., to the faculties of *Sharīʿah* and theology that had hitherto dominated the university's academic programme. This was the third and the most wide-ranging attempt following two similar instances of reforms in 1911 and 1930.

Al-Azhar was first opened in 361/972 by the Fatimid caliph Muʿizz al-Dīn and it began to offer courses in theology, logic, languages and astronomy etc. The academic programmes of al-Azhar had historically followed the traditional *madrasah* pattern which accorded considerable freedom of choice to both students and professors. The student chose both the subject of his study and the professor who taught it. The choice of subject was often focused on particular but well-recognised textbooks that a professor chose to teach in his class. The student in other words chose the text and the professor. At the end of the course of study in one or more texts, the student was interviewed by the professor and if the latter was satisfied as to the candidate's accomplishment, the student would be given a certificate of graduation. This certificate represented the academic credentials of the graduate and he could be employed on that basis as an instructor in his relevant field of specialisation by al-Azhar itself or by other *madrasahs*. This was normal practice at al-Azhar until the end of nineteenth century when the transition began to a modern educational system that was based on formal course structures, syllabi, timing and degree programmes.

The first academic governing body at al-Azhar was established in 1908 as a result of a statutory law that was promulgated in that year. Under the chairmanship of the *Shaykh al-Azhar*, the High Council of al-Azhar included among its members the Grand Muftī of Egypt and representative *'ulamā'* from each of the other three leading *madhhabs*, namely Mālikī, Ḥanbalī and Shāfi'ī, among others. This was the beginning of a stage where some of the decision making functions of the professor were overtaken by a university body. Academic freedom that professors and students had hitherto enjoyed was wide-ranging and unencumbered by hierarchy and officialdom of the kind that has since become normal practice in al-Azhar.[147]

The general picture that emerges from the foregoing discussion is that academic freedom is the normal and natural pattern in Islam and any restriction that is imposed must be justified and reasonable, if it were to be acceptable at all. Academic freedom in religious sciences is broadly subject to similar restrictions as would apply to *ijtihād*. The rational sciences are subject only to their own parameters and due observance of the goals and principles of Islam that promote, rather than destroy, the essential benefits (*ḍarūriyyāt*) on which normal life and order in society depend. We now turn to exploring the scope respectively of harmony and conflict between Islam and science.

VIII. Islam, Rationality and Science

The Qur'ānic concept of knowledge encompasses transcendental knowledge as well as knowledge that is based on sense experience and observation. The *Sunnah* has endorsed this and placed emphasis on beneficial knowledge that advances human welfare. This may be seen as a basic framework of harmony rather than conflict between Islam and science, yet it is a framework that does not preclude areas of disharmony and conflict between them. What is attempted here is a brief enquiry into the nature of the scientific method and the reason, if any, behind the common perception of an inherent conflict between religion and science.

The basic area of tension between religion and science is seen in the latter's experimental approach to reality that tends to preclude transcendental knowledge. The scientist does not speak, for example, of God and the creation of the first Man because he has no scientific data to refer to. The body of metaphysical discourse that draws attention to the intricacies of human body, the relationship and balance that can be noted among living creatures and the created world does not engage the scientist's attention. The likely response of the scientist may be that he cannot go beyond what can be found and proved by evidence. This scientific attitude is very different from that of the ancient Greeks and early Muslim thinkers, who took an ontological view of knowledge which went beyond observable reality. Science according to Aristotle is 'knowledge not only of fact but of reasoned fact.' Its aim is not merely to record observable connections in nature and calculate them in mathematical terms, but also (and mainly) to account for observable phenomena and throw light on their relations to their causes. Modern science aims not at ontological but at empirical knowledge. It denies the validity of the method of ontological science and believes in controlled observation, experimentation and generalisation. Scientific attitude and methodology do not accept revelation as a source of knowledge. The spiritual aspect of man is ignored and man is regarded as a biological and social phenomenon.[148]

Induction may be singled out as one of the basic tools of science. The inductive method in science is based on detailed observation of incidents and phenomena that eventually lead to the formation of a general conclusion. Nature in the sense of the observable world is the principal subject matter of science, but nature as spoken of in science includes, in addition to physical nature, society in all of its observable manifestations, human nature and human behaviour.[149] The scientific method attempts to make the chaotic diversity of sense experience correspond to a logically uniform system of thought, which is provable and convincing. Science is characteristically rational, consistent and coherent, capable of being applied and proved by evidence when its premises are challenged. Scientific truth is thus capable of being verified and vindicated by external and objective evidence.

Inductive reasoning is also accepted in the Islamic perception of knowledge. It is, in fact, the basis of the epistemological appeal of the Qur'ān in places where the text calls on people to think, reflect and reason on the basis of what they can experience and observe. In so many places the Qur'ān refers to the movement of the planets, the sun, the moon, and the observable world. Muhammad Iqbal went so far as to say in this connection that the Qur'ān marked the birth of the 'inductive intellect' and it is a religious obligation, therefore of every Muslim to master the inductive method to uncover the laws of nature and society.[150] Iqbal has given an insightful analysis of the Qur'ān in conjunction with Greek philosophy and Western views of science that have already been discussed.

The Qur'ān contains numerous references to knowledge that is obtained through the senses, and to man's responsibility for the proper application and channelling of his powers of observation, sight, hearing, speech, and intuition. The text provides on a striking note, for example:

والله أخرجكم من بطون أمهاتكم لا تعلمون شيئًا وجعل

لكم السمع والأبصار والأفئدة لعلكم تشكرون

God brought you out of the wombs of your mothers when you knew nothing, and He gave you ears, eyes and heart that you may be thankful. (16:78)

It is thus indicated that all knowledge is gained through sense perception and intuitive reflection, and the latter also seems to emanate from sense perception. It is of interest also to note that references to the use of the senses in the Qur'ān, especially to hearing and sight, are typically combined with a reference to intuition and understanding through the light of one's heart. This can be seen in the verse just quoted, and in another verse which reads:

إن السمع والبصر والفؤاد كلّ أولئك كان عنه مسئولا

'Verily the hearing and the sight and the heart will each be asked...' (17:36; 67:23)

Another passage refers to those who deny the signs of God in the world around them even when their experience would tell them otherwise '. . . but their ears and eyes and heart availed them not since they denied the signs of God.' (46:26; also 3:179)

فما أغنى عنهم سمعهم ولا أبصارهم ولا أفئدتهم من شيئ

إذ كانوا يجحدون بآيات الله

Also of interest here is that the reference to hearing consistently precede that of seeing, a point which has prompted one observer to note that hearing is more widely used in the acquisition of knowledge. As of the moment of birth of a child, unlike the eyes which open gradually, the hearing is immediately functional. Similarly, when a person falls asleep, the eyes close but hearing continues to be receptive to sound. It may further be noted in this connection that hearing (*al-sam'*) is the principal means of transmitted knowledge, whether by means of revelation (*waḥy*) or through narration of past events. If one hears one's teacher's voice without seeing him, one can follow him, but it would be difficult to achieve the same if one could only see but not hear one's teacher.[151] In another place the Qur'ān praises those 'who listen to the word and follow the best of it' (or make the best possible interpretation thereof). (39:18)

الذين يستمعون القول فيتبعون أحسنه

The text also takes to task those who listen to what the Prophet tells them but do not open their minds and hearts to what they hear (6:25). The Qur'ān is replete with reminders that in the observable world there are lessons for those who hear, for those who see, for those who think (*yasma'ūn, yubṣirūn, yatafakkarūn*) about the world, about the Qur'ān, their own selves and their Creator. This inducative and experimental method of the Qur'ān can also be seen in its phenomenology and occasions of revelation (*asbāb al-nuzūl*) in that a great deal of the Qur'ān was revealed in conjunction with actual events that were experienced by the early Muslims, and the Companions often asked the Prophet questions about them. The *asbāb al-nuzūl* is a much wider phenomenon but references to it can be found in at least fifteen Qur'ānic verses which begin with the phrase 'they ask you (*yas'alūnaka*)' about such and such, and then the text addresses the issue as the case may be. These are some of the ways in which the Qur'ān delivers its messages and in this respect the experimental and inductive method of science is by no means unfamiliar to the Qur'ān.

The basic harmony of faith and reason is also manifested in the Qur'ān through a series of exclusions which seek to clarify the correct from the misleading means and avenues of knowledge. These are manifested in at least four contexts that are summarised below:[152]

1) Rejection of conjecture (al-ẓann) vis-à-vis certitude (al-yaqīn):

This is a basic guideline that the Qur'ān advocates not only in religious disputation but also in the context of testimony and judgement, and indeed in most other areas of human affairs. Although certainty remains the ideal standard of knowledge, conjecture that inclines toward probability is nevertheless accepted in practical human affairs, such as in court decisions that are often based on probability (ẓann), for want of certainty, in order to facilitate resolution of disputes among people.

The Qur'ān altogether precludes conjecture and probability as a basis of belief, as faith must be based in conviction, which precludes ẓann. To this effect the Qur'ān takes the deniers of truth to task, for their blind faith in what is no more than conjecture: '... they follow but a guess, and a guess can never take the place of the truth.' (53:28)

إن يتبعون إلا الظن وإن الظن لا يغني من الحق شيئًا

Guesswork (ẓann) in this verse, as in many other verses in the text (10:36; 6:116) is used in contradistinction with knowledge (ʿilm), and it is ʿilm that is acquired through hearing, seeing and reasoning that command acceptance. This is what the Qur'ān has instructed its readers in another verse to '... follow not that of which you have no knowledge. Truly the hearing and sight and the heart are all accountable.' (17:36)

ولا تقف ما ليس لك به علم إن السمع والبصر والفؤاد

كل أولئك كان عنه مسئولا

2) Rejection of passion and untrammelled desire (hawā):

Qur'ānic references to hawā occur in contradistinction to correct guidance and truth. Thus it is provided in an address to the Prophet-King David: 'O David! We made you a vicegerent in the earth so that you judge among people with truth, and follow not the passion that sways you away from the path of God.' (38:26)

يا داود إنا جعلناك خليفة في الأرض فاحكم بين الناس بالحق ولا تتبع الهوى فيضلك عن سبيل الله

The impulses of passion, whether consisting of love, hatred or anger etc., can be so powerful as to obfuscate rational judgement. The basic message of this verse is that the best qualified of judges, even the Prophets, are not immune to the influence of *hawā*. Equally clear is the point that knowledge and truth must be pursued and vindicated through reasonable methods that are not influenced by personal sentiment and passion. The extensive influence of *hawā* is elsewhere indicated in the Qur'ān which reads in an address to the Prophet Muḥammad. 'Have you seen the (predicament of) one who chooses for his god his own passion? Would you then be a guardian over him?' (25:43)

أرأيت من اتخذ إلهه هواه أفأنت تكون عليه وكيلا

Passion can dominate a person's outlook totally in which case truth and reason can have but little place in his order of priorities. The Prophet Muḥammad has been repeatedly warned as to the little impact his teaching could possibly make on such persons. This evidence sustains the conclusion that the Qur'ān contemplates reason that is untainted by the vagaries of *hawā* as its principal means to knowledge, discovery of truth, and justice.

3) Rejection of blind imitation:
Islam's outlook on reason is also based on reason that is inspired by conviction, as opposed to blind imitation of the custom and legacy of the past. The objectivity of reason is to be ensured by its independence in that conventional practice does not necessarily provide the way to correct knowledge and guidance. The past must be judged in the light of reason and rejected if it is found misleading. The Qur'ān has to this effect recounted the attitude of its deniers and the typical response they have given to the Prophet Muḥammad that 'we follow the way of our ancestors, even if their ancestors did not know nor were they rightly guided.' (5:104; also 2:170)

قالوا حسبنا ما وجدنا عليه آبائنا أولو كان آباؤهم
لا يعقلون شيئًا ولا يهتدون

This was also the response that Prophet Abraham and many other prophets received from idol-worshipers but which they retorted it in such terms: 'both you and your ancestors were clearly misguided.' (21:52; 7:70; 11:87). The Qur'ān recounts these merely to highlight a certain continuity of values, and in this instance, also to confirm that knowledge and truth stand on their own merit independently of the custom and convention of the past.

4) Rejection of dictatorship:

The Qur'ān takes to task those who indiscriminately obey arrogant dictators and rulers who are averse to enlightenment and truth. Thus it is provided that the plea of those who say on the Day of Judgement that '…We obeyed our princes and great men and they misled us.' (33:66) وقالوا إنا أطعنا سادتنا وكبراءنا فأضلونا السبيل will have no merit. This is because, as the text explains, they rejected the correct guidance when it was conveyed to them. In another verse, the text refers to the Pharaoh who misled his people:

ولقد أرسلنا موسى بآياتنا وسلطان مبين إلى فرعون
وملإيه فاتبعوا أمر فرعون وما أمر فرعون برشيد

We sent Moses with our signs and clear evidence unto Pharaoh and his chiefs, but they followed Pharaoh's command which failed to give the right guidance. (11:96)

In another verse it is stated that the Pharaoh 'persuaded his people to make light (of Moses), and they obeyed him. They were none other but a wanton folk.' (43:54)

فاستخفّ قومه فأطاعوه إنهم كانوا قوما فاسقين

People are thus advised to use their own judgement and distinguish between guidance and misguidance in the light of reason. This is because they themselves, and not their self-styled leader, would ultimately be held responsible. The intrinsic value of truth and knowledge must therefore remain unaffected by the indulgent claims of oppressive men who often seek to subjugate others for their own selfish proclamations.

Muḥammad ʿAbduh (d. 1905) was of the view that there was no necessary conflict between religion and science. Both are founded in reason, and both study natural phenomena, albeit from different angles. Since the Qur'ān encourages the Muslims to study and investigate the universe, Islam should be considered as a friend, not the enemy, of science. ʿAbduh also observed that there was nothing against true Islam in modern civilisation and science, provided that Islam was rightly understood and rightly expressed. In saying this ʿAbduh emphasised those Islamic tenets and principles which are fundamental to Islam as opposed to those that are of local and temporary application.[153]

The western scientific approach to liberal education can be seen in the 1945 Harvard Committee Report entitled *General Education in a Free Society*,which divides knowledge into three classes: natural sciences, humanities, and social studies. General education is expected to develop certain capabilities of the mind which are 'to think effectively, to communicate thought, to make relevant judgements and to discriminate among values.'[154]

Effective thinking is described as having three phases: logical, rational and imaginative. Logical thinking is applicable to practical matters such as whom to vote for and whom to befriend; it is also the ability to extract universal truths from particular cases and infer the particular from general laws; it is also the ability to analyse a problem and recombine elements with the help of imagination.

By rational thinking the report means the ability to think at a level appropriate to a problem. The report adds that making relevant value judgement involves the ability of the student to clarify the impact of a whole range of ideas upon the area or object of experience. 'Discrimination among values' means the ability to distinguish various kinds of values, aesthetic, moral and intellectual and then to commit oneself to such values in the conduct of life.[155] The report excludes metaphysical knowledge and religious studies from the sphere of knowledge, and confines the attention of educationists to a concept of man for whom belief in God, or even pursuit of knowledge beyond the domain of senses do not have any special significance. One commentator noted that by ignoring religious studies the report failed to appreciate the effect of religion on personality and the direction that effective thinking might take as a result of the impact of religion on the whole person.[156]

Islamic thought in the Middle Ages did not admit of the ontological distinction between tangible entities that could be sensuously apprehended and entities of a spiritual or subliminal nature. This is certainly a sound and realistic view of reality than is allowed for by modern positivistic doctrines of science. Being is manifested at various levels and in several forms, none of which is less real than the other. Arabic thought employed the notions systematised in Stoic theory that divided being into three modes: verbal utterance, psychic representation, and reality. Fārābī took up this view, and assimilated psychic representation to the entities of reason. Others rehearsed this division with the addition of a fourth mode, that of Scripture. Being thus had a four-fold manifestation depending on whether the thing existed immediately in itself, or whether its like was graven in the mind (*dhihn, psyche*) composed of sounds, which together indicates the psychic representation, or was manifested in characters standing for sound and speech. All four have a basic characteristic in common, which is existence.[157] While some thinkers and scientists confined their typology of existence (*wujūd, ḥaqīqah*) to the two genera of the mental and the immediate, this did not render the verbal and the spiritual existentially suspect. They were all part of a theory of knowledge in which the immediate and literal were identified as basic and original existence, while existence in the psyche formed part of the field of figurative existence.

In all cases the truth, whether articulated in speech or represented in the psyche, consists of correspondence between a tangible immediate existent, a verbal existent, and a graphic existent. The ideal state of knowledge therefore is one which seizes the very immediacy of the object of knowledge in which the correspondence between concept and thing is complete. It is a state in which the object is so assimilated by its concept, or the concept to its object, that they are interchangeable. In fact it is in this sense that the manuals of psychology refer to memory as a depository of sensuous experiences, and to intellectual acts, as a combination of components so deposited. Knowledge thus relates to its object in that the object is apprehended visually or quasi-visually. The latter refers not only to gnosis but also to idealised knowledge in general, as is indicated by the use of the term *ʿilm*, and not *maʿrifah*, which is used to indicate mystical gnosis as opposed to articulated knowledge, which is science.[158] The object of a science is the region of 'sensuous and spiritual reality to which its topics appertain; indeed every reality accessible to the mind should have a science particular to it.' Such, for instance, are numbers, the object of arithmetic, and homothetic judgement, which is the object of jurisprudence.[159]

The view that Islam subordinates science to the teaching of religion finds support in Nasr who wrote that by contrast to the Western world which views the science of nature to be mainly concerned with 'quantitative aspects of things,' and where science is closely identified with technology and its applications, Islamic science 'seeks perfection and deliverance.' To understand it requires placing oneself within its perspective as a 'science of nature which has a different end, and uses different means from those of modern science.' The ultimate aim of Islamic science, Nasr added, has always been to relate the corporeal world to its basic spiritual principle through the knowledge of symbols which unite the various orders of reality. Islamic science should thus be judged and understood, in terms of its own perspectives.[160]

It is further added that 'the arts and sciences in Islam are based on the idea of unity' and its aim is to show the interrelatedness of all that exists. In contemplating the unity of the cosmos, man may be led to the unity of the Divine principle, of which the unity of Nature is the image.[161] Ausaf Ali, however, has expressed some reservation over Nasr's views when he wrote 'for me the true worth of science lies in helping us to understand nature. . . We need science and technology not to make us more spiritual, moral and ethical. . . but to make us more productive' and enable us to subdue and manipulate nature.[162] Soroush is of the view that modern science explains the world as if it was not created by a god, not denying his existence, but rather finding no need to postulate it. In other words, it is assumed that even if there were a god, science would nonetheless be able to explain the world without relying on his existence.[163] The experimental science has reached such a grandeur, according to Soroush, that 'it is now unassailable.'

Without wishing to delve further into these different strands of thought, I may briefly say concerning Ali's critique of Nasr that Nasr's main point was to stress the unitarian outlook of Islam on knowledge, and not as it were 'to make us more spiritual.' Be that as it may, Islam may be said to be supportive of scientific enquiry in so far as it does not promote agnosticism and denial of God's existence. Islam is also supportive of knowledge which promotes human welfare, not degradation and erosion of human values in the name of science.

Science is not value free as it has always interacted with cultural and historical factors and operated in that context. If Muslims understand science within their theistic perspective, without any wish to interfere with its methods and results, that by itself is not a distortion provided that the objectivity of science is otherwise maintained. Science is not necessarily expected to promote religion, yet religion may help to give science a sense of direction and purpose. According to Soroush, religion is not identical with science, nor is it 'a progenitor, an arbiter or a guide for it. At the same time, religion need not deny or oppose science.'[164] Science is of immense help in discovering knowledge of the means of human welfare, but it is ethically neutral and fails to guide us in the realm of the objectives of life, its values and norms and the nature of ultimate reality; it has the potential also to become a source of menace to human life.[165]

Quṭb observed that the greatest problems of science could not be resolved without believing in the ultimate Creator, and that Islam has succeeded in amalgamating the temporal with the spiritual, and also science and religion, into a harmonious system of thought.[166]

Ashraf and Quṭb have both criticised the preoccupation of scientists with technical goals, increased efficiency and immediate utility. Social consequences of inventions and experiments are ignored, and nature and society are exploited to their detriment. Forests are destroyed, rivers polluted and hills denuded, an indication perhaps of the inability of science to prevent environmental imbalance.[167]

The use and relevance of scientific rationality has also been questioned in certain contexts, such as witchcraft, and the role it plays in primitive societies. In a study Evans-Pritchard conducted concerning the Sudan Azande tribe, witchcraft and accusations of witchcraft were used as a way of dealing with and expressing social tensions. People who are otherwise considered to be capable of rationality persist in practices deriving from mystical belief about 'non-existent entities' (i.e. witches). Evans-Pritchard contrasted Azande tribal mentality to western scientific thought and thus the so-called rationality debate began. It was suggested if the criteria of rationality were internal to a certain culture, it was 'useless to speak of witches as non-existent entities.'[168] Witchcraft is a reality in the Azande context, and indigenous people, the like of Azande, do not draw much advantage from the highly developed form of western rationality. Science and its standards of rationality did not seem to be 'the right genre for understanding Azande witchcraft.'[169]

The definition of rationality is also problematic. It is, for example, not clear where rational stops and the irrational begins, or whether there is a diffused field between the two.[170] Rationality may seem identical to western scientific positivism and technological reasoning but it has wider connotations that may become more subjective in a particular context and take therefore local forms. Thus the Azande were considered 'capable of rationality' even though they believed in witches. Scientific rationality is not successful in understanding religion and culture as entities that convey meaning and affect the perception of reality among its followers.

Religion and science are not in total harmony, but the tension that exists between them need not be exaggerated. Human beings can remain spiritual and religious while enjoying the benefits of technology and science. The modern world has condemned ignorant and vulgar religiosity, but it has, in the meantime, allowed learned religion to prosper on a higher level. Scientific treatment of socio-political and economic affairs does not preclude a well-defined role for God and religion in human affairs.[171]

Science and secularism tend to go hand in hand. This also raises a question over the extent to which secularism has affected education in the Muslim countries.

Secularism, which is regarded as one of the greatest contributions of modern science is defined as the deliverance of Man 'first from religious and then from metaphysical control over his reason and language.' Secularism and modernisation have gone hand in hand and both tend to share a fundamental belief in rationality and scientific thought. They also had the effects that are often described as 'the de-sacralisation of politics' and 'deconsecration of values.' Just as nature is separated from the will of God, Man is 'freed' from the restrictive demands of religion.[172] Secularism in the Arab world has brought about considerable transformation in the institutions of learning, the judiciary and the status of religious scholars and *ʿulamā'*. Secularism in Arab countries and elsewhere in the Muslim world is also manifested in the replacement largely of *fuqahā'* by lawyers, and religious teachers by trained teachers in modern schools, especially when the *kuttāb/maktab*, the Qur'ānic schools were transformed into modern schools on Western models, even though the process was gradual and uneven.

The changes that took place were on a wider scale in other parts of the Middle East compared to Egypt, where for various reasons, al-Azhar kept its controls over primary education. In the

Maghreb, French colonialism divided the education system into a modern sector closely modelled on the French system and another, older sector, based on the *kuttāb*. The transformation was extended with the replacement of the *medersas* (sic), which used to teach the *fiqh*, the Qur'ān, the *hadīth* and elements of Arabic, by universities applying modern curricula. Drastically revised curricula were later, and somewhat reluctantly, introduced by institutions like al-Azhar, and Zaytunah, perhaps less drastically in the former. But Zaytunah was transformed so much that its status was reduced from a university to what is now a part of a modern university, known as the Faculty of Religious Studies. Changes in al-Azhar were not so radical as the new faculties, and their revised curricula, still remained under the umbrella of the old al-Azhar principles and traditions.

Turkey under Kamal Ataturk had imported the western secular education without even attempting to reform the traditional system. Indonesia, and Malaysia, although Muslim majority countries considered it wise to accept secularism and remain non-committal to the idea of a reformed Islamic educational system beyond retaining religious education as a subject in the school curricula.[173]

These changes led to a shift from a perception which saw public affairs, society and education through the prism of religion, to one that bore the imprint of modernity, or *nahḍah* (awakening), that implied openness to further modernisation. Changes were often accompanied by social upheavals that took place in Arab and Muslim societies for over a century that affected their education system and the judiciary more than most. The body of ʿ*ulamā*' was displaced from the leading places it had occupied in public life. The introduction of legal codes in many fields that were previously governed by the *fiqh* texts added to the marginalised status of the ʿ*ulamā*'. Formal constitutions introduced on the eve of colonialism in many Muslim and Arab countries were yet other instruments of secularism which articulated the ideas and foundations of the Western nation state in these countries.[174]

IX. Concluding Remarks

Religion is concerned with the totality of existence both in this world and the next. Science concerns itself with this world alone and that too in a restricted sense. The exact sciences, as they are known, concern themselves with nature whereas in social sciences both the natural and the social are combined. Religion is not as averse to science, one might say, as science is to religion. Ultimately however, science and religion can coexist if we agree that in religion we discover the will of God, and in science the law of nature. Then it may be said that knowledge of nature is the same as the knowledge of God in that the laws of nature represent God's ways with nature. Sayyid Ahmad Khan's (d. 1898) epithetical statement that 'the word of God, as expounded in the Qur'ān, cannot be contradictory to the work of God.' As the words of God are unchanging, so are the ways of God and the laws of nature. Science tries to discover the laws of nature.[175]

Islam is supportive of harmony between human beings and nature. In his capacity as God's vicegerent in the earth, Man also belongs to the total ecological community and his exploitation of nature must therefore be guided by the overall purpose of maintaining balance and harmony in God's creation and the use therefore of science for constructive purposes.

Islam also imposes an obligation, whether personal or collective, in respect of acquisition and dissemination of knowledge, science and education. The duty that is imposed is addressed both to the individual and the state to take all the necessary steps toward its fulfilment. The *Sharī'ah* also recognises education as a basic right of the individual especially in the case of children, who have a right to education and educating them is a duty both of the parents and the government.

Some commentators have identified education as a personal liberty and it is consequently regarded a matter of personal choice whether or not to have an education. The Islamic concept of *fard kifā'ī* is not in total harmony with this view of education, and it is in any case too important for the community to view education as a matter only of personal liberty and choice. Yet there is no inherent contradiction in identifying education both as a right and a basic liberty, for a basic liberty can sometimes change into a right or an obligation in different contexts and in relationship to individuals and subjects. Thus according to one commentator 'the freedom of education' in the Islamic context is not always a freedom but may become a right, an obligation, a recommendation, or a mere permissibility, depending on the type of knowledge/education and the party who is seeking it.[176] If the constitution or national charter of a Muslim country determines education to be a basic right, which it usually does, then that is where we stand, as the constitution is, from the *Sharī'ah* perspective, an ordinance of the *uli al-amr*, conformity to which becomes a requirement. To identify education as a basic constitutional right bears perfect harmony with the Islamic perspective and merits wider recognition and support.

The *'ulamā'* have discussed a certain order of priority in education and attempted to classify some under *farḍ 'ayn* and others under *farḍ kifāyah*. To recognise and proclaim education as a constitutional right would subsume both of these positions and the emphasis that is conveyed in the idea of *farḍ* would have consequently been achieved in a better way. Whereas some *'ulamā'* did not dispute the conventional dichotomy of knowledge into the religious and secular sciences, others have attempted a holistic approach and considered the idea of beneficial knowledge to be closer to the general objectives and *maqāṣid* of the *Sharī'ah*. A holistic approach to education that is also guided by the idea of applied and beneficial knowledge is obviously sound and in greater harmony with the Islamic perception of knowledge.

NOTES

1. Nasr, *Science and Civilization in Islam*, 65.

2. Cf. Yusuf Ali, *The Holy Qur'ān: Translation and Commentary*, note 5582; al-Sibā'ī, *Ishtirākiyyah*, 55.

3. Surah *Al-Raḥmān* (55:1–4).

4. Qaraḍāwī, *al-'Aql Wa'l-'Ilm*, 258.

5. Bukhārī, *Ṣaḥīḥ al-Bukhārī* (Muhsin Khan's trans.) vol. I, *ḥadīth* 86.

6. Ibn Mājah, *Sunan*, II, 1395, *ḥadīth* 4169.

7. Al-Suyūṭī, *Al-Jāmi' al-Ṣaghīr*, vol. 2, *ḥadīth* no. 9304; al-Nabhānī, *al-Fatḥ al-Kabīr*, III, 266.

8. Ibn Mājah, *Sunan*, I, 83, *ḥadīth* 229.

9. Bukhārī, *Ṣaḥīḥ al-Bukhārī* (Muhsin Khan's trans.), I, 56, *ḥadīth* 67.

10. Al-Suyūṭī, *Al-Jāmi' al-Ṣaghīr*, II, 97, *ḥadīth* no. 5264; Ghazālī, *Iḥyā'*, II, 90.

11. Id., II, 527, *ḥadīth* 8956.

12. Ghazālī, *Iḥyā'*, II, 90.

13. Ghazālī, *Iḥyā'*, II, 90.

14. Bukhārī, *Ṣaḥīḥ al-Bukhārī* (Muhsin Khan's trans.), I, 67, *ḥadīth* 22.

15. Id., I, 79, *ḥadīth* 98.

16. Id., I, 80, *ḥadīth* 101.

17. I have here paraphrased a *ḥadīth* al-Bukhārī has recorded on the authority of 'Abd Allāh b. 'Amr b. al-'Āṣ in his *Ṣaḥīḥ al-Bukhārī* (Muhsin Khan's trans.), I, 80, *ḥadīth* 100.

18. Tabrīzī, *Mishkāt*, vol. I, *ḥadīth* 203.

19. Tabrīzī, *Mishkāt*, vol. I, *ḥadīth* 221.

20. Al-'Īlī, *Ḥurriyyat*, 449.

21. Fu'ād 'Abd al-Mun'im Aḥmad, *Uṣūl Niẓām al-Ḥukm*, 278.

22. Cf. Al-Qurṭubī, *Tafsīr*, ɪv, 41; and Maḥmaṣṣānī, *Arkān Ḥuqūq al-Insān fī'l-Islām*, 197.

23. Kubrazada, *Miftāḥ al-Sa'ādah*, ɪ, 706; Shishānī, *Ḥuqūq al-Insān*, 581.

24. Both the Caliph Umar b. 'Abd al-'Azīz and Ḥasan al-Baṣrī are quoted in Qaraḍāwī, *Fiqh al-Awlawiyyat*, 58 and 60 respectively.

25. 'Izz al-Dīn al-Sulamī, *Qawā'id al-Aḥkām*, ɪɪ, 215.

26. Qaraḍāwī, *Fiqh al-Awlawiyyāt*, 68.

27. Cf. Ahwānī, *al-Tarbīyah*, 189.

28. Ghazālī, *al-Risālah al-Laduniyyah*, 40-41. See also Ahwānī, *al-Tarbīyah*, 241.

29. Cf. Ahwānī, *Tarbīyah*, 227–28.

30. Iqbal, *The Reconstruction of Religious Thought*, 3–4.

31. Id., 5.

32. Id., 127–28.

33. Cf. Nasr, *Science and Civilization*, 59.

34. Al-Ghazālī, *Iḥyā'*, ɪ, 21–22.

35. Tabrīzī, *Mishkāt*, vol. ɪ, *ḥadīth* 200.

36. Cf. Sibā'ī, *Takāful*, 104.

37. Ibn Ḥazm al-Zāhirī, *al-Iḥkām fī Uṣūl al-Aḥkām*, ᴠ, 121–123; see also Al-Ghazālī, *Iḥyā' 'Ulūm al-Dīn*, ɪ, 21–22; Shishānī, *Ḥuqūq al-Insān*, 589.

38. Cf. Fu'ād Aḥmad, *Uṣūl Niẓām al-Ḥukm*, 277.

39. Shāṭibī, *Muwāfaqāt*, ɪ, 65; see also al-'Īlī, *Ḥurriyyat*, 443; al-Badawī, *Da'ā'im al-Ḥukm*, 258.

40. Ghazālī, *Iḥyā'*, ɪ, 23–24.

41. Al-Ghazālī, *Iḥyā'*, ɪ, 28; al-'Īlī, *Ḥurriyyat*, 444.

42. Id., ɪ, 37.

43. Id., ɪ, 25.

44. Id., ɪ, 38–39.

45. Al-Suyūṭī, *al-Jāmi' al-Ṣaghīr*, ɪ, 196, *ḥadīth* no. 1506. Ibn Mājah, *Sunan*, K. al-Du'ā', b. Du'ā' Rasūl Allāh.

46. Id., ɪ, 447, *ḥadīth* no. 3323.

47. Id., ɪ, 448, *ḥadīth* no. 3324.

48. See Nasr, *Science and Civilisation*, 62–65; Ashraf, *New Horizons*, 33.

49. Cf. Ashraf, *New Horizons*, 35.

50. Al-Ghazālī, *Ḥuqūq al-Insān*, 211–212.

51. Cf. Qaraḍāwī, *al-'Aql Wa'l-'Ilm*, 162-63 (referring to Ibn 'Abd al-Barr, *Jāmi' Bayān al-'Ilm*).

52. *Conference Book*, 78. Extracts of this document also appear in Ashraf, *New Horizons*, Appendix D (i), 102–110.

53. Id., see also Ashraf, *New Horizons*, 26. (recommendations, sections 2, 2.1, and 2.2).

54. Id., 106.

55. Id., 106.

56. Id., 116.

57. Id., 119.

58. Recommendation of the Third Conference (General Principles). See Ashraf, *New Horizons*, 118.

59. Ashraf, *New Horizons*, 27.

60. Tabrīzī, *Mishkāt*, vol. II, *hadīth* 3376.

61. Abu'l-Ḥasan ʿAlī al-Qābisī, *al-Risālah al-Mufaṣṣalah li-Aḥwāl al-Muʿallimīn wa Aḥkām al-Muʿallimīn wa'l-Mutaʿallimīn*, appearing as an appendix in Aḥmad Fuʾād al-Ahwānī, *al-Tarbīyah fi'l-Islām*, Cairo: Dar al-Maʿārif, 1968, 267–351. Originally a PhD thesis, al-Ahwānī's book is also devoted, almost entirely, to al-Qābisī's views on education. See also Yūsuf al-ʿĀlim, *al-Maqāṣid al-ʿĀmmah*, 355; Fuʾād Aḥmad, *Uṣūl Niẓām al-Ḥukm*, 278.

62. Cf. Ahwānī, *Tarbīyah*, 103.

63. Cf. Ahwānī, *Tarbīyah*, 102f.

64. Id., 102, 251.

65. Cf. Ahwānī, *Tarbīyah*, 103–104.

66. Cf. Ahwānī, *Tarbīyah*, 105.

67. Ahwānī, *Tarbīyah*, 106.

68. Ahwānī, *Tarbīyah*, 108, 186.

69. Quoted in Ahwānī, *al-Tarbīyah*, 145.

70. Qābisī, *al-Risālah*, 316, also Ahwānī, *Tarbīyah*, 141f.

71. Qābisī, *al-Risālah al-Mufaṣṣalah* (appearing as appendix to Ahwānī, *Tarbīyah*), 321.

72. Cf. Ahwānī, *al-Tarbīyah*, 155.

73. Cf. Ahwānī, *al-Tarbīyah*, 156.

74. Ibn Saḥnūn, *Adab al-Muʿallimīn*, 356. This treatise also appears as an appendix to al-Ahwānī, *al-Tarbīyah fi'l-Islām*, 351–371, Ibn Saḥnūn has attributed the contents of this treatise to his father, Saḥnūn al-Tanūkhī.

75. Id., 358.

76. Ahwānī, *Tarbīyah*, 263.

77. Ibn Sīnā, *Risālah fi' Riyāḍat al-Ṣubyān* (unpublished manuscript) quoted in Ahwānī, *Tarbīyah*, 158 & 232.

78. Ghazālī, *Iḥyāʾ*, III, 70.

79. Id., VI, 136.

80. Ibn Khaldūn, *Muqaddimah*. Maṭbaʿah al-Bahiyyah), 399; also quoted in Ahwānī, *al-Tarbīyah*, 151, and 250.

81. Quoted from al-Anbānī's unpublished manuscript '*Risālah fī' Riyāḍat al-Ṣubyān wa Ta'limihim wa ta'dibihim*' by Ahwānī, *Tarbīyah*, 152.

82. Ahwānī, *Tarbīyah*, 183, & 318; Ibn Saḥnūn, *Risālah*, (Ahwānī's Appendix) at 358.

83. Ghazālī, *Iḥyā'*, iii, 71.

84. Id., iii, 70.

85. Ghazālī, *Iḥyā'*, i, 55.

86. Id., i, 59.

87. Id.

88. On this point, many other writers have considered it permissible to charge a fee even for teaching the Qur'ān.

89. Id., i, 61–63.

90. Cf. Ahwānī, *al-Tarbīyah*, 244.

91. Bukhārī, *Ṣaḥīḥ al-Bukhārī* (Muhsin Khan's tran.), i, 56, *ḥadīth* 67.

92. Id., *ḥadīth* 69.

93. Id., *ḥadīth* 70.

94. Id., *ḥadīth* 69.

95. Al-Ghazālī, *Iḥyā'*, i, 23.

96. Id., i, 15.

97. Id., ii, 336.

98. Ibn Khaldūn, *Muqaddimah*, 359ff.

99. Ibn Khaldūn, *Muqaddimah*, Eng. trans. by Rosenthal, vol. iii, 300–303; see also Nasr, *Science and Civilization*, 67–69.

100. Extended excerpts of the 1977 Conference Resolutions appear in Ashraf, Appendix D (i), 102–110, at 104.

101. Id., 112.

102. Id., 114–115 (excerpts of the Islamabad Conference proceedings appear in Ashraf, *New Horizons*, Appendix D (ii) 110–118.

103. Id., 120–121 (under Appendix D (iii).

104. Id., 121 at Appendix D (iii).

105. Id., 131, at Appendix D (iv).

106. Cf. Al-ʿĪlī, *Ḥurriyyat*, 448; Badawī, *Daʿāʾim*; see also al-Ghazālī, *Ḥuqūq al-Insān*, 210; Musaylihī, *Ḥuqūq al-Insān*, 110.

107. Ibn ʿĀbidīn, *Ḥashīyah Ibn ʿĀbidīn*, i, 32.

108. Cf. Sibāʿī, *Takāful*, 106; Fu'ād Abd al-Munʿim Ahmad, *Uṣūl Niẓām al-Ḥukm*, 277.

109. Id., 278.

110. Cf. Sibāʿī, *Takāful*, 101, 109; Shīshānī, *Ḥuqūq al-Insān*, 593–94.

111. Abū Zahrah, *al-Mujtamaʿ al-Islāmī*, 7; Shīshānī, *Ḥuqūq al-Islām*, 582.

112. Ḥadīth *Muthafaqun ʿalayh*, see al-Nawawī, *Riyāḍ al-Ṣāliḥīn*, *ḥadīth* no. 1387.

113. Long *ḥadīth* recorded in Mundhirī, *Targhīb*, i, 60; Haythamī, *Majmaʿ al-Zawā'id*, i, 164; Sibāʿī, *Takāful*, 101.

114. Cf. al-Sibāʿī, *Takāful*, 107.

115. Id., 106.

116. Al-Nabhānī, *Muqadimat al-Dustūr*, 420.

117. Maḥmaṣṣānī, *Arkān Ḥuqūq al-Insān*, 196. Qaraḍāwī has noted the *ḥadīth* that refers to China is often quoted as a *ḥadīth* but it is more likely to be a proverbial statement that many scholars have cited and its purport seems to have the support of general consensus (*ijmāʿ*), see Qaraḍāwī, *al-ʿAql wa'l-ʿIlm*, 224.

118. Muḥammad Yasif, 'al-Ḥaqq al-ʿIlmī fi'l-Islām,' in ed., M. Yasif, *Niẓām al-Ḥuqūq fi'l-Islām*, 69.

119. Al-Sibāʿī, *Takāful*, 111; Muṣaylihī, *Ḥuqūq al-Insān*, 110; Ahwānī, *Tarbīyah*, 255; ʿAfīfī, *al-Ḥuqūq al-Maʿnawiyyah*, 115.

120. Al-Ghazālī, *Iḥyā'*, i, 221; al-Sibāʿī, *Takāful*, 109-110.

121. Ibn ʿĀbidīn, *Ḥāshiyah*, ii, 6.

122. Cf. al-Badawī, *Daʿā'im al-Ḥukm*, 264; Fu'ād ʿAbd al-Munʿim Aḥmad, *Uṣūl Niẓām al-Ḥukm*, 278.

123. Cf. Muṣaylihī, *Ḥuqūq al-Insān*, 137.

124. Bukhārī, *Saḥīḥ al-Bukhārī* (Muhsin Khan's trans.) i, 56, *ḥadīth* 67.

125. Bukhārī, id., i, 80, *ḥadīth* 101.

126. Bukhārī, id., i, 96, *ḥadīth* 131.

127. Cf. Nasr, *Science and Civilization*, 65–66.

128. Ḥasan Ibrāhīm Ḥasan, *Tārīkh al-Islām*, vol. iv, 422; al-Badawī, *Daʿā'im*, 263; al-Azmeh, *Arabic Thought*, 223; Nasr, *Science and Civilization*, 70.

129. Nasr, *Science and Civilization*, 71.

130. Id., 70.

131. Its construction began in 457AH and completed in 459. Two of its renowned professors were Abū Isḥāq al-Shirāzī and later Abū Ḥāmid al-Ghazālī.

132. Nasr, *Science and Civilization*, 71–72.

133. Cf. Nasr, *Science and Civilization*, 73; Zuḥaylī, *Ḥuqūq al-Insān*, 273; Ismāʿīl Badawī, *Daʿā'im al-Ḥukm*, 263.

134. Al-Azmeh, *Arabic Thought*, 224.

135. Id., 226, 229.

136. See details on Zarnūjī in Ahwānī, *Tarbīyah*, 244f; al-Azmeh, *Arabic Thought*, 236.

137. Ibn Khaldūn, *Muqaddimah*, 375.

138. See details on these and other doctrines of *uṣūl al-fiqh*, Kamali, *Principles of Islamic Jurisprudence* which devotes a chapter each to the study of these topics.

139. See for details Kamali, *Punishment in Islamic Law: An Inquiry into the Hudud Bill of Kelantan*.

140. Abū Zahrah, *Tanẓīm al-Islām li'l Mujtamaʿ*, 194.

141. Wāfī, *Ḥuqūq al-Insān*, 232.

142. Cf. Shaltūt, *al-Islām ʿAqīdah wa Sharīʿah*, 547.

143. Cf. Kamali, *Freedom of Expression in Islam*, 62.

144. See for detail's Kamali, *Principles of Islamic Jurisprudence*, chapter 19 on *ijtihād*.

145. Cf. Shaltūt, *al-Islām ʿAqīdah wa Sharīʿah*, 548.

146. See for details on *ḥisbah, shūrā* and *naṣīḥah*, Kamali, *Freedom of Expression in Islam*, 63ff.

147. Cf. Farhud, 'al-Azhar', *Mawsuʿah al-Mafāhīm al-Islāmiyyah al-ʿĀmmah*, pp. 38–40.

148. Cf. Ashraf, *New Horizons*, 7–8.

149. Cf. Ausaf Ali, *Islam, Science and Islamic Social Ethics*, 18; Soroush, *Reason, Freedom and Democracy in Islam*, 50.

150. Iqbal, *Reconstruction of Religious Thought*, chapter 5.

151. Cf., Qaraḍāwī, *al-ʿAql wa'l-ʿIlm*, 234.

152. Cf. Qaraḍāwī, *al-ʿAql wa'l-ʿIlm*, 250–270.

153. Quoted in Siddiqi, *Modern Reformist Thought*, 92–93.

154. Harvard Committee, *General Education*, 64, quoted in Ashraf, *New Horizons*, 36–37. Physics, chemistry and biology are natural sciences whereas economics, political science and sociology are social sciences, and anthropology, psychology and psychoanalysis are classified as human sciences.

155. Quoted in Ashraf, *New Horizons*, 37.

156. Ashraf, *New Horizons*, 38.

157. Cf. al-Azmeh, *Arabic Thought*, 109.

158. Id., 109–112.

159. Id., 15.

160. Nasr, *Science and Civilization in Islam*, 39–40.

161. Id., 22.

162. Ausaf Ali, *Science, Islam*, 26.

163. Soroush, *Reason, Freedom and Democracy in Islam*, 122, 37; Ali, *New Horizons*, 8.

164. Id., 60.

165. Cf. Quṭb 'Islam and the Crisis of Modern Mind,' in ed., Khurshid Ahmad, *Islam, its Meaning and Message*, 251.

166. Cf. Quṭb, 'Islam and the Crisis of Modern Mind' 244.

167. Ashraf, *New Horizons*, 17–18.

168. Andre Droogers 'Cultural Relativism and Human Rights,' in An-Naʿim et al., *Human Rights and Religious Values*, 82.

169. Id., 84.

170. Id.

171. Cf. Soroush, *Reason, Freedom and Democracy in Islam*, 61.

172. Cf. Ashraf, *New Horizons in Muslim Education*, 8–9.
173. Cf. al-Azmeh, *Islams and Modernities*, 47; Ashraf, *New Horizons*, 52–53.
174. Cf. Id., 48.
175. Ausaf Ali, *Islam, Science*, 12.
176. Fu'ād Abd al-Munʿim Aḥmad, *Uṣūl Niẓām al-Ḥukm*, 276.

CHAPTER TWO

Right to Work (*Ḥaqq al-ʿAmal*) and Business Ethics in Islam

I. Definition and Summary

This chapter is presented in ten sections, beginning with a review of the Qur'ān and *Sunnah* that helps to characterise Islam's basic outlook on work. Thus it will be shown that Islam's concept of *ʿamal* comes close to the pursuit of righteousness and worship. Work that is undertaken with the intention of producing a lawful benefit and that which is intended to build and beautify one's home, neighbourhood and environment as well as work that brings personal prosperity and wealth, indeed all beneficial work, tends to acquire a religious and spiritual dimension in Islam. This has prompted the Muslim jurists to evaluate *ʿamal* on the familiar five-point-scale of *Sharīʿah* values. Work may thus fall under the category of *wājib* (obligatory) or *mandūb* (recommendable) or it may be neutral (*mubāḥ*), reprehensible (*makrūh*), or indeed forbidden (*ḥarām*). These will be discussed in further detail following our review of the Qur'ān and *Sunnah*. A brief but still related discussion follows on whether a Muslim may work and cooperate with a non-Muslim government. Section four provides a review and analysis of the Islamic work ethics which informs the reader on some of the most desirable attributes of workers and attitudes that Islam encourages toward work. The succeeding section advances an Islamic perspective on fair trading in the market place, which is then followed by a discussion of women's right to work and child labour in section six. Then we address the rights of workers in reference particularly to employment, fair wages, issues over accidents in the work-place and liability for loss. This is continued by a brief discussion of right to a fair work regime and leisure, right to association, pension rights, and issues of concern to minimum wages. Section eight discusses the responsibilities of an Islamic state and the role that it is expected to play in the development of industries, creation of employment opportunities and provision of an unemployment benefits scheme.

'Amal is basically an economic concept which is defined as 'physical or mental exertion by a human being that is made for generating economic gain, or for enhancing and developing an existing value.'[1] To quote a slightly different definition, *'amal* consist of 'self-exertion by a human being either individually or in collaboration with others in order to produce goods or render a particular service.'[2]

In modern Arab writings, expressions such as *'āmil* (worker), *'ummāl* (workers), *ḥaqq al-'amal* (the right of work), *ḥurriyyat al-'amal* (freedom of choosing one's profession and work) refer mainly to work in its legal and economic senses, yet *'amal* retains its general meaning and continues to be used, in the spoken language of the Arabs, both within and outside the context of religion. *'Amal* as such refers to human effort in all its manifestations, including, that is, speech, which is an activity of the tongue. *'Amal* may also be said to be an integral part of the dignity of the person that manifests his or her self-worth and contribution to society. *'Amal* is a means of earning a living for individuals just as it is the principal arena of man's compliance with, or defiance of, God's injunctions. *'Amal* is also a personal duty of every able-bodied Muslim just as it is a collective obligation generally (*farḍ kifā'ī*) of the community to build the earth and develop its resources for the benefit of humanity. References in the Qur'ān and *Sunnah* that often occur to 'work with one's hands' have led some to conclude that agriculture, industry, and commerce are the most meritorious of all works as they cater for the basic needs of life, not only of the humans, but of all life on earth.[3]

II. Evidence in the Qur'ān and *Sunnah*

The word *'amal* (work, action, conduct) in the Qur'ān, *Sunnah* and *fiqh* literature is often used in conjunction with *'aqīdah* and *īmān* (faith and dogma). The Qur'ān also uses *sa'y* (effort) as an equivalent to *'amal*—such as in the phrase '*sa'y fi'l-arḍ*,' which means 'making effort in the earth' (2:205; 79:22). *Sa'y* as such includes not only moving about in pursuit of a purpose but work generally, even if it does not involve any movement or travel. Other equivalent terms that occur in the Qur'ān are *fi'l* (to do) *juhd* (effort) and *kasb* (acquisition or gain) as are discussed below. The Qur'ān and *Sunnah* often highlight the spiritual dimension of *'amal*, whereas juristic literature on the subject sees *'amal* as an economic proposition in the first place. The juxtaposition of *'aqīdah* and *'amal* in the Qur'ān often conveys the message that the one generally complements the other.

Evidence suggests that basically no human activity, however slight, can be said to be totally devoid of value and consequence. The Qur'ānic vision of a good deed (*'amal ṣāliḥ*) is all-encompassing and not confined only to spiritual and purificational activities. Good deeds can be spiritual, social and economic. This may also be said of religion (*al-dīn*) which is not confined to a dogma and state of mind but extends to all areas of human activity. The substantive convergence of faith and action can thus be seen in the Qur'ān where the text declares 'Then shall everyone, who has done (*ya'mal*) an atom's weight of good, see it; and anyone who has done an atom's weight of evil, shall also see it.' (99:7–8)

ومن يعمل مثقال ذرة خيراً يره ومن يعمل مثقال ذرة شراً يره

Note also the verse which provides 'Those who have faith and do good works (*'amilū al-ṣāliḥāt*) shall have blessings and great rewards.' (35:7)

والذين آمنوا وعملوا الصالحات لهم مغفرة وأجر كبير

The reference to *'amal* in both of these passages may appear as if they carry a religious purpose, implying primarily acts of worship, charity, helping others or doing something so as to gain the pleasure of God. The correct understanding would however be that they refer to all good work. This is also the case in another verse when it is stated:

وقل اعملوا فسيرى الله عملكم ورسوله والمؤمنون

And say (you must) work, soon will God see your work, and so will His Messenger and the believers. (9:105)

The reference to ʿamal here is general which comprises devotional acts as well as work in order to earn a living, and work that brings a sense of pride and achievement to the entire community. A reference to ʿamal in its dominantly economic sense occurs in the verse which provides 'As for the boat, it belonged to some poor persons who worked in the sea. . .' (18:79)

أما السفينة فكانت لمساكين يعملون في البحر

and in another verse to the effect 'that they may eat of the fruit (of working on the land), and their hands worked it not, will they not then give thanks?' (36:35)

ليأكلوا من ثمره وما عملته أيديهم أفلا يشكرون

The fruit that is yielded by the soil is not, in other words, entirely due to one's manual work, but due also to the growth potential that God has endowed in the soil. A certain shift of emphasis may at times be noticeable in connection with the various manifestations of ʿamal in the Qur'ān, but it remains true that ʿamal ṣāliḥ includes earning and lawful living and all work that is undertaken with the intention to bring benefit to oneself, one's family and the society at large.

Jamāl al-Bannā writes that the International Islamic Labour Union (al-Ittiḥād al-Islāmī al-Duwalī li'l-ʿAmal) has in its charter (Art. 6) adopted the wider meaning of ʿamal in accordance with its Qur'ānic usage. ʿAmal as such is not confined to its economic conception but extends to the religious and spiritual dimensions of work.[4]

References to ʿamal occur in no less than 360 verses in the Qur'ān, and to its equivalent al-fiʿl in another 109 verses.[5] Several other equivalent terms, derived from such roots as kasb, juhd and saʿy also occur frequently in the text and they are all assertive of the value of work. The fact that Islam encourages productive work is evinced by the special concession, for instance, that is granted in respect of religious duties: According to an express statement of the text, the obligatory late night prayer (ṣalāt al-tahajjud) was later abrogated in Medina in order to enable the believers to pursue their economic goals with full strength (73:20). The text also declares that God Most High made the day light convenient for the people to go after their work to earn a living (78:11):

وجعلنا النهار معاشا

The Qur'ān condemns laziness and calls upon people to take full advantage of time by investing it in righteous work. One who does not utilise time actually becomes a victim of it and condemned therefore to perdition and loss (*khusr*). (103:1–3)

إن الإنسان لفي خسر إلا الذين آمنوا وعملوا الصالحات

The persistent engagement of the Qur'ānic discourse in *ʿamal* and its obvious prominence led many commentators to characterise Islam as a 'religion of action.' *ʿAmal* is clearly a major theme of the Qur'ān so much so that it prompted Ismāʿīl al-Farūqī to observe that 'filling this world, this space and this time with value is not only important for religion, but is the whole business of religion.'[6] The relationship between faith and action, *īmān* and *ʿamal* in Islam resembles that of root and tree, which substantiate each other's vitality and worth. Work is the sole criterion, besides faith, by which the real worth of a person is evaluated for purposes of reward and recompense. The Qur'ān thus provides:

ولكل درجات مما عملوا وماربك بغافل عما يعملون

To all are (assigned) degrees (or ranks) according to their deeds. For Thy Lord is not unmindful of anything that they do. (6:132)

ولكلّ درجات مما عملوا وليوفيهم أعمالهم وهم لايظلمون

And to all are (assigned) degrees according to what they have done, and in order that God may recompense their deeds, and no injustice is done to them. (46:19)

To read that degrees are attained on account of work accomplishment evidently suggests that people are endowed with different abilities and talents, and also that some people apply themselves better and excel over others. This also means perhaps that merit is attached solely to the work itself according to their deeds—*bi-mā ʿamilū:* 'That He may recompense their deeds—*li-yuwaffiyahum aʿmālahum,*' and not to any other criterion of distinction. Some people excel themselves in knowledge and professional skills over others, within the same line of work or profession, and they consequently accomplish better results. People are born equal in the essence of humanity, but this does not mean that they are also equal in their talents and natural gifts. But then when a naturally talented person does not apply himself and achieves nothing, the mere talent by itself would not be counted as a basis of reward or of ranking to a higher degree. Thus it is the results of those natural differentials in abilities which are relevant, and not the differentials themselves, for the purpose of evaluation and accomplishment. This analysis would apply equally whether one discusses work in the purely practical sense of the word or work that is an extension of *ʿibādah*, or even work that consists mainly of prayer and charitable deeds.

The Qur'ān speaks highly of persons who strive in order to seek 'the bounty of God.' This 'bounty' includes all means of livelihood. The special prayer that the Prophet taught and is consequently recited by Muslims while stepping out of a mosque—*Allāhumma innī as'aluka min faḍlika*—(O God I beseech you to grant me of your bounty) is both a reminder of the value of work as well as exhortation to strive for one's sustenance. 'The ethics of Islam' wrote al-Farūqī, 'clearly counsels against begging, against being a parasitic living on the labors of others. The noble *Sunnah* also recorded for us a number of occasions in which man's economic endeavour was praised and economic resignation condemned.'[7]

Al-Ghazālī has quoted the renowned sage Luqmān al-Ḥakīm to have impressed upon his son the value of earning one's livelihood through work (*al-kasb al-ḥalāl*). Luqmān thus told his son: make yourself self-reliant and independent of others through honest work. This will certainly relieve you of poverty and enhance you in honour. No one has been afflicted with poverty until he became neglectful of the values of his faith, wisdom, and personal honour (*muru'ah*), but even a greater calamity befalls people when their outlook changes such that work itself is looked down upon.[8]

The Qur'ān not only permits business but has given detailed instructions on the approved and disapproved varieties of business practices. The basic permissibility of business is thus augmented by practical legislation on the various modes of commercial transactions including sale, leasing, loan, mortgage and partnership. The Qur'ān also equates honest trading with acts of great spiritual distinction, just as it is equally forceful in its denunciation of exploitation, dishonest business practices and cheating. Justice and fair dealing in weights and measurements have been strongly recommended, and usury (*ribā*), gambling and fraud are forbidden. References to business and commerce occur in no less than 370 places in the Qur'ān, extensive enough to enable one researcher to write a doctoral thesis on them bearing the title 'The Commercial-Theological Terms in the Koran.' The author of this work noted that a considerable part of Qur'ānic theology is presented in business terms and the Qur'ān maintains a lively interest in matters of trade.[9]

Being the vicegerent of God on earth, man is made the trustee and custodian of the earth. The Qur'ān thus speaks of man's duty to work hard in order to build this world and to harness its resources in the best possible manner (11:61). The believers are urged to gain control of the world around them and develop it for their own benefit. (7:10; 62:10)

The faithful is certainly not expected in Islam to occupy most of his time with prayer and worship. The normal expectation seems to be that people should be observant of their religious duties but should otherwise engage themselves in productive work. Note, for instance, the reference to work in conjunction with the Friday congregational prayer:

فإذا قضيت الصلاة فانتشروا في الأرض وابتغوا من فضل الله واذكروا الله كثيرا لعلكم تفلحون

And when the prayer is finished, you may disperse in the land, seek of the bounty of God, and celebrate the praises of God that you may prosper. (62:10)

This juxtaposition of worship and work is on the one hand indicative of the value of work, which is placed next to obligatory prayer, and of the relative roles that each is given in the daily lives of Muslims on the other. The text informs, in other words, that worshippers are not required to stay in the mosque any longer than what is necessary for the performance of prayer. They should instead go after their livelihood as soon as the prayer is finished. The fact that the Qur'ān here refers to work in such words as 'seeking of the bounty of God' is further affirmation of the nobility of work in the eyes of God.

In a section of his *Iḥyā'* on earning a lawful living (*al-kasb wa'l-maʿāsh*) al-Ghazālī recounts an incident when the Prophet Jesus asked a man whom he saw on the street as to what he was doing for a living, and the man answered 'I occupy myself with worship.' Jesus then asked him 'Who is supporting you?' To this the man replied that his brother was supporting him, and Jesus said to him that 'your brother is more pious than you.'[10] Al-Ghazālī has followed this with several *ḥadīths* and narratives from the Muslim sages on the subject. The fact that he quoted a statement of Prophet Jesus on this is very likely intended to show the common perspective of Christianity and Islam on work.

The Qur'ān also refers to work as a means of earning a living in conjunction with the freedom of movement:

$$هو الذي جعل لكم الأرض ذلولا فامشوا في مناكبها وكلوا$$
$$من رزقه$$

He it is who made the earth subservient to you; so traverse through its tracts and enjoy the sustenance which He has provided. (67:15)

Work and travel are often inter-related in the sense that most work is done outside the home and a great deal of it also involves travelling. To utilise the resources of the earth and travel in its tracts necessitates work. Work and travel between them hold the essence of prosperity and the greatest potential for improvement. Any attempt therefore to deny lawful business and travel, or to try to impose undue restrictions on them would be deemed unwarranted and unlawful. The text encourages travel in the tracts of the earth which is deemed necessary for mankind to build the earth. Travel also brings familiarity and can be a means of closeness among people and can in the meantime open new avenues of opportunity for work. Thus when someone is unable to find a suitable work in the place of his residence, he is encouraged to travel and find his sustenance elsewhere. Freedom of movement is thus seen as a complementary and important dimension of the right to work.

The open outlook that the Qur'ān maintains on both of them is in turn related to the Qur'ānic principle of the vicegerency (*khilāfah*) of Man in the earth. The Qur'ān is expressive at once of the responsibility and power that are the necessary ingredients of this mission. The reference that immediately follows *khilāfah* is for mankind to build the earth:

$$ولقد مكناكم في الأرض وجعلنا لكم فيها معايش$$

It is We who have placed you with authority in the earth, and provided you therein with means for the fulfilment of your life. (7:10)

It is not the bare necessities of day-to-day living that is the focus of the text here but authority to exercise initiative and develop the abundant potentials of the earth so as to bring facility and enjoyment for its inhabitants. Man can only achieve this through ingenuity and self-application in the work place.

Elsewhere the Qur'ān addresses the Prophet Muḥammad to remind the believers of the value of work, and what it takes to make it a source of pride for the community and a firm basis by which to gain the pleasure of God:

$$\text{وقل اعملوا فسيرى الله عملكم ورسوله}$$

And say (you must) work. Soon will God observe your work, and His Messenger (and the believers). (9:105)

The emphasis in this verse is clearly on the collective responsibility of the entire community to ensure that its members excel in good work and that this can only be achieved through dedication and a watchful attitude on the part of the leaders. The affirmation that ʿamal is a concern directly of God and His Messenger automatically integrates God-consciousness into the calibre of ʿamal in Islam. The Qur'ān maintains this outlook in many of its passages in which ʿamal is made the litmus test and criterion of Man's success in both this life and the next: '...He created life and death so as to try you—which of you excel in deeds.' (67:2)

$$\text{هو الذي خلق الموت والحياة ليبلوكم أيكم أحسن عملا}$$

It is then declared that 'We shall not cause to waste the recompense of one who excels in ʿamal.' (18:30)

$$\text{إنا لا نضيع أجر من أحسن عملا}$$

Commentators have noted that the reference to ʿamal in these verses is to all work, both pertaining to the affairs of this world and to those of the next.[11]

The Qur'ān also reminds people of the beneficial character and effect of work on personality. If man were to have access to the means of livelihood without having to work for it, that would mean not only laziness but rebellion and corruption:

ولو بسط الله الرزق لعباده لبغوا في الأرض ولكن ينزّل بقدر ما يشاء

> If God were to enlarge the provision of His servants, they would surely rebel in the earth, but He sends down by measure as He wills. (42:27)

Life on earth has thus been planned such that human beings exert themselves to develop the earth and provide for their own needs. Work tends to control within bounds the ego of Man and helps to keep the relationship of Man with the universe and of men among themselves within the given perimeters of that plan.

The Prophet Muḥammad, like many of his predecessors among the Prophets, did not shun from hard work just as he also spoke highly of those who exerted themselves in useful occupations. He exemplified in his own lifestyle that all useful work, both within and outside the sphere of religion, whether manual or otherwise, is honourable and earns the pleasure of God. The Prophet thus declared:

ما أكل أحد طعاما قط خيرا من أن يأكل من عمل يده، وأنّ نبي الله داود عليه السلام كان يأكل من عمل يده

> No one has ever eaten food purer than food that is earned by the toil of one's hands. The (King cum) Prophet of God, David, peace be on him, used to earn his living by the toil of his hands.[12]

Reports indicate that Prophet David occupied himself with cloth making and that many Prophets before him also lived off the toil of their hands: Prophet Adam was a farmer, Noah was a carpenter, Idrīs was a tailor and Moses was a shepherd. It is also interesting to note that many of the learned personalities of Islam took pride in their works and chose to be called by names such as *al-Bazzāz* (cloth merchant), *al-Qaffāl* (locksmith), *al-Qaṭṭān* (cotton trader), *al-Jaṣṣāṣ* (painter), *al-Khayyāṭ* (tailor) and only exceptionally, they identified themselves by reference to their ancestors and tribes.[13] The fact that Prophet David was singled out in this *ḥadīth*, as Abū Zahrah pointed out, was to highlight a certain attitude, for he was a king and was in no need of manual work. The attitude conveyed by this *ḥadīth* is that work is a source of nobility and pride, and that no one should see it in the opposite light. To honour manual work is also tantamount to a rejection of the class system of the olden days whereby workers were denigrated and denied the nobility that Islam recognises for them.[14] Prior to the advent of Islam, 'workers were considered a low class with no recognised rights.'[15] Islam marked a turning point on this and a deliberate effort was made to eliminate this age-old attitude of discrimination toward work.

The same message is confirmed in yet another *ḥadīth*, wherein it is provided that 'The best earning is that which is obtained through unadulterated sale and the toil of one's own hands.'[16]

Further on the spiritual merit of work that is done with one's hands, the Prophet is reported to have said:

من أمسى كالا من عمل يده أمسى مغفورا له

One who sleeps a night while taking his fill out of the toil of his hands invokes (God's) blessings on himself throughout that night.[17]

Manual work has obviously been commended so as to make it an integral part of Islamic ethos. Circumstances have obviously changed. What is important is a sound attitude to work itself, manual or otherwise. Yet there may still be a lesson here to say that a society which shuns manual work does so to its detriment and may find it hard to be self-reliant. What we are seeing nowadays in some of the more affluent Muslim countries is perhaps reminiscent of the importance that Islam attaches to work with one's hands. For some of these societies have become dependent on foreign workers for their manual labour. The result is very likely to be a certain weakness not only in the economy but also in the outlook and even character of the people, and the social fabric of the society suffers as a result.

It is reported that upon his return from the battle of Tabūk the Prophet commented on some marks that he happened to see on the hands of one of his Companions. The Prophet asked the man: 'What is this that I see on your hand?' The man replied that it was due to 'the work that I do with the rope so that I can feed my family.' Upon hearing this the Prophet kissed the man's hand and said 'this is truly the hand that God and His Messenger love.'[18]

In Islam *'amal* becomes a dimension of *'ibādah* only when it is done well and to the best of one's ability. Work that is done with the intention to satisfy one's own legitimate needs, to support one's family and friends, and to realise a benefit to the community is equated in the Qur'ān with *jihād* in the way of God. Thus the Qur'ān promises with great reward those '. . . who travel in the land seeking of God's bounty, and others who fight in the way of God. . .' (73:20)

وآخرون يضربون في الأرض يبتغون من فضل الله
وآخرون يقاتلون في سبيل الله

Work that qualifies as service to God must necessarily be of a high calibre in which attention is paid to both quality and anticipated outcome, and it is free of dishonesty and cheating. Many prominent figures among the Companions and Successors, including 'Umar b. al-Khaṭṭāb, 'Abd Allāh b. Mas'ūd, Abū Qulābah, Ibrāhīm al-Nakhā'ī have held that occupying oneself in lawful and professional work is preferable to devotion and worship. The caliph 'Umar b. al-Khaṭṭāb thus told a group of people who had consecrated themselves to worship in the mosque that 'none of you should ever neglect work by which to earn a living and simply pray "O Allāh grant me sustenance," for you must know that heavens do not shower gold and silver on people.' 'Abd Allāh b. Mas'ūd is simply quoted to have denounced the predicament of an idle person who does not apply himself and is not engaged in work of any kind, whether worldly or religious, and is consequently a burden on others. Ibrāhim al-Nakhā'ī was once asked a question as to who commended greater merit—an honest merchant, or one who is devoted to worship—and he replied that the former attained greater merit as he engaged himself in *jihād* through honest business and fairness to others. The Companion Abū Qulābah has also been quoted to have said to 'a man' that 'I would love to see you occupied in earning a living more than seeing you committed (to worship) in the mosque.'[19] Al-Ghazālī, who recorded this information, went on to advance a somewhat unusual observation that devotion to worship is preferable to business for four types of worshippers. The first of these is one who occupies himself with the normal worship such as prayer and fasting, etc. Second is the person who is engaged, not so much in the physical aspects of worship, but in spiritual refinement of the self, the Sufi and mystic. Third is a learned person who helps the people in practical ways such as the jurisconsult (*muftī*) and Qur'ān teachers and the like. And last is the person who engages himself with what is of benefit for the community and advances their interests, such as the sultan, judge, witness and the like. People who devote themselves to any of the foregoing are in effect doing what is preferable to trading or commercial activity undertaken purely for purposes of earning a living (i.e. *al-kasb*).[20] It is obvious from this discussion that Ghazālī's idea of *al-kasb* was somewhat narrowly focused and did not include the work of the sultan, judges and lawyers. If *al-kasb* is strictly understood as work that involves trading in the sense of buying and selling, then to exclude judges and lawyers from the purview of *al-kasb* may be acceptable. But if one were to understand *al-kasb* more openly in the sense of work that is undertaken in order to earn a living, then *al-kasb* need not be confined to the conventional concept of handling merchandise or agriculture. Ghazālī maintains that these four types of *ʿibādah*, or worship and the work they involve are preferable to *al-kasb*. It is an interesting strand of thought, reflective perhaps of Ghazālī's own Sufi orientations, yet its harmony with the early precedent is somewhat uncertain. Once it is accepted that *al-kasb* is a wider concept and need not be confined to commerce then the rest of the discussion as to the superiority or otherwise of any of the said categories to *al-kasb* also collapses. It is not certain, for instance, whether the work of a *muftī* or a judge is spiritually superior to that of an honest trader. There is no question on the other hand over the validity of saying that dedication to the service of God and the community and work that brings benefit to the people is spiritually superior to business activity and trading. Basic evidence in the Qur'ān and *Sunnah* tends to maintain a broader view of the value of work in all varieties without any attempt at specification. Note, for example, the *ḥadīth* in which the Prophet is reported to have said: 'God loves it when a worker does a work that he does it well.'[21]

The Prophet has also said with reference again to *ʿamal* that 'God has prescribed beauty (*al-iḥsān*) on everything.' Al-Qaraḍāwī has observed concerning this *ḥadīth* that the word '*kataba*' (prescribed) therein indicates that it is an obligation in that everyone must aim for it.[22] This conscientious attitude to work finds further endorsement in the following saying of the Prophet:

ألا كلكم راع وكلكم مسؤل عن رعيته، فالأمير الذى على الناس راع وهو مسؤل عن رعيته، والرجل راع على أهل بيته وهو مسؤل عنهم، والمرأة راعية على بيت بعلها وولده

All of you are custodians and all of you are responsible for what is in their custody. The Amīr (ruler) is a custodian who is responsible for his subjects; the husband is a custodian and he is responsible for his family; and the wife is a custodian who is responsible for her household. . . [23]

Everyone is thus a custodian and trustee of what is placed in his or her custody. The reference is evidently to a responsible and conscientious approach to the performance of duty. Everyone in position of responsibility is included in the purview of this *hadīth*. The size and magnitude of that responsibility is decidedly greater in the case of the *amīr*, or head of state. Yet in principle the *hadīth* contemplates everyone to exert themselves to the best of their ability in the due performance of work that they undertake. According to another *hadīth* the Prophet addressed everyone to 'occupy yourselves with work, for everyone has a certain predisposition to doing certain things well.'[24]

اعملوا فكلّ ميسر لما خلق له

This also means that everyone should choose the kind of work that suits him well and agrees with his predisposition and talent. The advice of this *hadīth* confirms the individual's freedom of choice, and also the suggestion perhaps that a harmonious choice is likely to bring personal satisfaction.

The Qur'ān has in several places encouraged agricultural work that involves food production and land development. People are thus reminded to take advantage of the soil which God has made fertile and congenial for growth: 'And We produce therein orchards of date-palms and vines, and We cause springs to gush forth therein so that they may enjoy its fruits.' (36:33–35)[25]

وآية لهم الأرض الميتة أحييناها وأخرجنا منها حبّا فمنه
يأكلون وجعلنا فيها جنات من نخيل وأعناب وفجّرنا فيها
من العيون ليأكلوا من ثمره وما عملته أيديهم أفلا
يشكرون

Man may till the soil and sow the seed, but the productive forces of nature are not the handiwork of Man; they are a manifestation of God's providence for His creatures. The verse just quoted is worded in a way that implies that God Almighty combines His own exalted work with that of the human hand. To say that God has endowed the earth with many resources is another way of saying that God has accomplished His purpose and His work, and it is for Man to do his part in developing the resources of the earth.

The Prophet has taken the point further by indicating some of the ways in which agricultural work is counted as charity which brings benefit to all concerned.

ما من مسلم يغرس غرسا الّا كان ما أكل منه صدقة،
وماسرق منه له صدقة وما أكل السبع منه فهو صدقة، وما
أكلت الطير فهو له صدقة، ولايزرؤه (أى بنفقه) أحد الا
كان له صدقة

Any Muslim who plants a tree that bears fruit, which is then consumed by the inhabitants of the earth, it becomes a charity for him; it is counted as charity even when someone steals from it, or when it is eaten by animals and birds, or indeed when it is diminished in any other way—all of it becomes charity (*sadaqah*).[26]

Achievement on the work front is inevitably associated with a keen awareness of the value of time. This message can hardly be conveyed better than in the following *ḥadīth*:

ان قامت الساعة وفى يد أحدكم فسيله فان استطاع الا
يقوم حتى يغرسها فليفعل

When the final hour approaches and one of you has in his hand a seedling of palm for planting and thinks there will be time enough to plant it, then let him plant it if he can.[27]

With reference to trading and commerce the Qur'ān declares the permissibility of sale but prohibits usury (*ribā*). This is due to the fact that *ribā* consists of profit that is not earned through work but gained unjustly by exploiting works done by others (2:275). The text also provides:

يأيها الذين آمنوا لا تأكلوا أموالكم بينكم بالباطل إلا أن تكون تجارة عن تراض منكم

O you who believe! eat not up your properties among yourselves in vanities, but let there be among you traffic and trade by mutual consent. (4:29)

Eating up or misappropriation of the property of others is a broad concept that comprises almost all instances of unlawful activities including fraud, bribery, gambling, usury, usurpation and illicit enrichment. These are to be avoided, and the way to avoid them is through lawful trading by mutual consent. The Qur'ān here lays down the basic framework that all commercial activity and contracts must be founded on the consent of its participants. Mutual consent thus becomes the cornerstone of the Islamic law of transactions and contract.

In a reference to the use of navigation for purposes of trade, the Qur'ān reminds the believers:

الله الذي سخر لكم البحر لتجري الفلك فيه بأمره ولتبتغوا من فضله ولعلكم تشكرون

It is God who subjugated the sea to you that ships may sail through it by His command that you may seek of His bounty and you may be grateful. (45:12)

There are also allusions to the construction of houses, utilisation of mineral resources (16:80), and the military and other usages of iron (57:25), all of which are identified as potential sources of benefit, prosperity and wealth.

The Prophet further accentuated the merit of honest trading in the following *ḥadīth*:

التاجر الصدوق الأمين مع النبيين والصديقين والشهداء

The honest and trustworthy trader stands in the hereafter next to the Prophets, the truthful servants of God, and the martyrs.[28]

As previously noted many a leading Prophet including Abraham, Lot, and the Prophet Muḥammad occupied themselves with trading. In the early days of his youth the Prophet Muḥammad entered a partnership with one al-Sā'ib b. Abī al-Sā'ib when both of them lived in Mecca. The Prophet went on trading journeys to Sham (Syria) on behalf of Lady Khadījah, whom he later married. Even before these events, the Prophet had acquired a reputation for honesty, which is why he was known by the epiteth *al-Amīn* (the trustworthy).

The *Sharī'ah* validates trade in all of its varieties provided it does not proceed over unlawful substances and it is clear of exploitation and expropriation of the property of others. The government is also under a duty in *Sharī'ah* to keep open all the avenues of lawful trade, to remove obstacles in the way of free movement of goods and people, and not to burden free trade with the imposition of onerous custom duties. In its capacity as custodian of the benefit and *maṣlaḥah* of the community the state must ensure that all the avenues of permissible trade remain open to the people.[29]

Engagement in trading activity is not advisable for a government official who is normally entitled to a pay that should be sufficient for his needs. Al-Ghazālī has taken up this point and reminded his readers that when the first caliph Abū Bakr assumed the caliphal office he retained his business activity which had occupied him before. But many of the senior Companions advised him against it as business generated demand on his time which should be devoted to the affairs of the community. It seems that Abū Bakr still kept his business and also withdrew a salary from the Public Treasury (*bayt al-māl*), but then left a will to return to the *bayt al-māl* what he had received. Al-Ghazālī also noted that the caliph Abū Bakr considered it preferable to receive a salary at the time but had apparently intended to pay it back.[30]

One of the well-known Companions, Salmān al-Fārisī, has been quoted to have cast doubt on the efficacy of trading (*tijārah*) and said 'if any of you has an opportunity to go to the *Hajj*, fight a holy war, or build a mosque, let him do so, but let him not be a trader (*tājir*), nor a traitor (*khā'in*).' Ghazālī has quoted and discussed this partly because the derogatory reference to trading in it is divergent to the bulk of the evidence that is clearly supportive of trading activity as an honest trader is often praised in the *ḥadīth*. Ghazālī understands Salmān's statement to be referring to trading which is pursued for the sake, not of sufficiency for oneself and one's family, but for increase in wealth (*ithtikthār*) that are not expended on charitable causes, but simply to satisfy one's greed.[31] I may add here a brief note that the way Salmān spoke was contextual, which was to compare *tijārah* with certain devotional acts and his statement should just be read in that light. As for engaging oneself in trading beyond the level of sufficiency, this too is not reprehensible, provided that the necessary charity (i.e. *zakāh*) and other due payments are paid out of its earnings, and when this is the case, the general evidence of *Sunnah* is supportive of *tijārah*, and not otherwise, even if it is aimed at *istikthār*.

III. The Value (*Ḥukm*) of Work

Broadly speaking, work is a personal duty of every able-bodied individual in *Sharīʿah*. But the personal circumstances of the individual and the prevailing conditions of society tend to have a bearing on this obligation. The ʿulamāʾ have thus attempted to evaluate work on the familiar scale of *Sharīʿah* values either as recommendable (*mandūb*) or obligatory (*wājib*) on the one hand, and *makrūh* (reprehensible) or forbidden (*ḥarām*) on the other. To work for a living is a duty if it is the only way to prevent dependency on others and begging, and it is only recommendable above the level of sufficiency.

The Qur'ān praises those who 'beg not of men importunately (*ilḥāfā*)' (2:273),

ولايسألون الناس إلحافا

and the Prophet explained this by saying

من سأل منكم وله أوقية أو عدلها فقد سأل إلحافا

> 'Anyone of you who has an *awqiyah* or its equivalent and begs verily begs importunately.'[32]

The Prophet is also reported to have said:

اليد العليا خير من اليد السفلى، واليد العليا هي المنفقة
والسفلى هي السائلة

The upper hand is better than the lower hand, for the former is one that spends whereas the latter resorts to begging.[33]

Begging is permitted in dire necessity of which the *Sunnah* has specified only three situations as follows:

إن المسألة لا تحلّ إلا لثلاثة: رجل تحمل حمالة فحلت له المسألة، فسأل حتى يصيبها ثم يمسك، ورجل أصابته جائحة فاحتاجت حاله فحلت له المسألة فسأل حتى يصيب قواما من عيش . . . ورجل أصابته فاقة حتى سقول من ذوى الحجى من قومه قد أصابت فلانا الفاقة فحلت له المسألة فسأل حتى يصيب قواما من عيش، أو سدادا من عيش ثم يمسك

Begging is not permissible except in three cases: firstly, for a man who is unable to pay the blood-money (*diyyah*) that he owes. He may ask others for help until he is able to pay it and no more; and then for a man who is victim of calamity and loses all his assets; he may resort to begging until he can support himself; and lastly for a man who is afflicted with penury due to loss in business and three discerning persons of his group confirm it. Anyone who begs outside these situations commits a heinous act and devours what is forbidden for him.[34]

Work that is obligatory may consist either of a personal obligation (*farḍ ʿayn*), or a collective obligation (*farḍ kifāʾī*). To exert oneself in order to earn a lawful living is a personal obligation of every capable individual especially when work is undertaken for any of the following three purposes:

(1) In order to satisfy one's own personal needs for sustenance, because fulfillment of one's bodily needs and protection against destruction and disease is an emphatic duty (*farḍ ʿayn*) of every Muslim.

(2) Work may alternatively be undertaken in order to repay a debt with the income that is earned, in which case it is obligatory, if the debt in question cannot be otherwise repaid.[35]

(3) Work in order to support one's wife and family. According to the Qur'ānic directives on this subject the husband is to provide his

wife with a suitable dwelling that is within his means (65:6). He is under a similar obligation to support his family in a manner that is in accord with his financial standing (65:7 and 2:133 respectively). To work and to earn in order to support oneself and one's family is also a great act of merit, as in the following *ḥadīth*:

دينارا أنفقته في سبيل الله ودينارا أنفقته في رقبة ودينارا تصدقت به على مسكين ودينارا أنفقته على أهلك، وأعلاها أجرا الذى أنفقته على أهلك

If you spend a dinar in the way of God, and another with which to support your servant, and another that you give in charity to the poor, and yet another by which you support your family— the dinar that you spend on your family earns you the greatest reward.[36]

According to another report, the renowned Companion, Salmān al-Fārisī said the following to his fellow Companion, Abū al-Dardā:

قال سلمان لصاحبه أبي الدرداء: إن لربك عليك حقا وإنّ لبدنك عليك حقا وإن لأهلك عليك حقا فأعط كل ذي حقّ حقّه. فذكر ذلك للنبى صلى الله عليه وسلم فقال: صدق سلمان

Your Creator has a right over you; your body has a right over you; and your family has a right over you. So give every right-bearer his right. This was then mentioned to the Prophet to which he responded 'Salmān has said the truth'.[37]

Speaking of industries and professions, al-Ghazālī wrote that sustenance of basic industries such as agriculture, weaving, tailoring, medicine and even politics is a collective obligation (*farḍ kifāʾī*) of the community that must be upheld; for when a city is devoid of these, it will face decline and eventual destruction.[38]

With regard to the distinction between personal and collective obligations (*farḍ ʿayn, farḍ kifāʾī*) it is to be noted that personal obligations takes priority over collective obligations, especially in the event of a conflict arising between them. For instance, *jihād* is a collective obligation, whereas being good to one's parents (*birr al-wālidayn*) is a personal obligation and therefore takes priority over *jihād*. This is the purport of a *ḥadīth* reported by ʿAbd Allāh b. ʿAmr b. al-ʿĀṣ as follows:

جاء رجل الى النبي صلى الله عليه وسلم فاستأذنه في الجهاد فقال: أحيٌّ والداك. قال: نعم. قال: فيهما فجاهد

'A man came to the Prophet, peace be on him, and asked for permission if he could join the *jihād*. The Prophet asked him "Are your parents still alive?" to which the man replied "Yes", and the Prophet told him "go and serve your parents (you strive through serving them)".'[39]

Enforcement of collective obligations also tends to vary among peoples and communities. There are some which receive more attention whereas others are neglected. In the time of al-Ghazālī in the early sixth/eleventh century Baghdad, much attention was paid to the study of religious sciences and *fiqh*, which is a *farḍ kifāʾī*, and it is said that in the district where he lived there were about fifty *faqihs*, but only one non-Muslim physician. Notwithstanding the people's need for physicians and the fact that medicine is a field of learning that stretches across the religious and secular divides, it received evidently very little attention.[40]

A *farḍ kifāʾī* may occasionally be elevated to the rank of *farḍ ʿayn* in the event where only one person is available to discharge it. To illustrate this, should there be only one *faqīh* in a locality that can advise the people on religious issues, or one physician, scientist, architect or engineer, for that matter, who can serve the community, the *farḍ kifāʾī* concerning them converts to *farḍ ʿayn* and it becomes their personal obligation to offer their services to the community.[41]

Whereas *farḍ ʿayn* generally takes priority over *farḍ kifāʾī*, a certain order of priority can also be ascertained with regard to *farḍ ʿayn*. Here it may be said, for example, that *farḍ ʿayn* pertaining to the Right of Man takes priority in matters of enforcement over *farḍ ʿayn* pertaining to the Right of God. The Rights of God are on the whole open to a degree of leniency whereas the Rights of Man generally calls for rigorous enforcement. To perform the *ḥajj* pilgrimage, for example, is a *farḍ ʿayn* that belongs to the category of the Right of God, as opposed to the repayment of a personal debt, which is a *farḍ 'ayn* pertaining to the Right of Man. Should there arise a conflict situation between these, such as when a man has limited funds that are enough to repay a debt whereas he also needs to perform the *hajj*, the debt repayment takes priority over the *hajj*, unless his creditor allows him to perform the *hajj* first. It is due to the great emphasis that is placed on personal duties, especially on the repayment of debt that according to the terms of a *hadīth*, God forgives a martyr (*shahīd*) all his failings except for an unpaid debt (*dayn*). The *hadīth* on this simply declares that 'every sin is forgiven of a martyr except for an unpaid debt.'[42]

The obligatory duties, whether collective, or personal, take priority over what may be recommendable (*mandūb*) or merely optional (*mubāḥ*). To observe a supererogatory fast is only recommendable but not for a woman who does it at the expense of neglecting her more important tasks of looking after the welfare of her family and young children. Similarly a worker who observes recommendable fasting on Mondays and Thursdays and goes to work stricken by lack of energy and fatigue would clearly be advised against it. For work is a duty whereas fasting outside the Ramaḍān is merely recommendable.[43] As for those whose work involves hardship and it is not possible for them to stop working during the fasting month of Ramaḍān, be it for their own needs or the community's need for such work, they may open the fast. They should, however, start the day with fasting and open the fast only when the hardship becomes intolerable.[44]

According to the clear terms of *hadīth*, as quoted below, the best of all works, careers, and professions is one which brings greatest benefit to the people:

أحب الناس إلى الله أنفعهم وأحب الأعمال إلى الله عز
وجل سرور تدخله على مسلم، أو تكشف عنه كربة، أو
تقضي عنه دينا، أو تطرد عنه جوعا، ولأن أمشي مع أخي
المسلم أحبّ إليّ من أن أعتكف في المسجد شهرا

The most beloved to God of all people is the most beneficent (to others), and the best of all works in the eyes of God Most High is one that brings happiness to a Muslim, or alleviates hardship from him, or releases him from a debt (he cannot pay), or saves him from hunger. If I were to walk together with my Muslim brother who is in need, I would prefer this than a month-long worship and seclusion in a mosque.[45]

Work that promotes the best interests of the community and advances peace and harmony among people is also highly recommended—as proclaimed in the following *hadīth*, where the Prophet posed a question to his Companions:

ألا أخبركم بأفضل من درجة الصلاة والصيام والصدقة: إصلاح ذات البين، فإن فساد ذات البين هي الحالقة

Should I inform you of something which ranks even higher than obligatory prayer, fasting and charity? It is to bring peace where there is a conflict between two parties, for hostility between individuals is like a razor (that erases their faith).[46]

Commenting on these two *hadīth*s, Qaraḍāwī has noted that social welfare works and educational efforts that aim to prevent crime and corruption, and works that bring benefit to the poor and the sick and provide them with employment opportunities, or help them to meet their needs, all partake in work that the Prophet has so strongly recommended.[47]

The spirit of encouragement to good work, especially of work that sets an enduring example for others to emulate, is clearly manifested in the following *hadīth* of the Prophet:

من سنّ في الإسلام سنّة حسنة فعُمل بها بعده كُتب له مثل أجر من عمل بها ولاينقص من أجورهم شيئ ومن سنّ في الإسلام سنة سيّئة فعُمل بها يعده كُتب عليه مثل وزر من عمل بها ولاينقص من أوزارهم شيئ

One who sets a good example in Islam and it is followed by others after him, a reward will be written for him on account of every instance of compliance by others while nothing will be reduced from the reward of the followers. And one who sets a bad example in (the name of) Islam, which is then followed by others after him, it will be recorded in the accounts of both the leader and follower and nothing will reduce their burdens.[48]

Further in praise of good deeds of a durable kind, the Prophet declared:

إذا مات الإنسان انقطع عمله إلا من ثلاث: صدقة جارية، أو علم ينتفع به، أو ولد صالح يدعو له

The deeds of a person come to an end with his death except for three things: continuing charity, beneficial knowledge, and well-behaved offspring who prays for him.[49]

Abū Zahrah has observed that work which partakes in *fard kifā'ī* refers to all beneficial work that promotes community welfare such as working in agriculture and industries, building roads and hospitals and the like. If some people in the community undertake it, the duty is fulfilled generally but work of this nature may not be abandoned altogether. In the event when this happens, the government may compel to work those who are capable of doing it.[50]

Broadly speaking, the individual's freedom and right to work remain undiminished unless they partake in *darar* and become a means of inflicting harm on others, which would then fall under the purview of the renowned *hadīth* that 'harm may neither be inflicted nor reciprocated in Islam.' لاضرر ولاضرار في الإسلام Work that partakes in harm and corruption is generally unlawful and so is the revenue that is earned by it. No one may make a business out of defaming others nor profit through acts of oppression. The *Sharī'ah* thus prohibits sale of arms to rebels and to the enemy at war; it also prohibits sale of grapes to a winery and work that involves concluding or facilitating unlawful business deals and contracts. Work that involves prostitution, sorcery, gambling, fraud and wine drinking which either directly or indirectly promotes them all amount to *ma'siyah* and sin which must be avoided. The basic rule here is that whatever that leads to *harām* and is used as a means toward procuring *harām* also becomes *harām*.[51] A worker is consequently not entitled to any wages for the unlawful work he might have completed.[52] Work that violates a clear prohibition, or one which inflicts a manifest harm on another person is thus unlawful and may render the person liable to punishment or payment of compensation. Work that falls in between the two categories of *halāl* and *harām* should also be avoided if one can find alternative work which is clear of doubt. This would be in conformity with the instruction of the *ḥadīth* that 'one who keeps clear of doubts purifies his faith and his honour.'[53]

من اتقى الشبهات فقد استبرأ لدينه وعرضه

If no other alternative could be found, then one may undertake doubtful work to the extent necessary for fulfillment of his basic needs. Work that is clear of doubt is preferable even if it involves greater hardship.[54]

Should there arise a conflict between the fulfilment, on the one hand, of a personal obligation (*farḍ ʿayn*) and indulgence in unlawful work, on the other, the latter is tolerated, according to some *ʿulamāʾ*, including Imam Mālik, to the extent that is necessary. Suppose that someone lives in a place where he can find no other work to support himself and his family except by undertaking work that is *ḥarām*, and he cannot escape to another place either, he may engage in unlawful work to the extent that is necessary for his survival, but no more than that.[55] It is equivalent to the concession *Sharīʿah* has granted to a person who fears death from starvation, in which case he is allowed to consume unlawful food. This is an exceptional concession that falls under the rules of necessity (*ḍarūrah*). One of the salient legal maxims that needs to be invoked here simply declares that 'necessities make the unlawful lawful.' (*al-ḍarūrāt tubīḥ al-maḥẓūrāt*). But then another legal maxim lays down the proviso that 'necessity is to be measured according to its true proportions,' (*al-ḍarūratu tuqdaru bi-qadrihā*) which evidently means that unnecessary indulgence in forbidden activity would not be covered by the rules of necessity.

The most noble of all professions is intellectual work that involves teaching and academic research. This is because intellectual development and thought is the bedrock of all other areas of improvement. This is followed by productive professions which respond to the tangible needs of people for them. The *fiqh* literature of medieval vantage has also listed a number of professions under the broad category of lowly professions (*al-ḥiraf al-danīʾah*) which were considered to be compromising of personal dignity and decorum (*murūʾah*). The schools of law are not entirely in agreement on these but the common headings included rubbish collectors (*zabbāl*), barbers, dyers and tanners, iron smiths, finance workers, funeral workers etc. Some even included the surgeon, animal doctor, tailor and poet.[56] Looking further back in history, the available information suggests that work was generally looked down upon by the ancient cultures. The Romans considered trade as a lowly occupation and left it largely to the subjugated people and slaves. The Arabs on the other hand considered trade (*tijārah*) as a noble occupation but looked down upon agriculture and industrial work, which they too left for the inferior classes and slaves. Islam marked a departure and advanced a more dignified outlook on work generally.[57] The present writer is of the view that this aspect of the early literature is somewhat subjective and bears the influence of custom and public opinion of particular times, which may or may not enjoy unequivocal support in the sources. Some of these identifications also seem to have undergone a change whereby the present generation of Muslims may no longer see them in the same light in which they were seen earlier.

Questions have also arisen over a certain order of priority between the broader categories of work. Three areas are mentioned, namely of agriculture, industry, and commerce: which of these take priority and which, one might say, command greater spiritual merit? The reason as to why this question arose in the first place goes back to the reported ḥadīths, as quoted earlier, on the merit respectively of agriculture, industry and commerce.

Al-Nawawī has drawn the conclusion from his reading of the relevant *aḥādīth* that work which is done through the toil of one's hands is of greater merit and that would place agriculture and industry at the forefront and give them priority over commerce.[58] The jurists have occasionally attempted to recommend one more highly than the other of these three spheres of work. Imam Shāfiʿī is said to have ranked commerce to be of the greatest merit.[59] Qaraḍāwī's investigation led him to the correct conclusion, I believe, that none is to be given absolute priority over the other, but that preference may be given to one or the other in accordance with the people's need for it. Thus when there is a shortage of foodstuffs, agricultural work and food production would acquire greater merit, especially when this involves hard work and patience (*al-ṣabr*), yet also great benefit for the people and those who attempt it earn greater reward.[60] But if food supplies are adequate and the society is in need of industrial development so as to reduce imports from abroad, or develop new lines of industry, such as arms production for self-defence, then the industrial work is likely to acquire greater importance and preferable from the viewpoint of Islam.

In the event where both agriculture and industry are proportionate to the needs of the community, but there is shortage of foreign currency and imbalance in foreign trade, international trade may become a priority sector in the economy and may therefore be given preference as the circumstances may demand. If there be a case for soliciting legal advice and *fatwā* over priority that may be given to a particular line of work, the answer to this should reflect the advice of the legal maxim of *fiqh* that '*fatwā* may change with the change of time and place.' But since the basic position here is one of choice between the various types of lawful work, there may be no need for a *fatwā*, and the matter basically falls within the realm of government policy.

As far as the current needs of the *ummah* are concerned, science and technology tend to be among the priority areas where special attention is needed to upgrade the capabilities of the Muslim nations. This will require greater attention to education and training and preparations that are necessary to ensure progress therein. All of this partakes in meritorious work and should be given priority as far as possible.[61]

What follows next is still related to the value of work and provides a response to the question whether a Muslim may work, and cooperate, with a non-Islamic government.

IV. Participation in a non-Islamic Government

The question that is raised here is over permissibility for a Muslim to work and cooperate with a non-Islamic government. Many have answered this question in the negative including al-Qaraḍāwī who has given a detailed *fatwā* to the effect that a Muslim should not participate in a government which refuses to comply with Islamic principles. Qaraḍāwī has quoted several verses from the Qur'ān which ask the believers not to look for alternative rulings in the event where a decisive ruling is available in the ordinances of God and His Messenger (33:36 & 24:63). This normative position also demands total compliance with the teachings of Islam and rejects the eclectic attitude of one who accepts only some of God's commands while choosing to reject others (cf. Q. 2:85).

Having given a basically negative response to the question under review, Qaraḍāwī then seeks to abandon that position on grounds of what he calls as valid *Sharīʿah* considerations (*iʿtibārāt sharʿiyyah*) whereby he advocates the opposite of his initial response. The *fatwā* that he gives then allows a qualified participation for a Muslim in a non-Islamic government. The grounds of this *fatwā* may be summarised as follows:

a) Minimisation of oppression and evil to the extent of one's ability. If participation in a non-Islamic government by a concerned Muslim can bring even a partial relief to himself and other Muslims, an attempt should be made to seize that opportunity. This is the implied meaning of the Qur'ānic directive to the believers 'to fear God to the extent you can' (al-Taghābun, 64:16).

$$فاتقوا الله مااستطعتم$$

The same message has been endorsed in a renowned *ḥadīth* where the Prophet addressed his followers: 'When I order you to do something, you must do it to the extent of your ability.' The principle conveyed here is that Islam makes concessions in situations of necessity where circumstances might be such that total compliance with its own injunctions may be unfeasible.[62]

b) Opting for the lesser of the two evils (*akhaff al-ḍararayn*): This is the subject of a legal maxim of *fiqh* on whose basis the jurists have often given *fatwas*. One example of such a *fatwā* is to allow a person to remain silent in the face of an evil, if doing anything is likely to cause a greater evil. Thus if a Muslim is convinced that participation in a non-Islamic government is the lesser of the two anticipated evils, he may take employment with it.

c) Avoidance and removal of hardship (*rafʿ al-ḥaraj*). This is the subject of a number of Qur'ānic verses where it is provided

$$يريد الله بكم اليسر ولا يريد بكم العسر$$

God intends ease and facility for you, not hardship. (2:185), and

$$يريد الله أن يخفّف عنكم$$

God intends to lighten your burden... (4:28)

In another verse, it is provided that:

$$فمن اضطرّ غير باغ ولاعاد فلا إثم عليه$$

One who is compelled without being a transgressor or a rebel, does not incur a sin. (2:173)

A legal maxim that is drawn from these and a number of similar *ḥadīths* thus proclaims 'necessity makes the unlawful lawful.' When there is a way that hardship can be eased and overcome, an attempt should be made in that direction. In the event, for example, where a witness of upright character is not available in a judicial case, the judge may admit a witness of lower qualification if this is the only way that the court can prevent a manifest injustice.

In response to a question whether one should go to *jihād* if one has a choice either to go with a ruler who is strong but sinful, or with one who is pious but weak, Imam Aḥmad b. Ḥanbal gave preference to the former. For a ruler who is strong but commits sins, his sins are his own responsibility but his strength will benefit the Muslim community. As for the pious but a weak ruler, his piety benefits him personally but his weakness will affect the community as a whole. The former is therefore preferable, if one has to choose between them. Qaraḍāwī thus concludes that a person who is unable to secure any employment, he may lower his ideals and take the pragmatic step of working for a non-Muslim employer, if this would be beneficial to him and the Muslim community.[63]

Islam also advocates a measured and graduated approach to matters that cannot be achieved all at once. While stating this, Qaraḍāwī adds that establishing an Islamic system of government is a great yet ambitious task. One should strive for it but the fruits of that striving may take time. An illustration is given in this connection of the pious Umayyad caliph, ʿUmar b. ʿAbd al-ʿAzīz whose young and pious son, ʿAbd al-Malik, told the caliph one day as to why was he so hesitant in implementing the *Sharīʿah*. To this the caliph replied with caution and advised his son not to be in a rush, for 'God Most High condemned wine drinking twice and then banned it on the third ruling on the subject. I fear if I compel the people with truth all at once, they may abandon it all at once too and the result will be a tumult and *fitnah*.'[64]

The following conditions must, however, be observed in order to make participation permissible from the viewpoint of *Sharīʿah*.

First, participation should be in deed rather than words. A person's action does not create a binding basis of commitment, but his words may well do. The basic concern here is that participation is not such that can be used as a tool in the hands of others in such a manner that leaves nothing for the participant. The latter cannot, in other words, contribute to a good cause or try to prevent a bad one in even the slightest proportion.

Second, the ruler or employer is not renowned for oppression and transgression of the rights of others. For if it is totally oppressive and there is no opportunity for a Muslim to change anything for the better, it would be better for him to avoid participation.

Third, the participant is able to use his right of criticism when he is convinced of the efficacy of criticising an oppressive government. A clear example of this might be participation with the government of Israel despite its unjust occupation of Palestine and refusal to address the rights of refugees, and its oppressive policy of settlement of the newly arriving Jews in Palestinian territories.[65]

According to a *fatwā* issued by the Shāfiʿī jurist, ʿIzz al-Dīn ʿAbd al-Salām al-Sulamī, in the event where disbelievers conquer a Muslim territory and appoint therein rulers and judges who are committed to establish the rule of law, participation is allowed. If the non-Muslim rulers try to select from among Muslims qualified persons who can serve as judges and officials, it is permissible for the latter to participate and let their expertise be put to good use for the benefit of Muslims.[66]

Ibn Taymiyyah has issued a similar *fatwā* when he was asked a question as to the permissibility of a Muslim's participation in a non-Islamic government. He considered it permissible for a Muslim judge or *mujtahid* to serve in that capacity if he feels that his participation is likely to contribute to justice and bring benefit to the Muslims more than would be the case if a non-Muslim were to be appointed to that position. The judge in question may remain in a position he had occupied, or take a fresh appointment. It is not only permissible but preferable for him to participate.

The same analysis is extended to the case of the legal executor (*waṣī*) of orphans, the *waqf* administrator (*mutawallī*) and partner or employer in business partnership and the like. If they know that they will be unable to serve in their respective capacities and the benefit that they bring will discontinue unless they paid a portion of the assets they manage to oppressive non-Muslim rulers, they may pay it and continue to secure the benefit (*maṣlaḥah*) which would be lost otherwise.[67]

V. Islamic Work Ethics

A leading statement that sets the tone and framework of the work ethics of Islam is found in a renowned *ḥadīth* in which the Prophet is reported to have said:

إن الله يحبّ إذا عمل أحدكم عملا أن يتقنه

God loves it when any of you undertakes a work that he does it
to perfection.[68]

A similar message is conveyed in another *ḥadīth*, as earlier quoted,
where the Prophet accentuated the value of beautiful work when
he said: 'God has prescribed beauty (*iḥsān*) on everything.'[69] This
obviously inspires all capable and skilled workers to try to bring out
that beauty. The general tone of this *ḥadīth* also suggests that every line
of work has the potential of refinement and perfection and beauty is
created when perfection is achieved.

Perfection (*al-itqān*) in work performance means awareness of time,
an assiduous attitude, as opposed to inertia and lack of purpose, and
sincerity. If work is accomplished such that it brings satisfaction to
the concerned parties, it also earns the pleasure of God. For it means
due fulfilment of the trust (*amānah*) which God has required of the
believers, as in the following Qur'ānic verse:

يأيها الذين آمنوا لاتخونوا الله والرسول وتخونوا أماناتكم
وأنتم تعلمون

O believers! betray not God and the Messenger, nor betray the
trusts (that you carry) while you know it. (8:27)

Perfection in work performance is also known by reference to prevailing custom. The expectations that the industrial workplace, or the
society at large, may have of work that is done with care and perfection provide the measure by which to evaluate performance. This
applies to manufactured goods, to services, to academic work and virtually to all lawful work that is known to the *ʿurf* and experience of
society.[70]

It is a requirement of *itqān*, or the quest for perfection, that the
worker takes care of the tools of work which are entrusted to him.
The shepherd must take good care of the livestock in his care and so
must the office worker and engineer who take care of what is placed
in their trust; they must be alert and not negligent, and avoid harm to
others. This is the purport of the renowned *ḥadīth* as quoted earlier,
wherein the Prophet declared everyone as a trustee and guardian over
what has been placed in his custody. The Imam is a custodian of

his subjects, the man is a custodian of his family, the servant in the property of his employer and so forth. 'Beware that everyone of you is a custodian and responsible for what is in his care.'[71]

ألا وكلكم راع وكلكم مسئول عن رعيته

Al-Bukhārī has recorded a *hadīth*, narrated by 'Ā'ishah Ṣiddiqah, that 'The Prophet was once asked: "what work does God Most High like most?" He replied: "The most regular and sustained work, even if it be little", and he also said: "Do not take upon yourselves works other than what is within your ability." '[72]

عن عائشة رضى الله عنها قالت: سئل النبي صلى الله عليه وسلم أيّ الأعمال أحبّ إلى الله؟ قال أدومها

Sustained work is professional work which requires self-application on a regular basis. Continuity tends to lead to specialisation and achievement of excellence, especially in the knowledge-based professions.

The word *iḥsān* (beauty) in the *hadīth* quoted above is not confined only to work but applies to all spheres of human relations. Work and work relations seem nevertheless to be the immediate frame of reference, and *iḥsān* in this context can mean 'beauty', 'perfection' or 'fairness' on the part of both workers and employers. With reference to the worker, *iḥsān* means the kind of self-application that generates beauty in the sense of satisfaction and contentment that is achieved as a result. To produce a beautiful piece of workmanship, or to make the work environment a beautiful place and an enjoyable experience are all implied in the meaning of *iḥsān*. More objectively perhaps, *iḥsān* conveys the sense of working to perfection and creation of beauty in the visible manifestations of work. If God has 'written beauty on everything,' it is the perpetual human assignment to discover and secure it in every activity that is important to him. The Prophet has once again declared this succinctly when he said that 'God is beautiful and He loves beauty.'[73]

إن الله جميل يحب الجمال

In response to a request by Abū Dharr al-Ghaffarī who asked the Prophet if he could be employed to a government post, the Prophet showed signs of disapproval, and advised Abū Dharr against self-candidacy, which in his case was indicative of weakness. The Prophet told Abū Dharr that appointment to governmental positions was made on the basis of trust (*amānah*) for which only those who were strong and capable were best qualified.[74] These are the same qualities which occur in the Qur'ān, in a context where the daughter of the Prophet Shu'ayb (Jethro) recommended to her father that Moses (who later became Prophet Moses) was suitable to be employed as a servant: 'O father, employ him, for truly the best of employees you can employ is one who is strong and trustworthy.' (28:26)

يا أبت استأجره إنّ خير من استأجرت لقوي الأمين

These are the two principal components of what Ibn Taymiyyah has termed as the most suitable (*al-aṣlaḥ*) of employees who are appointed to government positions. This must strictly be on the basis of merit, regardless of such considerations as social status, family ties, race, locality and the like. Elsewhere the Qur'ān specified knowledge and physical capabilities as the grounds of God's own exalted selection of Saul as King over the leaders of Bani Israel. Thus in a reference to Saul (Tālūt) the Qur'ān declared that 'God has chosen him above others and has increased him abundantly in knowledge and in physical strength.' (2:247)

إن الله اصطفاه عليكم وزاده بسطة في العلم والجسم

The best of qualities that are consequently sought in a leader, caliph and head of state, according to the theory of caliphate, are the ability to carry out *ijtihād* and fitness to lead the army in *jihād*.

The two Qur'ānic verses, quoted above, on the best qualities of workers concur on the point that strength in relationship to work is to be determined by reference to the work itself, such as knowledge of military affairs and bravery in an army commander, trustworthiness (*amānah*) and knowledge of the *Sharī'ah* in a government leader and judge. Trustworthiness according to Ibn Taymiyyah refers to the fear of God to the exclusion, that is, of the fear of men, and a resolute attitude not to sacrifice one's principles, for a small price, as the Qur'ān puts it:

ولا تشتروا بآياتي ثمنا قليلا وإياي فاتقون

Not to sell My (God's) signs for a paltry sum, and be conscious of Me. (2:41)[75]

When the worker refuses to give his due measure and wilfully neglects his duty, he is guilty of betrayal of trust (*khiyānah*) and falls foul of the Qur'ānic directive quoted above (i.e. *al-Anfāl*, 8:27). In the event where a deliberate neglect of duty on the part of an employee causes destruction and harm, the employee in question is responsible for damages. But if the harm that is caused is not deliberate and fails to qualify as an act of *khiyānah*, the employee is not liable for damages. Similarly when damage is caused by an act in respect of which the employee has been granted permission, or when the later has acted on particular instruction, he will not be held liable for compensation.[76]

Workers are advised not to bear grudges nor be envious of the wealth and affluence of their employers. For envy eats into the good deeds of the faithful. Workers are advised to be trustworthy and loyal and give sincere advice to fellow workers and create a pleasant working environment. The employer is simply advised to be assiduous for the well-being of his employees like a trustee and custodian who must take good care of those God has placed under their custody. The employer should visit when his employee falls ill and take care of his needs.[77]

When the employee discharges his duty conscientiously, it is the employer's duty to reciprocate and grant him fair treatment. The employer must show diligence in giving the employee what is due to him. The first thing that the employer should do, as we read in the figurative language of the *hadīth* is to:

اؤتوا الأجير حقه قبل أن يجف عرقه

Give to the employee what is due to him (i.e., his wages) before the sweat of his brow dries up.[78]

Some jurists have understood this *hadīth* in the wider context of the worker's consideration of welfare and benefit. It may sometimes be for the benefit of the worker if his wages are paid at intervals of a month or such other period that may prove an incentive for him not to spend unwisely. If this be the case, then delay in payment is permissible.[79] It may be added perhaps that the *ḥadīth* before us is worded so that it conveys emphasis on payment itself rather than the timing of pay. The timing of pay should therefore be referred to customary practices, rather than the textual injunction as such. The clear message of the *ḥadīth* is on prompt payment without delay as soon as the work is completed. Any delay in payment that harms the worker must therefore be avoided.[80]

When the worker completes his work, his wages becomes a debt on the employer. Apart from the fact that repayment of a debt in accordance with its terms is an obligation, to be assiduous in payment is highly recommended. According to a *ḥadīth* which is unanimously reported (*muttafaqun ʿalayh*), the Prophet has said 'the best of you are ones who are best in repaying their debts.'[81] While quoting this *ḥadīth*, al-Ghazālī comments that the 'best in repayment' here refers to timely payment, as well as the quality of the goods, and in the case of repayment in kind, to give the best in quality. In the event one is unable to pay in time, he must keep firm in his intention to pay. God will help him and enable him in accordance with his sincerity and purpose.[82]

The other party to a debt, whether in the context of employment or of other transactions, is the creditor, of course, who is advised in turn to be tolerant and understanding in his demand for repayment in the event where the debtor may have difficulty to pay on time. Thus, according to a clear text of the Qur'ān, 'there should be a respite until the debtor's condition eases.' (2:280)

$$\text{وإن كان ذو عسرة فنظرة إلى ميسرة}$$

The instruction here is more than a moral advice but rather establishes a legal position that is taken into consideration by the court of justice. There is encouraging advice in the *Sunnah* for a creditor who is lenient in his demand and patience that he exercises earns him a spiritual reward. Hence the supplication of the Prophet 'May God be merciful to one who is easy when he sells, easy when he buys, easy when he makes a payment, and easy in his demand for payment.'[83]

$$\text{رحم الله رجلا سمحا إذا باع و إذا اشترى واذا اقتضى}$$

The Prophet has also declared, on the other hand, that 'delay in repayment by an affluent person is oppression.'[84]

مطل الغني ظلم

This *ḥadīth*, in turn, authorises the court to penalise a person who is able to repay but who refuses to do so.

The concept of *ḥalāl* and *ḥarām* is an integral part of the work ethics of Islam. The Prophet has drawn the people's attention to this and their accountability to God for unlawful gain especially when it becomes entrenched and develops into an attitude of aggressive exploitation of others, or of persistent failure to give others their due. The Prophet has thus warned:

كلّ لحم نبت من حرام فالنار أولى به

Every piece of human flesh that grows out of forbidden means shall become fuel to the fire of Hell (that burns him).[85]

The general terms of this warning, as will be noted, apply to the employer and employee alike, indeed to everyone, within or even outside the context of employment. The caliph ʿUmar b. al-Khaṭṭāb has been quoted to have said by way of an invocation: 'May God bless a man who restrains himself from indulgence in excessive speech, and a worker who exceeds the amount of work he is supposed to do.' The caliph then added: 'Be firm in the work that you undertake and this is done when you do not postpone today's work for tomorrow.'[86]

According to another report the caliph ʿUmar happened to be passing by a group of idle people in Medina and asked them a question: 'Who are you?' To this they replied 'We are the *mutawakkilūn* (ones who place their trust in God).' The caliph responded in a pun which conveyed his full message in one word, saying that 'No, but you are *muta'akkilūn* (spongers, devourers). For a *mutawakkil* is one who sows the seed in the soil first and then places his trust in God.'[87] One observer has taken this point further and drawn the conclusion that 'it is not permissible for anyone (able to work) to simply do nothing,' call himself *mutawakkil* and expect to be supported by others. No able bodied person may thus make himself a burden on society.[88]

The caliph ʿUmar's rigorous attitude on work is seen once again when he told the Qur'ān memorisers (*al-qurrā'*) in Medina to work and earn their living and even though they were a special category of people whose advice and counsel he often solicited himself, they were expected nevertheless to avoid being a burden on others and apply themselves in pursuit of earning their own livelihood through work.[89]

The caliph ʿAlī b. Abī Ṭālib accentuated the spiritual merit of work in one of his statements when he said 'one who seeks of the bounty of God and earns in order to support his family truly earns a reward greater than that of a warrior who fights in the cause of God.'[90]

The Prophet is reported to have said that 'God Most High loves a faithful person who is industrious.' إنّ الله يحب المؤمن المحترف [91]

'*Muḥtarif*' in this *ḥadīth* implies sustained self-application in a line of industry or skilled work. The Prophet encouraged this and tried to ensure continuity of such works in the towns and villages of Arabia under his rule. A practical incentive that Islamic law provides in this connection is that no *zakāh* is levied on the tools of production, machinery and equipment that are engaged in productive work, nor in fact on the means of transport that are used for transporting the products of such work.[92] The *Sharīʿah* also protects professional work in various other ways one of which is that the judge is authorised not to grant approval for dissolution of a partnership of two at the request of one if it would threaten collapse of the business for the other. But if dissolution and apportionment of assets (*qismah*) does not threaten continuity of the professional work, the judge may grant the request.[93] Another concession that is granted in this connection relates to inevitable stains and impurities on garments that work in certain professions may involve, such as an animal doctor, butcher, or surgeon whose clothes may frequently be stained. To wash the small stains repeatedly may involve hardship which is why it is permissible for such persons to perform ritual prayer in their work garments. In a similar vein, looking at the private parts of the human body is not permissible but a concession is granted for a physician who may examine a patient without incurring a violation that is otherwise attached to the exposure of *ʿawrah* (private parts of the body). A judge and a witness are likewise permitted to look at a woman who is otherwise accustomed to covering her face.[94]

The Prophet is also reported to have said:

إن من الذنوب ذنوبا لايكفّرها الصلاة ولاالصيام ولاالحج والعمرة. قالوا: فما يكفّرها يا رسول الله؟ قال: الهموم على كسب المعيشة

> Among the sins (people commit) there are some which are not expiated by prayer and fasting, nor by *hajj* nor *ʿumrah*. The Companions then posed the question: What would expiate for them then? The Prophet said: diligence in earning a living.[95]

In a discussion of the ethical aspects of business and market activity, al-Ghazālī (d.505/1111) has some advice for the traders which he expounds in seven points, as will be presently summarised. But a brief note may be added in advance: Much of the details with which al-Ghazālī concerns himself may have lost their relevance due to many changes that have taken place since his time, yet the substance of his advice is interesting and may in many ways be seen educational and relevant. Al-Ghazālī begins by addressing the subject of intention (*niyyah*) where he says:

(1) The merchant should enter his business with the right intention, which is a quest for sufficiency for himself and his family, and a dignified life that relieves him of the need to ask others for help or be covetous of them. He should be willing to offer sincere advice to others, be fair and treat others the way he would like to be treated. If this is his state of mind, his business will be a blessing for him and he is counted as a struggler in a sacred path (*mujāhid*).[96]

(2) The trader should be mindful of the social role his business activity plays. Most of the trading and industrial activity on which the people depend partake of a religious obligation (*min furūḍ al-kifāyāt*)— hence the people's need for them should be taken into consideration. If all the traders were to occupy themselves with the same line of business or industry, the people's needs would be neglected and market could not be expected to remain unaffected by distortion and neglect. The collective affairs of the community thus require cooperation in the marketplace and across professional divides. There should be no unbalanced concentration therefore in a single area of industry and trade, and traders should diversify their trading activities in accordance with the people's need for them.

The choice of a business or type of work should also reflect the ethical factor in that one should try to avoid work that is morally degrading, such as playing or working with musical instruments or such other businesses that do not merit commendation. Mentioned in this connection is jewelry business, especially when it means making gold rings for men, and a tailor who makes silk robes for men, selling shrouds for the dead, as it anticipates death for the living. Butchery is also criticised as it involves callousness, and so is street sweeping, cupping and tannery as they entail contact with filth. The renowned Followers, Ibn Sīrīn and Qatādah, are also quoted to have considered middlemanship reprehensible as it involves exaggeration in the praise and commendation of commodities as well as aggressive selling. Other lines of work that invoke mild disapproval are those that entail contact with women and children, such as weaving, cotton manufacture, spinning of yarn, and surprisingly enough, teaching. Al-Ghazālī goes on, however, to say that teaching the Qur'ān and *Sharīʿah* is praiseworthy and should be done free of charge. It is also a right of the Muslim over others to be given a decent burial, hence no business line is recommended to be made out of this.[97]

(3) The market-place of this world should not overwhelm the trader so much as to forget the market-place of the hereafter (*sūq al-ākhirah*) and that the merchant should frequent the mosque for congregational prayer and reminiscence of God.

(4) Piety (*taqwā*) is not confined to the four walls of the mosque. Praise of God and quiet recitation of religious phrases should not be neglected even in the market-place, especially when one knows that the market is a place of temptation, and the inner strength to fight it is gained through piety. Ghazālī then quotes a *ḥadīth*, narrated by Abū Dharr, which al-Tirmidhī has recorded, addressing the believer to 'fear God, wherever you are—*ittaqi Allāha ḥaythu mā-kunta.*'[98]

(5) One should not be too eager (*shadīd al-ḥirṣ*) in market activity and business, and should certainly not be the one who enters the market before everyone else and leaves it after everyone has left. This is, in fact, the rehash of a *ḥadīth* which Ghazālī has quoted himself and the purpose evidently is that one should contain one's drive for financial gain and have a sense of balance over things. One ought to be able, in other words, to resist greed and over-indulgence in an endless pursuit that is ultimately likely to compromise on other values.

(6) The purpose is not only to avoid what is prohibited (*ḥarām*) but that one should also avoid instances of doubt (*mawārid al-shubh*) as to the purity of one's earning. The advice given here is that one should determine this in the light of one's own insight and good judgment as well as the Qur'ānic guideline to the believers to eat of the pure things God has provided for His servants (20:81). This might involve some level of inquiry, which has prompted al-Ghazālī to refer to an incident wherein it is reported that someone presented to the Prophet some milk of which he drank but before he did so, he asked the person what

sort of milk it was, and the man answered that it was goat's milk, and then the Prophet asked as to where the goat was milked, and when he heard the reply, he drank the milk and said that he ascertained this so as to know that it was pure food that came from a lawful source.[99] Al-Ghazālī then concludes that in instances of doubt such as when a trader is unsure of the source and permissibility of his merchandise, he may ask two questions, one as to the object itself, and the other as to its origin, but to use more than this may be excessive and awkward. It is necessary for a trader, therefore, to look into the condition of his client and avoid dealing with people who might be involved in theft, fraud and usury, or even soldiers and government officers who are corrupt and oppressive. For these do not deserve to be helped, they should be shunned and avoided instead.[100]

(7) Lastly, the trader should carry out a thorough account of all of his dealings with at least one of his customers and find out in detail as to the propriety of all his transactions with him.

For this would give him insight and a good way to take stock of his activity, not only in this world but also to prepare his account for the hereafter. If he proves to be just and upright, he is one of the well-guided (ṣāliḥūn), and if he went a step further and acted with benevolence (iḥsān) to his client and others, he would have achieved closeness to God and stand among the muqarrabūn.[101]

VI. Fair Trading

In a section of Iḥyā' which is devoted to the subject of sale, al-Ghazālī has quoted the ḥadīth earlier cited on the value of an honest sale and followed it with a detailed commentary which may be summarised in the following paragraphs. The ḥadīth in question provided that 'the best earning is that which is obtained through unadulterated sale and the toil of one's own hands.' It is this concept of 'unadulterated or blessed sale bayʿun mabrūr' which is the focus of al-Ghazālī's comments. Yet he opens the discussion with a reference to two other ḥadīths, one of which is on avoidance of harm (lā ḍarar) which should manifest, especially in market activities, the essence of fraternity among the believers. The general advice here is that one should not do 'to his brother that which one would not like for oneself.' This too is a rehash of a renowned ḥadīth on the subject which al-Ghazālī has quoted and elaborated under the following four points:

(1) Abandonment of praise (*tark al-thanā'*): The seller must not praise the commodity he sells in any way that might be misleading or which unduly influences the buyer in its favour. What is accepted here is for the seller to explain the facts about the goods that are not obvious but which need to be brought to attention as a part of the basic description of the commodity he is offering. If the commodity in question is described for what is not in it then that is lying and misrepresentation (*tadlīs*). If the buyer acts on it then the seller's description amounts to a combination of injustice and lying (*ẓulm wa kidhb*). But even when the buyer does not act on the false description, the seller would have told a lie; if the lie in question is such that is widely encountered (*yurawwaj*) and not unusual, the seller would have compromised his integrity (*murū'ah*). If the seller's description is true, then it may amount to unnecessary expatiation (*hadhyān*) that is not advisable, unless 'he praises the commodity for what it is but which is not known to the buyer.' This would be acceptable. But even so, it is never advisable to resort to swearing even if one is telling the truth. 'For the material gain of this world is too low to warrant unnecessary invocation of God's illustrious name.'[102] Even when a commodity is praised for what is true, it is still reprehensible and should be avoided.

(2) It is obligatory (*wājib*) on the vendor to declare all the defects in his commodity 'both apparent and hidden, and must not conceal anything of it whatsoever.' For one who hides such defects is oppressive and fraudulent (*ẓāliman, ghāshan*), which are clearly forbidden. The vendor would have also fallen short of his positive moral duty to give sincere advice (*naṣīḥah*) to a fellow Muslim. Fraud of this kind is committed when a vendor shows only the good part of a cloth or when the good one of a pair is shown but not the other, which is unsound. The prohibition here is established on the authority of the *hadīth* wherein it is reported that the Prophet, peace be on him, passed by a man who was selling wheat, which pleased the Prophet, but when he entered his hand into the heap, he detected dampness. The Prophet then enquired and was told that the rain had caused the dampness, to which the Prophet responded that the damp part should have been put on top so that the people would see it, and then said 'one who cheats us is not one of us.'[103]

As for the duty to offer sincere advice through declaration of defect in merchandise, this is the subject of the unanimously reported *hadīth* (*muttafaqun 'alayhi*) of Jarīr b. 'Abd Allāh who said that when he embraced Islam and pledged his allegiance (*bay'ah*) to the Prophet, he was asked to give *naṣīḥah* to all Muslims.[104] Al-Ghazālī elaborates:

when Jarīr offered a commodity for sale he would expose its defects and would tell the buyer to buy it if he wished, or leave it. One of his customers told Jarīr that if he continued speaking that way, he may be unable to sell at all. To this Jarīr responded that when he pledged allegiance to the Prophet, it was accepted on condition that he offered sincere advice to every Muslim. This was also confirmed by another Companion, Wāthilah b. al-Asqāʿ, who is reported to have sold a camel to someone for three hundred dirhams but Wāthilah was distracted for a brief moment during which the man had taken the camel away. Then Wāthilah started running after the man and asked him whether he bought the camel for meat or for riding, to which the man answered that it was for riding. Then Wāthilah said to the man that the camel had a hole in its hoof which affected its pace and speed. The man returned the beast but bought it at the lower price of two hundred dirhams on which occasion Wāthilah said that when he pledged allegiance to the Prophet, he was asked to give sincere advice to every Muslim. Wāthilah also cited another *hadīth* that he had heard from the Prophet on the subject of sale. Al-Ghazālī has quoted the *hadīth*, and his commentator, Zayn al-Dīn al-ʿIraqī has added in his commentary on the margin of *Ihyā'* that al-Ḥākim al-Nīshāpūrī and al-Bayhaqī have considered it to be 'sound of *isnād*.' The *hadīth* provides:

> Sale is not permissible for anyone unless he declares its defect, and it is also not permissible for anyone who knows of it without explaining it first.[105]

To declare the defects of a commodity offered for sale is thus understood to be included in the meaning of *naṣīḥah* that one gives to his fellow Muslim. It is not a mere supererogatory concept of a moral type but one which is a duty, and those who practiced it did so with this understanding. Al-Ghazālī then adds that knowledge of this condition has caused many a pious individual not to occupy himself in trading as error and confusion can occur even when one tries to avoid them. But those who acted righteously in trade firmly believed in two things, one of which was that cheating and concealment of defects did not add to one's wealth but on the contrary took away all the blessings from their trade. This is once again, al-Ghazālī adds, based on the unanimously reported *hadīth* (*muttafaqun ʿalayhi*) wherein the Prophet declared:

> When the buyer and seller are truthful and advised one another sincerely, their trade will be blessed, but if they conceal and lie

concerning it all the blessing of their trade will be taken away and withdrawn.[106]

A similar *ḥadīth* which al-Ghazālī recorded on the same page is also reported by Abū Dāwūd from Abū Hurayrah as follows: 'God's "protective" hand is on the trading partners for so long as they do not betray their trust but when they do so, God's hand is lifted away from them.'

The second of the two points under review is the fundamental belief that the profit of the hereafter is better than that of the present world-for the former is lasting whereas the latter ephemeral. Those who are firm in this belief would not wish to trade their faith with a paltry of vanishing gain.[107]

Then it must be added, al-Ghazālī continues, that cheating and dishonesty are prohibited (*ḥarām*) equally in sales as well as in industrial work without any exception. It is not permissible for a manufacturer (*al-ṣāniʿ*) therefore to take a negligent attitude to his work in such a way that if he employed someone else to that work and did it for him, he would not like it. It is therefore all the more advisable to accomplish the work one undertakes to the best of one's ability. But if one applies oneself well and a defect still arises, one should declare it and in this way discharge one's responsibility. 'A transaction is therefore not complete, whatever the nature of the transaction may be, unless the defects therein are identified and declared.'[108]

I may hasten to add here that this is a totally different picture when it is compared to the Common Law doctrine of *caveat emptor*, which entitles the seller not to declare the defects of what he offers to sell. It is the responsibility, instead, of the buyer to investigate for himself and find out any defects that may exist in the subject matter of sale. The position of Islamic law is thus decidedly protective of the consumer's interests not only in respect of the duty it places on the seller to declare the defects in his goods, but also that the buyer is additionally entitled in Islamic law to an option even after the event. This is known as the option of defect (*khiyār al-ʿayb*) which the buyer may exercise in the event he discovers a defect in the goods after the purchase. The *Sharīʿah* makes the option of defect available to everyone regardless as to whether the parties might have stipulated for it or not-unlike certain other types of options which can be exercised only when the parties had stipulated for it when they concluded the bargain.

The third of the four points al-Ghazālī has made in his description of a valid sale is concerned with measurement and quantity. The seller must give exact measurement and refrain from any underhand tactics that deny to the buyer what is due to him. The Qur'ānic expression for those who give less when they sell to others but insist to have full measure when they buy themselves is *al-muṭaffifīn*, who do not fail to invoke God's displeasure and blame on themselves. The Qur'ān refers to them on several occasions, and it is known as a result that the Prophet gave a little extra on his side of the bargain when he bought or sold. Many pious Muslims followed this example and preferred to take a little less when they bought, for fear of any inadvertent violation of the Qur'ān.[109] The believers are thus directed to 'give full measure and weigh with justice and wrong not the people in respect of their goods' (11:85). The issue here is one of justice and honesty in trade and of fair treatment of the customer, which the Qur'ān has clearly emphasised, and set the standards which the jurists have elaborated in their discourse on contracts and transactions. Al-Ghazālī also gave some practical examples of *tatfīf* which included the butcher who actually commits *tatfīf* when he adds the bone with the meat in such a way that is not customary. This is also said of a cloth merchant who pulls out and stretches the cloth before he sells and thus becomes guilty of *tatfīf*.[110]

Lastly, the seller must be honest in pricing his commodity and avoid over-pricing. This is a complex issue which has received the Prophet's personal attention in connection with price distortion that was practiced by some traders at the time. The Prophet thus declared forbidden certain varieties of sale such as the false bidding sale (*al-najash*) and *talaqqi al-rukbān* (meeting the riders) in which prices were distorted. Unfair advantage was taken in these transactions of the ignorance of suppliers and purchasers over the market price of commodities. *Al-Najash* is a sale in which a disinterested party bids for a higher price with the sole purpose of enticing the buyer to pay the same. In *talaqqi al-rukbān*, the settled traders would go out of town to meet the newly arriving supplies and buy them before their arrival in the market of Medina, usually at a lower price, thus taking advantage of the ignorance of the sellers over the market price. The Prophet declared these transactions forbidden and advised that everyone, buyers and sellers alike, should be afforded the opportunity to trade at fair market prices that were not detrimental to either side. Thus the instruction is given in one *ḥadīth*: 'Do not intercept the riders to sell (their commodity.)'[111] More specifically, it was provided in another *ḥadīth*: 'Do not intercept the commodities until they reach the market.'[112]

The Prophet also forbade the sale of *muṣarrāt* wherein the seller of a milk-giving animal would not milk the beast for days prior to selling it, with a view obviously of creating a false impression of its yield. This type of sale also involved price distortion and the *ḥadīth* which addressed this issue declared that anyone who bought a *muṣarrāt* has the option either to accept the animal, or if he wished, to return it but to compensate the seller for the milk that might have been consumed during the interval. The amount of compensation was specified roughly at a 'bowlful of dates.'[113] Traders were thus directed not to take advantage of the people, nor of one another, through manipulation and dishonest methods, which undermined the integrity of the market-place.

VII. Work, Women and Children

The Qur'ān is affirmative on women's right to work and their right to what they earn as a result of it. There is, in principle, no distinction in this being a basic right of every individual without consideration of gender. Women are therefore entitled to take up all lawful occupations that they are capable of doing.[114] The Qur'ān thus declares in general and unqualified terms that 'men have a right to what they earn and women have a right to what they earn.' (4:32)

للرجال نصيب مما اكتسبوا وللنساء نصيب مما اكتسبن

One commentator has noted that this verse 'is a declaration of equality between men and women in regard to their basic right to work. It is therefore permissible for women to take up all works and professions that suit their conditions.' Women are also entitled to all the benefit of the work that they do.[115] This is further endorsed by the fact that the norm in *Sharī'ah* concerning matrimonial assets is separation of property which entitles the spouses to their own property before and after the marriage unless they choose otherwise. The wife also keeps her own family name and marriage does not affect her personal identity and financial independence. The substance of this last text has been endorsed in another verse where God Most High declared in an address to both men and women that 'I will not suffer the work of any worker among you to be lost whether male or female, the one of you being from the other.' (3:195)

أني لا أضيع عمل عامل منكم من ذكر أو أنثى بعضكم من بعض

Maḥmūd Shaltūt's commentary on this verse draws attention to the Qur'ānic phrase '*baʿḍukum min baʿḍ,*' which eliminates distinction between men and women and suggests substantive equality between them. This Qur'ānic phrase also signifies partnership and cooperation between men and women in family and society in the sense that both play equally important roles and there is no superiority of one over the other.[116]

The Qur'ān also entitles men and women equally to the exercise of *wilāyah*, (protection, authority) in respect of one another and also in the sphere of public affairs and government. This is the subject of another verse which declares 'the believers, men and women, are protectors (*awliyā'*, pl. of *walī*) of one another, they command good and they forbid evil.' (9:71)

والمؤمنون والمؤمنات بعضهم أولياء بعض يأمرون بالمعروف وينهون عن المنكر

In addition to validating *wilāyah*, cooperation, and support between men and women, this verse entitles them both to the most comprehensive of all *wilāyāt*, which is to promote good and to prevent evil, also known as *ḥisbah*. Government itself partakes in *ḥisbah*, which means that women are entitled to participation in government and leadership in political affairs. Women are therefore entitled to take up positions that may involve exercise of authority and *wilāyah* in legislative, judicial or executive spheres, for these are 'the various manifestations of the principle of *ḥisbah* which subsumes all walks of the public and political life of the community.' While making this observation, al-Shawāribī has quoted in support a number of other commentators including Muḥammad Rashīd Riḍā, Maḥmūd Shaltūt, al-Bahī al-Khūlī and ʿAbd al-Ḥamīd Mutawalli, all of whom have concurred in this conclusion and upheld women's equal right to work in all spheres of government.[117]

A professional woman who is separated from her husband, whether by death or divorce, is allowed to engage herself in work outside her home. She may leave her home in daytime and return at night.[118] But when a married woman engages herself in professional work, her husband may be relieved, according to the Ḥanafīs, from the duty of providing her with maintenance. The reason for this is that such a woman is no longer in a position to devote herself to her husband. Since this exclusive dedication (*iḥtibās*) is the basis of her right to maintenance and *iḥtibās* no longer obtains in that situation, so is her right to maintenance. The same ruling is extended to a woman who runs a full time business from her home.[119] On a similar note, a professional woman who occupies herself with full time work outside her home may be relieved of her right to the custody (*ḥaḍānah*) of her child if the work is such that she cannot take proper care of the child. The judge may, however, assess the situation and make a decision that is in the best interest of the child.[120]

Muḥammad al-Ghazālī and Ṣādiq ʿAfīfī have both concurred with Abū Zahrah to the effect that the *Sharīʿah* entitles women to work and to earn their living whenever they need to do so or when they can make a special contribution to society. But they add that it is preferable for women to devote their creative energy and work to motherhood since they can make a unique contribution in this area to the well-being of the family. It is then added that women may join the work force in the following four situations:

(1) When they have abilities and skills that are particularly valuable to the community as a whole. This is when they excel others, including men, and the role they can play here is considered almost as unique as they can play as mother and manager of the household.

(2) When they undertake work to which they are particularly suited such as working in child care, health services and education. Some ʿ*ulamāʾ*, including Ibn al-Humām al-Ḥanafī, have considered this kind of work as a collective obligation (*farḍ kifāʾī*) that applies particularly to women. As for the question of agreement between the spouses, the husband is advised not to stand in the way of his wife when she wishes to work in any of these capacities.

(3) When women work side by side with their husbands and family and they assist themselves and family members in their work. This is often the case in the countryside wherein women in farming families, small landholders and other low-income groups assist their men-folk in various capacities, often combining their duties as mothers and household managers with these other activities. Their contribution deserves special recognition and 'these are the exemplary women of our society; they are hardworking, efficient and compassionate, not like the ones who work as singers and dancers in the night clubs. . .'

(4) When a woman is in need of earning a living to support herself and her family and there is no one else to support her and her family, in which case she would have to work as a matter of necessity. Having said this al-Ghazālī adds that in an Islamic welfare state, this last category of women are entitled to support from the public treasury

(*bayt al-māl*) regardless as to whether she is a Muslim or a non-Muslim. For this is the purport of the *ḥadīth* in which the Prophet has declared 'whoever leaves behind property, it shall belong to his heirs, but if he leaves a debt or dependents in need, they shall be my responsibility.'[121]

The elderly and the child should not be engaged in strenuous work and it is a responsibility partly of the guardians and relatives in charge of the affairs of minors and women to ensure that this does not happen. The guardian is accordingly permitted to assign to his minor ward light work which is not harmful, but must avoid engaging him in work that might be harmful over a long term, or work that might affect the future well-being of the child concerned.[122] Child labour and assignment of paid work to minors below the age of majority is forbidden unless it has educational value and take place under the guardianship and supervision of the father.[123] Similarly women should not be assigned work that is incompatible with their feminine dignity, and this includes work that brings them into contact with doubtful characters or situations that involve mingling with strangers of the opposite sex. Women are otherwise permitted to work in trades and professions of their choice. They may work in order to earn a living and do what they wish with the income that is earned.[124] It is reported that Lady Zaynab bint Jaḥsh, the wife of the Prophet, used to work in tanning the hides and gave as charity the income she earned from it. It is also reported that Rā'iṭah, the wife of the renowned Companion, ʿAbd Allāh Ibn Masʿūd, earned by her own handiwork, and she asked the Prophet a question whether it was right for her to spend her earning on her husband and their child, for they had no other income than what she earned. She added that she could not spare to give any of it in charity. To this the Prophet replied 'you also earn a (spiritual) reward by spending it on your family. Spend as you wish.'[125]

For children below the age of discernment (*tamyīz*), which is about seven years, employment is totally prohibited. Minors below that age do not have the capacity to enter financial transactions and contracts either with or without the permission of their guardians. Children above this age have a partial legal capacity in that they may conclude a transaction and undertake work that is beneficial to them with the approval of their guardians provided that the work is appropriate to their condition. They may not undertake any work without the permission of their guardians and any undertaking they incur on their own is null and void. Consideration of child welfare at this stage requires a high priority to be given to education. Muslim jurists have spoken on the subject of work for children of tender ages in such terms that it is permissible if it would encourage the ability and confidence of the child and is undertaken in the spirit of inculcation of good work ethics on their part. This manner of approval is in reality a part of the early education of the child especially when one bears in mind that the rules of *fiqh* were formulated at a time when regular employment was not a feature of life even for adults. One is really talking of casual work such as undertaken during school breaks nowadays.

Some of the salient aspects of the juristic discourse on the role and responsibility of the guardian (*walī*) in work related matters may be summarised as follows:

First, the guardian of a child below the age of majority is entrusted with the authority to make decision concerning the choice of profession and employment for his ward. The work so chosen may not be morally degrading and sinful nor does it harm the child's present condition or his future.[126] To this one may now add the proviso that work at this stage must not obstruct child's education. If a part-time work, which may be with a close relative and in the nature of acquiring skill that inheres within the family, the guardian may allow it within reasonable bounds.

Second, a child above the age of discernment (*tamyīz*) has the legal capacity to enter a (simple) contract or transaction that is manifestly to his benefit with the prior or subsequent approval of his guardian. Thus when a minor of that age undertakes work and completes it well, he is entitled to be paid for it.[127]

Third, when the minor reaches the age of majority, which is 18 for purposes of financial transactions (also corresponding with school leaving age), any contract he may have entered under the supervision of his guardian becomes nullified and he has the choice either to revoke or endorse it. Upon completion of 18 years the child becomes an adult of full capacity to enter a regular employment contract.

Four, the employer of a discerning child must take into consideration his tender age and avoid therefore assigning him work that is onerous and punitive. He should also grant the minor rest periods and break times for prayer, just as he is required to pay him a fair wage.[128]

A child between seven and fifteen years of age is not qualified to conclude a valid contract of employment, and if he does, the contract would be null and void. The Ḥanafīs have added the detail that a contract entered into by a discerning child (*ṣabṭ mumayiz*) is not effective and will remain in suspense until it is ratified by the legal guardian (*walī*) of the child. If the *walī* had given advance permission to a discerning child and then he undertakes work, it would be deemed valid, according to the Ḥanafīs, but invalid according to the Shāfiʿīs. If a discerning child who is still under the care of his guardian undertakes work which he carries through and completes, he is entitled to the wages which shall belong to him. This resembles a gift that is given to a child which is valid and the permission of the guardian in this case is taken for granted.[129] Although on a strictly legal ground, work undertaken by a discerning child without the permission of the guardian does not generate its legal consequences, yet it is said that the result of the work done merits consideration. 'If the work is sound and it is well done, it becomes effective and the child is entitled to payment for it. Otherwise it would be a waste of the child's effort and inflict harm on him.'[130]

In the event where a child is injured or harmed in any way during the time he works, the person who has hired him becomes liable for damages, in which case he is not under obligation to pay for the work that might have been done–based on the principle that liability does not combine with wages.[131]

The father is entitled to assign his minor son work to do, as 'the father's authority over his minor child resembles the authority he has over himself, for his love of his son is like his love of his own self, since he is entitled to assign himself a work, he is entitled to do the same with regard to his son.'[132] Al-Kāsānī who wrote this went on to explain that the father is responsible for the upbringing and behavioral propriety of his minor son. He is within his rights therefore to employ his child to a work which 'partakes in discipline, moral education and physical exercise (*min bāb al-tahdhīb wa'l taʾdīb wa'l-riyāḍah*) and he considers the work to be conducive to the child's development.' The right also exists for the father's executor (*waṣī*) and failing him for the grandfather and then for the judge. For these are the guardians of the child who are entrusted with a responsibility. But it is unlawful for anyone other than these, that is the father or his *waṣī*, the grandfather and his *waṣī*, to employ a child below the age of majority. No other relative is entitled to the same authority over the child.[133] 'Don't you see?' Kāsānī explains that these other relatives have no right to interfere with the property of the child, and that position obtains even more so with regard to his person, unless the child is in their custody and lives with any of them, in which case they may, according to one opinion, employ the child. It is the fact of custody in this case that entitles the relative in question to a modicum of guardianship (*darban min al-wilāyah*). The relative in question is responsible for the 'upbringing and discipline of the child, and employing him in industries is a form of discipline (*al-ta'dīb*) which he is entitled to in the capacity only of *ta'dīb*.'

It is possible that a child is in the custody of a relative at a time when the child may also have a closer relative. The question arises as to whether this closer relative is entitled to employ the child to do some work. Suppose that a child is in the effective custody and care of his paternal uncle and his (child's) mother employs him. The mother is entitled to do so, according to Abū Yūsuf, whereas al-Shaybānī has held that she is not so entitled.

Al-Shaybānī explained his position by saying that the effective guardianship in respect of upbringing the child belongs to the relative with whom the child lives and not necessarily the closer relative and authority to employ the child also belongs to the former. Abū Yūsuf has held, on the other hand, that the basis of *wilāyah* in both cases is kinship (*qarābah*) and one who is closer to the child in this respect also enjoys a superior right of guardianship. As for the entitlement to any earning that is realised by the child's work, the relative who takes care of the child is entitled merely to receive it, but the money belongs to the child himself. The relative has no authority to spend it in any way, even on the child himself. For the authority here is only in respect of receiving (*al-qabḍ*) and in that respect it is similar to receiving a gift on behalf of the child. The gift would belong to the child and the relative in question has no authority to spend it or interfere with it in any proprietary capacity.[134] This is not to say, however, that the child himself cannot receive payment for work, or a gift, as the case may be. It is just that the relative with whom the child lives is also entitled to receive it on his behalf.[135]

I propose at this juncture to point at a certain imbalance in al-Shaybānī's opinion, especially in respect of suppressing the mother's wishes vis-à-vis a more remote relative who is in effective custody of the child. Abū Yūsuf has, I believe, corrected that imbalance. But there still remains a degree of bias in favour of male relatives in the general theory of guardianship (*wilāyah*) as developed by Muslim jurists of earlier times, which I have addressed elsewhere but merely wish to refer to it here.[136] It is not accidental here to see the reference to the executor (*waṣī*) of the father, to the grandfather and then to his *waṣī*, taking priority in matters of guardianship over the mother. This I believe is to some extent reflective of a certain gender bias of juristic discourse of medieval vantage, which is not borne out by the basic guidelines of the Qur'ān and *Sunnah*. Almost every reference in the Qur'ān to the parents which invites the children to treat them with love, dignity and respect is to both the parents (*al-wālidayn*), and not only to the father. The *Sunnah* of the Prophet has moreover placed an unusually strong emphasis on the mother's status. Yet in matter of *wilāyah* one notes that the mother's right gives way to the *waṣī* of the father and even to the *waṣī* of the grandfather, a position which fails to reflect the underlying principles of *wilāyah* and may therefore call for a review.

The child himself is entitled, upon attaining the age of majority, to refuse to undertake any work and may abandon any agreement or contract that might exist regarding any work assignment for him. If he then wishes, as an adult to complete it, he may do so, but may abandon it if he wishes even if the contract is validated by his father. For continuity in that capacity and completing the assignment may well be harmful to him, and may compromise his personal image. Imam Abū Ḥanīfah has in this connection made the following comment: suppose that the child becomes an adult and become a *faqīh*, or a judge, and then to think that he was assigned to serve others is demeaning and undermines his image of himself. Abū Ḥanīfah has also held that if the discerning child is employed by a *waṣī* of the father or grandfather for himself, the latter is required to pay a fair wage which is equivalent to the market value of the work involved.[137]

It remains to be said, however briefly, that the climate of opinion and custom in the late 6th/12th century seem to have influenced, not only the juristic rules on child's employment, but also the overall perspective of the child's upbringing. The early attitude concerning children's upbringing was geared toward the purpose of preparing the child for manhood, and there was a tendency in those times to treat the (discerning) child almost like a man. This outlook was reflected in the fact that the child was taught the kind of working skills that he would be expected to take up as an adult. Another influential factor in this regard was the desire to give the child a grounding in religion and morality and a sense of responsibility to conform to the teachings of Islam. Al-Ahwānī who recorded this information in the context of the 4th/10th century writing of al-Qābisī on child education added the remark that there was in the meantime an awareness that the child should be given his freedom to enjoy his childhood, but that did not mean to exclude work. Work was not seen as something contrary to the child's happiness and it was to be carefully guided by the father and close relatives.[138] Ahwānī recognises nevertheless that the child should not be burdened with the concerns of adulthood. What is equally important to emphasise is that the child's natural development in an atmosphere of freedom should be encouraged. This also means that he should have the freedom to work and to earn some income.[139]

Due to considerable changes in culture, social environment, and education, especially the availability now of compulsory schooling for children on a universal basis up to a certain stage, it now seems necessary to take this into consideration. There is ample evidence in the works of the Muslim jurists themselves on the value that is attached, almost above all other considerations, to the interest and welfare of the child in matters of custody and guardianship (*ḥaḍānah, wilāyah*). Children of discernible age should naturally be free to do casual work to earn some money during vacation and also to help their parents in some respects, but none of this should come in the way of the child's education. No one should now have the right to sign a contract of employment on behalf of a child of eight or nine years of age, or of any schooling age, up to the completion of high school. These are some of the realities of the present time and merit to be considered no less than some of the rulings that were formulated earlier that reflected the outlook and values of that time.

VIII. Workers' Rights

The discussion that follows in this section occurs under four sub-headings, namely right to employment, right to fair wages, work accident and liability for loss, and right to a fair work regime and leisure.

RIGHT TO EMPLOYMENT

It is a basic right of the individual vis-à-vis the state to be availed of the opportunity to work, and it becomes consequently a duty of the ruling authorities to employ, as far as possible, all able-bodied and willing persons in suitable works. For those who have skill but lack the tools of trade, they are entitled to government help to provide them with the necessary tools of trade.[140] This conclusion is derived from a general reading of the evidence in the Qur'ān and *Sunnah*. The state and community's basic role as the vicegerents of God in the earth places in them the responsibility to build and develop the natural resources at their disposal and this necessitates adequate utilisation of labour. The state is also under duty to promote the essential interests (*maṣāliḥ ḍaruriyyah*) of the people, which include life, and that necessitates the means of livelihood and the ability to earn a living through employment.

To enable everyone to earn a lawful living is a requirement also of the Qur'ānic principle of *hisbah*, that is enjoining good and forbidding evil. Unemployment in the face of necessity and need becomes an evil which must be prevented as far as possible. The duty of *hisbah* falls first and foremost on the government and it is also a collective responsibility of the community. The state's responsibility to fulfil the need for basic necessities of its citizens must naturally begin by enabling the individual to meet his own needs and those of his family and dependents through work. It is the responsibility of the officer in charge of *hisbah* (i.e. *muhtasib*) to put a stop to begging by forcing, if necessary, all able-bodied beggars to work and thereby to earn their living. He can even punish them if they do not comply with his orders.

It is a duty of the state, according to Ibn Taymiyyah, to fight unemployment and provide jobs for those who are unable to find one or set up their own businesses.[141] This responsibility becomes all the more pressing in a society where the majority of the populace depend on employment and wage earning. Justice required, Ibn Taymiyyah added, that everyone should have an equal opportunity to be productive and engage in business, and that no one should be allowed to create a monopoly so as to deny others the right to work and trade.[142]

Abdul Rauf has quoted Muḥammad al-Ghazālī and Yūsuf al-Qaraḍāwī in support of his own view, all of whom have spoken in support of equal treatment for non-Muslim citizens with respect to employment. In al-Ghazālī's view, Islam treats non-Muslims who live peacefully among Muslims in the same way as it treats Muslims and that the social support system of Islam, which is based on mutual cooperation (*ta'āwun*) applies equally to all. There is no objection also for a Muslim to work under a non-Muslim and vice-versa. Qaraḍāwī has similarly held that the basic principle of *Sharī'ah* in the sphere of economic relations is equality between Muslims and non-Muslims. Non-Muslims enjoy equal rights and also bear similar obligations to those of their Muslim compatriots.[143] Abdul Rauf also alluded in this context to the change of circumstances that Muslims have experienced in the course of history: There was admittedly little room for the *dhimmis* to assume a role in government during the early decades of the advent of Islam due mainly to the fact that 'Islam was in a seriously precarious condition' and that the element of trust between the Muslim and non-Muslim communities could not be taken for granted. But it is noted nevertheless that the Prophet himself and his Companion Abū Bakr, upon their migration to Medina, employed a polytheist, ʿAbd Allāh b. al-Arqaṭ, as their guide and trusted him enough to lead them to their destination. Added to this is the fact that there are now Muslims residing in the countries of Europe, North America and Australia who 'have been granted full citizenship and on the whole suffer no legal incapacities.'[144] Then it is noted that many of the applied constitutions of Muslim countries today, including those of the Islamic Republic of Iran (Art. 3 and 13) grant equal rights and protections to their non-Muslim citizens in the sphere of economic activity and employment.[145] The Islamic state's welfare commitment, including its commitment to provide employment opportunities for its citizens thus proceeds on the premise of equality between all of its citizens, Muslims and non-Muslims alike.

While discussing the legal capacity of the individual to conclude a valid contract or execute a commercial transaction in the market, al-Kāsānī wrote that being a Muslim is not a requirement. Contracts such as sale, lease, hire, partnership and the like that include interaction between Muslims and non-Muslims, or non-Muslims on their own may be concluded without any hindrance. For most of the market transactions in these areas consist of commutative contracts which involve exchange of value for value, and the religious identity of the participant in them is immaterial. It is of interest also to note Kāsānī's response to the question as to whether a non-Muslim woman may be employed as a wet nurse to suckle a Muslim child. Al-Kāsānī's answer to this question is that there is no objection to this as the woman's disbelief in Islam does not affect the quality of her milk.[146]

RIGHT TO FAIR WAGES

Workers are, as a general rule, entitled to fair wages for their work. Any attempt on the part of the employer to deprive the worker of a fair wage, or even to unduly delay it, is a transgression. The Qur'ān provides the guideline that wages must be decided by mutual consultation and consent—as in the case of young Moses when the Prophet Shuʿayb (Jethro) employed him and they negotiated the wages (28:26–27). It is important therefore that wages are determined through mutual agreement, which subsumes consultation. Everyone bears personal responsibility to fulfil scrupulously whatever is placed under their custody. This responsibility naturally extends to one's job, and it matters little what the nature of the job or assignment might be, provided that it is lawful. For the Qur'ān enjoins upon Muslims to 'discharge your trusts (*al-amānāt*) to whom that they belong, and when you judge among people, you judge with justice.' (4:58) '*Amānāt*' in this verse clearly include faithful discharge of responsibility by both the employer and employee. Faithful discharge of *amānah* is first and foremost achieved, in the context of employment, by the determination of fair wages. It is also a part of the responsibilities of the market inspector, that is, the officer in charge of *ḥisbah*, to ensure that workers are paid their fair wages and that the employers are not oppressive to them.[147]

To pay less than what a worker deserves is tantamount to extortion and exploitation of the sort that the Qur'ān has clearly forbidden. The text thus enjoins the believers: 'And withhold not from the people that which they are entitled to have.' (7:85). This is confirmed in another verse which provides 'Whosoever does work of an atom's weight shall see its reward. . .' (99:7). Work is also rewarded in accordance with qualifications and work record of the one who undertakes it, and this is the purport of another verse which declares: 'and for all there will be ranks for what they do, that He may pay them for their deed; and they will not be wronged,' (46:19). The notion of fair wage must accordingly reflect the record of achievement and professional standing of the employee.

ولاتبخسوا الناس أشياءهم

ومن يعمل مثقال ذرة خيرا يره

ولكل درجات مما عملوا وليوفيهم أعمالهم وهم لايظلمون

Broadly speaking, a worker remuneration must be sufficient to cover his needs for essentials, including food, clothing and accommodation that is deemed suitable for him and his peers. The worker must be paid his due, but the worker too must give what is due to the employer and it is only then that the Qur'ānic directive referred to above is implemented. In the event of a wide discrepancy between remuneration and the cost of living, the worker is likely to be either the victim of injustice (*ẓulm*),[148] or of fraud and prejudice (*ghabn wa ḍarar*).[149] This is the purport of a *ḥadīth* in which the Prophet is reported to have given the following instructions:

من كان لنا عاملا ولم يكن له سكن فليتخذ مسكنا، ومن لم يكن له زوج فليتخذ زوجا، ومن لم يجد خادما فليتخذ خادما، ومن لم يجد دابة فليتخذ دابة، ومن اتخذ غير ذلك فهو غال أو سارق.

Whoever is working for us but has no dwelling, let him be provided with a dwelling. If he has no spouse, let him get married. If he has no servant, let him get one. If he has no riding beast, let him be provided with one. But to charge beyond these needs makes him either a swindler or a thief.[150]

Sibāʿī has observed, and rightly so, that the Prophet has in this *ḥadīth* spoken in his capacity as the head of state. The fact that he envisaged giving assistance to unmarried workers as well as helping them with the means of transport are indicative of a long term benefit scheme that the Prophet had contemplated for workers. For employers cannot be expected to provide these for all workers, especially for those who completed their work in a short time of say days, or even months. The basic responsibility of the employer is to pay a fair wage and apply a reasonable work regime, and not necessarily to help the worker with his marriage expenditures. When the Prophet referred to these additional long-term benefits, he was speaking of the responsibility of the state to provide a benefit scheme for workers that was additional to a fair wage. The said benefits were to be given in the event where the workers' basic earning was not enough for them to meet their needs.[151]

The meaning of *ghulul* (cheater, swindler) has also been explained in another *ḥadīth*, reported by Buraydah that the Prophet said: 'When we employ someone and assign him a living, what he then takes after that means that he becomes *ghulul*.'[152]

Workers and employers are advised to take what is due to them in a paid job. This is the purport of a *ḥadīth* in which one Ibn al-Sāʿidī said: 'The caliph ʿUmar, may God be pleased with him, employed me to collect the *zakāh*. When I finished the task assigned to me he ordered that I should be paid. I said that I did it only for the sake of God, but he told me to take what is due to me. For 'I (ʿUmar) was employed during the time of the Prophet and he paid me for my work.'[153]

No work must be assigned without remuneration. For the *Sharī'ah* forbids forced labour and entitles every worker to full and fair payment for the work accomplished. This is indicated in the Qur'ānic passage where the young Moses was addressed by Prophet Shu'ayb's daughter: 'My father invites you that he may pay you for having watered for us.' (28:25)

إن أبي يدعوك ليجزيك أجر ما سقيت لنا

Then it is stated elsewhere that 'the Pharoah exalted himself in the earth, divided its people, a tribe among them he oppressed, killing their sons and sparing their woman. He was an agent of corruption.' (28:4)

إن فرعون علا في الأرض وجعل أهلها شيعا ويذبح أبنائهم ويستحي نسائهم إنه كان من المفسدين

This was on account of Pharoah's attempt to subjugate the people to forced labour. He was thus declared as an agent of corruption and a tyrant.

Since forced labour is forbidden, it is not lawful to employ anyone, especially an orphan, without wages, even if it be for a relative or teacher. The mother presents an exception as it is held that the orphan may do unpaid work for his mother.[154] The Prophet is reported to have conveyed in a *ḥadīth* Qudsī, the concern over the treatment of workers and payment of fair wages for the work done:

قال الله تعالى: ثلاثة أنا خصمهم يوم القيامة، رجل أعطي بي ثم غدر، ورجل باع حرأ ثم أكل ثمنه، ورجل استأجر أجيرا فاستوفى منه ولم يعط أجره

God Most High said: I shall be the opponent of three people on the day of judgment: the man to whom I gave generously but then he cheated; the man who sold a freeman into slavery and ate up its price, and the man who hired a worker and took his due measure from him but did not pay him his (fair) wages.[155]

Fair wages are determined in due regard for the capacity of the worker, the nature of the work and the time in which it can be completed. Remuneration may be in cash or in kind, usufruct or service, including for example, the worker getting married to someone and undertaking to serve the latter in lieu of the dower he might otherwise be unable to pay.[156] Remuneration may not, however, consist of a substance that is not valuable from the *Sharīʿah* point of view and this includes such things as liquor, pork, dead carcass and unlawfully possessed property.

Fair wages must qualify equal wages for equal work. Workers with similar skills who are assigned similar duties should be similarly paid. Equal pay for equal work also means that other factors such as the individual needs of the workers do not lead to wage differentials, although some have maintained otherwise. Thus a worker with a large family is not necessarily paid more than the one without a family for the same work. All of this, however, does not mean commitment to a linear equality. Workers in the same line of work may be paid differently in accordance with their individual capabilities.[157]

Since a worker's pay is most likely to be his or her only means of livelihood, it is held that any undue delay in payment amounts to prejudice. Moreover, the right to a suitable remuneration takes it for granted that the quantities involved, namely the amount of work and its payment, are specified in advance in order to prevent fraudulent practices and conflict. This is the subject of a *ḥadīth* narrated by Abū Saʿīd al-Khudrī which declared 'the Prophet prohibited employing a worker without specifying and declaring his wages.'[158] The same message has been conveyed slightly differently in another *ḥadīth*: 'Whoever hires a worker must specify and declare his wages to him.'[159]

من استأجر أجيرا فليسمّ له أجرته

A contract of hire which falls short of this and does not specify the wages is consequently held to be irregular and voidable (*fāsid*) as it is likely to lead to conflict.[160] Lease and hire (*al-ijārah*) is a binding contract in Islamic law and it binds its signatories to due fulfilment of their contractual obligations (cf. *al-Māʾidah*, 5:1). *Ijārah* is like sale in that both involve exchange of values, the only difference being that in *ijārah* one side of the bargain consists of usufruct (*manfaʿah*) such as labour or service. It is a binding contract which cannot be dissolved or terminated by one side only. The contract of *ijārah* is open to stipulation as the parties may wish to insert. The parties may thus agree to make it prompt or deferred or absolute, the last of these means unstipulated *ijārah* which is not contingent on any conditions. Whichever of these is opted by the parties the result will accordingly vary. The right of the parties in regard to stipulation in *ijārah* is validated in the *ḥadīth* which declares that 'Muslims are bound by their stipulations.'[161] A prompt *ijārah* entitles the worker to payment as of the time of the agreement. The worker is consequently entitled to exercise full proprietary rights over it, which means that he may give it away in gift or charity or spend it in any way he pleases. Indeed all the rights that a seller acquires over the price of the goods he has sold, the worker/artisan acquires over the wages he has earned as he has sold his labour. In the event of delay in payment by the employer, the worker is entitled to retain the goods at his disposal until he is paid. This is once again analogous to the right of the seller to hold on to his goods until the buyer pays the price for it. This right of retention is available to both the common employee (*ajīr mushtarak*) as well as the individual employee (*ajīr khāṣ*). An individual employee would thus be entitled under a prompt *ijārah* to withhold his services, or not to make himself available until he is paid.[162]

In the event where the parties to an employment contract agree on a deferred *ijārah*, the consequences of *ijārah*, including salary and payment, will be deferred until the work is done, or in the case of manufacture of goods, until the delivery of goods. In the case of an absolute *ijārah* where the parties have not stipulated any time frame, the worker is entitled to payment only after completion of work, or when the goods are made by an artisan or manufacturer and delivered to the client.[163]

There is a certain difference of opinion among the Ḥanafīs and Shāfiʿīs over the consequences of an absolute *ijārah* and the precise time the worker becomes entitled to payment. The question here is over delivery and possession, which is physically possible with regard to objects such as manufactured goods but not so with regard to service. Labour and service are in the nature of usufruct (*manfaʿah*) which materialises gradually until the work is completed, or the job is done, hence the entitlement to payment in arrears. The Shāfiʿīs have differed and maintained that even in absolute *ijārah* the effects of the contract for both sides materialises immediately as of the signing of contract and the employee who gives his service is entitled to pay as of that time. As for the artisan or a common employee, it is generally agreed that payment becomes due upon delivery of the manufactured goods.[164]

Should there be substantial ambiguity in the determination of wages such as when it is said 'work for me and I shall pay you; or I shall make you happy'—the contract is voidable (*fāsid*). If the work is completed under such terms the worker will be entitled to an equivalent wage (*ujrat al-mithl*).[165] This also applies to a situation where the specified wages are oppressively low. An exception to this is noted by ʿIzz al-Dīn al-Sulamī concerning work the payment for which is customarily known, such as brokerage fees, barber's charges, medical charges etc., in which case the usual wages will be payable even if no specific figure is mentioned at the outset.[166]

When ignorance over the wages of a worker, or work that is assigned to him is such that it is likely to lead to a dispute between the parties, the hire contract is invalid due to excessive uncertainty (*gharar*) and it becomes voidable (*fāsid*) as a result. This level of ignorance will obstruct effective completion and delivery of its subject matter as the parties would not know exactly what they are supposed to expect from one another.[167] The wages in a contract of hire is tantamount to the price in the contract of sale and the rules of *gharar* apply to both in their respective capacities. This also means that whatever is acceptable to be given as price in a sale is also acceptable to be given as wages in *ijārah*, which means in effect that it must be a valuable asset that is clearly determined (*māl mutaqawwim maʿlūm*). This would normally consist of money but it could also be a commodity, which is known and identified by direct viewing, counting and quantification, or if not present, by price description that eliminates ignorance.[168]

The Ḥanafīs are of the view that the worker's pay may not consist of a similar work, such as gardening for gardening, or domestic work for its equivalent, but there is no objection if gardening work is paid by its equivalent in domestic work. The Shāfiʿīs maintain that differential of genus is not a requirement. The Ḥanafī position here is again based on a distinction between corpus (*ʿayn*) and usufruct (*manfaʿah*). If both of the counter values in *ijārah* consist of usufruct which materialise gradually over time, it might partake in *ribā*, and also *gharar*. The Shāfiʿīs validate the exchange of both sale and hire to consist of either *ʿayn* or *manfaʿah*, as both are *māl* and may be given in price or in wages.[169]

Another requirement of a valid *ijārah* is that it should be possible of fulfilment or that its subject matter can be delivered. Thus if a worker is given an impossible assignment, such as digging manually a well into what turns out to be solid rock-the contract would be held to be incapable of fulfillment.[170] And lastly that the subject matter of contract is lawful. A contract of hire in which the employee is given an unlawful assignment such as to commit murder, abduction and theft would be void and unlawful.[171] A woman may not be hired for prostitution, nor may a Muslim enter employment in a wine making factory. A question has arisen whether a Muslim is entitled to payment for carrying a load of a prohibited object such as wine. Whereas the two disciples of Abū Ḥanīfah, Abū Yūsuf and Al-Shaybānī, have answered this in the negative, Abu Ḥanīfah himself has held that the act of carrying itself is not unlawful and the carrier is entitled to his payment. For after all it is possible that the wine may be intended to be poured away and destroyed, but if both the employer and employee knew that it was meant for drinking, then it is unlawful and does not create a right to payment. The Qur'ānic authority quoted here is the verse which addresses the believers to 'cooperate not in transgression and hostility.' (5:2)[172]

ولاتعاونوا على الأثم والعدوان

It is unlawful for a person to hire his parents to serve him, due once again, to the Qur'ānic injunction which prescribes dignified treatment and respect for the parents (17:23). Disrespect of this kind is unlawful and *ḥarām*, regardless as to the status of the parent and off-spring, and whether the parent is a Muslim or a non-Muslim.[173] The ruling here would seem also to apply by analogy to one's grandparents. The basic cause and rationale of this prohibition is to prevent disrespect for the parents through a humiliating kind of employment in which a son or daughter employs his or her parents, as a personal servant, for example, but if the employment is intended on the contrary to help one's parents in a dignified capacity, it is submitted that there should be no objection, as this would in fact qualify the terms of the preceding portion of the same Qur'ānic verse, quoted above, which enjoins the believers to 'cooperate in good work and righteousness' (5:2). وتعاونوا على البر والتقوى Dignified employment would as such qualify as an act of merit and recommendable.

No one may be employed to work that is essentially the personal obligation of the worker in the first place. For no one, in principle, is entitled to be paid for performance of a personal duty. An example of this would be to employ someone to take care of the latter's own child or wife, or for that matter to perform the obligatory prayer (*ṣalāh*) on the employer's behalf.[174] This is the basic principle, but some disagreement has arisen over subsidiary issues, such as the charging fees for teaching the Qur'ān, or teaching the due performance of prayer and fasting. Some Ḥanafīs have suggested that this sort of teaching partakes in the religious duty of all Muslims to disseminate knowledge of the Qur'ān, whereas the Shāfi'īs have held it permissible for such teaching to be paid for. There is disagreement over this even among the Ḥanafīs. The Imam Abū Ḥanīfah himself has disallowed charging a fee, but it is reported that subsequent *'ulamā'* in the Ḥanafī school have issued *fatwā* to the contrary. This was because experience showed, at a very early stage that people did not volunteer to teach the Qur'ān for free. The knowledge of the Qur'ān suffered as a result—hence the ruling that it is permissible to charge a fee for it.[175]

There is evidence in the *ḥadīth* to the effect that no one may ask to be paid for leading a prayer, nor may any one ask to be paid for taking part in *jihād*, especially when it becomes a personal duty. *Jihād* in general is a collective obligation (*farḍ kifā'ī*), as opposed to a personal obligation (*farḍ 'ayn*) but it is elevated from the former to the latter when the community has to repel imminent aggression that threaten everyone's life. One may similarly not charge a fee, as Kāsānī wrote for 'bathing a deceased person—*ghusl al-mayyit*,' but may do so for 'carrying its coffin, and also for digging a grave'.[176] This is due to the authority in a *ḥadīth* which proclaims some such activities as to be partaking in the right of Muslims over one another. To give yet another example, it is not permissible for a wife to ask her husband for wages for what is a part of her domestic duties, but that it is permissible if the wife wished to pay her husband a wage for taking care of the domestic work. The reason given here is that domestic work is normally not a part of the husband's duty who may therefore be paid for it.

It is also unlawful for a person to be paid in lieu of work that benefits him in the first place, for this would be tantamount to self-employment. An example of this is as follows: it is permissible for a women to employ her husband to take care of a flock of animals that she owns, for this is not a part of the husband's duty and may therefore be paid for his work. But if it so happens that shepherding those animals is also beneficial for the husband, he may not ask for remuneration—as he would in this case, become his own employee.[177]

It now remains to be seen that some of these rulings of *fiqh* may be said to have been formulated in the light of the custom and prevailing conditions of earlier times. Custom (*'urf*) is a recognised basis of judgment and it is correct, as a matter of principle, to acknowledge the role of custom in social and commercial affairs. Should there be a subsequent change in the custom and living conditions of the people, then it would follow that a parallel adjustment in the initial judgment and *fatwā* may be necessary. To take one or two of the examples given above, we noted that a prayer leader may not charge for leading the prayer, nor may a fee be imposed on bathing the corpse of a deceased person. Due to the change of conditions that urbanisation and city life have brought about both of these activities are now conducted on a professional and organised basis. The Imam is paid a salary for his work as is the undertaker and funeral director. Change of custom in these cases leads to the conclusion that earning a wage for these works is permissible under the present circumstances.

Fair wages are further described as that rate of earning which enables the worker to live decently in the station of life to which he or she is accustomed.[178] Ibn Taymiyyah refers to it as 'the wage of the equivalent' (*ujrāt al-mithl*) which refers to equivalence in the exchange of value as well as equivalence with the market practice that prevails. It is a parallel concept to that of equivalent price (*qīmat al-mithl*), which is the regular market price under normal conditions of supply and demand. While the market value of labour must be left, in principle, to the market forces of supply and demand, it is more specifically determined in normal circumstances by the agreement of the employer and employee. Bilateral bargaining thus plays a role in the determination of wages. But there is an element of objectivity in the *ujrat al-mithl* which gains prominence in cases of imperfections in the market. For example, if people are in need of the services of farmers or of those engaged in textile production or in construction, but workers in these industries are not prepared to give their services and make unreasonable demands, the authorities may in this case fix the wage of the equivalent, so that the employer cannot reduce the wage of the worker nor does the worker demand more than the established 'fair wage.'[179]

In response to the question whether the state may fix wages to ensure their fairness, Ibn Taymiyyah has observed that wage fixing may become necessary as part of the state's responsibility for the settlement of labour disputes in particular situations, but not under normal conditions. Ibn Taymiyyah regards labour as a value or commodity that carries a market price, and therefore treats wage fixing analogously to price fixing. His term for wage fixing is the 'pricing of labour' (*tas'īr fi'l-a'māl*). Ibn Taymiyyah has maintained a similar position on price fixing or price control (*al-tas'īr*) which should normally not be attempted, but may be attempted in the event only of serious distortion and market irregularities. Wages and prices may have to be regulated by the state as the situation may demand in order to check exploitation and protect the interests of the people.[180]

Another issue that arises concerning fair wages is the introduction of a minimum wage law. Islam's emphasis on workers' welfare has prompted some Islamic economists to suggest that the wages should at least be sufficient to fulfil the basic needs of the wage earner, even if it means introducing a minimum wage law. Yet it has been suggested that fixing minimum wages might have negative effects such as driving many people out of employment and that it is, in any case, not a solution to the problem of poverty. Minimum wages tend to benefit those that are employed at the cost of those that are not employed. Minimum wage laws also tend to drive prices up. This may benefit a small group but the vast majority may suffer as a result. Moreover, many people such as the self-employed, retired persons and casual workers tend to fall outside the scope of minimum wages. But the basic critique here is that wages are not determined on the criterion of need, otherwise two workers doing the same work would be entitled to different wages. Nor is it the responsibility of the employer to guarantee the parity between wages and needs. Wages are determined by reference to market conditions. If marketable wages are not sufficient to fulfil the basic needs of some workers, that should be taken care of through other methods of distribution. The overall conclusion that is often drawn is that in a system where a comprehensive scheme for need fulfilment is available, minimum wage law would not be generally needed.[181]

It is suggested that under normal circumstances, there should be no interference in the natural flow of supply and demand in the economy and wages should be no exception. Only when distortion and irregularity disrupt normal conditions may the government intervene in the wages market. To do so is also in line with the general requirements of justice and prevention of oppression.[182]

It is for the government to ensure that wages and salaries are generally fair and commensurate with the demands of work. In its supervisory role the government is also advised to encourage suitable incentives for workers to make their best contribution to the development of the economy and increased production.[183] Adequate regulations should also be made to encourage promotion to higher grade and pay for those who qualify.[184] In order to ensure a fair regime of labour law and its due enforcement, it is suggested that a supervisory body should be assigned the role of general supervision on labour relations, salaries and incentives so as to keep the law abreast with reality and also implement the Qur'ānic directive 'And withhold not from people that which duly belongs to them.' (7:85)

ولاتبخسوا الناس أشياءهم

WORK ACCIDENT AND LIABILITY FOR LOSS

Wages are determined on the basis of either work or of the time spent on completing it. This is also the basis of the distinction between the private and common employee (*ajīr khāṣ, ajīr mushtarak*). Common employees such as tailors, carpenters and craftsmen are paid on the basis of the work they accomplish. They are entitled to retain the product or article that is placed in their possession until their wages are paid, and this they may do without even seeking permission of the authorities. They are entitled, and so are the *ajīr khāṣ*, to do this and their right to remuneration remains unaffected even in the event where a deficiency in the contract of employment becomes known and renders the contract voidable (*fāsid*).[185]

There may be other methods of determining the wages, such as the ones based on the number of items involved, or a job lot and so forth. Any method that is accepted by custom (*'urf*) and is free of uncertainty and deception would be acceptable from the viewpoint of *Sharī'ah*.[186] The common employee is, however, liable for any loss or damage to the goods that are placed under his custody until such a time when the goods are returned to the owner. In the event where the common employee does not complete the work for which he has been hired, he is not entitled to any wages, and no wages are payable for unfinished work either.[187]

If the object that is retained by a worker in lieu of his wages is damaged or destroyed while in his possession, he is not liable for compensation unless it is proven that he was negligent or acted wrongfully.[188] He is still entitled to his wages, if he has discharged his duty properly in the first place. According to a variant opinion, when the article is destroyed in the worker's possession, he also loses his entitlement to wages, as it may otherwise mean that a harm (*ḍarar*) is inflicted on the employer. The preferred view, however, is the first one, which is that the employee's entitlement to wages remains intact.[189] If the employee does not complete the work he has undertaken, he is only entitled to his pay if the part that is completed is of benefit to the employer, such as a wall that is partially built. But if the partially completed work is of no benefit to the employer, the worker will not be entitled to any wages.[190]

In the event where the employer is indebted and his creditors demand to be paid while he has also employed workers whose wages are unpaid—priority is given to the latter. The employee has a priority right simply because he may need to support himself and his family with the wages he earns. Also based on this premise is the *fiqh* ruling which exempts worker's wages from interdiction (*al-ḥajr*) by court order in the event where the workers themselves face creditor claim for repayment of debt. The worker's wages may not be subjected to interdiction unless the wages in question are in excess of the living needs of the worker.

Workers are also protected against the risk of unfair contracts of employment. Thus if a landowner hires a worker on such terms as to make his wages payable from the yield of the land by a certain proportion or percentage of the yield, this kind of partnership is not permitted for fear of crop failure and possible harm to the worker.[191] The worker is also entitled to seek annulment of a contract that stipulates fraudulent wages or conditions that partake of the same. This also entitles the worker to seek compensation from the employer for the harm he might have suffered as a result of such stipulations.[192]

The issue of liability for loss (*ḍamān*) has received much attention. The two criteria that are usually considered most relevant in the determination of *ḍamān* are effective control or possession of the assets involved, and also negligence of duty or fault. This is illustrated by a simple example of a person hiring another to carry a container of cooking oil for him. The owner helps the porter but as the owner tries to lift the load, the oil container breaks almost still in the hands of its owner. The porter will not be liable for loss in this case, but he may be held liable if he destroys the load when it is in his possession, according to one view attributed to Abū Yūsuf, but not so according to al-Shaybānī.[193] Suppose that the porter destroys the oil due to a slip of the foot along the way, or due to the crowd pressing against him, he will not bear liability for loss either as he could not be said to have been negligent.[194]

In the event where destruction and loss is due to transgression or manifest negligence of the employee, he will bear liability for it regardless of his status as a private or a common employee. A certain distinction has been drawn in this connection in regard to whether the worker has acted in the context of what was expected of him to do, or whether he acted outside this framework. The likelihood of his being held liable for loss is greater in the latter case than in the former, and this likelihood increases further in the case of a common employee (*ajīr mushtarak*) compared to a private one (*ajīr khāṣ*). This is partly due to the ruling of *ijmāʿ* whereby the common employee is expected to observe a higher degree of care and will generally be held liable for loss and destruction of goods that are placed in his custody.[195] Another example of a common employee Kāsānī has given is that of a shepherd who takes the village cattle to the pasture, and while crossing a bridge the cattle rush and panic, which causes some of them fall as a result into the river below and die. The question as to whether the shepherd would be liable for loss will be determined by reference to his use of the whip in driving the animals. If he used the whip in the way he normally did and what would be expected of him to do, then he is not liable, but he would be liable if he acted abnormally and deliberately caused panic by the harsher use of the whip. For this would be a case of liability for loss due to transgression (*taʿaddī*) that falls beyond the scope of normal practice.[196]

In the event where a pupil or a trainee causes accidental damage, the trainer/employer bears liability on his behalf, if the accident had occurred in the progress of normal work, but not otherwise. To illustrate this, suppose a young trainee who works with a master tailor accidentally drops a lamp which causes damage to a cloth that belongs to a client. The trainer will in this case be liable for compensation to his client. But if this happens to the cloth which is temporarily deposited at the tailor's shop, the latter will not be held liable to compensation. The difference in these two positions relates to the differential legal standing of the master-trainee. In the first of these examples, the master is responsible for safekeeping of the cloth he has received from his client as he charges a fee for the work he has undertaken, whereas in the latter case, he has not received the cloth in the capacity of a guarantor, and he is in any case doing another person a favour. Liability for damage that is caused by the pupil's act is therefore born by the pupil himself.[197]

Should a disagreement arise between two persons, one of whom is a trustee who has received goods in his custody on behalf of the former, credibility is given to what the trustee might have to say. Suppose that a sea freight operator receives goods from someone to transport to a destination, but when the goods are being delivered at destination, the owner claims that they are not the same goods. The operator maintains that they are the same goods. The operator's version of the case prevails if he would take an oath to certify it. The cargo operator is also not responsible for any claim of damage to the goods. This is because he received the goods in his custody as a trustee. The owner of goods is, however, not required to pay for the labour unless he acknowledges the goods as his and receives them.[198] The common employee is also a trustee (*amīn*) who receives the goods of his clients in that capacity, and a trustee is normally not liable for loss to the goods in his custody. But according to a ruling of the fourth caliph ʿAlī, this position was changed on grounds of public interest (*maṣlaḥah*). The common employee was consequently held responsible for loss unless he proved that he had not been negligent in any way, or that the damage was caused by events beyond his control.

The question of entitlement to wages and liability for loss is also determined by reference to completion of task and also whether the result of that work benefits the employer as in the following examples:

(1) Suppose that Ahmad employs a baker to bake bread out of a quantity of dough that Ahmad puts at his disposal. The baker takes the bread out of the oven but it falls back accidentally and burns before it is taken out. The baker will not be entitled to a wage simply because the work he undertook has not been completed and its result has not benefited Ahmad. The work would have been accomplished if the bread had been produced. The case here is similar to the accidental spillage or destruction of milk before it is all taken out of the udders of the animal, for which no wages would be payable either. Nor is the worker liable for any compensation as he had no control over the accident, only that he forfeits his entitlement to wages.

(2) Suppose on the other hand that the baker makes the bread for Ahmad, not in his bakery, but in Ahmad's premises. He takes the bread out of the oven but then it catches fire and is burnt for no fault of his. The baker would in this case be entitled to the agreed upon wages and also bears no liability for the loss. He is entitled to wages because he completed the task that was assigned to him and placed the bread at Ahmad's disposal. He is not liable for loss simply because he had not caused it and he cannot therefore be held liable for it.[199]

(3) Suppose also that a resident of Kufa hires a man to deliver a manuscript of his to someone in Basra. The man takes the manuscript to Basra only to find that the person to whom it was to be delivered had died. So the manuscript is returned to its owner in Kufa. Imam Abū Ḥanīfah has held concerning this case that the worker is not entitled to any wages as the purpose of his employment had not been met. The Imam's disciple al-Shaybānī held, on the other hand, that the man is entitled to be paid for the fact that he went to Basra and that this was the material factor as far as the worker was concerned, and not, as it were, its delivery to the intended person.[200] In the present author's opinion, al-Shaybānī's view seems preferable as the unknown element in this case did not involve any fault or negligence of the employee.

In the event where the worker or artisan making a mistake about the quality, attribute or quantity of the goods and delivers something different to what has been ordered, the employer/customer is entitled to an option whether to take what is produced and pay the cost of the production, or else to accept an equivalent in compensation. The worker/artisan would thus be required to compensate the customer the equivalent of what has been placed in his custody in the first place plus any decrease in the value of the goods. Al-Kāsānī illustrates this as follows:

(1) Ahmad takes a piece of white cloth to the dyers to be dyed green but due to an error on the part of the dyer the cloth is dyed red. The owner shall in this case have the option either to take the cloth and pay for the cost of the dye, if the dying is deemed to have enhanced the value of the cloth, or else to ask the dyer for the price of a white cloth as a replacement. The reason for this option of guarantee (*khiyār al-taḍmīn*) is the dyer's failure to meet the need/purpose of his client and it is as if the dyer has destroyed the cloth. But if the dying is deemed to have reduced the value of the material, the dyer should compensate the owner of the cloth for the loss in value.[201]

(2) A man takes a piece of gold to the jeweller and orders his name to be engraved on it, but the jeweller makes an error and engraves a different name, in which case the jeweller would bear liability to replace what has been placed in his custody, and will not be entitled to any payment for his work. This is because liability for loss (*ḍamān*) does not combine with payment/reward (*al-ajr*). It is as if the jeweller had destroyed what was initially placed in his custody. A similar example would be when the owner of a building hires

a contractor to paint the building blue but it is painted a different colour. In this case the contractor is not entitled to any payment for his work as liability (*ḍamān*) cannot combine with payment/reward, but he may be paid the cost of the paint if this has added to the value of the premises, or else to compensate the owner if the wrong paint has reduced the value of the premises.[202]

There is a difference, al-Kāsānī maintains, between an error that affects the genus as opposed to one that affects only the attribute of an object. Error in regard to the genus is a total error, such as in the foregoing examples, but error in regard to attribute is deemed as a lower degree of error which does not disqualify the worker/artisan from payment of fair wages, although the client would still have the option of guarantee whether or not to accept the product, and if he does not accept it, he will also not have to pay for the work. Al-Kāsānī has illustrated this by an example in which a person gives to a weaver a quantity of cotton to make a light weight cloth for him, but the weaver produces a heavy weight cloth, or vice versa. The weaver has here made an error in regard to what may be said to be an attribute; he has used the same material but the error occurred in regard to an aspect of the cloth. The owner has the option either to accept a replacement of his cotton in which case the cloth shall belong to the weaver, or to take what is manufactured and pay a fair price (*ajr al-mithl*) which does not however exceed the agreed price (*al-ajr al-musammā*).[203] The worker is entitled to wages because error in regard to the attribute meant that the contract had been basically fulfilled but it was deficient. This is somewhat similar to the case of someone buying a defective item, in which case the buyer is entitled to the option of defect (*khiyār al-ʿayb*). The buyer either accepts the defective item as it is, or returns it and claims the price he paid for it.[204]

An error in regard to measurement and quantity on the part of the worker/manufacturer also entitles the client to an option either to take what is produced and pay the price as agreed, or to claim for a replacement of what he had initially placed in the custody of the worker. There are two possibilities here, one of which is that the manufacturer has given a large measure or quantity, or that he has given less. An example of the former would be when someone gives a quantity of wool and asks for a piece of cloth to be made measuring seven feet by five feet, but the weaver exceeds this measurement. The owner may take what is produced and pay the agreed wages (*al-ajr al-musammā*) or to ask for a replacement of his wool, in which case the cloth shall belong to the weaver.[205]

In the event where the weaver manufactures a cloth which is smaller in measurement than what was ordered, there are two views, one of which entitles the weaver to wages in proportion to the measurement of the cloth, and the other which entitles him to a fair wage (*ajr al-mithl*), that is, the market rate for the amount of work done. In both cases, the situation resembles a defective contract of hire (*ijārah fāsidah*) that only entitles the employee to compensation for the work done but not to agreed-upon wages. This is because the employee has failed to meet the specific purpose of the client, so the client also pays a rough wage, not the agreed upon wage. In both of these views, the client is entitled not to accept the cloth and ask for a replacement with an equivalent amount of wool.[206]

In the event where the employer acts aggressively toward the employee, or reduces his wages, or when he faces the employee with excessive demands, the market controller (*muhtasib*) may intervene to put an end to aggression and ensure that proper wages are paid.[207] Only when the employee fails to carry out his duty and is negligent to the extent that the expected benefit of work is not secured by his work, or that the employer is harmed as a result, the worker stands to lose his entitlement to wages. In the event where neglect of duty leads to a manifest harm and financial loss to the employer, the employee in question may be held liable to pay compensation.[208]

To sum up, the basic notions of justice and fair dealing run through the detailed *fiqh* rulings on liability for work-related accident and damage that originate in malicious or careless acts of the workers. Much of the *fiqh* guidelines on these matters were evidently formulated before the advent of industrial revolution and legislation on accident insurance that has followed suit. Work related accidents have also changed character to some extent, as a result of unprecedented development in technology and science. When one imagines the range and diversity of technical skills that go into production say of a car, airplane, or advanced technological goods, one is not always sure how to evaluate the worker's responsibility for accidents of a highly technical nature under these conditions. The scale of mechanisation and precision engineering that interact and interrelate until the final product materialises is often too broad to be entirely covered by the *fiqh* rules of medieval origin on liability and *damān*.

How much of a certain accident is the result of a poor design of a certain machine tool, computerised and automated input in a certain line of product, and how much of it could be related to negligent performance of the worker are among the questions that need to be asked when determining personal liability for damage. One would not wish to depart too far from the conventional *fiqh* analysis of work-related accidents, yet it would appear that work-related accidents are now addressed through labour legislation and accident insurance that are informed by the prevailing realities, the nature of work and its related matters. Sometimes the cost of a work-related accident may be so high that it bears little relationship to the earning, whether actual or potential, of a worker or workers that may be involved in a chain of events. Modern legislation on work-accident in the Muslim countries should naturally be guided by the basic ideals of justice and fair dealing (*ʿadl wa-iḥsān*) of the *Sharīʿah* as well as the valuable contribution of *fiqh* on the subject. All of this would in the meantime need to reflect on the current realities of the work place, customary changes, adequate protection of workers and concern for the wider interests of the community.

RIGHT TO A FAIR WORK REGIME AND LEISURE

As already noted, the *Sharīʿah* requires fair dealing on the part both of the employer and employee and this is achieved through due fulfilment of their respective rights and obligations. The employer is thus directed to be attentive to the welfare needs of the employee by paying him fair remuneration and ensuring a work environment that is free of exploitation and hardship for the worker. According to ʿIzz al-Dīn al-Sulamī, the rest periods at work must be adequate. Thus he wrote by way of illustration 'if an employment contract stipulates such that the employee works day and night for a month, without allowing any breaks for sleep and rest, it is null and void.'[209] No one should burden a worker so that he can only sustain it for a day or two and then fails to be able to continue. The pattern of rest and recreation is usually determined by reference to prevailing custom.[210] Workers should be treated such that their productive energy remains a source of sustained benefit both for themselves, their families, and the community at large. To deny the workers' welfare needs for leisure and a healthy work regime, their productive force will decline. Working hours and work-load as well as the physical environment of work are among the factors that call for particular attention. These are also the conclusions that contemporary writers and commentators on the subject have drawn from the basic evidence of the Qur'ān and *Sunnah*.[211] The broad message of this evidence is conveyed in the

Qur'ānic verse that 'God intends for you facility and ease and He does not intend to put you in hardship.' (2:185)

$$ يريد الله بكم اليسر ولايريد بكم العسر $$

In another verse of the same chapter it is proclaimed that 'God does not burden a soul beyond its capacity.' (2:286)

$$ لايكلف الله نفسا إلا وسعها $$

The Prophet addressed the subject succinctly when he said in a *ḥadīth*: '...if you assign work to your servants/employee that is beyond his capacity, then you should help him to do it.'[212]

$$ ولاتكلفوهم مايغلبهم فإن كلفتموهم فأعينوهم $$

One commentator has drawn the conclusion from this evidence that 'Islam demands gentleness in the treatment of workers and shuns harshness and oppression concerning them.'[213] The level of what may be said to be bearable is often determined by general custom or prevailing practice in the relevant professions. It is now generally accepted, for example, that eight hours of work per day with the necessary breaks in between is normal and a demand to engage the worker for much longer than this is excessive, although a certain margin of flexibility should be acceptable. If there is an agreement on overtime between the employer and employee, then any work in addition to the eight hour limit should be separately paid. It thus appears that a fair wage is also one that is customary and consistent with what is accepted in a particular locality or profession.[214]

In following the purport of the *ḥadīth* quoted above, ʿIzz al-Dīn al-Sulamī wrote that the daily working hours should be such that do not impose an oppressive demand on the capabilities of the worker. Workers must be allowed sufficient breaks to enable them to take rest in addition to the time that is required for meals, obligatory prayers and the calls of nature. They should also have a day of rest on a Friday for example. Al-Nawawī has stated that a contract of hire takes for granted break allowances for obligatory worship and other necessary break periods which must be given without any deduction from wages. This also applies to the Friday congregational prayer where a longer break is usually needed.[215] The Prophet has instructed the workers to avoid a work regime that would drive them into exhaustion: 'You are required to work to the extent of your abilities, for God is not impatient unless you yourselves become impatient.'[216]

عليكم بما تطيقون، فوالله لا يملّ الله حتى تملّوا

This evidently encourages the workers to exert themselves to the extent only that they are capable of, but tells them in the meantime to be aware of their own limitations and avoid over-indulgence and fatigue. The Prophet has advised everyone who exerts themselves mentally and physically whether in paid work or unpaid occupation to 'Refresh your hearts hour by hour (every now and then), for the heart tends to go blind when it is denied a reprieve.'[217]

روحوا القلوب ساعة فساعة، فإن القلوب إذا كلت عميت

Rest and relaxation in other words is just as necessary for the well-being of people as is the work itself. Vacation and rest should therefore be given due attention in the determination of rules that regulate labour relations. This is also the purport of the *ḥadīth* earlier quoted that 'Your body has a right over you,' and one of those rights is to avail it of rest and recreation at regular intervals.[218] One should be able, in meantime, to see to one's other responsibilities as a husband and father as the case may be. For these are likely to suffer in the event where a worker is over-exhausted due to a working regime that puts excessive demands on his energy. The Prophet has in yet another *ḥadīth* warned against over-exertion and advised the individual to guard against inflicting severity upon themselves:

لا تشدد على أنفسكم فيشدد عليكم، فإن قوما شددوا
على أنفسهم شدد عليهم فتلك بقاياها في الصوامع

Do not be severe on yourselves, for if you are, others will also treat you with severity. When a people inflict hardship upon themselves, then hardship is visited upon them as a matter of course.[219]

Al-Bukhārī has also recorded a *hadīth*, instructing the believers: '... When God Most High puts one's brother under one's command, one should feed him of what one eats, and clothe him of what one wears, and should not ask him to do what is beyond his capacity. And if he asks him to do a hard task at all, he should help him with it.'[220]

فمن جعل الله أخاه تحت يده فليطعمه مما يأكل وليلبسه مما يلبس ولايكلفه من العمل مايغلبه، فإن كلّفه مايغلبه فليعنه عليه

One way whereby such help can be given, according to Sibāʿī, would be to pay a worker overtime for additional work he is asked to do.[221]

Cleanliness and health of the worker and workplace are the shared responsibilities of the employer and employee. The *hadīth* which declares that 'cleanliness is a part of faith'[222] الطهور شطر الإيمان is addressed to both employer and employee. In another *hadīth*, the Prophet is reported to have said 'God requires every Muslim to take a bath (at least) once in every seven days. If he has perfume, he should wear it (now and then).'[223]

Since cleanliness is a religious requirement, it is also one of the duties of the market inspector (*muhtasib*) to supervise individuals, the market-place and factories to ensure standards of cleanliness and health.[224] The flour mills are thus to be supervised so that earth and sand is properly removed from wheat before it is grinded into flour. Bakeries must use clean water for making dough, just as the dough makers are instructed not to knead with their feet and should also wear something over their mouth and nose when they knead.[225]

Removal of hardship (*rafʿ al-haraj*) is a Qur'ānic principle (5:6) which is the basis of numerous concessions that the *Sharīʿah* grants to the sick, the traveller, the pregnant and lactating women to ease their hardship. With regard to the sick and the invalid, the Qur'ān stipulates that 'hardship may not be inflicted on the blind, the lame and the sick...' (24:61)

ليس على الأعمى حرج ولا على الأعرج حرج ولا على المريض حرج

Ibn Ḥazm (d. 456/1064) has drawn the conclusion that the wealthy individuals in every city are responsible to take care of the poor and the State may compel them to contribute toward that end if the State revenues are insufficient.[226] This naturally includes the sick people who are also poor and cannot afford to pay for their sustenance. Another renowned jurist, Qāḍī Khān, spoke of a certain allocation of the funds of public treasury for the medicinal needs of the poor. Since the workers' only asset that enables them to earn their living is their fitness and good health, and the community's welfare also depends on their welfare, their health is a joint responsibility of the employer and the State.[227]

It is interesting to note that the Prophet has advised the same attitude with regard to prayer and worship. These too should not be overdone to the limit of exhaustion. There are several *ḥadīths* on this subject, including the one that follows:

إذا نعس أحدكم في الصلاة فليرقد حتى يذهب عنه
النوم، فإن أحدكم إذا صلى وهو ناعس لعلله يذهب
يستغفر فليسبّ نفسه

When any of you feel sleepy while praying, then let him lie down until you are refreshed. For if you pray in that state, you might be confused and might turn a supplication into a word of insult.[228]

The prayer leader (*imām*) is also instructed in the *ḥadīth* of the Prophet not to make his recitations too lengthy lest the weak and elderly members (and those who are engaged in demanding work) of the congregation find them hard to endure, just as lengthy recitations are likely to discourage people from attending the congregational prayers.

The 1989 Islamic Declaration of Human Rights (*al-Iʿlān al-Islāmī li-Ḥuqūq al-Insān*) (Art. 24—ratified by member countries of the Organisation of Islamic Conference in its 17th Session in Tehran)[229] entitles every employee to break periods during the daily hours of work, and periodical holidays during which the employee remains entitled to his or her normal emoluments.

We do not have space to discuss a detailed account of the international labour movement, treaties and developments within and outside the framework of the International Labour Organisation (ILO).

Suffice it to note, however briefly, that legislation within the member states of the UN and international treaties sponsored by the ILO have repeatedly formulated and emphasised worker's right to leisure, a fair work regime in the work place, pension rights, right to association, and restrictions on hours of work as well as protective legislation against discrimination, forced labour, child labour and so forth.[230]

The following Qur'ānic verse and *ḥadīth* have been quoted in support of a right to pension for workers and employees in both the public and private sectors.

إلا الذين آمنوا وعملوا الصالحات فلهم أجر غير ممنون

Those who have faith and do good and righteous work—for them there is recompense beyond bounds. (95:6)

The recompense of good work and a successful record of such work by persons of upright character should be generous and should be such that offers them peace of mind and help when they are in need of it. The Prophet is reported to have said:

إذا مرض العبد أو سافر كتب الله له من الأجر مثل ماكان يعمل صحيحا مقيما

When a person falls ill or travels, God Most High grants him with reward similar to what he might have been doing if he were in good health at his place of residence.[231]

Al-Māwardī wrote in reference to the entitlement of the employees of the armed forces that the jurists have differed as to whether their pay should continue after disability and old age. Some have held the view that payment is normally made for a work done, and if the employee is no longer able to work, his entitlement to pay also collapses. A second view recorded on this is that the pay should continue even if the soldiers are unable to serve. This would help encourage the people to enter the armed forces.

As for the continuation of salaries after the person passes away, once again two different views have been recorded on more or less the same grounds. One view holds that salary should discontinue after the death of the employee as of that event. If his family is entitled to support, this should be given from the *zakāh* and other poor support funds. The second view on this entitles the surviving relatives to the salary of their deceased relative. For this will encourage the people to take on public service duties and it is in any case a more dignified option and bears greater harmony to the Qur'ānic proclamation on the human dignity (17:70) and fair treatment (*iḥsān*) (16:90).

Based on the above, the model Islamic constitution drafted by Abū Bakr al-Jazā'irī, and the 1981 Universal Declaration of Human Rights (Art. 17—bearing the title: Status and dignity of workers) provides: 'Islam honours work and the worker and enjoins Muslims not only to treat the worker justly but also generously. He is not only to be paid his earned wages promptly but is also entitled to adequate rest and leisure,' and The 1989 Islamic Declaration of Human Rights of Tehran (Art. 23) have all entitled workers to pension rights and recommended that adequate provisions should be made to that effect. It was also recommended that pension rights are additional to any other entitlement that the workers might have to welfare benefits from the public treasury.[232]

IX. Workers Associations

The *fiqh* literature does not address this subject in any details as workers unions did not exist in earlier times. Yet there seem to be no objection to them especially if trade unions would see themselves and their objectives so as to comply with Islamic teachings on fair dealing and justice for both the employer and employee.[233]

Jamāl al-Bannā who wrote a book on the subject maintains that trade unions are not only permisible but that they are required in order to prevent exploitation and ensure justice. 'If justice is what the workers unions seek to obtain, this is also the goal and objective of Islam.'[234] The Qur'ān clearly validates help for the victims of oppression (42:39) and even encourages them to leave the land of oppression and migrate rather than tolerate injustice (4:97). In the *ḥadīth* also the faithful is directed to 'assist your brother—*unṣur akhāka*' and 'support one another as if you were the component parts of a building.' The *ḥadīth* also directs anyone who sees an evil to change it by any means he can, by words of mouth, through taking action, or through silent denunciation. The purport of these directives should also apply to industrial action that is not hostile to society but seeks to fight oppression.[235]

A *Sharīʿah* compliant workers union must, however, internalise Islamic values and conduct its activities as a carrier of its message, which is the quest for justice in the first place. It should neither be aligned with socialism nor capitalism, nor should it become a partisan movement that only fights for a faction at the cost of the common good of the society. An Islamic workers union should distinguish itself from the conventional one by its distinctive perception of work. The conventional view of work is confined to the four walls of economics, work, wages and benefits which, however, leaves out the spiritual dimension of *'amal*. Work in Islam has a spiritual dimension that makes it tantamount to the service of God and must therefore integrate the meaning of religion and its teachings on trust, honesty and God-consciousness. Islam's teachings on trade and transaction also seek to keep the work environment clear of usury, gambling, fraud and trading in alcohol and drugs, teachings that must be observed by workers and their unions.[236]

Al-Bannā develops this theme by reference to the work of an eight/fifteenth century Muslim jurist, Tāj al-Dīn ʿAbd al-Wahhāb al-Subkī (d. 771), in particular his *Muʿīd al-Niʿam wa-Mubīd al-Niqām* (*Harbinger of fortune and extinguisher of misfortune*) where al-Subkī spoke of the professions, their religious/ethical framework and what was unlawful in their activities. A brief summary of this extant work anticipates the basic rationale of a self-regulatory association of the professions. As-Subkī thus wrote:

> The construction workers should ascertain that the site which they build is clear of living creatures. Building works should not be rushed such that it entraps animals underneath or that unclean substances are mixed and used in construction materials. Textile workers and tailors should not make pure silk garments for men nor should they draw inappropriate pictures and designs on their cloths. Dyers and tannery workers must also avoid using unclean substances in their line of work. The use of blood in dying is one such example, which is unlawful. Transport workers and those who rent out animals for transport should refrain from being a party to the procurement of sin—such as taking people to gambling circles. Prison governors and guards must allow Muslim prisoners to perform their Friday congregational prayers unless the judge has ordered against it. The judge is authorised to disallow it on grounds of public interest. They must also help prisoners whom they know to be innocent to seek their release. Weavers must ensure not to include pig hair in the cloth which Muslims may use as prayer mat or wear during the performance of prayer. Water carriers must ensure that drinking water is clean of impure

substances. It is a part of their Islamic duties to be watchful in this regard. Then it is added that if any of these classes of workers are misled or pressurised by the corrupt and powerful elements of society to violate their professional ethics, they must resist the pressure in order to preserve their purity of character and piety.

Jamāl al-Bannā also refers to as-Subkī's views and then concludes, that taking effective measures, including the formation of workers unions, that can help resist illicit pressure and ensure good standards in trade and in the work place is not only permitted but highly recommended in Islam.[237]

X. Role and Responsibility of Government

This may be summarised under five sections as follows:

(1) The Islamic government and its leaders (i.e. the *ulū al-amr*) are under duty in *Sharīʿah* to protect the basic interests (*maṣāliḥ*) of the community and take necessary measures, within the broad framework of *siyāsah sharʿiyyah*, for their development and growth.[238] The source evidence of *Sharīʿah* is affirmative on the individual's right to enter the work force and everyone is entitled to choose the work they wish to do. Islam also imposes 'a duty on the state to provide employment for all who are capable of it.'[239] With regard to the selection of employees, the government is under a similar obligation to apply equal standards that are free of discrimination and sectarianism.

The basic guideline of *Sharīʿah* to be observed here is to select the most suitable (*al-aṣlaḥ*) person to government positions based entirely on their qualification for the job in question. Religion is also not a ground of discrimination, although the jurists have recorded divergent opinions on this. The choice of the fittest (*ikhtiyār al-aṣlaḥ*) basically does not contemplate religion as a criterion, except perhaps in the sphere of religion itself, or the kind of work that involves decisions based on religious principles. A certain adjustment of the earlier juristic discourse on this may be called for in the light of the change of circumstances. Note, for example, Ibn Taymiyyah's discussion on the identification of the fittest (*maʿrifat al-aṣlaḥ*), in his renowned work, *al-Siyāsah al-Sharʿiyyah*,[240] which has a distinctly religious tone that was more suitable for his time, but since religion is not the sole determinant of employment in contemporary Muslim societies, selection of employees and officials need not be too strongly influenced by the religious affiliation of the candidate or his ranking on the scale of religious piety. Moral standards and dedication to good values will always be relevant, but beyond that the choice of the most suitable person for a particular position in government must refer to the Qur'ānic criteria of strength and trustworthiness, as we have earlier discussed.[241]

In the area of labour relations, the government must supervise over the smooth running and efficiency of essential industries and ensure that a fair and balanced regime governs labour relations in the community. The government may from time to time introduce new rules, or change and adjust the existing ones, so that the law regulating the rights of workers and relations between the employer and employee is kept abreast with the changing conditions and realities of the market place. The government must play a supportive role, as Ibn Qayyim pointed out, in the promotion of industries by providing necessary training for workers in various professions, and provide, as far as possible, appropriate means and procedures for this purpose. Since the people are in need of agriculture and industries, then it must mean that promoting and protecting these is a *farḍ kifā'ī*. It is a duty in principle of the government to provide the necessary educational and training facilities to keep these professions alive, and may even compel people's participation in them if necessary.[242] The role of the Islamic government in this resembles that of a partner in businesses and industries rather than an outside observer. As such it is the proper role of government to facilitate economic development through the establishment of factories and production centres either directly or in partnership with others and also to encourage private enterprise for these purposes.[243]

Since work is a duty of all able-bodied individuals, the state should not make idle living a viable option and may, if necessary, compel the qualified people to work in order to keep the essential industries and services available. By the same token, the state is under a duty to provide employment opportunities to absorb the available work force. Every one, it is pointed out, should take up work which they are capable of and suit their capabilities and talents.[244] Commentators have noted that when an able-bodied person or a skilled worker fails to find suitable employment, they may request the government for assistance in their search for employment and the latter must assist them to fight unemployment by all means at its disposal.[245] All members of the community, including the government leaders, are expected as the Qur'ān has addressed them, 'to cooperate in good and righteous work' (5:2). To help the unemployed find a suitable work undoubtedly falls within the ambit of this address. The ruler is also the trustee and custodian of the people who must look after their welfare, and employment in beneficial occupations is a way of doing just that.[246] Training schemes and programmes should be made available to all but should in the meantime be so designed as to encourage the most capable individuals to specialise in the various fields of industry and science.

Abū Zahrah has suggested a pyramid-like worker training programme which is open to everyone at the beginning but ends up by focusing its resources on the training of specialists in various areas of industry, technology and science. The trainees and specialists are in turn faced with an Islamic obligation to play their role for the benefit of the community and realisation of their legitimate interests.[247] Zuḥaylī has noted that due to the greatly enhanced role and presence of the modern state in the economy and the resources that it has at its disposal, it can, to that extent, be more effective in creating employment opportunities by embarking on industrial and agricultural projects of scale that can absorb the available labour force into the employment market.[248]

(2) The government should also supervise the smooth running of trading practices and prevent price distortion, wage hikes, and profiteering that inflict injustice and hardship on the community. The government should, in principle, not interfere with the natural flow of supply and demand in the determination of prices, and in this way refrain from making price control (*al-tasʿīr*) into a policy instrument of first resort.[249] But when unfair monopolistic and subversive practices interfere with the smooth flow of trade and disrupt the price of commodities and labour to the extent that they become a source of mischief to the public, then *al-tasʿīr* is not only permissible but may become a necessary instrument of policy by which to restore normal order to the market.[250]

(3) As already explained the *Sharīʿah* demands fair remuneration and treatment for the workers, it also permits recourse to all reasonable means that would facilitate realisation of these objectives, including trade unions and associations for protection of the legitimate rights and interests of workers. When the purpose of such associations is to ensure fair dealing and prevent capitalist exploitation and exorbitant discrepancy between the pay scale and the costs of living, then there is no objection to the formation of labour associations, and the government should play a supportive role to ensure that they are well

regulated and managed. The *Sharī'ah* does not, however, permit trade unions or any other party and organisation to use their collective influence in a manner as to deprive the community of essential goods and services. In such an eventuality the government must take initiative and adopt necessary measures to ensure continued availability of essential goods and services, and compel, if necessary, recalcitrant workers and their associations to fulfil their collective obligation toward the community.[251]

(4) The government must protect and safeguard the right of all citizens to employment and their basic liberty to pursue the work and profession of their choice. Forced labour is prohibited in Islam and any threat, whether real or potential, that compromises the integrity of the right of the individual to earn a living and acquire wealth through all lawful means should be fought and eliminated.[252]

(5) Government in Islam is committed to the welfare of its citizens, and it is therefore responsible to provide adequate unemployment benefits for unemployed workers who are prepared to work but have fallen victim of adversity. If the state can create employment opportunities to absorb the unemployed workers into the work force, this should be given priority, but the state must in the meantime have an unemployment benefit scheme which caters for the basic needs of the unemployed, both Muslims and non-Muslims, who cannot support themselves and their immediate families.[253] These will fall under the category of the poor and indigent (*al-fuqarā'*) and a subject of numerous Qur'ānic declarations where the text is affirmative of their entitlement to financial assistance. The Qur'ān gives the poor a right in the wealth of the affluent members of the community (51:19, 70:25) who are consequently under a duty to provide them with the basic necessities of life.[254] The *Sunnah* is equally explicit on the rights of the poor to assistance and support, from the funds of the public treasury (*bayt al-māl*).

In case the funds of the *bayt al-māl* are insufficient to meet the welfare needs of the poor, the government is entitled to compel the affluent members of the community to provide the poor among them with their basic necessities.[255]

To sum up, the *Sharī'ah* takes an affirmative stance on encouraging all capable persons to apply themselves and work not just for their self-improvement, but also to gain the pleasure of God and make a worthy contribution to the community. These levels of achievement can best be realised by those who aspire to a conscientious attitude to work that can qualify as service to God and a cause therefore of personal satisfaction. In the sphere of labour relations and the rights and duties of employer and employee, the moral guidelines of Islam and the legal directives of its *Sharī'ah* are inspired by justice (*'adl*) and fair treatment that are informed not only by the idea of conformity to rules but by the spirit of cooperation in good works (*ta'āwun*), and beneficence (*iḥsān*). A good Muslim must learn to be a good worker, and a good employer, assiduous at work and eager to build a fair and healthy working environment that is conducive to prosperity and growth.

One can hardly over-emphasise the importance of social reality and new developments in science and technology in the formulation of juridical responses to new issues. For *fiqh* by definition necessitates a sound understanding of reality and the issues it brings forth and then finding solutions for them from the source materials of *Sharī'ah* that are also informed by the broad and basic goals and guidelines of the *Sharī'ah*. The *fiqhī* responses that are so obtained should promote the well-being of the people through fair, balanced and *ijtihād*-oriented responses that address the issues as they are found. One must therefore avoid the temptation of subsuming new issues and solutions under *fiqhī* rules of ancient origin that need themselves to be adjusted in the first place. A sound knowledge of the heritage of *fiqh* is necessary to enable one to formulate well-informed solutions that are marked by continuity of values. When concept and reality are contemplated in the light of the broad principles of the Qur'ān and *Sunnah*, veritable *fiqh* develops as a result.

NOTES

1. Cf. Al-Dughmī, *Naẓariyyah al-Amn al-Ghadhā'ī*, 63–64.

2. Qaraḍāwī, *Mushkilat al-Faqr*, 38.

3. Al-Nawawī, *Rawḍat al-Ṭālibīn*, III, 281; 'Abudī, *Al-Ḥurriyyat al-Ijtimā'iyyah*, 45; Al-Dughmī, *Naẓariyyah al-Amn*, 64.

4. Jamāl al-Bannā, *al-Islām wa'l-Ḥarakah al-Niqabiyyah*, 135.

5. Cf. Mushtaq Ahmad, *Business Ethics*, 10, and al-Bāqī, *Al-Mu'jam al-Mufahras li-Alfāẓ al-Qur'ān al-Karīm*.

6. Ismā'īl al-Farūqī, 'Is the Muslim Definable,' in Khurshid Ahmad ed., *Islamic Perspectives*, 188.

7. Id., 155.

8. Ghazālī, *Iḥyā 'Ulūm al-Dīn*, II, 64.

9. Charles C. Torrey, *The Commercial and Theological Terms in the Koran*, Leiden: E. J. Brill, 1982, 3ff; see also Mushtaq Ahmad, *Business Ethics in Islam*, 15.

10. Al-Ghazālī, *Ihyā'*, II, 64.

11. Cf. Al-Husarī, *Al-Dawlah wa Siyāsat al-Hukm*, 322.

12. Tabrīzī, *Mishkāt*, vol. II, *hadīth* 2759.

13. Cf. Qaradāwī, *Mushkilat al-Faqr*, 44.

14. Abū Zahrah, *al-Mujtamaʿ al-Insānī*, 182-83; al–Niʿmah, *al-ʿAmal wa'l ʿUmmāl*, 4.

15. Sibāʿī, *al-Takāful*, 153.

16. Tabrīzī, *Mishkāt*, vol. I, *hadīth* no. 1290; Ghazālī, *Ihyā'*, II, 63.

17. Al-Mundhirī, *Al-Targhīb wa'l-Tarhīb*, II, 524; Muhammad al-Ghazālī, *Huqūq al-Insān*, 178.

18. Al-Ghazālī, *Huqūq al-Insān*, 178; al-ʿĪlī, *Hurriyyat*, 479.

19. Ghazālī, *Ihyā'*, II, 64–65.

20. Ghazālī, *Ihyā'*, II, 65.

21. al-Suyūtī, *al-Jāmiʿ al-Saghīr*, *hadīth* 1891; Qaradāwī, *Fiqh al-Awlawiyyāt*, 48.

22. Muslim, *Mukhtasar Sahīh Muslim*, 327, *hadīth* no. 1201.

23. Muslim, *Mukhtasar Sahīh Muslim*, 338, *hadīth* 1249; Qaradāwī, *Fiqh al-Awlawiyyāt*, 48.

24. Bukhārī, *Sahīh al-Bukhārī*, Muhsin Khan's trans., vol. VIII, *hadīth* 236.

25. Other references to agriculture can be found in suras *al-Anʿām*, 6:33; *al-Hijr*, 15:20; and *Qāf*, 50:9.

26. Muslim, *Mukhtasar Sahīh Muslim*, 258, *hadīth* no. 978. A similar but shorter version of this *hadīth* also appears in Bukhārī, *Sahīh al-Bukhārī*, K. al-Adab, *hadīth* 1926.

27. al-Suyūtī, *Al-Jāmiʿ al-Saghīr*, I, 359, *hadīth* 2668.

28. al-Suyūtī, *Al-Jāmiʿ al-Saghīr*, I, 456, *hadīth* 3392.

29. See for details Badawī, *Daʿā'im al-Hukm*, 440-457; Dughmī, *Nazariyyah al-Amn*, 106 and 144.

30. Ghazālī, *Ihyā'*, II, 65–66.

31. Id., II, 65.

32. Al-Bājī, *Al-Muntaqā bi-Sharh al-Muwattā*, VII, 324. An *awqiyah* is the equivalent of 40 dirhams. See also Zuhaylī, *Huqūq al-Insān*, 288.

33. Bukhārī, *Sahīh al-Bukhārī*, Muhsin Khan's trans. vol. VIII, hadith 448.

34. Muslim, *Mukhtasar Sahīh Muslim*, 154, *hadīth* 568.

35. Al-Shaybānī, *Al-Iktisāb fi'l-Rizq al-Mustatāb*, 32; al-Shishānī, *Huqūq al-Insān*, 307; Badawī, *Daʿā'im*, 381; Dughmī, *Nazariyyah al-Amn al-Ghadhā'ī*, 66.

36. Muslim, *Mukhtasar Sahīh Muslim*, 234, *hadīth* 885.

37. Nawawī, *Riyāḍ al-Ṣāliḥīn*, *ḥadīth* no. 153; also al-Badawī, *Daʿāʾim al-Ḥukm*, 383.

38. Al-Ghazālī, *Iḥyāʾ*, i, 28; See also Ibn Taymiyyah, *al-Ḥisbah fiʾl-Islām*, 44 who quotes al-Ghazālī, Abī Farāj, Ibn al-Jawzī and others and then concurs with them.

39. Bukhārī, *Ṣaḥīḥ al-Bukhārī*, Muhsin Khan's trans., vol. viii, *ḥadīth* 3.

40. Al-Ghazālī, *Iḥyāʾ*, i, 28; al-Qaraḍāwī, *Fiqh al-Awlawiyyāt*, 141.

41. Cf. Al-Qaraḍāwī, *Fiqh al-Awlawiyyāt*, 144.

42. Muslim, *Mukhtaṣar Ṣaḥīḥ Muslim*, 287, *ḥadīth* 1084.

43. Cf. Qaraḍāwī, *Fiqh al-Awlawiyyāt*, p. 137.

44. Ibn ʿĀbidīn, *Ḥāshiyah Ibn ʿĀbidīn*, ii, 114; Qalaʿjī, *Al-Iḥtiraf*, 35.

45. Suyūṭī, *Al-Jāmiʿ al-Ṣaghīr*, *ḥadīth* 176; Qaraḍāwī, *Fiqh al-Awlawiyyāt*, 106.

46. Suyūṭī, *Al-Jāmiʿ al-Ṣaghīr*, *ḥadīth* 2595.

47. Qaraḍāwī, *Fiqh al-Awlawiyyāt*, 106.

48. Muslim, *Mukhtaṣar Ṣaḥīḥ Muslim*, 491, *ḥadīth* 1859.

49. Muslim, *Mukhtaṣar Ṣaḥīḥ Muslim*, 264, *ḥadīth* 1001.

50. Abū Zahrah, *Tanẓīm al-Islām*, 51; Shīshānī, *Ḥuqūq al-Insān*, 509; al-Badawī, *Daʿāʾim al-Ḥukm*, 382.

51. Ibn Qayyim al-Jawziyyah, *Iʿlām*, iii, 147; Ibn Rushd, *Bidāyat al-Mujtahid*, ii, 111.

52. Al-Nawawī, *Rawḍat al-Ṭālibīn*; Dughmī, *Naẓariyyah*, 70–72.

53. Al-Bukhārī, *Ṣaḥīḥ al-Bukhārī*, K. al-Īmān, b. man faḍl man istabraʾ li-dīnih, *ḥadīth* 50; Muslim, *Ṣaḥīḥ Muslim*, K. al-Musaqat, b. akhdh al-ḥalāl wa-tark al-shubhat, *ḥadīth* 2996.

54. Cf. Shīshānī, *Ḥuqūq al-Insān*, 458.

55. Cf. Al-Shāṭibī, *Al-Iʿtiṣām*, ii, 300; Shīshānī, *Ḥuqūq al-Insān*, 457; Shāṭibī wrote that Ibn al-ʿArabī and Ghazālī held similar views.

56. Cf. Qalaʿjī, *al-Iḥtiraf*, 12.

57. Cf. Ibrāhīm al-Niʿmah, *al-ʿAmal waʾl-ʿUmmāl*, 26.

58. Al-Nawawī, *Rawḍat al-Ṭālibīn*, iii, 281; see also al-Dughmī, *Naẓariyyah*, 65.

59. Id., vii, 281.

60. Cf. Qaraḍāwī, *Fiqh al-Awlawiyyāt*, 119.

61. Cf. Qaraḍāwī, *Fiqh al-Awlawiyyāt*, 120.

62. Qaraḍāwī, *Min Fiqh al-Dawlah fiʾl-Islām*, 179-80.

63. Id., 182.

64. Id., 184, referring also to al-Shāṭibī, *al-Muwafaqāt*, ii, 94.

65. Qaraḍāwī, *Min Fiqh al-Dawlah*, 185.

66. al-Sulamī, *Qawāʿid al-Aḥkām*, i, 85.

67. Ibn Taymiyyah, *Majmuʿ Fatāwā Shaykh al-Islām Ibn Taymiyyah*, xxx, 356f.

68. Al-Suyūṭī, *Al-Jāmiʿ al-Ṣaghīr*, *ḥadīth* 1890.

69. Muslim, *Mukhtaṣar Ṣaḥīḥ Muslim*, 348, *ḥadīth* 1249.

70. ʿAbd al-Salām al-Sulamī, *Qawāʿid al-Aḥkām*, ii, 127.

71. Bukhārī, *Ṣaḥīḥ al-Bukhārī*, (Muhsin Khan's trans.) vol. ix, *ḥadīth* no. 252.

72. Id., vol. viii, *ḥadīth* 472.

73. Muslim, *Mukhtaṣar Ṣaḥīḥ Muslim*, 20, *ḥadīth* 54.

74. Muslim, *Mukhtaṣar Ṣaḥīḥ Muslim*, 328, *ḥadīth* 1204.

75. See for details Ibn Taymiyyah, *Al-Siyāsah al-Sharʿiyyah*, 8–9.

76. Cf. Ibn Qudāmah, *al-Mughnī*, v, 496; al-Badawī, *Daʿāʾim al-Ḥukm*, 414.

77. Cf. Al-Niʿmah, *Al-ʿAmal waʾl-ʿUmmāl*, 71.

78. Ibn Mājah, *Sunan Ibn Mājah*, ii, 817, *ḥadīth* no. 2443.

79. Cf. Shīshānī, *Ḥuqūq al-Insān*, 466–467.

80. Ibrāhīm al-Niʿmah, *al-ʿAmal waʾl-ʿUmmāl*, 48.

81. Al-Ghazālī also quotes a *ḥadīth* to the effect that as of the moment one intends to pay one's debt, God Most High appoints an angel, who guards the debtor and pray for his until he actually pays his debt. Ghazālī, *Iḥyāʾ*, ii, 83.

82. Ghazālī, *Iḥyāʾ*, ii, 83.

83. Tabrīzī, *Mishkāt*, vol. ii, *ḥadīth* 2790.

84. Abū Dāwūd, *Sunan*, K. al-Buyūʿ, b. fiʾl-matl, *ḥadīth* 3345; Kāsānī, *Badāʾiʿ*, ii, 910.

85. Ibn Mājah, *Sunan Ibn Mājah*, vol. ii, 1297.

86. Abu ʿUbayd, *Kitāb al-Amwāl* (Ghiffar's trans.), 4.

87. Al-Manāwī, *Fayẓ al-Qadīr*, vi, 88; al-Badawī, *Daʿāʾim al-Ḥukm*, 565.

88. Musaylihī, *Ḥuqūq al-Insān*, p. 153.

89. Ibn ʿAbd Rabbih, *Al-ʿAqd al-Farīd*, iii, 27.

90. Al-Saʿīd, *al-ʿAmal waʾl-Niẓām al-Ijtimāʿī fiʾl-Islām*, 57; Badawī, *Daʿāʾim al-Ḥukm*, 367.

91. Tabrīzī, *Mishkāt*, vol. ii, *ḥadīth* 2759.

92. Kāsānī, *Badāʾiʿ*, ii, 833; Dughmī, *Naẓariyyah*, 84.

93. Ibn ʿĀbidīn, *Ḥashiyah*, ii, 647.

94. Ibn ʿĀbidīn, *Ḥashiyah*, ii, 647; Qalaʿjī, *al-Iḥtiraf*, 37–38.

95. Nabhānī, *Al-Fatḥ al-Kabīr*, i, 418.

96. Ghazālī, *Iḥyāʾ*, ii, 84.

97. Id., ii, 85–86.

98. Id., ii, 87.

99. Id., ii, 87.

100. Ghazālī, *Iḥyāʾ*, ii, 88.

101. Id., ii, 88–89.

102. Ghazālī, *Iḥyāʾ*, ii, 76–77.

103. Id., ii, 77; Muslim, *Mukhtaṣar Ṣaḥīḥ Muslim*, 334, *ḥadīth* 1235.

104. Muslim, *Mukhtaṣar Ṣaḥīḥ Muslim*, p. 329, *ḥadīth* 1210; Ghazālī, *Iḥyāʾ*, ii, 77.

105. Id., II, 77; Tabrīzī, *Mishkāt*, vol. II, *ḥadīth* 2802.

106. Al-Ghazālī, *Iḥyā'*, vol. II, p. 78.

107. Id.

108. Id., II, 78.

109. al-Ghazālī thus quoted the *ḥadīth* recorded by Tirmidhī that when the Prophet bought something he would tell the person who weighed (in a barter sale) to 'weigh and give a little more—*zin wa arjiḥ*'.

110. Id., II, 80.

111. Tabrīzī, *Mishkāt*, vol. II, *ḥadīth* 3847.

112. Id., vol. II, *ḥadīth* 2849.

113. Id., vol. II, 80.

114. Cf. al-ʿAbūdī, *Al-Ḥurriyyat al-Ijtimāʿiyyah*, 84; al-Zuhaylī, *Ḥuqūq al-Insān*, 218 and 287.

115. Muṣaylihī, *Ḥuqūq al-Insān*, 154.

116. Shaltūt, *al-Islām, ʿAqīdah wa Sharīʿah*, 195.

117. See for details al-Shawāribī, *al-Ḥuqūq al-Siyāsiyyah li'l-Mar'ah fī'l-Islām*, 85ff.

118. Ibn Qudāmah, *Mughnī*, VII, 572; Qalaʿjī, *al-Iḥtirāf*, 35.

119. Qalaʿjī, *al-Iḥtirāf*, 35.

120. Cf. Id., 34.

121. *Ḥadīth* reported by all the major collections of *Ḥadīth* (i.e. *muttafaqun ʿalayhi*): Abū Dāwūd, *Sunan*, K. al-Kharāj wa'l-Imārah wa'l Fay', b. fī arzāq, *ḥadīth* 2954; Muḥammad al-Ghazālī, *Ḥuqūq al-Insān*, 134–35.

122. The *ʿulamā'* of India, *Al-Fatāwā al-Hindiyyah*, IV, 410; Qāḍīkhān al-Farghānī, *Fatāwā Qāḍīkhān*, on the margin of *Al-Fatāwā al-Hindiyyah*, II, 314; Badawī, *Daʿā'im*, 404.

123. Cf. Al-Nawawī, *Rawḍat al-Ṭālibīn*, V, 250; al-Dughmī, *Naẓariyyah*, 78.

124. Cf. al-Shīshānī, *Ḥuqūq al-Insān*, 535; Badawī, *Daʿā'im*, 404.

125. Abu ʿUbayd, *Kitāb al-Amwāl*, (Ghiffari's tr.), 490; Ṣanʿānī, *Subul al-Salām*, II, 143.

126. Cf. Qāḍīkhān, *Fatāwā Qāḍīkhān* on the margin of *al-Fatāwā al-Hindiyyah*, II, 314.

127. *Fatāwā al-Hindiyyah*, IV, 410; Shīshānī, *Ḥuqūq*, 477.

128. Id., VI, 429.

129. Kāsānī, *Badā'iʿ*, V, 2560.

130. Id.

131. Kāsānī, *Badā'iʿ*, V, 2560.

132. Id., V, 2564.

133. Id.

134. Kāsānī, *Badā'iʿ*, V, 2564–65.

135. Id, V, 2565–66; and VI, 2621.

136. See for further details on *wilāyah*, Kamali, *Islamic Law in Malaysia: Issues and Development*, 105f.

137. Id., v, 2565–66; and vi, 2621.

138. Ahwānī, *al-Tarbīyah fi'l-Islām*, 198; See for further detail on Qābisī the first chapter of volume on education.

139. Id., 199.

140. Māwardī, *Aḥkām*, 214; Dughmī, *Naẓariyyah*, 69; Mushtaq Ahmad, *Business Ethics*, 131.

141. Islahi, *Economic Concepts of Ibn Taymiyya*, 183.

142. Id., 179.

143. Muḥammad Abdul Rauf, *Ummah, the Muslim Nation*, 48-49.

144. Id., 52.

145. Id., p. 219. The report on ʿAbd Allāh b. al-Arqaṭ also appears in Kāsānī, *Badā'iʿ*, v, 2556.

146. Kāsānī, *Badā'iʿ*, v, 2561.

147. ʿAbd al-Hādī, *Al-Fikrah al-Idāriyyah al-Islāmiyyah*, 246; Mushtaq Ahmed, *Business Ethics*, 84.

148. Ibn Ḥazm, *Al-Muḥallā*, vi, 156; Shīshānī, *Ḥuqūq al-Insān*, 463.

149. Abū Zahrah, *Tanẓīm al-Mujtamaʿ*, 58.

150. Tabrīzī, *Mishkāt*, vol. ii, *ḥadīth* 3751; Abū Dāwūd, *Sunan Abū Dāwūd*, K. al-Kharāj wa'l-Imārah, b. fi arzāq al-ʿummāl, *ḥadīth* 2945. There is a slight but immaterial variation in the two available versions of this *ḥadīth*.

151. Sibāʿī, *al-Takāful*, 1.

152. Abū Dāwūd, *Sunan*, K. al-Kharāj wa'l-Imarat wa'l-Fay', b. fi ārzaq al-ʿummāl, *ḥadīth* 2943.

153. Id., *ḥadīth* 2944.

154. Ibn Nujaym, *Al-Ashbāh wa'l-Naẓā'ir*, 228; al-Dughmī, *Naẓariyyah*, 78.

155. Ibn Mājah, *Sunan*, ii, 816, *ḥadīth* no. 2442.

156. Cf. *Surah al-Qaṣaṣ*, 28:27.

157. Al-Niʿmah, *al-ʿAmal wa'l-ʿUmmal*, 40–42.

158. Al-Shawkānī, *Nayl al-Awṭār*, v, 293; Shīshānī, *Ḥuqūq al-Insān*, 464.

159. Kāsānī, *Badā'iʿ*, v, 2555.

160. Ibn Qudāmah, *Al-Mughnī*, v, 404.

161. Kāsānī, *Badā'iʿ*, v, 2630.

162. Id.

163. Id.

164. Id., v, 2631.

165. Al-Nawawī, *Rawḍat al-Ṭālibīn*, v, 160; al-Dughmī, *Naẓariyyah*, 71; Shīshānī, *Ḥuqūq al-Insān*, 465.

166. ʿIzz al-Dīn ʿAbd al-Salām, *Qawāʿid al-Aḥkām*, ii, 130; Dughmī, *Naẓariyyah*, 77.

167. Kāsānī, *Badā'i'*, v, 2569.

168. Kāsānī, *Badā'i'*, vi, 2606.

169. Id., vi, 2608–9.

170. Id., v, 2586.

171. Id., v, 2591.

172. Kāsānī, *Badā'i'*, v, 2999.

173. Id., vi, 2600.

174. Id., vi, 2602.

175. Cf. Kāsānī, *Badā'i'*, vi, 2603; Abū Zahrah, *Uṣūl al-Fiqh*, p. 219.

176. Kāsānī, *Badā'i'*, vi, 2603.

177. Kāsānī, *Badā'i'*, vi, 2604.

178. Islahi, *Economic Concepts of Ibn Taymiyya*, 84.

179. Ibn Taymiyyah, *Al-Ḥisbah fi'l-Islām*, 34; Islahi, *Economic Concepts*, 85.

180. Id. 179.

181. Cf. Iqbal, *Distributive Justice*, 18.

182. al-Ni'mah, *al-'Amal wa'l-'Ummāl*, 45.

183. Ghazālī, *Iḥyā'*, ii, 139; Bājī, *al-Muntaqā*, iv, 80.

184. Cf. Dughmī, *Naẓariyyah*, 79–80.

185. Ibn Rushd, *Bidāyah*, ii, 200; Ibn Ḥazm, *Al-Muḥallā*, viii, 249; Abū Zahrah, *Fi'l-Mujtama' al-Islāmī*, 58.

186. Cf. Shīshānī, *Ḥuqūq al-Insān*, 465.

187. Kāsānī, *Badā'i'*, vi, 2634.

188. Ibn Qayyim, *I'lām*, iv, 32; Kāsānī, *Badā'i'*, iv, 208.

189. Cf. Shīshānī, *Ḥuqūq al-Insān*, 520.

190. Al-Nawawī, *Rawḍat al-Ṭālibīn*, v, 16; al-Bājī, *Al-Muntaqā*, v, 114; Dughmī, *Naẓariyyah*, 76.

191. al-Ni'mah, *al-'Amal wa'l-'Ummāl*, 48–49.

192. Id., 108.

193. Kāsānī, *Badā'i'*, vi, 2646.

194. Id., vi, 2648.

195. Id.

196. Id.

197. Kāsānī, *Badā'i'*, vi, 2650.

198. Kāsānī, *Badā'i'*, vi, 2670.

199. Kāsānī, *Badā'i'*, vi, 2633–34.

200. Id., vi, 2636.

201. Id., vi, 2658.

202. Id., vi, 2659.

203. Id.

204. Id., vi, 2661.

205. Id., vi, 2660.

206. Id., vi, 2661.

207. Al-Māwardī, *Al-Aḥkām al-Sulṭāniyyah*, 255.

208. Ibn Qudāmah, *Al-Mughnī*, v, 496; al-Shīshānī, *Ḥuqūq al-Insān*, 466.

209. ʿIzz al-Dīn al-Sulamī, *Qawāʿid al-Aḥkām*, ii, 186; Dughmī, *Naẓariyyah*, 76.

210. Cf. Al-Nawawī, *Rawḍāt al-Ṭālibīn*, ix, 119; Dughmī, *Naẓariyyah*, 76.

211. Cf. Muḥammad al-Ghazālī, *Ḥuqūq al-Insān*, 258; al-ʿĪlī, *Ḥurriyyat*, 485; Badawī, *Daʿāʾim*, 402; Shīshānī, *Ḥuqūq al-Insān*, 478.

212. Muslim, *Mukhtaṣar Ṣaḥīḥ*, 238, ḥadīth 904; al-Shawkānī, *Nayl al-Awṭār*, vii, 3.

213. Musaylihī, *Ḥuqūq al-Insān*, 158.

214. Cf.Sibāʿī, *al-Takāful*, 157.

215. ʿIzz al-Dīn ʿAbd al-Salām, *Qawāʿid al-Ahkām*, ii, 128; Al-Nawawī, *Rawḍat al-Ṭālibīn*, v, 260.

216. Al-Suyūṭī, *Al-Jāmiʿ al-Ṣaghīr*, ii, 139, ḥadīth no. 5585.

217. Al-Suyūṭī, *Al-Jāmiʿ al-Ṣaghīr*, i, 603, and 202.

218. Nawawī, *Riyāḍ al-Ṣāliḥīn*, ḥadīth 153.

219. Tabrīzī, *Mishkāt*, vol. i, ḥadīth 181; Ghazālī, *Ḥuqūq al-Insān*, 202.

220. Bukhārī, *Ṣaḥīḥ al-Bukhārī* (Muhsin Khan's trans.), vol. viii, ḥadīth 76.

221. Sibāʿī, *al-Takāful*, 157.

222. Tabrīzī, *Mishkāt*, vol. i, 281.

223. Ibn Qayyim, *Zād al-Maʿād*, iii, 155; Shīshānī, *Ḥuqūq al-Insān*, 474.

224. Māwardī, *al-Aḥkām al-Sulṭāniyyah*, 257.

225. al-Qurshī, *Maʿālim*, p. 89; Shīshānī, *Ḥuqūq al-Insān*, 474.

226. Ibn Ḥazm, *Muḥallā*, vi, 156.

227. Cf. *Fatāwā Qāḍīkhān* on the margin of *al-Fatāwā al-Hindiyyah*, ii, 314; Shīshānī, *Ḥuqūq al-Insān*, 476.

228. Muslim, *Mukhtaṣar Ṣaḥīḥ Muslim*, 106, ḥadīth 286.

229. The original Arabic text of this document appears as an Appendix in Muḥammad al-Zuḥaylī's *Ḥuqūq al-Insān fiʾl-Islām*, 400-409 (in 25 Articles).

230. See for details Zuḥaylī, *Ḥuqūq al-Insān*, 291f.

231. Tabrīzī, *Mishkāt*, vol. iii, ḥadīth 5144; also quoted in Dughmī, *Naẓariyyah*, 90.

232. Abū Bakr al-Jazāʾirī, *Al-Dustūr al-Islāmī*, 63–65; Dughmī, *Naẓariyyah*, 90.

233. al-Niʿmah, *al-ʿAmal waʾl-ʿUmmāl*, 79.

234. Jamāl al-Bannā, *al-Islām waʾl Ḥarakah al-Naqābiyyah*, 68.

235. Id., 92.

236. Id., 107–111.

237. Jamāl al-Bannā, *Al-Islām waʾl-Ḥarakah al-Naqābiyyah*, 92–96.

238. See for details on *Siyāsah Sharʿiyyah* my article 'Siyasah Sharʿiyyah or the Policies of Islamic Government,' listed in the bibliography below.

239. Cf., Muṣayliḥī, *Ḥuqūq al-Insān*, 156.

240. Cf. Muṣayliḥī, *Ḥuqūq al-Insān*, 155.

241. Cf. Ibn Taymiyyah, *al-Siyāsah al-Sharʿiyyah*, 23 (chapter on *al-wilāyāt*).

242. Ibn Qayyim al-Jawziyyah, *Al-Ṭuruq al-Ḥukmiyyah*, 247.

243. Cf. Al-Ghazālī, *Iḥyā' ʿUlūm al-Dīn*, v, 174.

244. Ibn Taymiyyah, *Al-Siyāsah al-Sharʿiyyah*, 16; see also Dughmī, *Naẓariyyah*, p. 68; Zuḥaylī, *Ḥuqūq al-Insān*, 288.

245. Badawī, *Daʿā'im*, 387; Dughmī, *Naẓariyyah*, 68; Jazā'irī, *al-Dustūr al-Islāmī*, 62.

246. Cf. Qaraḍāwī, *Mushkilat al-Faqr*, 52.

247. Abū Zahrah, *Tanẓīm*, 55.

248. Zuḥaylī, *Ḥuqūq al-Insān*, 288ff.

249. See for details on *al-tasʿīr*, M. H. Kamali, 'Tasʿīr or Price Control in Islamic Law,' *The American J. of Islamic Social Sciences*, ii (1994), 25–38.

250. Cf. Al-Ghazālī, *Ḥuqūq al-Insān*, 187.

251. Abū Zahrah, *Tanẓīm al-Islām*, 51; Jarīshah, *Iʿlān al-Dustūr al-Islāmī*, 49.

252. Cf. Badawī, *Daʿā'im*, 390; Dughmī, *Naẓariyyah*, 69; Mushtaq Ahmad, *Business Ethics*, 31.

253. Cf. Al-Shīshānī, *Al-Ḥurriyyat al-ʿAmanah*, 521; Badawī, *Daʿā'im*, 391.

254. Cf. *al-Baqarah*, 2:273; *al-Ḥashr*, 59:8 and passim.

255. Ibn Ḥazm, *Al-Muḥallā*, vi, 156.

CHAPTER THREE

Right to Welfare
(*al-Takāful al-Ijtimāʿī*)

I. Introductory Remarks

Al-takāful ijtimāʿī (social support) also known in Arabic as *ḥaqq al-ḍamān al ijtimāʿī* (right to social security) refers to the right of the individual to the necessities of life. *Takāful* in Arabic means mutual *kafālah*, or mutual guarantee of social help within the community. It is a right of the citizen vis-à-vis the community and state which remains dormant in the event the community does not possess the means to support its members, but it becomes active when the state does have the necessary means at its disposal. The right exists only in respect of individuals who are unable to support themselves and unable to earn their living. The right to social security is also closely related to the individual's contribution to the common wealth through productive activity and work.

Everyone who contributes when he can is entitled to welfare support, not only in old age but also at times when he or she may be unable to work and may not have the resources to support himself and his dependants. Workers who fall victim to illness, accident and disability may be forced to stay away from work, just as there will be cases where a person is fit and willing to work but unable to find a suitable employment, in which case he or she would have a right to social assistance from public funds. And then the right to social support is naturally not confined to workers, but extends to individuals who may be afflicted with poverty and disease, or such other conditions that undermine their ability to earn a living.

This would not only include the elderly and the disabled but also those who might be responsible for their care and service as well as those who look after a child or take care of a dependant who would otherwise be left without help. The evidence reviewed in the following pages indicates that the support in *Sharīʿah* for a welfare system for all citizens is independent of such considerations as race, colour and creed. There is also a certain entitlement for those who die in poverty as the *Sharīʿah* makes it a collective obligation of the community to give them a decent burial and the expenditure that is incurred as a result constitutes a charge on the public treasury.

The social system of Islam can be seen to be operative in four areas, beginning with the family unit, then the community at large, followed by cooperation among smaller groups and associations such as neighbors and local residents, and lastly support given through the legal payments of alms *(zakāh)*, and voluntary charities.

Islamic law has devised an elaborate system of family support which entitles close relatives to maintenance *(nafaqah)* among themselves. The duty is naturally addressed to the affluent members of the family to help their needy relatives. Should there be no resources within the family, the duty falls on the community and can be fulfilled through the levy of *zakāh* and other taxes. *Zakāh* is basically designed to cater for the needs of the poor and certain other categories of individuals whom the law has specifically identified. These two levels of support have been specified in the Qurʾān and can, at least partially, be operative, whether one lived in a Muslim majority state or a minority Muslim community. There are, however, certain sub-varieties of *zakāh*, such as the tithes and tax on mineral resources, etc., which would be difficult to administer without government intervention. The other two levels of social support that Islam has envisaged also address the individual believer and can once again be operative anywhere. They consist basically of voluntary and recommended charities, charitable endowments, the *fiṭr* obligatory donations, and the expiations *(kaffārāt)* which can be given directly to the poor even independently of a government. But the welfare system that is expounded in the following pages is for the most part predicated on the state and its administrative machinery, some basic charities can be given individually, but a social welfare system involving collection and distribution of funds would seem to necessitate a governmental framework.

The discussion that follows begins with a review of basic evidence in the Qurʾān and *Sunnah* on social cooperation and fraternity in

Islam. This is followed in section three by an analysis of welfare, and the contributions of jurists and economists to the debate on social justice and the criteria of asset distribution in the Muslim community. The discussion continues in section four to expound family support system as manifested in the obligatory rules of maintenance (*nafaqah*), and criteria of entitlement to such support. Section five examines the rules of *zakāh* and criteria of its collection and distribution, which is followed in the succeeding section, by a similar account of the *fiṭr* and *Aḍḥā* charities, and a series of similar items of revenue that accrue upon agricultural produce, mineral resources, and escheats etc. The succeeding section addresses voluntary charities, especially the charitable endowments of *awqāf* which have historically played a significant role in the provision of welfare benefits. This is followed by a brief review of the expiations (*kaffārāt*), and then a similarly brief description of the public treasury (*bayt al-māl*) as an instrument of welfare assistance, collection and distribution of assets in the fiscal system of Islam.

II. Affirmative Evidence

The Qur'ān provides basic authority for the individual's right, not just to a minimum, but to an adequate level of subsistence and support. The Qur'ānic proclamations on this subject have in turn been endorsed and elaborated by the *Sunnah* of the Prophet, and then the practice of Pious Caliphs after him. The *Sunnah* that is examined in the following pages consists basically of sayings and instructions that the Prophet issued in his Prophetic capacity, and those which he might have issued in his capacity as the Imam and first head of the Islamic state of Medina. It is admittedly difficult to draw a clear distinction between the two, yet some of the *hadīth*s that are reviewed below were evidently pronounced in the latent capacity of the Prophet as the head of state, which he became after some thirteen years of the beginning of his prophetic mission. It then becomes even more important to note that in his capacity as the head of state the Prophet saw it as a firm commitment of his community and state to protect the citizens of Medina against poverty and disease. The textual evidence that is examined here consists both of general declarations as well as specific provisions in the Qur'ān and *Sunnah* on welfare assistance. The general provisions shall be reviewed first before moving on to examining the more specific aspects of textual guidelines on the subject.

The Qur'ānic declaration on dignity (*karāmah*) as a natural right of all human beings also implies, in addition to the spiritual dimensions of dignity, the individual's right to an honourable life. Personal dignity is seriously compromised in the face of crushing poverty and degradation. The right to dignity therefore envisages a concomitant right to the provision of basic needs. The general Qur'ānic declaration on human dignity, quoted below, may even be said to have actually contemplated this conclusion:

ولقد كرّمنا بني آدم وحملناهم في البر والبحر ورزقناهم
من الطيبات وفضلناهم على كثير ممن خلقنا تفضيلا

We have bestowed dignity on the progeny of Adam. We carry them on land and sea and have made provision of good things for them, and have given them distinction above many of those whom We created. (17:70)

The fact that reference to human dignity in the first clause of this text is followed, in the second clause, by a reference to the provision of 'good things' and transportation on land and sea is indicative of a certain linkage between human dignity and the provision of necessities through the utilisation of resources and commerce. God tells mankind, in other words, that 'your dignity' is achieved through 'your effort and success' in the realisation of a decent standard of living. The Qur'ān also declares in a number of places that man's natural environment has been endowed with vast potential to nurture for human needs but that man would need to make the effort to turn that potential into reality.

Textual allusions of this kind, in turn, form a basis of responsibility for everyone to engage in productive activity so as to cater for his own needs. It is a shared responsibility of the individual and community also to utilise the resources of the earth for welfare purposes:

ولقد مكّنّاكم في الأرض وجعلنا لكم فيها معايش قليلا ماتشكرون

And We have given you (mankind) power in the earth, and appointed for you therein a livelihood. Little do you thank! (7:10)

To thank God for His grace and generosity relates to the proper use of the power that man has been endowed with. The Prophet is reported to have said in this connection: 'The world is green and pleasant and God has put it under your charge to see how you will manage'[1]

إن الدنيا حلوة خضرة وإن الله مستخلفكم فيها فينظر كيف تعملون

The Qur'ān and *Sunnah* thus make it a joint responsibility of both the individual and community to ensure that they apply themselves and work to harness the resources of the earth, to meet their own welfare needs, and by doing so also make the world a pleasant place to live. The collective aspect of this responsibility also features elsewhere in the Qur'ān where the text enjoins cooperation (*ta'āwun*) in beneficial work. That is one way in which people can be more effective, not only in meeting their practical needs, but also in aspiring to high ideals and acting in way that is more meaningful and conducive to human dignity. To quote the text:

وتعاونوا على البرّ والتقوى ولا تعاونوا على الإثم والعدوان

Co-operate with one another in good work (*al-birr*) and righteousness (*al-taqwā*) and cooperate not in transgression and hostility (5:2).

Cooperation in good work naturally includes economic cooperation and mutual support in all worthwhile pursuits that are meaningful to the individual and promote the people's welfare. Cooperation in good work can, of course, extend to such other areas of concern as combating criminality and fighting for human rights. Cooperation as such is therefore not confined to a strictly religious framework. The address here is also to all people, Muslims and non-Muslims, and all who can cooperate in pursuit of a worthy cause. Muslims and non-Muslims can join hands in charitable and humanitarian work, indeed in all beneficial work. The word *al-birr* (good deeds) in the Qur'ān carries the meaning of being good in dealing with others, especially with one's parents (19:32); it also means performance of the obligatory duties of prayer and *zakāh* (2:44). Yet the most explicit meaning of *al-birr* is found in the verse which begins with these words: 'You shall not attain *al-birr* unless you spend of that which you love, and God is aware of whatever you spend (in His cause).' (3:92)

لن تنالوا البر حتى تنفقوا مما تحبون وما تنفقوا من شيئ

فإن الله به عليم

The other key term in the verse under review is *al-taqwā* (righteousness) which is a broad term that carries a variety of meanings, including honesty and truthfulness (39:33), uprightness of character (5:8); due fulfillment of promises (9:4), but also helping others in their moments of need, giving to the poor (51:19) and giving sacrifice with one's property and in personal deeds (9:44).

Elsewhere the Qur'ān characterises the Muslim community as one in which care and protection must become the driving force of its unity. It is also significant that the text on this subject makes this a shared responsibility of men and women alike:

والمؤمنون والمؤمنات بعضهم أولياء بعض يأمرون

بالمعروف وينهون عن المنكر ويقيمون الصلوة ويؤتون

الزكوة

And the believers, men and women, are protecting friends (*awliyā'*) of one another. They enjoin good and they prevent evil, they establish prayer and they give charity. (9:71)

'Protective friendship' or *wilāyah* is taken a step further in another place where the text declares the believers to be related to one another in a bond of fraternity: 'Truly the believers are brethren. So help your brethren to live in peace with one another' (49:10).

إنما المؤمنون إخوة فأصلحوا بين أخويكم

'To live in peace' with one another in an atmosphere of fraternity is not possible in the face of crushing poverty and abundant wealth side by side. Fraternity must therefore mean that the needy is entitled to welfare assistance through equitable distribution of wealth.

The Qur'ān has imposed the *zakāh* on affluent members of the community for the purpose specifically to meet the needs of the poor. The importance of *zakāh* is manifested in the fact that references to *zakāh* in the Qur'ān occur side by side with obligatory prayers (*ṣalāh*) and it is, like the *ṣalāh*, a pillar of the Muslim faith. To give charity and pay *zakāh* manifests one's sincerity in faith. These are the pillars of fraternity in the Qur'ān where the text speaks about the disbelievers in such terms that 'if they repent, perform the prayers, and pay the *zakāh*, they become your brethren in the faith.' (9:11)

فإن تابوا وأقاموا الصلوة وآتوا الزكوة فإخوانكم في الدين

In a similar vein, the Qur'ān describes as '*muḥsinīn*' (people of excellent character) 'those who perform the *ṣalāh*, pay the *zakāh* and believe in the Last Day'. (Luqmān, 31:3)

الذين يقيمون الصلوة ويؤتون الزكوة وهم بالآخرة هم يوقنون

The obligatory character of *zakāh* is also conveyed in the clear injunction of the text wherein the Prophet was addressed to 'Take from their (the wealthy) assets the alms, so that they are cleansed and purified by it'. (9:103)

خذ من أموالهم صدقة تطهّرهم وتزكّيهم بها وصلّ عليهم
إن صلوتك سكن لهم

The personal wealth of a Muslim thus remains unpurified unless the *zakāh* is duly paid out of it. The text also implies that poverty and need constitute the grounds of entitlement to financial support from the revenues of *zakāh*. Yet there is no indication in the text to suggest that *zakāh* would be sufficient to eliminate poverty. This is confirmed by the fact that the Qur'ān and *Sunnah* impose other taxes, in addition to *zakāh*, so as to provide additional support for the poor. These include war booty (*ghanīmah* and *fay'*) as in the following verse:

مآ أفآء الله على رسوله من أهل القرى فلله وللرسول
ولذي القربي واليتمى والمساكين وابن السبيل كي لايكون
دولة بين الأغنياء منكم. . . للفقراء المهاجرين الذين
أخرجوا من ديارهم وأموالهم

What God has bestowed as spoil *(fay')* unto His Messenger (and taken away) from the people of the townships belongs to God and His Messenger, and for the near of kin and the orphan, the needy and the wayfarer, in order that it may not (merely) make a circuit between the wealthy among you. . . it is for the poor fugitives who have been driven away from their homes and their belongings. (59:7–8)

This verse legalises *fay'*, that is, wealth received from the enemy without engaging in combat, such as ransom money, that is given in order to prevent war, or indeed other assets that are surrendered without fighting. All of this is payable to the public treasury (*bayt al-māl*) to be spent, in turn, on welfare purposes, as the text itself has specified.

Fay' is technically different from *ghanīmah*, the latter consists of war booty of movable items that is taken from the enemy as a result of fighting. On this the Qur'ān also provides that one-fifth of it is 'assigned to God, to the Messenger, to the near kin, the orphans, the needy and the wayfarer.' (8:41)

One-fifth of the war booty is thus allocated for welfare purposes and the remaining four-fifths were to be given to the soldiers themselves. This is explained by the fact that during the Prophet's lifetime there was no organised army and the warrior themselves bore the costs of war, hence they took four-fifth of the *ghanīmah* as remuneration and compensation for actual expenditures. The *fay'* revenues were, on the other hand, to be entirely spent on welfare assistance whereas only a fifth of *ghanīmah* was assigned to welfare purposes. These two items of revenue, together with the obligatory *zakāh*, constituted the principal income of the *bayt al-māl* during the time of the Prophet and that of the Pious Caliphs, but the significance of war booty as an item of revenue dwindled in course of time as wars of conquest gradually subsided. We do not therefore propose to delve into the details of *fay'* and *ghanīmah* as they are no longer practiced and institutionalised armies are nowadays recruited and maintained independently of revenues from booty.[2]

The Qur'ān provides direct authority which entitles the poor to basic welfare assistance—as in the following verse:

وفي أموالهم حقّ للسائل والمحروم

And in their wealth there is a right (*ḥaqqun*) for the destitute and the deprived. (51:19)

The text here simply establishes 'a right' for those in need in the wealth of the affluent but does not say what this right actually involves. *Zakāh* is certainly included in this 'right' but it seems that the right in question is not confined to *zakāh*. The right of the poor in the wealth of the rich naturally implies a corresponding duty on the part of the latter, and by extension on the state, to provide the poor with basic necessities. It is also understood from the general language of the text that every 'poor and deprived' person, regardless of race, age, religion and status in life is entitled to the basic necessities of life.[3]

While *zakāh* is a duty to be enforced, the Qur'ān also recommends voluntary help to the indigent and speaks in praise of those

(1) Who remain patient in times of affliction, they are steadfast in prayer and spend willingly of what We have given them. (22:34)

والصابرين على ما أصابهم والمقيمى الصلوة ومما رزقهم ينفقون

(2) And those who feed, for the love of God, the poor, the orphan and the captive. (76:8)

ويطعمون الطعام على حبه مسكينا ويتيما وأسيرا

The Prophet has also described his own mission as one that seeks to accomplish high moral objectives:

بعثت لأتمم حسن الأخلاق

I have been sent in order to accomplish that which is morally virtuous.[4]

The right to social support is evidently grounded in Islam's commitment to moral virtue. For it is immoral and unjust to deny support to those who may have fallen victim to adversity, especially when they have shown to be assiduous and hard working, and those who have contributed to public welfare when they had the ability to do so. This moral purpose is further accentuated in a *ḥadīth* where the Prophet resembled the Muslim community to an edifice which can only stand firm when all of its parts support one another:

المؤمن للمؤمن كالبنيان يشدّ بعضه بعضا

The believers are to one another like a building in which its various parts support and reinforce one another[5]

The same message is conveyed even more vividly in another *ḥadīth*:

$$\text{مثل المؤمنين في توادهم وتراحمهم وتعاطفهم مثل الجسد}$$
$$\text{إذا اشتكى منه عضو تداعى له سائر الجسد}$$

In their love, compassion and cooperation for each other the believers are like the different organs of a body; when a single organ is afflicted with pain, the rest is visited by restlessness and fever.[6]

In yet another *ḥadīth*, the Prophet addressed his followers in the following terms:

$$\text{لايؤمن أحدكم حتى يحب لأخيه ما يحب لنفسه}$$

None of you is a (true) believer unless he loves for his brother that which he loves for himself.[7]

The wider fraternity of mankind is the subject of another *ḥadīth* where the Prophet declared the people, and not just the believers, as one family related to one another through their Creator:

$$\text{الناس عيال الله، أحبهم إلى الله أرحمهم لعياله}$$

People are God's children and those dearest to God are the ones who treat His children with kindness.[8]

In his capacity as the head of state, the Prophet verified his commitment to the welfare, particularly of his employees, when he said:

$$\text{من كان لنا عاملا ولم يكن له سكن فليتخذ مسكنا، ومن}$$
$$\text{لم يكن له زوج فليتخذ زوجا، ومن لم يجد خادما}$$
$$\text{فليتخذ خادما، ومن لم يجد دابة فليتخذ دابة، ومن اتخذ}$$
$$\text{غير ذلك فهو غال أو سارق}$$

When someone takes employment with us and has no dwelling, let him take a dwelling (with the help of *bayt al-māl*); if he is unmarried let him get married, and if he has no beast for riding then let him acquire one, but one who takes more than that is either fraudulent or a thief.[9]

The fact that the worker is entitled not only to his wages but also to a shelter, transport and even marriage tends to go beyond the familiar heads of benefits that workers are entitled to even in our own times. This is indicative of Islam's unusually strong commitment to people's welfare. The workers' welfare needs are thus to be met by rewarding them adequately for their achievements and the contribution they make to the common good.

Poverty and depravition are evils that eat not only into the material assets of men but also into their moral integrity and faith. This is the clear message of a *ḥadīth* in which the Prophet made the following supplication:

اللهم إني أعوذ بك من الكفر والفقر

O God! I seek refuge to Thee from disbelief and poverty.[10]

The juxtaposition of disbelief and poverty in this *ḥadīth* tends to suggest as if poverty can lead to disbelief. Islam has admittedly an ascetic side to its teachings which does not encourage over-indulgence in materialist pursuits at the expense of spiritual awareness, but this should not be equated with condoning poverty, as the *ḥadīth* just reviewed clearly testifies.

The basic commitment of an Islamic system of government to the welfare of its citizens is borne out in a number of *ḥadīth*s, as quoted below, in which the Prophet-cum-head of state spoke of himself as the protector and guardian of those who need protection:

الله ورسوله مولى من لا مولى له

God and His Messenger are the guardians of one who has no guardian.[11]

السلطان ولي من لا مولى له

The ruler is the guardian of one who has no guardians.[12]

من ترك مالا فلأهله ومن ترك ضياعا فإليّ وعليّ

One who leaves behind property, it shall belong to his heirs, but if he leaves a debt or dependents in need, they shall be my responsibility.[13]

من ولّاه الله شيئا من أمر المسلمين فاحتجت دون حاجتهم وخلتهم وفقرهم احتجب الله عنه دون حاجته وخلته وفقره

He whom God Almighty has made administrator over the affairs of Muslims and he turns his back on their needs, their necessities and their poverty, God will turn His back on his needs, necessities and poverty.[14]

The Prophet is also reported to have said:

وأيما أهل عرصة أصبح منهم أمرؤ جائع فقد برئت منهم ذمة الله تعالى

The inhabitants of a locality wherein a person is inflicted with hunger have no claim to the clemency of God Most High.[15]

According to yet another *ḥadīth* reported by ʿAlī b. Abī Ṭālib, the Prophet said:

إن الله فرض على أغنياء المسلمين في أموالهم بقدر الذي يسع فقرهم ولن يجهدوا الفقراء إذا جاعوا وعروا إلا بما يصنع أغنيائهم، ألا وإن الله يحاسبهم حسابا شديدا ويعذبهم عذابا أليما

God has made it obligatory on the wealthy among Muslims to give to the poor to the extent of their need. If the poor starves or goes unclad it is because of the conduct of the wealthy among them. Beware that God the Almighty and the Exalted will take a stern account from them and punish them with a painful punishment.[16]

The *ḥadīth* literature is replete with directives and advice on the subject of assisting the poor. The overall message that is conveyed is that the Muslim community, including the individuals and the state, are responsible for the poor among them. In its capacity as the community's representative, the state is consequently under an obligation to support and protect the poor.[17] Muslim jurists have consequently concluded that it is a responsibility of the Imam to collect the *zakāh*, if necessary by force, and ensure its distribution among those entitled to it. For this is what the Prophet did himself when he appointed *zakāh* collectors and sent them to places to collect the *zakāh*. The Pious Caliphs did the same after him, and the first Caliph Abū Bakr went so far as to wage war on those who refused to pay the *zakāh*.

The state responsibility to provide for the poor is also indicated in a report that the Prophet's daughter Fāṭimah, who was married to ʿAlī, asked her father if she could be provided with a servant. The Prophet declined her request and said:

لاأعطيكم وأدع أهل الصفة يلوى بطونهم من الجوع

> I shall not grant this while the Ahl al-Ṣuffa (a group of poor immigrants who slept in the mosque for lack of shelter) suffer from hunger and I do not find enough to cater for them.[18]

Bilāl al-Ḥabashī, the muezzin of the Prophet, who was also in charge of giving assistance to the poor, spoke in response to a question put to him by a fellow Companion, ʿAbd Allāh al-Hāzani as follows:

كنت أنا الذى ألي ذلك منذ بعثه الله إلى أن توفى، وكان إذا أتاه الإنسان مسلما فرأه عاريا يأمرنى فأنطلق فاستقرض فاشترى له البردة فأكسوه وأطعمه

> I was in charge of the *nafaqāt* (expenditures) ever since the beginning of the Prophet's mission until his demise. Whenever an unclad human being and Muslim came to him, he would order me to see to his needs. I would often borrow and buy clothes for him and feed him.[19]

This *ḥadīth* indicates that the needs of the poor were given priority even if it meant recourse to borrowing at times when Prophet had no funds to give at his disposal. The social support system that the *Sharī'ah* has envisaged is, however, meant only for those who are unable to fend for themselves. The conclusion is thus drawn that the collective duty that is addressed to the Muslim community and state does not obtain in the case of those who are not poor and those who are fit to work to earn a living, but who refuse to pull their weight. This is the purport of the following *ḥadīth*:

> One who begs others for help when he has enough to get by verily exceeds the limits.[20]

من سأل منكم وله أوقية أو عدلها فقد سألها إلحافا

We may repeat the following *ḥadīth* which we reviewed in the previous chapter.

> Begging (or receiving charity) is not permitted except in three cases: for one who has to pay indemnity to others, begging is permitted for him until he pays up and then he stops; for one who is struck by a calamity that wipes out his wealth; begging is permitted for him until he gets enough to subsist; and then for one who is starving and three persons of sound character from his people confirm it. Begging is then permitted for him until he has obtained enough to support himself.[21]

In response to a question whether the contents of the above *ḥadīths* apply equally to those who ask the ruler (*sulṭān*) for financial help, Muslim jurists have held that asking the ruler for help is permitted for anyone who has a right in the *bayt al-māl*. This is because the ruler is a representative (*wakīl*) of the people; it would be as if a person asks his own *wakīl* for help to be given from assets deposited with the latter. It thus appears that asking the ruler for help is permissible.[22]

One of the conclusions drawn from the foregoing *ḥadīths* is that a debtor, or one who has to pay blood money (*diyyah*) for unintentional homicide or reconciliation money to another may be assisted from the funds of *bayt al-māl* even if he is not on the bread line. Similarly those who lose their assets due to natural calamities and they are left in penury and need may be assisted from the funds of *bayt al-māl*. And lastly a person who is left penniless due to losses in business is similarly entitled to assistance from the public treasury after producing three witnesses to confirm it.[23]

The basic guideline remains, however, that able-bodied people who can help themselves must avoid asking others for help. It is reported that whenever persons who could work to earn a living approached the Prophet for charity, he politely refused to oblige. 'On one occasion when he was distributing charity two men approached him and asked if they could be given something. The Prophet looked at them only to find that they both looked fit and capable and were consequently told that they were not entitled to receive charity but if they insisted he could give them (something)'.[24]

The Prophet encouraged able-bodied individuals to earn their living through work. Thus he helped a man to sell his belongings, a quilt and a bowl, to buy an axe with which to cut wood. The man complied with the Prophet's advice and prospered as a result. A conclusion is drawn from this and similar other *ḥadīths* that the government is authorised to order able-bodied individuals to take up employment. The government should facilitate this and help the unemployed by providing them with the tools of trade, if they have any skill, so that they can earn their living and be productive.[25]

The Prophet put it succinctly on another occasion:

$$طلب كسب الحلال فريضة$$

To earn one's living through lawful means is an obligation.[26]

This has been further specified in another *ḥadīth* earlier quoted: 'any of you who resorts to begging while he possesses an *awqīyah* or its equivalent would be committing a transgression.'[27]

III. An Historical Sketch

A public welfare programme has been in force since the very early days of the inception of the Islamic State of Medina as welfare service was seen a vital duty of the State.[28] As an inalienable part of Islam, public welfare remained to be given a high priority in the state programme and policies. The precedent of the Pious Caliphs clearly exhibited a basic commitment to public welfare. The second caliph 'Umar evidently saw it as his duty to support the poor and ensure a fair distribution of wealth in the community. The caliph thus declared that God Most High had charged him with the responsibility of preventing the people from asking God for financial help. ʿIzz al-Dīn ʿAbd al-Salām al-Sulamī who quoted the caliph ʿUmar on this drew the conclusion that the ruler is responsible to fulfill the needs of the people so that they are not compelled to pray to God for the fulfillment of their needs.[29] The caliph evidently made this rather unusual statement with the purpose to address the issue of poverty entirely on its material grounds. If there is a spiritual aspect to poverty, it was not to be confounded with ʿUmar's positivist stand on the matter. The caliph has also been reported to have stated in a public address that everyone had an equal right in the community's wealth and that if he lived long enough, he would ensure that even the shepherd in Mount Sinai received his due share from that wealth.[30] Furthermore, the caliph made the following statement during the year of the famine in Medina:

> If I had no money to fulfill the needs of the people and the only way left were to make every household share their provisions with an equal number, everyone being only half fed until God gave us rain, I would have done so. For men can still survive on half the food that they need.[31]

Reports indicate that during the time of the caliph ʿUmar b. al-Khaṭṭāb, the state revenues were increased and he consequently established a state register (*dīwān*) for a regular system of distribution of the cash grants (*al-aʿṭīyah*) and distribution of foodstuffs (*arzāq*) such as wheat, oil and vinegar to deserving individuals and families. The assistance scheme also included salaries (*waẓāʾif*) that were paid to civil servants as well as those who were engaged in military service. The needs of the individuals, the number of people per household, and the number of children were taken into consideration in these allocations.[32] The caliph also made it known that anyone in need of support should approach him directly: 'Whoever wants to ask me for financial assistance should come to me. For God has entrusted me to be the keeper of (His) treasury and its disburser.'[33]

The Caliph was so conscious of his responsibility that he thought it applicable even to animals: 'if a camel dies unattended on the bank of the Euphrates, I am afraid God would hold me accountable for it.'[34]

The Dīwān register contained the names of the beneficiaries with the relevant details. The beneficiaries were issued with pension cards and ration cards which contained the name of the beneficiary, his tribe, and the amount of entitlement. Mobility of the population as well as births, deaths and other changes called for frequent revision of the Dīwān listings which was undertaken at intervals. The Caliph had intended to extend these benefits to the entire population but this objective was not realised due to insufficiency of resources. The list of beneficiaries in the Dīwān, although extended consistently to cover larger numbers 'never covered the whole population.'[35] Caliph ʿUmar was also the first to fix rations and set up ration depots where foodstuffs such as flour, dates, raisins and other provisions were stored for free distribution to the general public as well as wayfarers, visitors and guests.[36]

As already noted, evidence in the *Sunnah* suggests personal need to be the valid criterion of welfare assistance at the expense even of some quantitative inequality:

عن عوف بن مالك أن رسول الله صلى الله عليه وسلم
كان إذا أتاه الفيء قسمه في يومه، فأعطى الآهل حظين
وأعطى العزب حظا. . . فدعينا وكنت أدعى قبل أدعى
عمار فدعيت فأعطانى حظين وكان لى أهل، ثم دعى
بعدى عمار بن يسار فأعطى له حظا واحدا

ʿAwf b. Mālik reported that the Prophet used to distribute the revenues of *fay'* (from conquered lands) on the day of arrival. He gave a married man double the portion of a single. 'So I and ʿUmmār bin Yasār went and I received double the portion of ʿUmmār as I was married but he was not.'[37]

The early Caliphs apparently saw welfare assistance an integral part of their moral commitment and piety. This is perhaps vividly conveyed in the following report:

The caliph ʿUmar b. ʿAbd al-ʿAzīz was once found anguished and weeping, and when asked as to the cause of his distress he gave the following answer: 'I have taken charge of the affairs of the community of Muḥammad. I am apprehensive about the predicament of the hungry and poor, the unattended sick, the warrior in the cause of God, the oppressed, the prisoner in alien lands, the very old, and those with many dependants but who have little money. . . '[38] And then the same Caliph is reported to have addressed the people to assure them that he would try as best as he could to meet the needs of 'anyone of you to the extent possible whenever it comes to my notice.'[39] Reports also indicate that the caliph ʿUmar b. al-Khaṭṭāb and ʿUmar b. ʿAbd al-ʿAzīz both appointed salaried employees to serve the blind and the invalid. The former is also reported to have provided transport for the needy and the latter has provided financial grants for young persons to get married.[40]

Saʿd Ibn al-Waqāṣ, governor of Egypt under the caliph ʿUmar b. al-Khaṭṭāb commented concerning the latter: 'He gives a camel if someone loses his own, gives a servant if someone lacks one, gives money if someone is in need of it.' Ziyād the governor of Iraq under ʿUmar I also declared in his first speech 'I shall not hide myself if a needy person comes to me even in the middle of night.'[41]

There is also evidence to suggest that state assistance was extended, as a matter of priority to those who were enlisted in the military service. During the time of ʿUmar b. al-Khaṭṭāb and his successors, it was generally recognised that regular pensions presupposed military service in the past, present or future. Those who received a pension also presupposed it as a moral obligation to discharge military service whenever they were called upon to do so.[42] Traders were excluded from the list because they could not devote themselves to war. When ʿAbd al-Malik (d. 86/705) ordered the dispatch of an army unit to Khurasan, the pensioners transferred their pensions to those who could represent them on the battlefield. Umar II issued orders which entitled the army to fixed pensions, but for the rest of the population, he gave priority to townsmen over countrymen because the latter did not participant in war efforts.[43] This was in line with the precedent of ʿUmar I who also gave priority in pension allocations to town dwellers who rendered military service. As for the distribution of foodstuffs, Zaman has quoted al-Baladhurī in support of the conclusion that these were actually meant for all Muslims.[44] This would suggest that pension benefits were extended on the basis of need. A merit based pension system seems to have been in operation even earlier when it is noted that generous pensions were allocated to the Prophet's widows and relatives, those who participated in the battles of Badr and Uḥud (and their sons) or those who migrated to Abyssinia and later accompanied the Prophet to Medina.[45]

The Prophet's widow ʿĀ'ishah headed the list with a pension of 12,000 dirhams a year. After the Prophet's family (*the ahl al-bayt*) came the Emigrants and Helpers, each with a pension according to his precedence in embracing Islam. About 4,000 to 5,000 dirhams per annum was the average allotment to each person in this category.

At the bottom came the mass of Arabian tribes arranged in the register according to military service and knowledge of the Qur'ān. The minimum for an ordinary warrior was 500–600 dirhams; even women, children and clients (*mawālī*) were included in the register and received annuities ranging from 200 to 600 dirhams.[46] When it is remembered that a master builder in those days (and even much later into the Umayyad period) could be hired for a dirham a day and the ordinary labourer for about a third of a dirham, it becomes clear how relatively generous these pensions and annunities were.[47]

Abū ʿUbayd has observed that the caliph ʿUmar I entitled the countrymen to *fay'* but he did not grant them regular pensions as he did in the case of town dwellers. Instead, he, like the Prophet, peace be on him, supported them whenever they fell in need. It is then added that ʿUmar I had intended eventually to extend welfare assistance equally to all Muslims, and that this was what he actually did in the year of the famine.[48] By the time of ʿAbd al-Malik (d. 86/705) a large number of the Companions who were on high pensions had died and with that the inequality in the scale of pension allocations had also been narrowed down. A sizeable number of villagers joined townsmen and volunteered for military service and the number of beneficiaries expanded as a result.[49]

ʿUmar I gave rations to the people of the suburbs of Medina to which his successor ʿUthmān added clothes. ʿUmar had also entitled the Qur'ān memorisers to fixed allowances which he later discontinued. The Umayyad Caliph Muʿāwiyah (d. 60 AH) entitled to a hospitality allowance those who had entertained guests, and Walīd b. ʿAbd al-Malik (d. 96 AH) added to the list of beneficiaries all the destitute and invalid persons. The caliph ʿAlī had earlier increased the pensions of his followers in Iraq whereas Muʿāwiyah scaled down the pensions of honour (*sharaf*) by a substantial amount. ʿUmar II granted an allowance for pilgrimage to the *ḥajj* and continued the earlier policy of giving allowance to the destitute and the weak. He is also reported to have spent public funds in bearing the marriage expenses of the poor.[50] ʿUmar II abolished in the meantime the practice of giving allowances to the newborn but entitled them to a fixed sum from the age of weaning. He also discontinued special pensions to the privileged.[51]

The Prophet and the caliph Abū Bakr distributed the revenues equally, but ʿUmar I took into consideration personal merit and contribution in the entitlement to pensions and benefits although he also wanted to move in the direction of equality. After caliph ʿUmar the higher scale of pensions could not be curtailed for fear of resentment of their recipients most of whom were senior Companions. But they could not be increased due to scarce resources. Notwithstanding this element of constraint, the caliph ʿAlī maintained equality in all other distributions. Somewhat similar to what the Prophet had done, ʿAlī expedited distribution of funds whenever they became available. There are reports of instances where he distributed revenues received from outlying provinces within days of arrival and entitled everyone to an equal share.[52] Muʿāwiyah seems to have followed this precedent. On one occasion he is reported to have addressed the people and announced: 'some funds remain in your *Bayt al-Māl* after the distribution of pensions. They are now being given to you. If a surplus remains the next year, it will be distributed in the same way'.[53]

Pensions were paid twice a year while rations were issued every month. The pensions reached the recipients in a well-organised manner. At the outset, the administration followed the pattern set by the Prophet in the organisation of the army units. The army commander had under him group commanders, each controlling a number of contingents; each contingent was represented by a flag-bearer who controlled the tribal units. Each tribal unit was led in turn by a tribal chief who remained in contact with a commander (*ʿarīf*) who was in charge of ten persons. The (*ʿarīf*) was responsible for distribution of salaries and allowances to individuals in their houses. The system was called *Aʿshār*, the system of tens, and it continued until the founding of Kufa and Basra after which it was changed.[54]

There were instances in the precedent of the pious Caliphs of punishing unruly conduct by reduction of pension of rights. Thus it is reported that ʿUmar I cut the pension of a poet for ill-considered poetry. The caliph ʿUthmān temporarily suspended ʿAbd Allāh Ibn Masʿūd's pension but later apologised to him and paid it with arrears. ʿUmar II deducted two dinars from a pension because 'the pensioner spoke incorrect Arabic.' Even the prince Walīd, the son of ʿAbd al-Malik, lost his *sharaf* honorarium due to his father's annoyance with him. Muʿāwiyah had earlier made it his official policy to deduct pensions in lieu of compensation for crime (*diyyah*). He wrote to the judge of Egypt asking him to ascertain the nature of the wound of the wounded persons and send a note on that account to the master of registers so that the wounded can receive his *diyyah* entitlement out of the pension of the offender.[55]

Al-Walīd himself is credited with a number of initiatives on welfare services. He was probably the first ruler in medieval times to build hospitals for persons with chronic diseases, and the many lazar houses which later 'grew up in the west followed the Muslim precedent'.[56] Al-Walīd's period (705–717 CE), was one of comparative peace and opulence. He took so much interest in architecture and building that during his reign when people in Damascus met together, fine buildings formed a topic of conversation. He enlarged and beautified the great mosque of Mecca, rebuilt that of al-Madīnah, erected in Syria a number of schools and places of worship and endowed institutions for the lepers, the lame and the blind.[57]

IV. An Analysis of Welfare

An Islamic welfare state, according to Ibn Taymiyyah (d. 728/1328) seeks to guarantee social and economic justice for its citizens. One of its primary tasks in this connection is fulfillment of such essential needs as food, clothing, shelter, health and education, extending also to such policy measures as may be deemed necessary concerning price control, fixing of wages, opening of employment opportunities, intervention in property rights, and prohibition of usury. The state must also strive to eradicate poverty and realize economic stability and balance.[58] The whole purpose of government authority in Islam, according to Ibn Taymiyyah is 'to rule with justice and give to the people whatever that belongs to them, uphold the essential principles of a just policy (al-siyāsah al-ʿādilah) and establish good government (al-wilāyah al-ṣāliḥah)'.[59] Eradication of poverty is an obligation of the state. If an obligation cannot be met without acquiring certain other means then acquiring those means also becomes an obligation.[60] 'There is general consensus', Ibn Taymiyyah wrote 'that whoever is unable to earn sufficiently must be aided with money to suffice his needs and it matters little whether he is a traditional beggar, an army man, a trader, artisan or a farmer.' The revenues of zakāh are to be expended on their welfare needs. The artisan whose conditions of work are not adequate or the trader who does not earn enough to meet his needs, or the army man whose land grant (iqṭāʿ) is not adequate—all have a valid claim to assistance from the zakāh revenues.[61]

The criterion of distribution of basic provisions, according to ʿIzz al-Dīn ʿAbd al-Salām, is need fulfillment and so long as considerations of equality and justice are pursued, the actual quantities that are allocated might differ. For need fulfillment is the greatest purpose of distribution of available assets among its recipients, and not necessarily to distribute equal quantities among them.[62] It is necessary therefore to ascertain the people's needs, as those who are married with a child, or those who may own a horse or have to take care of an animal would be entitled to receive more. It is also important to take into account the prices and cost of living of the locality and such other factors that have a bearing on the needs of people. When an army man dies, his entitlement is given from the *bayt al-māl* to his wife and young children to the extent that satisfies their needs and this may be discontinued when his widow and daughter get married. It must be noted, however, that the assets of the *bayt al-māl* belong to the community and anyone who squanders or destroys them would be liable to compensate for them. No one may take anything from *bayt al-māl* without the authorisation of the Imam.[63]

Muslim jurists maintain that fulfilling the needs of the destitute is a collective obligation (*farḍ kifā'ī*) of the community. Since protection of life is one of the cardinal objectives of the *Sharī'ah*, this would require fulfillment of the basic needs. Al-Ghazālī (d. 505/1111) thus observed that the *Sharī'ah* is designed to protect the five basic values. These are religion, life, property, human intellect, and progeny. Religion can only be preserved through acquiring knowledge and through the performance of obligatory duties, both of which presume 'physical fitness, survival, and availability of a minimum of clothing, housing and other provisions.'[64]

Al-Shāṭibī (d. 790/1388) has also confirmed that fulfillment of the basic welfare needs is a collective duty of the community and a *farḍ kifā'ī* that is addressed not to any particular individual but to the totality of all individuals. This is designed to protect the common interests which cannot be realised by any one individual. These interests are predicated on the preservation of human life and require collective action. 'That is why God Most High has entrusted the fulfillment of common needs of mankind to the community as a whole. This is also the very reason for the existence of the state, in order to assume this responsibility.'[65] Al-Shāṭibī thus held that the ultimate responsibility to assist the needy and poor rests with the ruling authorities. Al-Shāṭibī's views on this are in conformity with those of al-Ghazālī who considered it to be 'incumbent on the ruler to help the people when they are faced with scarcity, starvation and suffering especially during a famine or when prices are high... The ruler should in these circumstances feed the needy and provide them with financial assistance from the public treasury.'[66] This collective duty according to al-Nawawī (d. 675/1280) includes 'elimination of suffering by providing food to the hungry and clothes to the unclad.'[67] Ibn Ḥazm al-Ẓāhirī is even more emphatic in declaring it 'a duty of the rich in every country to support the poor. If the revenues from *zakāh* and spoils of war are insufficient to cater for their needs, the ruler may obligate the rich to fulfill their responsibility.' The State may thus impose, whenever necessary, additional taxes for the purpose of providing the poor with food and clothing for summer and winter and a shelter to protect them from rain, heat and sun and give them privacy.[68]

Siddiqi's analysis of the welfare responsibilities of the Islamic State has also led him to the conclusion that 'the Islamic state has a right to tax the rich to ensure need fulfillment, should the normal sources of revenue not suffice for this purpose.'[69] He added that the welfare responsibility of the state to the extent of need fulfillment 'ranks highly in the objectives of *Sharīʿah*, because it relates to the survival of the individual realisation of any other objective of the *Sharīʿah*, presupposes the implementation of this principle.'[70] Historical precedent on the imposition of welfare tax on the wealthy is, however, less than explicit, and so is the early juristic literature, due probably to what Siddiqi has explained that such a situation 'rarely obtained' and that the normal revenue of the public treasury was sufficient for the purpose of meeting the welfare needs of the poor. Whenever the need for additional taxation arose, the jurists did not hesitate to affirm the state's right to impose additional tax.[71]

The emphatic tone of the source evidence on basic need fulfillment has, moreover led some prominent *ʿulamāʾ*, including Ibn Ḥazm al-Ẓāhirī, to the conclusion that it is lawful for a starving individual to take whatever will sustain him from any place irrespective of whether it is the property of the individual or the state.

In response to the question whether a starving person who has taken food belonging to another to fight starvation is obliged to pay for it, the jurists have given two different verdicts. The first verdict given is that it is necessary for him to pay the price and the owner is obliged to sell it to him at the market price. If the starving man cannot pay the price, then he acquires the food on credit, which means that he would have to pay for it later when he is able to do so.

The second of the two verdicts maintains that food and water for personal consumption should be given free to one who is in desperate need. Ibn Taymiyyah maintains, however, that if the person in distress is unable to pay, no compensation is required, but he must pay if he is affluent. Ibn Ḥazm and a number of other jurists have extended this ruling by analogy to cases of stressing need for clothing and shelter, and Anas Zarqā has suggested its extension also to medicine.[72]

Basic needs include, in addition to food, clothing and shelter as well as drinking water, fuel and electricity, medical care and basic education. Transportation, 'especially in big cities,' survival assistance to the blind and the invalid, assistance toward repayment of debt, and aid for purchase of trade tools, as well as assistance with the costs of getting married. To include all of these in the welfare assistance package constitutes 'necessary provision to ensure survival with efficiency and dignity.'[73] If a county is poor and no great surpluses are available for welfare assistance, the standards of assistance will be defined more by the requirement of survival. But if a country is rich and the revenue from *zakāh* and other sources are enough to provide for welfare assistance at a level closer to the average living standards in that country, it should aim at those standards.[74]

'There can be hardly any disagreement' wrote one observer 'that in an Islamic state basic needs must be provided,' regardless of the extent of interference with the market it may involve, but should preferably be done with the minimum possible interference.[75] The issue of 'basic needs' and who may be regarded as 'poor' are, however, not devoid of difficulty and commentators have differed over details. Whether basic needs are to be identified by reference to 'minimum subsistence, minimum adequacy, or minimum comfort' are questions that can neither be ignored nor easily answered. General response to some of these can, however, be found in the works of al-Ghazālī and al-Shāṭibī. Whereas the former spoke of the need for preservation of the five essential values including one's own life and physical well-being, al-Shāṭibī held that satisfaction of wants, including comforts and adornments of life is permissible and lawful in Islam. The Qur'ān and *Sunnah* also encourage enjoyment of the good things of life that God created for the use and service of mankind.

Numerous writers have concurred that need fulfillment should cover basic necessities, education and transport. Many have also included medical treatment and, whenever necessary, domestic help. Modern Arab writers tend to subsume these welfare needs under the umbrella term, *al-takāful al-ijtimāʿī*, the social support system to which the Islamic State and society are committed.

As earlier noted, there is much support in the sources and in early juristic writings to include assistance from the public funds to enable individuals of marriageable age to get married. This is because the Qur'ān and *Sunnah* encourage marriage for all who are capable and fit. The Prophet, peace be on him, has also spoken of marriage as his *Sunnah* and on many occasions helped his Companions who wished to get married to achieve that purpose. The following Qur'ānic verse is also quoted in this connection.

وأنكحوا الأيامى منكم والصالحين من عبادكم وإمائكم إن يكونوا فقراء يغنيهم الله من فضله والله واسع عليم

And marry such of you as are solitary and pious. If they be poor, God will enrich them of His bounty. God is of ample means, aware. (24:32)

Muslim jurists have often stated that marriage is obligatory (*wājib*) on those who are fit and find themselves in fear of falling into sin without it. If such a person has no means at his disposal, his affluent relatives must help him to get married in the same way as they help him with the provisions of food, clothes and shelter. The majority (*jumhur*) position on this is to include marriage within the concept of obligatory maintenance (*nafaqah*). This is especially the case with regard to the father and son who are entitled to help from one another to get married.[76]

It is also suggested that the need fulfillment programme should be committed to the provision of basic needs for at least one calendar year. Al-Qaradāwī has spoken of the 'right to full protection (*ḥaqq al-kifāyah al-tāmmah*)' to the extent of sufficiency that is granted 'to all individuals under the *Sharī'ah* for all of their basic needs including food, clothing, shelter and medical treatment, indeed all the necessities of life.' The individual himself is duty bound, however, to earn his living through lawful work in the first place, failing which it becomes the responsibility of his close relatives who are capable of supporting him to meet his needs. In the event where the relatives are unable to help, the duty falls on the state to provide assistance from the *zakāh* revenues. Should there be sufficient funds available, the need fulfillment should not be confined to the provision of basic minimum but should aim at the threshold of sufficiency (*ḥadd al-kifāyah*). In holding these views Qaradāwī has referred to the writings of jurists who have included such things as books and tools of trade in the category of needs, which is why the definition of welfare needs should not be confined to the minimum of survival but reach the extent of adequate fulfillment of needs. Qaradāwī has quoted the Shāfi'ī jurist al-Nawawī to the effect that entitlement to support extends for the duration of life for a person who has no means to support himself.[77] To quote al-Nawawī: 'if a poor man does not practice any profession nor knows artisanship nor trade and has no means to earn a living, he will be given an amount sufficient for him for his whole life according to persons of his age group in the town of his residence, and sufficiency for one year will not be the criterion in this case.'[78] Qaraḍāwī further added that the State's commitment to welfare is by no means confined to the *zakāh* revenues but extends to all the resources of the public treasury. If the *zakāh* revenue falls short of meeting the basic needs of the poor, the state may levy additional tax on the affluent in order to raise funds for this purpose.[79]

The schools of law have differed somewhat on the quantitative aspect of sufficiency. The Ḥanafīs maintain that sufficiency (*ḥadd al-kifāyah*) means taking a person from the state of poverty to that of affluence (*ghinā*), and this is measured by reference to the quorum of *zakāh*. Thus when a person has enough of any type of assets which makes him liable to pay *zakāh*, he is considered to be affluent and has reached the level of sufficiency, but it is permissible to give him more. Abū Ḥanīfah's disciple, al-Shaybānī, has been quoted in this connection to have urged the caliph Hārūn al-Rashīd to 'fear God Most High in the expenditure of (public) assets and spend it on those who are entitled to it. You should not leave any poor person without giving his due from the revenues of *zakāh* and charities until he and his family become affluent.'[80]

The Mālikīs, Shāfiʿīs and Ḥanbalīs have held that sufficiency means fulfillment of needs. When the poor is given an amount that is sufficient for him to remove his needs, there is no further obligation to give him more. Sufficiency according to this view refers to the fulfillment of needs for food, clothes, and shelter and all that which a person has to have for himself and his dependants, in order to live in accordance with his conditions without excess or undue frugality and restriction. This also extends to medical needs, payment of debt and marriage.[81]

The basic evidence that is relied upon by both groups is open to interpretation but may be said to favour generosity in giving. Abū ʿUbayd has thus recorded a statement from the caliph ʿUmar b. al-Khaṭṭāb: 'when you give (to the poor) give until they become affluent, and give repeatedly (if necessary) even if you have to give one person a hundred camels.' This would suggest that a person may be given repeatedly from the charities until his needs are met and he becomes affluent. Hamid Hassan commented that the caliph ʿUmar was not merely aiming at giving to the poor only an amount that allayed his hunger and immediate needs but aimed at taking him out of that predicament until he became affluent.[82] Commentators have also included education within the meaning of welfare needs and in doing so, they have cited in authority the *Sunnah* of the Prophet to the effect that the Prophet hired teachers to teach Muslim children literacy. Later during the time of the caliph ʿUmar al-Khaṭṭāb when the state revenues increased, the state also hired teachers and established schools for the same purpose.[83]

Abū ʿUbayd has also recorded a report in which the caliph ʿUmar b. ʿAbd al-ʿAzīz instructed his *zakāh* collectors to pay the outstanding debts on behalf of those who were under the burden of debt. In reply to this, his officials wrote back: 'What if we find a man who has a dwelling, a servant, house and furniture?' The Caliph wrote to them again: 'It is necessary for a Muslim to have a house in which he lives, a servant who spares him the trouble of his chores, and a horse on which he wages *jihād* against the enemy—and he must have furniture in his house. Yes, pay the debt on his behalf, for he is a debtor.'[84]

According to al-Nawawī, a man who owns landed property that he occupies and cultivates but the income he obtains from it falls short of being sufficient is a poor man in need. He will therefore be given assistance from the *zakāh* funds to the extent that his needs are met and he will not be obliged to sell his property.[85] Ibn Qudāmah (d. 620/1223) earlier held the same view albeit that he referred to a certain monetary sum that occurs in some reports. Thus a man who has landed property, or an estate, 'equal to ten thousand dirhams, or less or more, which does not furnish him with the means of subsistence, he may be given assistance from the *zakāh*.'[86] Al-Kāsānī (d. 578/1180) had also noted that one who owned a house, furniture, a servant and horse, weapon, clothing and books 'if he belongs to the class of the learned' may still receive assistance from the *zakāh* funds. For the Companions of the Prophet used to give *zakāh* to one who owned less then thousand dirhams, being the total cost of the horse, weapon, servant and house.[87]

When people are living at a subsistence level, the *Sharīʿah* demands that absolute poverty should be addressed first, and the question of paying attention to what may be regarded as 'relative poverty' may be said to be irrelevant to the subject of basic need fulfillment. Yet issues are not as clear-cut as they may sometimes appear. Food is obviously the first item in any need fulfillment agenda. Even if one limits food to what is needed to protect life, for example, the answer is not straightforward. A diet may be sufficient to keep a person alive for the time being, but improvement in the diet may decrease proneness to disease and increase life expectancy. The question then arises whether an improved diet should be considered necessary? If so, where does one draw the line? How does one determine the level of need fulfillment which should be guaranteed. The prevailing living standards of a given society would evidently provide the basic framework, but that too does not provide specific answers nor even adequate guidelines to all the relevant questions.[88]

Leading scholars and 'ulamā', including Mawdūdī (d. 1979), Sayyid Quṭb (d. 1966), Abū Zahrah (d. 1974), Muṣṭafā al-Sibāʿī (d. 1964), Bāqir al-Ṣadr (d. 1980), Muḥammad al-Mubārak, Yūsuf al-Qaraḍāwī have all spoken in support of the principle that the basic needs of every human being who resides within the territorial domains of the Islamic state must be fulfilled, and everyone is entitled to a minimum living standard that is above the threshold of abject poverty and degradation.[89] There is also general agreement that the zakāh revenue, even if they were fully realised, would not be sufficient to meet the welfare commitment of the state and that the Islamic state may still need to allocate additional resources for this purpose. Siddiqi has stressed that responsibility for the fulfillment of basic needs is in the nature of farḍ kifāyah which is basically addressed to everyone. 'The individual himself, his close relatives, the neighbourhood and the society must all recognise this,' but he added that the 'ultimate responsibility, in practice, rests with the Islamic State.'[90]

The long term objective of welfare assistance should be to enable the needy to acquire the necessary means to fulfill their needs on their own, making social security assistance unnecessary. This long term objective should not, in the meantime, be pursued at the expense of the short term objective of meeting the need for basic necessities of life. The long term and the short term objectives should in other words, be pursued simultaneously.[91]

There is a consistent line of agreement among scholars to the effect that those who can work may not ask for charity and unless they are willing to work, they are basically not entitled to social insurance benefit from the state. The state should also not extend benefit to them but help them instead to find suitable work. Ibn Taymiyyah expounded that it is highly recommendable and 'one of the best of deeds for the authorities to differentiate between the deserving and the undeserving and to do justice in the distribution of means of livelihood.'[92] The value and merit of the effort that is undertaken to achieve this in order to establish a carefully researched welfare programme can thus hardly be over-estimated.

The stigma that Islamic teachings tend to attach to reliance on charity provides a disincentive that is deeply embedded in Islamic ethos. There is evidence to suggest that the Companions took the Prophet's advice not to ask for charity very seriously. Siddiqi has recorded this information but then he also expressed doubt as to whether the disincentive effect referred to here will be strong enough to prevent abuse. He has stated that the 'individual's incentive to work is likely to be weakened by the prospect of his receiving an income without working or of his needs being fulfilled by others.'[93] The experience of the welfare state in Europe and elsewhere tends at least partially to confirm Siddiqi's apprehension, but Siddiqi has rightly acknowledged that the 'critics of the welfare state have failed to come up with an alternative way of dealing with absolute poverty and unfulfilled needs.'[94]

Muslim commentators have spoken in support of including medical care in the welfare assistance scheme. Many have reached the conclusion that it is an important component of welfare assistance that the citizen should receive from the state. Thus according to one observer 'medical care should be provided for all' and that 'the minimum to begin with is a state-funded hospital in every region supplying free services to the poor.'[95] Those who can afford to pay for the service should do so themselves, but the state bears responsibility to assist the poor. It is then added, and rightly so, that 'Muslim countries have a long way to go before they implement such a programme,' in which case, it is suggested that a detailed phased programme should be worked out by each Muslim country in which the type of medical care and its quantitative aspects are specified in proportion to their capabilities in each case. Until such time when this becomes available, reliance may be had on an income transfer programme, and any direct assistance that can be given to the poor to enable them to fulfill their needs from the market.[96]

It is not our purpose here to provide an exhaustive account of the *Sharīʿah* evidence on the importance of health and medical care, but merely to say that the textual sources are not expected to speak directly on the details of a health care agenda, but they provide nevertheless supportive advice and encouragement. The Prophet is thus reported to have said that 'a believer who is strong (and healthy) is superior and loved by God more than a believer who is weak, but there is good in all of them.'[97]

المؤمن القوي خير وأحب إلى الله من المؤمن الضعيف،
وفي كلّ خير

The fact that the *Sharī'ah* prohibits consumption of intoxicants and alcohol, dead carcass and unclean food also points to the same conclusion. On an affirmative note, protection of life and intellect have also been identified among the overriding goals and objectives of *Sharī'ah*. These must be protected against danger and destruction at all costs.

Both the Qur'ān and *Sunnah* encourage the believers to avoid courting danger and prompting themselves into situations that threaten their safety. 'Throw not yourselves deliberately into perdition' is the Qur'ānic guideline to everyone to avoid endangering their life and health. This would be the Qur'ānic advice against illnesses that can be avoided through personal care and precaution. The substance of this guideline is also upheld in the general proclamation of the *ḥadīth*-cum-legal maxim that 'harm may neither be inflicted nor reciprocated (*lā ḍarara wa lā ḍirar*).' Encouraging advice is also found in the *ḥadīth* wherein the Prophet declared:

ما أنزل الله داء إلا أنزل له شفاء

God did not create an illness without creating a cure for it.[98]

This is clearly a refutation of the fatalism and inertia that are sometimes erroneously subsumed under predestination, which is admittedly an aspect of Islam, but which is basically an article of faith rather than a guide for action, and it is valued in respect of matters which are beyond the knowledge and control of the individual. People do not know their destiny, but they must not let that to lead them to inertia in confronting danger and disease.

To say that physical health is the concern of religion is also seen in the *ḥadīth*, addressed to the individual, in such words وإنّ لبدنك عليك حقا 'Truly your body has a right over you...'[99] which evidently means avoidance of abuse to oneself and due regard for one's physical well-being and health. Caution is also advised in the *Sunnah* with regard to contagious disease: one should not enter the locality where plague has broken out, nor should one travel outside if one has already contracted it. And then, of course, the

Sharī'ah provides numerous exemptions to the sick and traveler in the performance of their obligatory duties, such as the daily prayer, and fasting during the month of Ramaḍān. Similar concessions have been granted to pregnant women, and persons of advanced old age.[100]

The caliph 'Umar b. al-Khaṭṭāb used to advise everyone to take care of their health and 'avoid obesity, for it is an obstacle,' and also to avoid 'overeating as it undermines one's ability to keep up the *ṣalāh*, corrupts one's body and leads to illness.'[101] It is also reported that a group of eight people came to Medina and embraced Islam, but the climate of Medina did not suit them and they complained of illness to the Prophet. The Prophet assigned them a place near the grassy pastures of Medina to have rest, 'enjoy access to fresh air and drink of the milk of the animals' until they regain their normal health.[102] Towards the end of first/seventh century, the Umayyad Caliph, Walīd b. 'Abd al-Malik established hospitals (*bīmāristān*) and leprosy centers, as well as free medical services and food to the destitute and the invalid.[103]

What has been said so far is enough perhaps to warrant the conclusion that the *Sharī'ah* does not leave health as a matter of concern entirely of either the individual or the State but makes it a joint responsibility of both and places a duty on the State to help the ill and the invalid who are unable to help themselves to fight disease. The level of state involvement is not even confined to material assistance but also to moral support and compassion. This is clear from a number of *ḥadīths* conforming the fact that the Prophet himself used to visit the sick and also instructed his followers to do the same. The caliph 'Umar b. al-Khaṭṭāb not only visited the sick himself but ensured that his governors in outlying regions also did. The sick must be assured that the community and its leaders cared for their well-being and health. This too is a manifestation of the fraternity that Islam advocates among the community of believers.[104]

The Universal Declaration of Human Rights 1948 entitles every individual to work, to a free choice of employment and to unemployment benefit (Art. 23). It is further stated in Article (25):

(1) Everyone has the right to a standard of living adequate for the health and well-being of himself and his family, including food, clothing, housing, medical care and necessary social services, and the right to security in the event of unemployment, sickness, disability, widowhood, old age or other lack of livelihood in circumstances beyond his control.

(2) Motherhood and childhood are entitled to special care and assistance. All children, whether born in or out of wedlock shall enjoy the same social protection.

The 1981 Universal Islamic Declaration of Human Right (Art. 18: Right to Social security: 'Every person has the right to food, shelter, clothing, education, and medical care consistent with the resources of the community.' It is further provided that this entitlement extends to 'all individuals who cannot take care of themselves due to some temporary or permanent disability.'

The 1989 Declaration of Human Rights in Islam (*al-Iʿlān al-Islāmī li-Ḥuqūq al-Insān*) which was deliberated in the various sessions and committees of the Organisation of Islamic Conference (OIC) and finally ratified in the nineth session of the OIC Foreign Ministers in Tehran contains the following provisions on citizen's right to welfare.

i) Every human being is entitled to live in a clean environment that is free of corruption and moral vice so as to enable him to attend to his spiritual well-being. The society and State are to facilitate this.

ii) Every human being has a right over the community and State in which he lives—to be provided within the limits of feasibility with all the facilities and services which the individual requires.

iii) The State guarantees to every human being the right to a life with dignity whereby he is availed of all of his welfare needs for himself and his dependents, and this includes food, clothing, dwelling education, medical treatment and other basic needs.[105]

A perusal and comparison of these two documents shows a basic line of harmony between them in regard to both the general objectives and specific details. The provisions of the Islamic Declaration may also be said to be in substantial harmony, in regard to the basic right to welfare with most of the other well-recognised international instruments and declarations of human rights.[106]

V. Obligatory Maintenance (*Nafaqah Wājibah*)

The *Sharīʿah* rules concerning maintenance among close relatives may be seen as the starting point of the social support system of Islam. Family support is the first recourse in that the duty to support a person does not fall on the public treasury and the state unless the person himself and then his immediate family are unable to support him. This is because welfare assistance is a form of cooperation (*taʿāwun*) and family is where cooperation must begin. Only when the person has no family or no one in the family is able to give help, the duty of co-operation falls on the larger family and the state undertakes the responsibility in its capacity of representing the community.

Family relations are divided into two groups, one of which include blood relatives (*aqārib*) such as one's ascendants, descendants and collaterals, and the other which include distant kindred (*dhaw al-arhām*). The former are entitled to inheritance from one another whereas the latter, which include aunts and uncles, cousins, nephews and nieces and their descendants—are on the whole not entitled to inheritance. Whereas close relatives are entitled to *nafaqah* the *Sharīʿah* recommends cooperation and assistance among all relatives. Observance of the ties of kinship (*sillat al-rahim*) in its broader sense is the theme of numerous directives of Islam. Those who observe them are promised with great rewards and those who sever and neglect them are warned of spiritual depravity and loss.[107]

The *Sharīʿah* imposes an obligation on the affluent members of the family to provide customarily sufficient maintenance for a poor relative who is unable to earn a living. This is to include food, clothing and shelter and the quantities involved are determined by reference to the prevailing custom. In the case of certain relatives such as one's wife the right to maintenance does not refer to the criteria of need, nor of her ability to work, nor even to the husband's financial condition. This means that the husband's duty to maintain his wife and young children is almost unconditional and absolute. There is consensus to the effect that a man may be compelled to provide maintenance for his wife, young children and parents and that these relatives are entitled to enforce their right by taking legal action against their defaulting relatives.[108] The *Sharīʿah* obligates the husband to provide for his wife but the wife is under no obligation to support her husband. Only the Ẓāhirīs have held that in the event the wife is affluent, she too is under a duty to support her destitute husband. The Ẓāhirī view here refers for its validity to the Qur'ān in which marriage is described as 'friendship and compassion' (30:21), which is naturally reciprocal as all friendships involve reciprocity and cooperation.

The parents' entitlement to support is determined on the basis of need, even if they are able to work, provided that the donor has the means to support them. A person with sufficient means is thus obligated to provide for his needy parents, needy offspring for as long as they are minor, and for such adult offspring as are incapable of providing for themselves due to disability and illness. The Qur'ān and

Sunnah speak emphatically of friendship and support among close relatives. Thus it is proclaimed:

$$\text{إن الله يأمر بالعدل والإحسان وإيتاء ذي القربى}$$

God commands justice and fair dealing and giving of financial assistances to the relatives. (16:90)

The faithful is also enjoined to 'worship God and join not any partners with Him, and be good to the parents, relatives, the orphans and those in need...' (4:36)

$$\text{واعبدوا الله ولاتشركوا به شيئًا وبالوالدين إحسانا وبذي}$$
$$\text{القربى واليتامى والمساكين}$$

The Qur'ān also speaks of an appointed right of the relatives and addresses the believers to 'give to the kindred their due, to those in want and to the wayfarer...' (17:26)

$$\text{آت ذا القربى حقه والمسكين وابن السبيل}$$

The duty imposed here is then reinforced by a decisive threat when the Prophet declared in a *ḥadīth*: 'one who breaks the ties of kinship shall not enter paradise.'[109]

$$\text{لايدخل الجنة قاطع}$$

Close relatives are thus entitled to a greater right to financial assistance than the more remote ones. This is also indicated in the Qur'ānic order of the right to inheritance within the family: If the relatives are entitled to inherit each other's property after they die, they are also entitled to assistance when they need it while alive.

Qur'ānic authority on obligatory maintenance is more specifically provided in the following three verses:

(1) Let him who has means spend according to his means, and he whose provisions are measured, let him spend of that which God has given him. God does not burden a soul beyond its capacity. (65:7)

لينفق ذو سعة من سعته ومن قدر عليه رزقه فلينفق مما آتاه الله لايكلّف الله نفسا إلا ما آتها

(2) As for the offspring, the father is to provide them with food and clothing in a suitable manner (or according to custom). (2:223)

وعلى المولود له رزقهن وكسوتهن بالمعروف

(3) With reference to the wife's right to maintenance the text declares:

Let them reside in the same manner as you do and in due proportion to your capability. (65:6)

أسكنوهن من حيث سكنتم من وجدكم ولاتضآرّوهن لتضيقوا عليهن

Specific quantities of *nafaqah* may be determined on the basis of the average means of the donor by reference to prevailing custom, and the needs of its recipient. The strength of the kinship tie is naturally always taken into consideration. In actual practice, these criteria often work together and guide judicial decisions in disputes over *nafaqah*. Detailed juristic conclusions are often drawn from these passages. The somewhat categorical language of the text in the second of these verses has led Imam Shāfiʿī, for example, to the conclusion that entitlement to *nafaqah* is confined to parents and children.[110] The textual reference to residence for one's wife in the third of these verses also implies her right to maintenance. Marriage itself is the cause of this obligation according to the Shāfiʿīs, whereas the Ḥanafīs maintain that it is detention (*al-ḥabs*) of the wife, in the household of her husband that is the cause of *nafaqah*.

So long as there is a valid marriage and the wife takes residence with her husband, she is entitled to maintenance regardless as to whether she is in need of it and whether or not she is able to support herself.[111]

The Qur'ān enjoins the offspring to be good to their parents in every respect.

وقضى ربك ألّا تعبدوا إلا إياه وبالوالدين إحسانا

And your Lord has determined that you do not worship any other diety save Him, and that you be good to your parents. (7:23)

To be good to one's parents naturally includes giving them financial support. This may indeed be the best manifestation of *iḥsān*.[112] The purport of this verse is also confirmed in other passages in the Qur'ān. The juxtaposition, in the verse just quoted, of God mentioning the parents next to His own illustrious self occurs once again in an address as to the faithful who are tersely told:

$$ أن اشكرلي ولوالديك إلّ المصير $$

You should thank me and your parents. Unto Me is your final return. (31:14)

It is reported that a Companion, Muʿāwiyah ibn Hayda, asked the Prophet a question as to who was the most entitled to his beneficence, to which the Prophet replied: 'Your mother, your mother, your mother, then your father, and then the nearest in kinship that may follow.'

$$ أمك ثم أمك ثم أمك ثم أبوك ثم الأقرب فالأقرب $$

The way to express one's gratitude to one's parents is to offer them service and material help. The text has elsewhere enjoined the believers to offer the same standards of help to their parents even when they happen to be non-Muslim. The faithful has thus been directed to be good to their non-Muslim parents and help them in all matters, with only one exception, which is that they do not renounce Islam in order merely to please their parents (29:81).

Maintenance to a relative should be sufficient for the latter's needs. The criterion of need here includes, not only the basic needs, but also what is customary among people of the same social group and locality. This is indicated in the *ḥadīth* in which the Prophet instructed Hind the wife of Abū Sufyān, to 'take (from the property of your husband) what is sufficient for you and your child in a decent manner (or according to custom)'[113]

$$ خذي لك ولولدك مايكفيك بالمعروف $$

Al-Kāsānī wrote that 'obligatory *nafaqah* for a close relative must be to the extent of sufficiency (*bi-qadr al-kifāyah*)'. What is deemed sufficient also refers to personal needs which include food, drink, clothes, shelter, fosterage in the case of a child, and a servant in the case of one who is dependent on it.[114] Food and clothing should be adequate for summer and winter, and shelter includes necessary furniture. Al-Qaraḍāwī who has summarised the juristic views on the subject includes maintenance for the wife and children, and also medical treatment. With reference to this last item, it is stated that early juristic discourse tended to be silent on health care as a part of *nafaqah*.[115] This is a fair statement. The relative silence of the early writings on this may be reflective to some extent of the conditions of medieval times. A certain adjustment of the juristic rules to include medical treatment in *nafaqah* is not only in harmony with the spirit of the source evidence but also justified due to availability at present of better medical facilities and services. This conclusion may be said to be implied from references to prevailing custom in the sources.

The Qur'ānic term *bi'l-maʿrūf* may also be said to be comprehensive enough to subsume a variety of relevant factors in the determination of *nafaqah*, but the criteria of entitlement to *nafaqah* among relatives varies according to the various schools. The Ḥanbalīs consider entitlement to inheritance to be the valid determinant. A poor or incapacitated relative is accordingly entitled to maintenance from his affluent kin if the latter would inherit from the former in the event of death, that is, when the poor relative is assumed to have died intestate. Should there be a number of affluent relatives in that category, their liability to provide maintenance will be in proportion to their respective shares of inheritance. A legal maxim of *fiqh* that is relevant here simply declares: 'liability is linked to gain' (*al-gharamu bi'l-ghanam*). The obligation to provide maintenance is thus linked to one's right of inheritance.

The Ḥanafīs on the other hand entitle to maintenance relatives such as uncle, aunt, nephews and nieces that may or may not be legal heirs.[116] They have taken the prohibited degrees of marriage as their criterion of entitlement to maintenance. If two persons are closely related to one another such that they would be forbidden to marry if one of them were supposed to be a female, then that would establish their entitlement to maintenance from one another. As noted earlier the Shāfiʿīs entitled to *nafaqah* only the ascendants, that is, parents and grand parents, and the descendants, that is, the children and grandchildren. The Mālikīs have on the other hand confined the scope of obligatory maintenance to the wife, parents, and children, that is, one's father, mother, son and daughter, but exclude all other relatives. These differential rulings are all reflective of the different interpretations that the schools of law have advanced from more or less the same evidence that occur in the Qur'ān and Sunnah.[117] Their differential conclusions would appear to be reflective of the customary practices of their locality and time as well as their differential approaches to interpretation and *ijtihād*.

Difference of religion is not a bar to obligatory maintenances in the case of one's wife and parents. A Muslim son whose father or mother happens to be non-Muslim is under duty to support them when they are in need of it. Similarly when the son is a non-Muslim and his affluent parents happen to be Muslim, he is still entitled to *nafaqah* from them when he in unable to support himself.

Difference of religion is, however, a bar to *nafaqah* in the case of other relatives. The obligation to provide *nafaqah* is basically addressed to those who have enough assets to disqualify them from being a recipient of *zakāh*, which is possession of means in excess to one's own basic needs and those of his wife and children. This is the Ḥanafī position, but the majority have held that *nafaqah* becomes due when a person has enough for himself and immediate family for a day and a night—anything in excess should then be given to the relative in need.[118]

It is provided in a *ḥadīth* that 'the giving hand is the superior hand; let your giving begin with your family, your mother and father, sister and brother, then those who follows in a descending order.'[119]

$$\text{يد المعطى العليا. ابدأ بمن تعول أمك و أباك و أختك}$$
$$\text{فأخاك وأدناك وأدناك}$$

According to another *ḥadīth*, 'the best of charity is to give to the next of kin who is in straightened conditions.'[120]

$$\text{إن أفضل الصدقة الصدقة على ذي الرحم الكاشح}$$

As for the threshold of poverty and the question as to what level of poverty entitles one to *nafaqah* from one's relatives, the jurists have once again referred to *zakāh*. One whose poverty level is to the extent that qualifies him to be a recipient of *zakāh*, and is himself exempt from paying it, he is entitled to claim *nafaqah*. According to another opinion, anyone who is afflicted with hardship (i.e. *mu'sir*), and has no assets is entitled to *nafaqah*. The two views are not very different perhaps. The question has still arisen concerning a person who has a house and a servant but who is in hardship—can he be called a *mu'sir*? Two different answers have been given, one of which is that such a person is not entitled to *nafaqah*, as he can sell or rent his house out and live in a cheaper place and also release the servant. The second answer given, which is preferable according to al-Kāsānī of the Ḥanafī school and the prevailing view of the Shāfi'īs and Mālikīs, is that such a person is still entitled to *nafaqah* as it may be difficult for him to sell the house and live elsewhere. To share a place with others is also not always possible. To sell a part only of the house is even more impractical. Al-Kāsānī concluded that 'the preferred view therefore is that no one may be ordered to sell his house but that the (affluent) relative may instead be ordered to support him.'[121]

Qaraḍāwī concurs and adds that the *Sharī'ah* envisages reasonable and dignified living that is in harmony with the Qur'ānic affirmation of human dignity. What is actually considered to be dignified and suitable also tends to vary from time to time and by reference to prevailing circumstances.[122]

A person who is fit to work and is not afflicted with illness and yet refuses to take employment that is on offer is basically not entitled to *nafaqah*, with the exception of one's wife and parents. An able-bodied person who refuses to take a suitable job incurs a sin as is proclaimed in the following *ḥadīth*. 'It is grave enough of a sin for a man to let go of an opportunity that earns him his livelihood.'[123]

$$\text{كفى بالمرء إثمًا أن يضيّع من يقوت}$$

It is provided in another *ḥadīth* that: 'charity is not permissible to the affluent nor to one who is strong and healthy.'[124]

$$\text{لا تحلّ الصدقة لغني ولا للذي مرّة سوي}$$

An exception is made here in favour of students who may be able to work but who devote themselves to their studies. As for those who refuse to fulfil their obligation in respect of a valid claim of a close relative for *nafaqah*, the affluent relative may be imprisoned, even if it be the father of the plaintiff, by the court. The judge may also quantify the entitlement to *nafaqah* and make it payable at suitable intervals.

VI. Inheritance and Bequest

We may begin the discussion here by giving a general characterisation of the Islamic law of inheritance, and in particular to note that the welfare orientations of *Sharīʿah*, and its concern for a fair distribution of wealth can also be seen in its scheme of inheritance. Inheritance is in many ways a continuation of the Qur'ānic principle of cooperation (*taʿāwun*) within the family that is manifested through *nafaqah* among the living, and it is manifested after the death of a family member through inheritance and bequest.

One of the salient features of inheritance in Islam is its obligatory character in that the basic entitlements of close relatives to shares in the estate of their deceased relative have on the whole been prescribed in the clear text of the Qur'ān which calls for enforcement on an objective basis. The objectivity of these entitlements is manifested in the principle that the father has no right to disinherit his own children, for example, of their right to inherit his estate after him. The legal heirs will receive their shares of inheritance as a matter of due enforcement of the law, which is precisely what the judge would be expected to order in the event of a dispute concerning these rights. The owner of the estate is entitled, on the other hand, to dispose up to one third of his assets by way of bequest while he is still alive. It is advisable for him to use his prerogative in respect of this one-third so as to rectify any irregularity that might be expected to arise from a strict enforcement of the law of inheritance. A relative may sometimes be excluded from inheritance due to the presence of a closer relative, such as a son's son, in the presence of a son. But suppose that the son's son is poor or invalid while the son is healthy and affluent. A strict enforcement of the rules of inheritance cannot overcome the inequity of that situation but a recourse to bequest can offer a remedy. This is, in fact, what the Qur'ān has recommended (4:8), which is to assign something by way of bequest to a deserving relative who may not otherwise receive a share. Having said this, it is basically up to the person himself to use his right of bequest in any way he or she wishes.

Some jurists have taken the Qur'ānic instruction a step further to provide for what is known as 'obligatory bequest' (*waṣiyyah wājibah*) for deserving relatives that are excluded from inheritance on technical grounds. Some Muslim countries, including Egypt, have in fact adopted this provision as a basis of new legislation on the subject.[125] The right to make a bequest may, of course, be used for other beneficial and charitable purposes, or it may be used to help a deserving person outside the family. A portion greater than one-third may also be assigned in bequest if the existing legal heirs are all in agreement, but not otherwise. It is, however, preferable not to interfere with the Qur'ānic scheme of inheritance, and bequest is generally seen as a main source of such interference. This may explain why the law does not permit bequest to a legal heir who is in the meantime recipient of a share in inheritance. For this is bound to affect the shares of other heirs and thus amount to interference in their entitlements.

The basic purpose of inheritance in Islam is distribution, as opposed to accumulation, of wealth, and the scheme is so designed that a single relative whether a son, or a daughter, can hardly expect to inherit the whole estate in the presence of other relatives. The immediate offspring admittedly inherit the largest share but they would have to share some of it with such other relatives as the spouse, parents and even grandparents of the deceased. Brothers and sisters also take a share in the presence of a daughter or daughters. The law thus entitles close relatives to greater share but it still pursues the purpose of wider distribution of assets among a larger number of persons.

As already noted, inheritance proceeds on the basis of kinship and not, as it were, on the basis of personal need. But even so, the question of need is not totally neglected. This can be seen in the entitlement to a much larger share of the offspring compared to the parent, although in respect of blood tie (*qarābah*) parents and children stand in the same degree of closeness to the deceased. The reason for this is that one's children are more likely to be in need of help than one's parents, especially when the former are young and have not realised their earning potential, whereas the parents may have already made their way in life and accumulated sufficient amount for their needs.

With reference to women's share in inheritance, the fact that the *Sharī'ah* entitles the male to a double share of the female relative in the same degree of relationship to the deceased is also said to be predicated on equitable distribution that is based on need. The most important consideration here is that the responsibility to provide *nafaqah* normally falls on the male relatives in the family such as the father, spouse, brother etc., who must provide for their young children as well as their minor and adult female relatives. Being responsible in respect of *nafaqah*, the assignment of a double share in inheritance to the male relative in the same degree of relationship thus contemplates the need of the male link for greater assistance.[126]

The fact that more and more women have entered the work force in recent times and earn regular income has often meant that they also contribute more effectively to the family budget. Women have also acquired a high profile in education and the acquisition of skills, and often tend to obtain even better results in universities and places of work than their male peers. These are some of the new realities that have given rise to questions of equality and fair treatment of women in inheritance. The present writer has known of cases in Malaysia where a woman supported her father in his old age and her brother practically did very little to help their father when he was alive and needed his help. But when the father died, the brother claimed his entitlement to twice the share of his more deserving sister. In situations such as this, conformity to the letter of the text may actually violate its spirit of providing equitable treatment for the female relative in question. On purely juristic grounds, I might propose the application in such cases of the principle of juristic preference or *istiḥsān*, which is the *Sharīʿah* equivalent of the western law doctrine of equity. *Istiḥsān* is designed to remedy certain exceptional irregularities that may arise from a strict application of the normal principles of the law in particular cases. This is when the jurist is faced with an unsatisfactory situation and is convinced as a result that a departure from the normal rule is preferable in favour of an alternative ruling if such a ruling would help to provide a better and more equitable solution. Even this brief description of *istiḥsān* helps to clarify some of the main differences between *istiḥsān* and such other doctrines of *uṣūl al-fiqh* as considerations of public interest *maṣlaḥah* and analogical reasoning (*qiyās*) etc. Whereas these other doctrines are normally applied in the absence of a textual ruling in the Qurʾān and *Sunnah*, *istiḥsān* applies, one might say it can only meaningfully apply, in the presence of a textual ruling in the sources, which, however, runs into difficulty when it is applied to a particular case.

I do not want to indulge in technicalities here. I merely want to suggest that *istiḥsān* can offer a way out of such anomalies as I depicted above. There is even a precedent available in the decision of the second caliph ʿUmar b. al-Khaṭṭāb in the renowned case of *al-Mushtarakah*. To sum it up briefly, a woman died and left behind her mother, husband, two germane, and two uterine, brothers. The husband took a half of the estate, the mother one-sixth, the two uterine brothers, being Qur'ānic sharers (*dawu al-furūḍ*) took one-third. The estate was exhausted and nothing was left for the full brothers, who were naturally disappointed and brought their case to the caliph ʿUmar. The Caliph decided, contrary to normal rules and what seems to be a typical case of *istiḥsān*, that the four brothers should share the one-third equally between them, which is why the case became renown by the name *Mushtarakah* (the apportioned).

Having cited this example, it is proposed that in exceptional cases where the literal application of the rule of double share to the male proves to be patently unfair as in the example I gave earlier, the more deserving sister should be entitled to an equal share to that of the negligent brother. I note in this connection, however, that *istiḥsān* can only offer a solution, as indicated above, in exceptional cases and it cannot replace the normal rules. It cannot therefore be generalised in the sense that it contemplates a case-by-case application preferably by a court of appropriate jurisdiction.[127] A partial remedy to such situation can also be found through bequest (*waṣiyyah*) to which a reference has already been made. With regard to patently unfair or difficult situations of inheritance, the law may make provisions to regulate instances of recourse to *istiḥsān* compulsory and authorise the judge to apply it when he is satisfied that it would serve the higher objectives of justice and fair distribution of wealth in the family in a better way.

Before I leave this subject, I may also mention in passing that commentators including Muḥammad Shahrūr and Selim al-Awa have advanced the argument, and rightly so, that the double-share-to-the-male rule is not as black and white as it appears and that it needs to be seen in operation in particular cases, as it is possible that a female relative sometimes gets a larger share without any gender-based disadvantage.[128] I do not, however, propose to enter technical details and hope that these additional contributions would eventually make an impact on the attitude of jurists and judges which has hitherto not been open to fresh approaches on this issue. Judges of *Sharīʿah* courts are inclined to follow the letter of the text even when they see unsatisfactory results arising from a literalist approach to the *Sharīʿah*.

Lastly, it is of interest to note that the Islamic law of inheritance has assigned fixed shares mainly for female relatives within the family which has strengthened their position in the general scheme of inheritance to what it used to be before the advent of Islam. Female relatives were often excluded from inheritance altogether. The other point to note is that relatives on the mother's side, such as the maternal aunt, became entitled to inheritance. This too was a new development compared to the pre-Islamic Arabian practice which excluded such relatives from inheritance altogether. The welfare concerns of Islamic law for a fair distribution of the family wealth can thus be seen in its laws of inheritance generally and in strengthening the position of women in particular. The overall pattern of the law of inheritance is also conducive to distribution, as opposed to accumulation, of wealth in a few hands. To avoid accumulation of wealth among the rich only is in fact a clearly stated purpose of the Qur'ānic legislation on inheritance, family laws and taxation (cf. al-Ḥashr, 59:27).[129]

VII. Legal Alms (*Zakāh*)

Literally meaning 'purification' *zakāh* commonly refers to the obligatory tax that all affluent Muslims are required to pay. It is sometimes referred to as *ṣadaqah*. The difference between the two terms being that *ṣadaqah* is wider than *zakāh*. Whereas *ṣadaqah* includes both obligatory and voluntary alms; *zakāh* only denotes the obligatory variety. *Zakāh* too is not a single item of taxation but a compound term that includes a variety of taxes which the jurists have often discussed under separate headings, but which are basically all the sub–varieties of *zakāh*. Thus the *ṣadaqat al-fiṭr*, which is essentially a religious poll tax that is payable at the end of the fasting month of Ramaḍān, the ʿ*ushr*, or tithe, that is levied on agricultural produce, and *rikāz*, that is, tax on treasure troves and mines, as well as sacrificial meats (*al-aḍāḥî*) of cattle slaughtered on the festive occasion of ʿĪd al-Aḍḥā, all fall under the broad heading of *zakāh*. The main reason that the jurists have discussed these separately is due to their differential rates and also the heads of expenditure to which they might have been specifically assigned. The present discussion also follows this practical division of *zakāh*, albeit on a selective basis, but begins with expounding the main variety of *zakāh* first. The discussion then continues to provide an overview of voluntary charities including the *awqāf* (charitable endowments) and other charities.

Being a religious duty and one of the five pillars of Islam, *zakāh* is seen by the faithful, as a mark of personal piety, and a manifestation of their commitment to the humanitarian teachings of their religion. As such, pious Muslims often pay the *zakāh* directly to the poor at their own initiative without any official demand by the state authorities. Muslims have also paid and continue to pay other taxes to their governments, but they usually do so in conformity with the laws of government. Taxes other than *zakāh* were thus viewed differently in that they were not integrated into the religious ethos of Muslims in the same way as the *zakāh*.[130]

Modern writers on Islamic economics have underlined the economic significance of *zakāh*, which they have generally characterised as 'a microcosm of the entire Islamic economic system... *zakāh* has played a crucial and extended role in affecting, shaping and directing the Islamic economy virtually in all of its important ramifications.' *Zakāh* is designed to 'eradicate poverty, ensure equitable distribution of wealth... stimulate economic growth... and promote social welfare.'[131] *Zakāh* also signifies an indispensable socio-economic commitment of Muslims to meet the needs of the poor 'without putting the entire burden on the public exchequer, which socialism and the secular welfare state have unwittingly done.'[132]

In response to the question whether a Muslim government can introduce taxes other than *zakāh* and levies that were operative during the time of the Prophet and those of Pious Caliphs, early Muslim scholars have generally held that introduction of additional levies should be confined to exceptional situations. A perusal of the earlier opinion on this indicates that in situations of necessity when the public treasury is depleted of funds and the government cannot defend its territory nor administer justice and when hunger and starvation threaten the lives of the poor, only in such situations may the government levy additional taxes on the affluent members of the community. However, scholars of the later periods have recorded a different view to say that the government has authority to levy additional tax, not only in exceptional but also under normal conditions. This is due mainly to the extended role that the modern state plays in the economy and the fact that the scope of its activities is much wider compared to what it was in the early decades of the Islamic era. 'Given the emerging fiscal scenario in a large number of Muslim countries, the right of an Islamic state to raise additional revenue cannot be challenged.'[133] Many scholars in recent times including Yūsuf al-Qaraḍāwī, Muḥammad Hamidullah, Nejatullah Siddiqi, Hasanuz Zaman and Umar Chapra, among others, have spoken in support of this position.[134] The only proviso that is stipulated here is that taxation should be just and proportionate to the ability of the taxpayer, and also that it should promote the goals and objectives of *Sharī'ah* (*maqāṣid al-Sharī'ah*).

Charity serves two main purposes, one of which is to subjugate selfishness through generosity and achieve control of one's inner self by giving away something one would like for oneself, and the other is to advance solidarity and cooperation among human beings. These objectives are conveyed in the Qur'ānic references to charity as a purifier of both the donor and the property from which it is given (9:103). The text also speaks in condemnation of those 'who hoard gold and silver and spend it not in the way of God'. (9:34)

والذين يكنزون الذهب والفضة ولاينفقونها في سبيل الله فبشرهم بعذاب أليم

Charity is not limited by the boundaries of religious fellowship but contemplates human need and cooperation. So the Qur'ān says concerning the non–Muslims

لاينهاكم الله عن الذين لم يقاتلوكم في الدين ولم يخرجوكم من دياركم أن تبرّوهم وتقسطوا إليهم

'God does not forbid you to act righteously and justly toward those who have not expelled you from your homes.' (*al-Mumtahinah*, 60:8)

It is reported that the Prophet entitled a Jewish family to assistance from the *ṣadaqah* and it was being paid to them. The report here indicates as if it was an allocation that was regularly paid out.[135] The Prophet's wife, Lady Safiyyah, also gave *ṣadaqah* to her two Jewish relatives of certain items which they then sold for thirty thousand dirhams.[136]

Abū 'Ubayd has recorded a comment attributed to Ibn Jurayj concerning the Qur'ānic verse which entitled the prisoners to financial assistance. The verse in question is as follows:

ويطعمون الطعام على حبه مسكينا ويتيما وأسيرا

And they give food, for the love of God, to the poor, the orphan and the captive. (76:8)

At the time when this verse was revealed, it is noted that 'there were no other prisoners except for the idolaters.'[137] The love of God could, in other words be earned and manifested by feeding all prisoners regardless of their religion.

Muslim jurists have described the *zakāh* as 'wealth which is taken from the rich and distributed among the poor.' Other Qur'ānic terms which are used in conjunction with charity are *infāq* (spending) and *ihsān* (benevolence). *Zakāh* is payable by every Muslim who has enjoyed for one complete year full ownership of assets above the quorum (*nisāb*). The rate of *zakāh* for various types of assets was determined by the Prophet at two and a half per cent per annum on all productive wealth, land, livestock, business capital and merchandise. The rate goes up to five or ten percent (depending on whether irrigated or dry land) on agricultural produce including grains, pulses and fruits, and it is levied at twenty per cent on mines and treasures found underneath the earth. A new item that Qaradāwī has listed is buildings and factories which he held to be *zakāt*able items by analogy to agricultural land, as they two are sources of periodical income. And then also dairy products that attract *zakāh* by analogy to honey, at the rate of one-tenth. The fact that two other items, namely, vegetables and horses, were exempt from the *zakāh* was most probably due to the arid climate of Arabia and also continued warfare. I submit that these exemptions were circumstantial and may be regarded as temporary legislation (*tashri' zamanī*). These exemptions may still apply under similar circumstances, but not in cases or countries where trading in these items constitute substantial items of revenues, in which case, *zakāh* may be imposed on them. *Zakāh* is, according to Ibn Taymiyyah, a right of the people in the same way as prayer (*salāh*) is the right of God. Prayer and *zakāh* are very often mentioned in the Qur'ān together as the two pillars of Islam. They are also spoken of as the two principal ordinances of all the other revealed scriptures conveyed to Abraham, Moses and Jesus.[138]

Historically *zakāh* has been one of the most important sources of revenue of the early Islamic state, and the state was responsible for its collection and administration. *Zakāh* revenues are to be reserved for welfare assistance and should not be mixed with the general state budget. *Zakāh* is also not a state revenue in the ordinary sense of the word as the end-use of its fund is predetermined and ear-marked. The Qur'ān has in this context identified eight groups of recipients of which the poor and needy top the list:

إنما الصدقات للفقراء والمساكين والعاملين عليها والمؤلفة
قلوبهم وفي الرقاب والغارمين وفي سبيل الله وابن
السبيل فريضة من الله والله عليم حكيم

Alms (*ṣadaqāt*) are only for the poor (*fuqarā'*), and the needy (*masākīn*), and those who collect them (*'āmilīn*), and those whose hearts are to be reconciled (al-*mu'allafah qulūbuhum*) and (to free) the captives, and those in debt (*al-ghārimīn*) and in the way of God, and for the wayfarer, a duty from God, and God is Knower, Wise. (9:60)

This verse was revealed in Medina at a time when the foundations of Islam were firmly laid and Muslims had established a government. *Zakāh* is here referred to by its generic name *al-ṣadaqāt* (charities), but the concluding words at the end of the verse describes it as as *farīḍah*, that is, an obligatory duty, which makes it clear that the text refers to the obligatory alms of *zakāh*. *Mu'allafat al-qulūb* referred to both Muslims and non-Muslims, even rich and influential pagans whose support was important for the advancement of Islam. They were people 'to whom the Prophet gave gifts and grants to reconcile their hearts,' and it seems that they included non-Muslims who were recruited as soldiers but were not given a fixed wage. Some jurists have held the view that the *mu'allafat al-qulūb* came to an end and no longer existed after the demise of the Prophet.[139] They were in any case given a share in the *zakāh* revenues that was later discontinued by the second caliph 'Umar. A new equivalent of this share was later given under the Abbasids, to new converts to Islam who were in need of help to make adjustment to their new conditions.

It is not obligatory to spend the *zakāh* on all of the eight categories equally, nor is it necessary that all the eight heads of expenditures be included. The share of each category may be determined on the basis of need but if some of the potential beneficiaries are not available at a given time, their portion may be allocated to other similar charitable purposes.[140] The eight categories may be classified into basically two, one of which is entitled to *zakāh* because of need and this includes the poor (*fuqarā'*), the needy (*masākīn*), the wayfarer, freeing the poor slaves and the insolvent debtors (*ghārimūn*). The second group receives the *zakāh* on the basis of their contribution and benefit to society, and this comprises the *zakāh* officials, the *mu'allafat al-qulūb*, and the warriors. Ibn Qayyim al-Jawziyyah has consequently observed that in the absence of either of these criteria, namely need, and benefit to the community, no one is entitled to receive the *zakāh*.[141] Caliph ʿUmar I advanced consumer loans as well as business loans from the funds of the *Bayt al-Māl* whereas ʿUmar II wrote to his governors to relieve the debt burden of insolvent debtors with government funds. On a similar note ʿUmar II is reported to have advanced agricultural loans to farmers.[142]

A distinction has also been made between the first two classes of *zakāh* recipients namely the poor (*faqīr*) and needy (*miskīn*) in that the former is one who is in need but does not beg the people for help whereas the *miskīn* does.[143] The former should be given priority over the latter. According to yet another interpretation attributed to the caliph ʿUmar b. al-Khaṭṭāb, *fuqarāʾ* refer to poor among Muslims whereas *masākīn* refer to poor among non-Muslims[144] Later still, a practical distinction was drawn between *fuqarāʾ* and *masākīn* in that the former meant persons whether Muslim or *dhimmī*, who were afflicted with poverty, whereas *masākīn* meant those who were able to work but lacked the means to secure employment.

Abject poverty is not a requirement in either case. Thus if a person has some property but his income falls below his sufficiency level, he is a *faqīr* and therefore entitled to receive *zakāh* and may not be compelled to sell his property. There is some difference of opinion among the *madhāhib*, but broadly speaking, owning a house, furniture, books and a horse and also having a servant do not necessarily disqualify a person from being recipient of the *zakāh* assistance if his income is insufficient to meet his needs and those of his family.[145]

The *ʿāmilīn* (employees) category comprises *zakāh* collectors and officials employed to administer and distribute the *zakāh* funds. This may naturally include auditors and supervisors who are involved in the task as well as expenditure that is necessary to facilitate efficient administration of the *zakāh* revenues. The Prophet himself entitled the *zakāh* collectors to a share in its revenue.[146]

Gharīm is the insolvent debtor who is entitled to assistance to clear his debt which is not due to criminal causes. Historically, it is known that the Jews, Romans and pre-Islamic Arabs permitted enslavement of the *gharīm*, which Islam prohibited, except in the cases of a wilful defaulter. One who was able but refused to pay his debt was a transgressor who could be imprisoned on the authority of a renowned *ḥadīth* that 'procrastination by an affluent debtor is injustice.'[147] (مطل الغنى ظلم) To help the debtor in this way was undoubtedly an unprecedented development of its time, but it is perfectly understandable in the Islamic setting due especially to the prohibition of usury *(ribā)*. Since usury was prohibited, giving a benevolent loan *(qarḍ ḥasan)* was encouraged and equated to an act of charity *(ṣadaqah)*. To entitle the debtor to support was also meant to protect the benevolent creditor who had after all responded to the call to help the needy. The poor were generally indebted and were to be helped to be relieved of their debts. The prohibition of usury in earlier times involved charging of onerous interest on borrowed assets. The poor often borrowed at high rates of interest for fulfillment of their basic needs, and due to their inability to pay back entered the ranks of the *ghārimīn*.[148]

An affluent person who is temporarily in hardship may also be helped from the *zakāh* funds. The caliph ʿUmar also added a new dimension to this: Instead of outright grants, he used to give loans to help people meet an emergency. These loans, of course, carried no interest.[149] It is further suggested that only a living debtor may be helped from the revenues of *zakāh* but not a deceased person who has left behind unpaid debts. This is partly because the debts of the deceased are transferred together with his assets to the surviving heirs.[150] In a letter that the Umayyad caliph ʿUmar b. ʿAbd-ʿAzīz wrote to the governor of Kufa, Zayd b. ʿAbd al-Raḥmān, the following instruction was given: 'I learned that you have some funds left after payment of the army allowances. I write this to ask you to pay out of this fund people who are indebted without mischief or those who wish to get married but need assistance.'[151] Thus, if indebtedness is due to indulgence in lawlessness, it would not qualify for help.

Ibn al-sabīl (wayfarer) is one who is stranded en route to his destination and has depleted all his resources. He is entitled to assistance from *zakāh* funds enough to enable him to reach his place of residence. The wayfarer is entitled to assistance even if he is affluent in his home town. The wayfarer can also be any traveler, Muslim or non-Muslim. No distinction need be made in the offer of help or hospitality to them. In view of the extensive travel facilitates that have become available nowadays, this category may be extended, perhaps, to cover the entire range of tourist facilities including, that is, the building of roads and bridges, provision of facilities for travelers to ensure their safety on the road and in the place they stay as well as provision of healthy food and health care services for them. The Caliph ʿUmar ensured that wayfarers had water and shelter along the route between Mecca and Medina. His governor Abū ʿUbaydah had rest houses built for this purpose. ʿUmar II's predecessors, Walīd and Hishām, also built guesthouses and facilities along passenger routes.[152]

The two heads of expenditure in the verse under review, namely 'in the cause of God', and 'for those whose hearts are to be reconciled' are also understood to mean that the *zakāh* funds may be expended on the defence and propagation of Islam and help to the armed forces. Some flexibility is thus available, as noted above, over the distribution of *zakāh* revenues. Priority must be given, however, to the needs of the locality, town or region from where the *zakāh* funds are realised. *Zakāh* collected in one region may only be transferred to another region after meeting the needs of that region first. It is for the government to decide, in the event of a dire need for transfer of assets of *zakāh* from one locality to another, whether a transfer should be made. A transfer of this kind is basically not recommended unless it is validated on grounds of exceptionally stressing circumstances.[153]

Zakāh is to be assessed annually except in the case of agricultural produce, mineral and marine products, on which *zakāh* is payable as and when they materialise. *Zakāh* may be disbursed in cash or kind.

There is no prescribed limit on what a single person or family may receive out of *zakāh* funds during a year, but the jurists tend to be in agreement that the entire expenditure for a year of a recipient may be disbursed from the *zakāh* revenue when sufficient funds are available. This is based on the analysis that *zakāh* itself is collected annually and the need of its recipients should also be considered on that basis. This does not, however, mean that assistance should be discontinued after one year. Assistance from *zakāh* may be continued for longer, or be given in lump sum to the extent of sufficiency whereby the recipient is no longer in need of assistance. There is evidence in the *Sunnah* and in the precedent of the Pious Caliphs that the purpose is to fulfill the needs of the poor to an extent, as far as possible, to take them out of that condition to the state of sufficiency, and this is not necessarily a goal that can be confined to a particular time frame.[154]

Entitlement to assistance is also not limited to food, clothing and shelter but includes marriage expenditure as this too is considered to be included in basic needs. Professional and skilled persons who become victims of adversity may be assisted in the purchase of their tools of trade and the amount of assistance may vary considerably from case to case. A tailor, carpenter or baker may need considerably less to activate his business compared to a jeweler or dealer in precious stones. Each one is entitled to assistance to enable them to earn a living. Those who are engaged in pursuit of beneficial knowledge, whether of religion or other useful disciplines, may also be assisted in the purchase of books and whatever they may need to enable them to function in their respective capacities. It is interesting to note here that Muslim jurists do not entitle to assistance one who devotes himself entirely to worship, but they do entitle to such assistance those who devote themselves to pursuit of knowledge. This is because worship is not a full-time occupation whereas pursuit of knowledge usually is. Al-Qaraḍāwī has observed, and rightly so, that children's education and medical care should also now qualify for assistance from the *zakāh* funds.[155]

The quorum of *zakāh*, or *niṣāb*, differs with different kinds of assets. With regard to silver, it is 200 dirhams, or 595 grammes, and for gold, it is 20 *mithqāls* or 85 grammes. For merchandise of all kind, the value is calculated on the basis of a silver standard. The *niṣāb* of cereals is five *awsaq*, which is equal to 653 kilogrames. Except for agricultural produce, all of this refers to assets that have been owned for one calendar year (*al-ḥawl*). The assets so owned must also be in excess of personal needs and clear of liabilities and debts.[156]

Spending in the way of God (*infāq fī sabīl Allāh*) which also occurs in the verse of *zakāh* is broadly understood by Qur'ān commentators to mean spending on what realises benefit for the community as a general and continuous item of state expenditure. This is also implied elsewhere in the text which enjoins Muslims to 'spend in the way of God and throw not yourselves into danger by your own hand.' (2:195)

وأنفقوا في سبيل الله ولاتلقوا بأيديكم إلى التهلكة

Spending in the cause of God thus means spending on maintenance of peace and security, economic development and industrial projects as well as welfare purposes of the community as a whole.[157] More specifically the jurists have identified three levels of benefits to be secured by such expenditures: the essential benefits (*al-maṣāliḥ al-ḍaruriyyah*) such as internal security, basic necessities of life, and administration of justice; complementary benefits (*ḥājiyyāt*) which aim at removal of hardship from the people although life can continue without them. A great deal of economic development matters and provision of public services fall under this category. And lastly the desirabilities and embellishments (*taḥsīniyyāt*) which means securing benefits that bring beauty and comfort to the people. These three classes of benefits are not exclusive as the categories may converge into one another, yet the division is naturally meant to suggest an order of priorities in the allocation and expenditure of funds for welfare purposes.[158]

In distributing *zakāh* to deserving persons in the locality, the principle of equality is to be observed. If some prove to be more pious then others, their reward is a matter between them and their Creator as was stated by the first caliph Abū Bakr. Local welfare needs and public expenditure on peace and administration of justice will also take priority in the allocation of *zakāh* funds. Should the funds of *zakāh* be less than the items of expenditure that are given in the verse of *zakāh*, priority is given to the needs of the poor who are to be given their due first, and the remainder to be equally distributed among the other deserving categories. In the event where the *zakāh* revenues exceed the identified heads of expenditure, the balance is to be deposited in the public treasury in order to be utilised on general welfare objectives of the community.[159]

As noted earlier, *zakāh* was collected and disbursed by the state in the early periods of Islamic history. Since the time of the caliph ʿUthmān, the right of government to demand payment of *zakāh* was confined to the openly visible assets such as crops and livestock whereas assessment of the less visible assets such as cash, gold and silver was left to the conscience of the individual. This was partly due also to increase in the state revenues and some difficulty that was encountered in the calculation of such assets.[160]

The state's prerogative to collect *zakāh* has in fact been indicated by the allocation of a share in *zakāh* revenues to *zakāh* collectors in the verse of *zakāh* (9:60). This shows that the text authorises the imam to appoint collectors and administrators for the purpose. The reference to ʿāmilīn in the said verse has thus established an undisputed right for the state to enforce the *zakāh*.[161] As a pillar of the faith, the faithful may still assess and pay *zakāh* as an when it falls due on their assets. For the greater part of Islamic history conscientious Muslims have actually paid the *zakāh* as a religious duty, just as they also supported other Islamic activities on a voluntary basis.[162] In the case of those who evade due payment of *zakāh*, Islamic law does not confiscate the property at issue as a penalty but penalises the defaulter instead. Thus according to Ibn Qudāmah, if the Imam is able to collect it from the defaulter, he does so and punishes him 'for neglecting the duty of *zakāh* with *taʿzīr*, but he takes no more than the amount of the *zakāh* that is due. All the Sunnī schools agree on this'.[163]

Zakāh is at present collected and distributed by the state only in some countries such as Pakistan, Saudi Arabia, the Sudan, and to some extent also in Malaysia and Bangladesh where state agencies are involved in the administration of *zakāh*. In many other Muslim countries and countries with Muslim minorities, there are numerous regional and local organisations administering *zakāh* on a voluntary basis. But a sizeable part of *zakāh* is given by the *zakāh* payers directly to the poor in the locality. This has also meant disparities in the practice and administration of *zakāh* which call for uniform policies. To provide help for the able-bodied poor from the *zakāh* funds and enable them to earn their living is one such area where a uniform policy decision would be helpful. It is important especially for Muslim minorities, to adopt models of *zakāh* administration which respond to their particular needs.[164]

As already noted, *zakāh* is a special right of the poor and it is best to be distributed directly among the poor and not to be paid to the *bayt al-māl*. But even if it is paid into the *bayt al-māl*, as indeed it was in the time of the Pious Caliphs, it is to be segregated and not mixed with other state revenues. With this one exception, all other state revenues from whatever source they come are payable to the *bayt al-māl* and as such they become public property which is expended on general government expenditures.[165]

VIII. The *Fiṭr* and *Aḍḥā* Charities

Each year on the occasion of *ʿĪd al-fiṭr* celebration that marks the end of the fasting month of Ramaḍān, every Muslim, male and female, minor and major is required to pay the *fiṭr* alms. Anyone who has food for himself and his family for more than a day and a night is required to give a specified amount as charity for himself and his dependants; that is, his wife, young children and parents. But if the dependants have property of their own, it is payable from their own property. The *fiṭr* charity thus amounts to an annual poll tax, which is payable in staple food, such as wheat, barley and dates at the rate of one *ṣāʿ*, that is about 2.75 kilogrammes per person. This is determined in a *ḥadīth* which provides that 'the Prophet, peace be on him, prescribed the *zakāh* of *fiṭr*, ending the Ramaḍān, at a *ṣāʿ* of dates or barley on every Muslims, freeman and slave, man and woman, child and adult all alike.'[166]

عن ابن عمر رضي الله عنهما قال: فرض رسول الله صلّى الله عليه وسلّم زكاة الفطر صاعًا من تمر أو صاعًا مِن شعير على العبد والحرّ والذّكر والأنثى والصّغير والكبير من المسلمين

As will be noted, the *fiṭr* charity in this *ḥadīth* has also been referred to as *zakāh*, which is obligatory according to general consensus (*ijmāʿ*). It is a tax not only on the affluent but on every person to compensate for any imperfections incurred in fasting and also to help the poor. Whenever possible, it should be handed over directly to the deserving party preferably in kind, but may also be paid in its monetary equivalent, according to the Ḥanafīs. The head of the household who is responsible for the maintenance of his wife, child and servant is also responsible for paying the *fiṭr* charity for them. Many contemporary writers have concurred with the Ḥanafī ruling and have considered monetary payment now to be more convenient for both the donor and recipient. Reports also indicate that prominent figures among the followers such as ʿUmar b. ʿAbd al-ʿAzīz, Ḥassan and ʿAṭā used to give the monetary equivalent to the poor. This charity is generally payable to those who are eligible to receive *zakāh*. Unlike the *zakāh*, however, the *fiṭr* charity was not collected nor administered by the state in earlier times, but there is nothing against intermediation if it is deemed beneficial. Abū Maysarah narrated a *ḥadīth* that 'the people used to pool their *fiṭr* alms with him of which he then gave some to the Christian monks.'[167] The *fiṭr* alms may thus be given to anyone in need including non–Muslims. Smaller population centers in earlier times made person-to-person transfer relatively easy. Since the densely populated metropolis of the modern era tends to present difficulties, intervention by voluntary organisations to collect and distribute their charity has consequently been accepted and widely practiced.[168]

The possible yield of the *fiṭr* alms may be estimated as follows: if we assume a country in which poverty is spread to the extent that 20 per cent of its people do not possess more than one day's food on the night of ʿĪd al-fiṭr, this would mean that among ten citizens there are two on whom the *fiṭr* charity is not obligatory and eight on whom it is. Thus it may be said that there would be four persons paying this charity for each person receiving it. Hence the average amount that is due to be received by each individual is about ten kilogrammes of foodstuffs.

The other annual charity to be mentioned here is that of ʿĪd al-aḍḥā, the annual feast at which animals are sacrificed and meat is distributed among the poor. Every affluent person (i.e., a niṣāb holder) is to sacrifice a head of cattle each year on certain days of the twelfth month of the Islamic calendar commemorating the sublime sacrifice of the prophet Abraham. One family may slaughter a larger head of animal on behalf of the entire household. This is upheld in a ḥadīth 'from ʿĀʾishah the Prophet's widow that the Prophet's household sacrificed one bull on the occasion of the last ʿĪd (before the Prophet passed away).'[169]

عن عائشة زوج النبي صلى الله عليه وسلم نحر عن آل محمد في حجة الوداع بقرة واحدة

Basic authority for the alms of aḍḥā is found in the Qurʾān which enjoins the faithful to 'pray unto thy Lord and sacrifice.' (108:2)

فصل لربك وانحر

The prayer meant here is also the aḍḥā prayer that is offered on the occasion. The jurists are, however, divided between the two positions as to whether the slaughter of aḍḥā is obligatory (wājib), or an emphatic Sunnah (sunnah muʾakkadah) only. The two positions are probably not very different as among the Muslim masses the sacrifice of aḍḥā is very much a living tradition, especially noticeable during the ḥajj ceremonies in Mecca, but also in other Muslim countries almost everywhere.[170]

It will briefly be noted that a separate organisation was established under the Abbasids toward the end of second/eighth century for the administration of charities and social welfare allocations. This was the Dīwān al-Birr waʾl-Ṣadaqāt which was complementary to the main treasury department (Bayt al-Māl) and supervised the collection of zakāh and other charities such as tithes and booty. The revenues collected were assigned to charitable causes as the Qurʾān had specified. The head of this department, known as Ṣāḥib Dīwān al-Birr waʾl Ṣadaqāt, was selected from among pious and virtuous individuals, and so were the employees of his department. The assets collected by this department were segregated in that they could not be utilised for other purposes nor were they to be mixed with other items of state revenues. A provincial branch of this Dīwān was also established in every province and the principle that guided their activity was that the revenues collected were to be expended in the locality of their origin. The local officials occasionally solicited the guidance of the *qāḍī* in the conduct of their affairs. The near equivalent of the Dīwān al-Birr wa'l-Ṣadaqāt in the present-day Middle East is the Ministry of Social Welfare (*Wazarat al-Shu'ūn al-Ijtimā'iyyah*), which has inherited many of the welfare functions of the Dīwān al-Birr wa'l-Ṣaqadāt.[171]

IX. Tithe, Land Tax, and Poll Tax (*'Ushr, Kharāj, Jizyah*)

There is no *zakāh* on agricultural land and dwellings, but there is a tax called *'Ushr*, which is a variety of *zakāh* imposed on the produce of the land. Although it is known as *'Ushr*, or the tenth part, the actual rate of tax on produce is imposed variously according to the type of land. The rate is one-tenth of the produce for dry farming land, and it is reduced to one-twentieth if the land is irrigated by artificial methods. The tax is to be paid at harvesting time by the land owner to the public treasury. The lower rate on irrigated land is due to the higher cost of labour and investment. *'Ushr* is, like *zakāh*, an obligatory tax which is to be distributed among the same eight categories of people as the Qur'ān has specified for *zakāh*.[172]

The *'Ushr* tax also comprised custom duties that were introduced on import and export of merchandise during the time of the second caliph 'Umar b. al-Khaṭṭāb. Muslim merchants who traded their goods in foreign lands had to pay a tenth of its value in tax to the non-Muslim government, a fact which prompted the Caliph to impose the same on a reciprocal basis on foreign merchandise imported into the Muslim territories. The *'Ushr* revenues that were so realised were also payable to the *bayt al-māl*.[173]

Kharāj is tax on land that is conquered by the Muslims but which is in the possession of their owners, while *jizyah* is a poll-tax levied on non-Muslims who are permanent residents of Muslim dominated territories. All revenue from *kharāj* and *jizyah* is payable to the *bayt al-māl* to be spent on community welfare purposes, but not necessarily on the same classes of people as the text has specified for *zakāh*. Muslims pay the *zakāh*, but since *zakāh* is a religious tax, it is not imposed on non-Muslims, who pay instead the *jizyah*. The term *jizyah* implies the idea of recompense (from the root word *jazā*) as it is paid in order to compensate the state for security and protection that it provided for the non-Muslims. *Jizyah* was levied only on adult, able-bodied non-Muslim males, but not on their women and children, nor on those stricken by old age and disease. *Jizyah* is lifted once a non-Muslim citizen embraces Islam.[174]

The *kharāj* tax is imposed on agricultural land owned by non-Muslim citizens. It is a tax that is attached to the land and not to the person owning it, which is why it does not cease by conversion to Islam of its owner or of the person who is farming it. The *kharāj* tax is also not associated with the religious denomination of one who pays it. It is a land tax that is payable by all landowners and it need not even retain that name.[175]

Due to historical reasons and the obvious change of circumstances, neither of these two taxes can be meaningfully applied under the present conditions of uniform taxation that currently prevails. This is not to say, however, that the basic concepts of *kharāj* and *jizyah* have become invalid, it is just to say that the effective cause (*ʿillah*) and rationale on which they were founded are not present under the prevailing tax regimes. If it is admitted that the current tax laws in contemporary Muslim countries impose a uniform tax regime on all citizens, Muslims and non-Muslims alike, and that non-Muslim citizens are also required to serve in the armed forces side by side with their fellow Muslims, then to impose additional taxes on them in the name of *kharāj* and *jizyah* will be manifestly unjust. If *jizyah* was originally levied as compensation money in lieu of state protection then participation in the armed forces would have invalidated that logic. Should there be an unexpected change of conditions and situations change drastically so as to justify a separate regime of taxation on the basis of the religious following of citizens, then *kharāj* or *jizyah* may well be restored as they would have in principle remained valid.

X. Mineral Tax (*Rikāz*) and Unclaimed Assets (*Dawāʾiʿ*)

Rikāz is an obligatory tax that is payable to the *bayt al-māl* and it is, as such, a means of wealth distribution in the community. Anyone who finds a mine or treasure trove beneath the surface of either owned or unowned land must pay one-fifth of it to the public treasury. Mineral resources of all kind as well as wealth found in the deep sea fall under the broad heading of *rikāz*. One who finds *rikāz* thus pays one-fifth to the treasury and retains the four-fifth. The *rikāz* tax is normally payable on the day a treasure is found or when its benefit is realised.

The heads of expenditure for *rikāz* and the manner of its expenditure and distribution have not been specified. The Imams Shāfiʿī and Ibn Ḥanbal have held, however, that *rikāz* revenue should be spent in the same way as the *zakāh* with the aim of need fulfillment and eradication of poverty among the designated beneficiaries.[176]

There is some disagreement as to the precise meaning of *al-rikāz*. The jurists of Iraq understood it as a broad term which comprised mines and treasure trove of which one fifth is payable to the *bayt al-māl*. The jurists of *Hijaz* (Mecca and Medina) held on the other hand that *rikāz* only applies to treasure trove but not to mineral wealth. Only the former is subjected to on-fifth but the latter is liable to the normal rules of *zakāh*. Imam Mālik and a number of other jurists have thus held that a mine partakes in the status of a farm. *Zakāh* is imposed on the produce of farms and the same applies to mineral wealth. This disagreement over the precise meaning of *rikāz* has not been resolved in view of the fact that both of the above mentioned schools have quoted *ḥadīth* in support of their positions and claim to have provided the correct understanding of that evidence.[177]

Those who draw a distinction between treasure trove (*kanz*) and mineral find (*maʿdan*) maintain that the former is buried wealth that belongs to a human being whereas the latter is God-given wealth. The rules of *rikāz* basically apply to mineral finds and its application to treasure trove is secondary and tropical. Juristic details also distinguish between treasure trove that is found in privately owned land, and land which is not so owned. According to the Imams Abū Ḥanīfah and Mālik, four-fifths of the treasure trove that is found in private land belongs to the owner of land, but according to Abū Yūsuf, it belongs to anyone who actually finds it, and no distinction in this respect is made between Muslim and non-Muslim and even children who are entitled to it in the same way as anyone else.[178]

Dawāʾiʿ includes any property or asset whose owner is neither known nor traceable and this includes lost property (*luqṭa*) and also property left by a deceased person who has no legal heir to inherit. Due diligence must be made to find the owner of such assets who would have priority to it failing which, the assets in question are payable to *bayt al-māl* and may be spent on public welfare purposes.[179]

XI. Expiations (*Kaffārāt*)

One other area where assistance to the poor has been integrated into the structure of religious duties is expiation for crime and sinful conduct. *Kaffārah*, which literally means 'a concealer', is supposed to act as an atonement that hides the crimes and makes up for failure in the observance of certain religious duties. The *Sharī'ah* has thus specified a number of instances where a *kaffārah* has to be given and it is often given in terms of charity and financial assistance to the destitute.

Kaffārah may in certain cases be the only compensation for sin or it may be supplementary to a punishment. *Kaffārah* is thus the principal atonement for a sin such as taking a false oath, or dishonouring an oath that is duly taken, and the transgressor is liable to a *kaffārah* of '... feeding ten poor persons with the kind of food you take with your family, or providing clothes for them.' (5:89)

لا يؤاخذكم الله باللّغو في أيمانكم ولكن يؤاخذكم بما عقّدتم الأيمان فكفّارته إطعام عشرة مساكين من أوسط ما تطعمون أهليكم أو كسوتهم

The *kaffārah* for failure to fast during the month of Ramaḍān without a valid excuse is one of the following three options: to release a slave, to fast for two months, or to feed sixty poor persons. This is also the expiation which must be observed by one who has sexual intercourse with one's spouse during daytime in Ramaḍān. In early Arabian society one who committed *ẓihār*, in which a person resembled his wife to his mother actually incurred a divorce. The divorce in question was, however, not specified by the law whether revocable or final. But if the husband wished to resume marital relations with his estranged wife he was required to give a *kaffārah* of the same order and type as the Qur'ān had specified for failure to observe the fast of Ramaḍān (58:4). The *fiqh* texts are elaborate on this and specify many other instances of transgression where a *kaffārah* falls due, in which case the person who gives the expiation normally gives it directly to the poor. If sixty poor persons cannot be found, it is acceptable, according to the Ḥanafīs at least, to feed one person sixty times, or for that matter ten persons on six occasions.

Expiation that supplements another punishment occurs in the Qur'ān in conjunction with unintentional homicide, and according to some jurists also in conjunction with intentional killing of another human being. These are offences for which the *Sharī'ah* provides a punishment, but the killer is required in the meantime, to repent and make his repentance good by an atonement which consists, once again, of either releasing a slave, fasting for two consecutive months, or feeding/clothing sixty poor persons (4:92).

The *Sharīʿah* provisions pertaining to *kaffārāt* are designed not only to promote acts of devotion but also acts that seek to strengthen the bonds of fraternity and cooperation in the Muslim community.[180] The *kaffārāt* are generally self-imposed and not justiceable, as they normally fall outside the jurisdiction of courts and governments.[181] In the event where the practicalities of life in crowded cities make it difficult to find deserving individuals, or poor persons to receive the *kaffārah*, it should be acceptable to pay the sums involved to an orphanage or poor peoples homes, and the authority may act in ways that may facilitate the collection and administration of the *kaffārāt*. Releasing a slave is obviously not feasible now due to the abolition and termination of slavery. A near equivalent of this might be to pay for a poor person's medical operation or an expensive surgery that would not be feasible without a generous charitable donation.

What has so far been discussed all belong to the broad category of 'obligatory charities,' which according to many economists, have enormous potentialities for mobilising sizeable funds dedicated mainly to the eradication of poverty. The estimates are that the annual yield of obligatory charities a Muslim country would be able to pool together can easily be around three per cent of its gross domestic product.[182] A carefully designed system of collection, management and distribution of these assets can go a long way to alleviate poverty and provide for a welfare assistance programme.

XII. Voluntary Charities

These are addressed under two headings, namely *taṭawwuʿ* (supererogatory) and *waqf* (charitable endowment) as follows:

SUPEREROGATORY CHARITIES (*ṢADAQAT AL-TAṬAWWUʿ*)

There is evidence in the Qurʾān and *Sunnah* to the effect that the legal alms of *zakāh* is the minimum that is levied for the purpose of welfare assistance. According to the expressed terms of *ḥadīth* 'there is a right in property other than the *zakāh*.'[183]

إن في المال حقا سوى الزكوة

The poor is, in other words, entitled to more than the *zakāh*. Voluntary charity is not regulated nor quantified as such and may be given any time to the poor or given in support of a good cause. Voluntary charity that is recommended in the Qur'ān and *Sunnah* falls under the general category of *ṣadaqat al-taṭawwuʿ* for which no minimum nor maximum has been specified. Charity should be given in the way of God; it may be given openly or given discreetly so as not to undermine the self-esteem of its recipient.

This latter method of giving charity is, in fact, highly recommended in the Qur'ān as in the following verse:

الذين ينفقون أموالهم في سبيل الله ثم لايتبعون ما أنفقوا منّا ولاأذى لهم أجرهم عند ربهم ولاخوف عليهم ولا هم يحزنون قول معروف ومغفرة خير من صدقة يتبعها أذى

As for those who spend their wealth in the way of God, then do not follow up what they have spent with reminders of their generosity nor do they annoy the recipient, they shall have their reward from their Lord. Kind speech and forgiveness is better than charity followed by injury. (2:262–3)

Elsewhere the Qur'ān speaks in praise of those who feed the poor, the orphan and the captive for the love of God (saying), 'we feed you for the sake of God alone without expecting from you any reward or gratitude.' (76:8)

ويطعمون الطعام على حبه مسكينا ويتيما وأسيرا إنما نطعمكم لوجه الله لانريد منكم جزاء ولاشكورا

The scope of voluntary charity is not confined, as is indicated in the following verse:

وما تقدموا لأنفسكم من خير تجدوه عند الله هو خيرا وأعظم أجرا

And whatever good you send forth for your soul you shall find it
in God's presence, indeed a better and greater reward. (73:20)

The Prophet has also praised those who give charity discreetly and
conceal their generosity such that the left hand does not know what
the right hand gives.[184] Priority is given, among the recipients of
charity, to those who do not ask for it but are actually in need of
help (cf. Qur'ān, 2:273). And then a relative also has a prior claim to
one's assistance and generosity.

Neighbours are yet another category in respect of whom the
Qur'ān and *Sunnah* recommend generosity and kindness (*iḥsān*).
The text in this connection speaks of three types of neighbours,
the neighbour-cum-relative, neighbour who is not a relative, and
companion in a journey, or one who may be sitting next to one in a
meeting or a public place (4:36). Acts of kindness among neighbours
(*al-Māʿūn*) is the title, in fact of a Qur'ānic sura where the text closes
on a striking note:

$$\text{فويل للمصلين الذين هم عن صلاتهم ساهون الذين هم}$$
$$\text{يراءون ويمنعون الماعون}$$

So woe to those who pray, but who do not think of what it means;
those who do an act of goodness in order (merely) to be seen,
and refrain from (a small) act of kindness. (107:4–7)

Commentators have understood *al-Māʿūn* as being helpful in lend-
ing a utensil to a neighbour and small acts of generosity in giving of
foodstuffs and presents. Even the use of kind words is considered a
charity in this context (cf. Qur'ān, 17:23). Charity is indeed a broad
concept in Islam and includes a vast number of opportunities in the
daily lives of the faithful. Activities such as greeting the people with
kind words, removing or alleviating hardship from others, even cleanliness and removing of any object of obstruction from a public path
etc., are all mentioned in *ḥadīth* as acts of charity especially for those
who may be unable to give charity in material and monetary terms.
To be good to one's neighbour includes Muslims and non–Muslims
alike. The renowned Companion Mujāhid has thus reported that he
happened to be visiting his fellow Companion. ʿAbd Allāh b. ʿUmar,
who had slaughtered a sheep and told his servant to give some meat to
his Jewish neighbour. He repeated this several times until the servant
told him why he was repeating himself, to which Ibn ʿUmar replied

that the Prophet advised his Companions so persistently on this that
he almost thought that the Prophet would assign to the neighbour a
share in inheritance.[185]

ما زال جبريل يوصيني بالجار حتى ظننت أنه سيورثه

Voluntary charity also includes giving of a benevolent loan (*qarḍ
ḥasan*), or vowing to give a special charity i.e. *al-nadhr* as thanksgiving
for a happy turn of events. Making a will to promote a good cause or
help a person who needs support for such a cause are also included in
the broad concept of voluntary charity. The *Sharīʿah* allows this up to
the maximum of one-third of one's property.[186] I propose, however,
not to dwell on all of them, but to address one of these namely the
charitable endowment (*waqf*) in some detail due to the significant role
it has played in the history of voluntary charities.

CHARITABLE ENDOWMENTS (*AWQĀF*)

Notwithstanding the fact that *waqf* is a voluntary charity, it has
played an historically more significant role than most of the obligatory
charities, in providing a stable source of support for a wide range
of beneficial activities. Literally meaning 'dedication', *waqf* may be
defined as a transfer of wealth from private ownership to collective
ownership for a beneficial purpose. Almost every type of property
that is capable of yielding an income or benefit, including agricultural
land, orchards, wells, baths, bakeries, and schools have been assigned
into *waqf* by pious individuals throughout the Muslim world. The
scale and size of *waqf* properties that currently obtain in some Muslim
countries is large enough for them to assign a special ministry for
their administration usually known as the Ministry of Awqāf. When
the owner of a property voluntarily assigns his property into *waqf*, he
relinquishes his personal right of ownership concerning that property,
simply because in theory the dedicated property is transferred to
the ownership of God. This may explain why no one exercises
proprietary rights over the *waqf* property but the income from it is
spent on a beneficial purpose that is usually specified in the deed of
waqf.[187] The legality of *waqf* is established in a *ḥadīth* wherein Ibn
ʿUmar reported that his father, ʿUmar b. al-Khaṭṭāb acquired land in
Khaybar and then told the Prophet that 'I have never had property
more valuable to me than this.' The Prophet suggested to him: 'if you
wish, you may retain its principal and give its yield in charity.'[188]

'Umar b. al-Khaṭṭāb is said to have done so in light of the Qur'ānic declaration: 'you will not attain (spiritual) excellence unless you spend out of that which you (really) love for yourselves.' (3:92)[189]

$$\text{لن تنالوا البرّ حتى تنفقوا ممّا تحبون}$$

Historically *waqf* endowments supported education and mosque-related activities, animal welfare, health facilities ranging from hospitals to homes for the disabled, provision of drinking water, welfare of prisoners, rest rooms for travelers, helping young persons to get married and the like, all on a voluntary basis by pious individuals throughout the Muslim World.

Numerous residential units in Mecca in the vicinity of the Holy Mosque have thus been assigned into *waqf* for the use of the *ḥajj* pilgrims. The number of such endowments increased to an extent that some jurists gave *fatwā* which declared invalid renting out such properties to the pilgrims during the *ḥajj* period. The reason given was that nearly all of them were *waqf* properties that were initially assigned for the use of the pilgrims. Hence they should not have to pay rent.[190]

The management of *waqf* property is normally entrusted to a supervisor, or *mutawalli*, of *waqf* who is often nominated by the dedicator (*wāqif*). Some deeds of *waqf* also nominate a second person who is then designated to succeed the supervisor when the latter becomes incapacitated or dies.

Historically, the state intervention in the management of *waqf* generally remained at a low level but the courts of justice had powers nevertheless to look into any complaints that arose concerning mismanagement and waste of the *waqf* properties. In course of time, however, the state became increasingly active in the management of *awqāf* due to many causes, chief among which was widespread mismanagement and abuse of office by *waqf* supervisors. Another reason given for the active State involvement was the fact that *waqf* properties were exempt from tax as they were also exempt from *zakāh*. This prompted the State to take over control of some *waqf* properties, as a rapidly growing *waqf* sector was likely to reduce the fiscal resources of the state.[191]

A *waqf* property is not a state property, just as it is not a private property either. Once it is made, a *waqf* endowment is permanent and irrevocable. Historically the *awqāf* endowments had a cumulative effect as private properties passed into *waqf* but the reverse could not take place. Inefficient management and the fact that the *waqf* sector largely operated outside the competitive property market caused problems so much so that *waqf* properties failed on the whole to operate at optimal levels of productivity and good management.

Another problem area concerning the *awqāf* was the family *waqf* (*waqf ahlī*, also known as *waqf dhurrī*) as opposed to benevolent *waqf* (*waqf khayrī*), or public *waqf*, the latter of which is not confined to the family and seeks to promote public welfare objectives. The family *waqf*, although remaining under control of the family, is also not always locked into the family circle as such. Family *waqf* may be designed such as to end up to become a public charitable *waqf* after the first one or two generations. In the event the family line discontinues the *waqf* that is dedicated in its name also terminates and converts into a *waqf khayrī*.[192] Notwithstanding the doubtful basis in law of the family *waqf*, it was nevertheless practiced by individuals who wished to keep the capital assets of *waqf* within the family and dedicate only its revenue to charitable causes. Problems arose because sometimes the dedicator defined the purpose of *waqf* either too narrowly or too vaguely which gave, in turn, the family members the flexibility to utilise the property according to their own wishes.[193] This would explain why in recent times, legislation in Muslim countries has generally sought to abolish the family *waqf*. Syria and Egypt introduced legislation in 1949 and 1952 respectively, which abolished family *waqf* altogether and other countries have generally followed suit.[194]

The *awqāf* are in need of further reformist legislation to overcome many of their long-standing problems. The increased state intervention in the *awqāf* was initially prompted by dissatisfaction, as already noted, over the activities of their supervisors. Yet instead of exerting a moderate influence to check individual abuse, the state itself added to the problematics of *waqf* through the introduction of heavy bureaucracy that proved to be inefficient, and generally suppressed personal initiative. The situation reached a critical stage to an extent as to prompt one observer to say that '*awqāf* are becoming extinct' mainly because people are not encouraged to establish them anymore.[195]

Two other problems concerning *waqf* that may briefly be mentioned are concerned with land reform legislation, and the rigidity of *waqf* assets respectively. Recent land reform legislation in many countries including Egypt, Turkey, Syria, Bangladesh and Pakistan has confined individual ownership of land to certain quantitative limits, and this has encouraged, in turn, the splitting up of agricultural estates among family members. This has proved to be another disincentive for agricultural *awqāf* by individuals who no longer owned larger estates that had previously encouraged setting up of *waqf* endowments.[196]

The *awqāf* properties are also difficult to convert into more liquid assets, giving rise to the difficulty therefore to reinvest the *waqf* assets into more profitable forms of investment in the event the *waqf* in question is no longer profitable. This has been a long-standing problem with many *awqāf* estates that were poorly managed and generated low income. Transfer of *waqf* assets into other investment vehicles naturally gave rise to issues over authorisation and ownership, which often proved to be complex, and as such positively discouraged any subsequent changes into the original deeds of *waqf* and the expressed will of its dedicator. These are, however, among the issues which fall beyond the immediate concern of this study.[197]

To give one example of the problematics of *waqf* in the Indian subcontinent, we note that there are close to 400,000 *awqāf* properties in India but a great number of them are faced with difficulties. Many have been deserted due to mass migration of Muslim populations during partition to Pakistan, and similar problems have been caused by internal migration of Muslims to different localities. The *waqf* properties are consequently left behind without anyone taking responsibility for their upkeep. One significant development has, however, been the sitting up of Waqaf Boards which are vested with powers to make decisions concerning the individual *awqāf* under their jurisdiction in co-operation sometimes with a *Sharīʿah* judge and scholar. Deserted and desolate *awqāf* can be sold and the proceeds can be invested in a new and more viable *waqf.* In a 1997 Fiqh seminar held in Mumbai, the seminar requested the Secretary General of the Islamic Fiqh Academy of India to form a committee to facilitate 'the necessary amendments in the Waqf Act along with valuable suggestions to the Parliamentary Committee formed by the government of India for Muslim Awqāf.'[198]

Notwithstanding the problematics of *waqf,* the vast properties that have been assigned into *waqf* in almost every Muslim country by wealthy individuals have made a rich contribution to the advancement of welfare activities and fulfilment of the needs of the poor. The *awqāf* sector made a visible impact on wealth distribution and mitigation of financial inequality in Muslim countries.

There is, at present, apprehension, over the increasing scale of appropriation of *waqf* property by the state. This has happened especially in countries with Muslim minorities where the state may not be supportive of religious endowment activities. Government attitude and policy have thus posed difficulties and often worked as disincentive for people to create charitable endowments. The increased Islamic awareness in recent decades among minority Muslim communities has, on the other hand, drawn attention to the important role *waqf* can play in support of certain religious purposes for which the state is not expected to allocate funds.

The emergence, in recent years of Islamic financial institutions, trusts and charity foundations that volunteer to play a role in welfare activities is also a hopeful sign for the future of *awqāf*. New legislative reforms of *waqf* may hopefully be introduced to encourage participation in the *waqf* sector by the Islamic charitable as well as investment organisations. Supportive legislation of this kind in the Muslim countries may open new possibilities for *waqf* endowment to enable them to play a greater role in welfare support programmes in their respective communities.[199]

XIII. Public Treasury (*Bayt al-Māl*)

Numerous references have been made, in the course of this study, to the *bayt al-māl*, which is why, it is proposed now to say a few words on it with the purpose specifically to note that *bayt al-māl* has historically been associated with the welfare objectives of Islam so much so that its commitment to welfare dominated the whole of the *bayt al-māl*.

Bayt al-māl was for the first time established by the second caliph ʿUmar b. al-Khaṭṭāb whose reign saw an unprecedented expansion of the territorial domain of the early caliphate. The sources of revenue which were hitherto almost totally confined to the *zakāh* and spoils of war had rapidly expanded to include other items of revenue. Parallel expansion was also evident in the state expenditures, from administration and defence, to welfare objectives whereby the state played an increasingly important role in the material well-being of its citizens. In a general sense, *bayt al-māl* or Public Treasury in an Islamic polity is entitled to receive all assets which have no known owner and also the general revenues of the state through taxation. The unowned assets may in this connection include the *waqf* endowments that have no known administrator and no one as its designated beneficiary so long as this does not contravene the stipulated conditions of the *waqf*.[200] The state is entitled also to borrow on credit or impose additional taxes on the affluent in the event where the *bayt al-māl* runs out of funds and the security and other needs of maintenance of law and order in the community cannot be met without them.[201]

The revenues of *bayt-al-māl* are varied and they are naturally not confined *to zakāh*. The full range of *bayt al-māl* revenues that were known in earlier times were on the whole of two types, namely regular and periodical revenues such as the *zakāh*, land tax (*kharāj*), poll-tax (*jizyah*), the tithe, and taxes that were imposed on a variety of agricultural produce and merchandise, including custom duties. The second category of revenues were the irregular and *ad hoc* type which were realised at times and were absent or discontinued at other times. Included in this category were the war booty (*ghanīmah*) and assets realised in the conquered lands without any war, unclaimed inheritance, loans and credits and also other assets that had no owner or beneficiary.[202]

As of the time of the second caliph ʿUmar b. al-Khaṭṭāb, the *bayt al-māl* was divided into four separate branches, each of which became recipient to certain items of revenues and also acquired responsibility for certain types of expenditures. A closer look at the organisation of *bayt al-māl* and its division into various branches helps to reflect the extent of its commitment to welfare objectives. Al-Kāsānī who lived in the latter part of sixth/twelveth century described the four departments of the *bayt al-māl* as follows:

(1) The *bayt al-māl* of *zakāh*, which was the main recipient of the *zakāh* in all of its varieties. The revenues that were received by this branch were entirely devoted to the eight heads of expenditure as were specified in the Qur'ān. Notwithstanding their strong Islamic features, *zakāh* revenues were not only given Muslims, the poor and destitute among Muslims and non-Muslims were entitled to assistance from its revenues. This was in keeping with the precedent of the caliph ʿUmar, who was known to have assigned allowances from the *zakāh* funds to non-Muslims.[203] Often quoted in this context was the case of an elderly Jewish man whom the Caliph saw begging in the market place. The Caliph enquired into his condition and then asked the keeper of *bayt al-māl* to assign him an allowance that he would receive during his old age.

(2) *Bayt al-māl* of booty, mineral resources, and treasure troves: The revenues of this section of the *bayt al-māl* were also assigned to welfare assistance to the poor, as in the first section above.

(3) *Bayt al-māl* of land tax and poll tax (*kharāj* and *jizyah*) and that which could be subsumed under these headings. The funds in this section of the *bayt al-māl* were assigned for general state expenditures,

including salaries of the army personnel, judges, other state officials, building of mosques, bridges, rest houses for travelers and allocations to the *ʿulamā'* who gave *fatwā* on government affairs.[204]

(4) *Bayt al-māl* of escheats and unowned assets (*al-ḍawā'iʿ*): Revenues from this part of the *bayt al-māl* were expended on health care for the ill, unprotected children (*al-laqīṭ*) and orphans, maintenance for the unemployed and those who were unable to work and also on their dependants. Other items in this category were funeral expenditures on the deceased persons who had left no assets behind.

The caliph ʿUmar described his own standing vis-à-vis the *bayt al-māl* as a 'guardian of the orphans' who was under duty to spend out of its assets with a high sense of responsibility and trust. The Caliph also went on record to say that 'there is not one person among Muslims who did not have a claim over the *bayt al-māl*'.[205] The State was clearly a trustee and caretaker of the public funds, committed to providing welfare assistance, and committed to ensure proper administration of the *bayt al-māl*.

XIV. Concluding Remarks

Issues over the feasibility of welfare support programmes and availability of means by which the state may be expected to meet its responsibilities call for fresh appraisal and commitment in the modern context. It is unfortunate that the vast majority of Muslim countries are not economically strong enough to be able to provide an adequate, let alone a comprehensive, unemployment and welfare benefits programme for their citizens. The level of national income in most Muslim countries is insufficient even to meet the basic needs of its citizens. What the *Sharīʿah* requires, in other words, is not within the available means of governments in most Muslim countries, although some of the more affluent states of the Gulf, Saudi Arabia and even Malaysia can afford to have a basic programme of need fulfilment. Some steps have also been taken toward the realisation of welfare programmes in these countries.

It is a matter of priority for a Muslim state to articulate its commitment to the citizens welfare. Ibn Taymiyyah has so long ago considered it as one of the defining characteristic of an Islamic welfare state to accept legal responsibility for the well-being of all its subjects, over and above even its responsibility for the maintenance of law and order and defence of territory. The material well-being and survival of the poor and the unemployed are too important to be left to individuals and families, customary and charitable initiatives of persons. The state must clearly make the provision of welfare benefits as its basic responsibility but also to encourage private initiative, and help with the collection and distribution of religious taxes and charities. Thus it is suggested that the state's responsibility in this respect should be clearly articulated in the constitutions of the Muslim countries.

The constitution should contain a clause that spells out the stat's commitment to the citizens welfare. The strong and unequivocal position that Islam takes on people's welfare and need fulfilment would help ensure support among the Muslim masses for such a commitment. There should also be a way for those actually in need of food, clothing and shelter to have their needs fulfilled through a direct and easily accessible method that does not involve lengthy procedures. No other conditions should be attached to this facility except the actual need. While the recipient of help may subsequently be obliged to work in order to earn a living, this should not be a precondition of receiving assistance for the basic necessities of life. The basic outline of a policy and commitment along these lines should be clearly determined in the light of prevailing conditions.

If a country is poor and has no surplus funds at its disposal, the need-fulfilment issue would naturally have to be addressed within the limitations of the available means. If a country is affluent, on the other hand, the scope and dimension of its welfare duty should not be confined to the basic minimum but that the standards of assistance that is provided should aim higher to include better facilities. The more affluent Muslim countries are thus expected to put in place a more diversified welfare programme that is in consonance with their economic capability and resources.

The network of obligatory alms and other charities that the *Sharī'ah* has stipulated are not enforced in most of the contemporary Muslim countries, or else that they are only partially enforced. Modern tax laws have generally replaced and subsumed the religious framework of taxation and charities. Voluntary charities are evidently left to the initiative of the individual. Voluntary charities and obligatory alms are an entrenched part of Islam which must naturally remain so, but the state has in the meantime a responsibility to play a supportive role in their collection, utilisation and management. From the viewpoint of Islamic jurisprudence, the lawful government and those in charge of community affairs (*ulū al-amr*) are authorised to turn the recommendable (*mandūb*) into *wājib* should the benefit and *maṣlaḥah* of people require such. Hence, any affirmative legislation that aims at greater efficiency in realising the people's welfare would be acceptable within the rubric of *Sharīʿah* and would also be likely to enlist public support.

Zakāh is an obligation and the Islamic polity has a responsibility to ensure that it is duly collected and administered within its proper framework. Since it is a separate tax that is designed to be distributed among the poor, it can be administered side by side with other tax laws. It may even be collected together with the general income tax but should be separately identified and made tax-deductible. This might mean that the state collects *zakāh* on an obligatory basis, side by side with the income tax, but provides tax relief on religious charities , indeed all charities. The tax system, including the religious taxes, must in all cases be fair and affordable to the taxpayer. Ways and means should also be found within the general framework of a *Sharīʿah*-oriented policy (*siyāsah sharʿiyyah*) to administer a just and balanced tax regime that is in harmony with the welfare objectives and purposes of *Sharīʿah*. Policy measures and affirmative action thus play a role no less important than the legal text and religious principle. It is a momentous challenge for virtually every Muslim government, indeed all governments in the developing countries, to take a pragmatic approach to welfare that is informed by the Islamic outlook, but even more importantly to develop the economic resources that is the prerequisite of a comprehensive welfare programme.

NOTES

1. Tabrīzī, *Mishkāt*, vol. ii, *ḥadīth* 3086.

2. See for details on *fay'* and *ghanīmah* Ibn Qudāmah, *al-Mughnī*, vi, 455f; Abū ʿUbayd, *Kitāb al-Amwāl* (Ghiffari's tr.), 17ff; Zarqā, 'Islamic Distributive Schemes,' 185f.

3. Al-Dughmī, *Naẓariyyah al-Amn al-Ghazāʾī*, 140; and Mushtaq Ahmad, *Business Ethics*, 53.

4. Tabrīzī, *Miskhkāt*, vol. iii, *ḥadīth* 5096.

5. Muslim, *Mukhtaṣar Ṣaḥīḥ Muslim*, 472, *ḥadīth* 1773.

6. Id., 472, *ḥadīth* 1774.

7. Al-Nawawī, *Riyāḍ al-Ṣāliḥīn*, 113, *ḥadīth* 118.

8. Abū Dāwūd, Sunan, *K. al-Kharāj Waʾl-Imārah, b., fī arzāq al-ʿummāl, ḥadīth* 2945; Zuḥaylī, *Ḥuqūq al-Insān*, 297.

9. Tabrīzī, *Mishkāt*, vol. ii, *ḥadīth* 3571.

10. Al-Nasāʾī *Sunan*, K. al-Istiʿādhah, b. al-istiʿādhah min sharr al-kufr; Qaraḍāwī, *Mushkilat al-Faqr*, 14.

11. Tirmidhī, *Sunan*, Abwāb al-Farā'id, b. mā jā'a fī mīrath al-māl.

12. Abū Dāwūd, *Sunan*, K. al-Nikāḥ, b. al-walī; Tirmidhī, *Sunan*, Abwāb al-Nikāḥ, b. mā jā'a lā nikāḥ illā bi-walī.

13. Tirmidhī, *Sunan*, Abwāb al-Farā'id, b. man taraka mālan fa li-warathatihi. For a slight variation of the same *hadīth* see Muslim, *Mukhtaṣar Ṣaḥīḥ*, 263, *hadīth* 999.

14. Abū Dāwūd, *Sunan*, K. al-Kharāj wa'l-Fay' wa'l-Imārah, b. fī mā yalzam al-īmān.

15. Ahmad b. Ḥanbal, *Al-Musnad*, *hadīth* no. 4880; Zuhaylī, *Al-Fiqh al-Islāmī*, v, 526.

16. Abū 'Ubayd, *Al-Amwāl*, 595; Zuhaylī, *Al-Fiqh al-Islāmī*, v, 526.

17. Cf. Al-Bayātī, *Niẓām al-Siyāsī*, 141; al-Dughmī, *Naẓariyyah*, 165.

18. Ahmad Ibn Ḥanbal, *Al-Musnad* (Cairo edn. by A.M. Shakir), vol. ii, *hadīth* 596.

19. Abū Dāwūd, *Mukhtaṣar Sunan Abī Dāwūd*, K. al-Kharāj wa'l-Imārah, b. al-imām yuqbal hadayah al-mushrikīn.

20. Tabrīzī, *Mishkāt*, vol. i, *hadīth* 1849.

21. Abū Dāwūd, *Sunan*, K. al-zakāh, b. mā tajūzu fihi mas'alah.

22. Al-Ṣan'ānī, *Subul al-Salām*, ii 145; Dughmī, *Naẓariyyat al-Amn*, 148.

23. Cf. Al-Dughmī, *Naẓariyyat al-Amn*, 149

24. Al-Sarakhsī, *Al-Mabsūṭ*, vol. 30, 271.

25. Abū Dāwūd, *Sunan*, K. al-zakāh, b. mā tajūzu fihi mas'alah; al-Māwardī, *al-Aḥkām al-Sulṭāniyyah*, 214.

26. Al-Tabrīzī, *Mishkāt*, vol. ii, *hadīth* 2781.

27. Al-Bājī, *Al-Muntaqā bi-Sharḥ al-Muwaṭṭā*, vii, 324. Imam Mālik who reported this *hadīth* said that an *awqīyah* amounts to 40 dirhams. See also al-Dughmī, *Naẓariyyah*, 66.

28. Hassanuz Zaman, *Economic Functions*, 315, 29; al-Sulamī, *Qawā'id al-Aḥkām* (al-Ḥusaynniyya edn.), 148. See also Siddiqi, *The Role of the State*, 11.

29. Al-Sulamī, *Qawā'id al-Aḥkām fī Maṣāliḥ al-Anām*, 148; see also Siddiqi, *The Role of the State*, 11.

30. Ibn Ḥazm, *al-Muhallā*, vol. vi, 58.

31. Ibn Sa'd, *Al-Ṭabaqāt*, vol. iii, 317; See also Siddiqi, *The Role of the State*, 18.

32. Ibn Kathīr, *Al-Bidāyah wa'l-Nihāyah*, vii, 136; Hazanuz Zaman, *Economic Functions*, 299; Dughmī, *Naẓariyyat al-Amn*, 142.

33. Ibn Kathīr, *al-Bidāyah wa'l-Nihāyah*, vol. vii, 46.

34. Ibn Sa'd, *Ṭabaqāt*, iii, 305. See also Siddiqi, *The Role of the State*, 11.

35. Ibn Kathīr, *Al-Bidāyah wa'l-Nihāyah*, ix, 57; Ṭabarī, *Tārīkh*, ii.1028; Hazanuz Zaman, *Economic Functions*, 301 & 306.

36. Zaman, *Economic Functions*, 319.

37. Abū Dāwūd, *Mukhtaṣar Sunan Abī Dāwūd*, K. al-Kharāj wa'l-Imarāt wa'l-Fay', b. fī qismat al-fay'.

38. Ibn al-Asīr, *al-Ta'rikh al-Kāmil*, vol. v, 24.

39. Ibn al-Ḥakam, *Sīrat ʿUmar bin ʿAbd al-ʿAzīz*, 41; Sibāʿī, *Takāful*, 354.

40. Id., p. 67, and Abū ʿUbayd, *Kitāb al-Amwāl*, 251; Siddiqi, *The Role of State*, 16.

41. Ṭabarī, *Tārīkh*, ii, 275, also quoted in Zaman, *Economic Functions*, 321.

42. Hasanuz Zaman, *Economic Functions*, 301.

43. Abū ʿUbayd, *Kitāb al-Amwāl*, 559.

44. Hasanuz Zaman, *Economic Functions*, 300.

45. The sums allocated varied from a high of 12000 down to 2000 dirhams and even lower for other categories. See for details Zaman, *Economic Functions*, 303.

46. Hitti, *History of the Arabs*, 172.

47. Id., 327.

48. Abū ʿUbayd, *al-Amwāl*, 58f; Zaman, *Economic Functions*, 300.

49. Zaman, *Economic Functions*, 301.

50. Abū ʿUbayd, *al-Amwāl*, 20 and 621.

51. Id., 586; Zaman, *Economic Functions*, 304.

52. Cf. Zaman, *Economic Functions*, 301–302.

53. Abū ʿUbayd, *al-Amwāl*, 620.

54. See for details, Zaman, *Economic Functions*, 303.

55. Ibn Saʿd, *Ṭabaqāt*, iii, 1; Ibn Kathīr, *al-Bidāyah*, ix, 57; Zaman, *Economic Functions*, 305–306.

56. Hitti, *History of the Arabs*, 221.

57. Id.

58. Islahi, *Economic Concepts of Ibn Taymiyyah*, 177–78.

59. Ibn Taymiyyah, *al-Ḥisbah*, 16.

60. Ibn Taymiyyah, *Majmuʿah Fatāwā*, vol. 29, 279; Islahi, *Economic Concepts*, 18.

61. Id., vol. 29, 570; also quoted in Islahi, *Economic Concepts*, 181.

62. ʿIzz al-Dīn ʿAbd al-Salām, *Qawāʿid al-Aḥkām*, vol. i, 71–72; see also al-Dughmī, *Naẓariyyah*, 141.

63. Al-Buhūtī, *Kashshāf al-Qinnāʿ*, iii, 103; see also al-Dughmī, *Naẓariyyah*, 141

64. Ghazālī, *Al-Iqtiṣād fi'l-Iʿtiqād*, 214.

65. Al-Shāṭibī, *Muwāfaqāt*, vol. 2, 177.

66. Al-Ghazālī, *Al-Tibr al-Masbuk fī Nasā'ih al-Mulūk*, 94; see also Siddiqi, *The Role of the State*, 14.

67. Al-Nawawī, *Minhāj al-Ṭālibīn*, 125.

68. Ibn Ḥazm, *Al-Muḥallā*, vol. vi, 156.

69. Siddiqi, *The Role of the State*, 22.

70. Id., 15.

71. Id., 22.

72. Ibn Ḥazm, *Al-Muhallā*, vol. vi, 159; Zarqā, 'Islamic Distributive Schemes,' 191.

73. Siddiqi, *The Role of the State*, 15.

74. Id.

75. Munawar Iqbal, ed., *Distributive justice*, 10.

76. Abū Zahrah, *Tanẓīm*, 152; Qaraḍāwī, *Khaṣā'is*, 79; Sibāʿī, *Takāful*, 194.

77. Qaraḍāwī, *Khasa'is*, 79-80.

78. Al-Nawawī, al-*Majmuʿ Sharḥ al-Muhadhdhab*, iv, 194, also quoted by Hamid Hassan, *Right to Social Security*, 23.

79. Qaraḍāwī, *Khaṣā'is*, 80.

80. Sarakhsī, *al-Mabsūṭ*, K. al-zakāh, ii, 18. See also Hamid Hassan, *Right to Social Security*, 25.

81. Nawawī, *al-Majmuʿ*, vi, 190; Ibn Qudāmah, *al-Mughnī*, ii, 670; Rayyān, *al-Riqābah al-Maliyyah*, 179.

82. Abū ʿUbayd, *al-Amwāl*, b. adna mā yuʿta al-rajul al-wāḥid min al-ṣadaqah, sections 1772-1774, 472. See also Hamid Hassan, *Right to Social Security*, 19; Rayyān, al-Riqābah, 179.

83. Dusūqī, *Ḥāshiyat al-Dusūqī*, ii, 181; Rayyān, *al-Riqābah*, 179.

84. Abū ʿUbayd, *al-Amwāl*, b. dhikr al-ṣadaqah al-ladhīna yatib lahum akhdhuhā, 495; also quoted by Hassan, *Right to Social Security*, 20.

85. Nawawī, *al-Majmūʿ*, K. al-Zakāh, iv, 192.

86. Ibn Qudāmah al-*Mughnī*, K. al-Zakāh, ii, 664; see also Hassan, *Right to Social Security*, 26.

87. Kāsānī, *Badā'iʿ al-Ṣanā'iʿ*, ii, 912; also quoted in Hassan, *Right to Social Security*, 27.

88. See for a discussion Munawar Iqbal, *Distributive Justice*, Introduction and passim.

89. Al-Sibāʿī, *Ishtirākiyyat*, 204; Abū Zahrah, *Tanẓīm*, 146; al-Ṣadr, *Iqtiṣādunā*, 701; Qaraḍāwī, *Mushkilat al-Faqr*, 121; al-Mubārak, *Niẓām al-Islām*, 133ff; Sayyid Quṭb, *al-ʿAdālah*, 240.

90. Siddiqi, *The Role of the State*, 14.

91. Id., 23.

92. Quoted in Islahi, *Economic Concepts of Ibn Taymiyyah*, 182.

93. Siddiqi, *The Role of the State*, 65-66.

94. Id., 66.

95. Siddiqi, *The Role of the State*, 28.

96. Id., 29.

97. Ibn Mājah, *Sunan*, K. al-Zuhd, b. al-tawakkul wa'l-yaqīn, *ḥadīth* 4168.

98. Bukhārī, *Mukhtaṣar Ṣaḥīḥ al-Bukhārī* (Abyani's edn.) K. al-Ṭibb 511, *ḥadīth* 1870.

99. Nawawī, *Riyāḍ al-Ṣaliḥīn*, *ḥadīth* 153.

100. For further details on this see Kamali, *Right to Life, Security, Privacy and Ownership in Islam* (especially the first chapter on 'The Right to Life.')

101. Ḥasan al-ʿĪlī, *al-Ḥurriyyat*, 490.

102. Tabrīzī, *Mishkāt*, vol. I, *ḥadīth* 181.

103. Zaman, *Economic Functions*, 320 & 335.

104. Cf. Ḥasan al-ʿĪlī, *al-Ḥurriyyat*, 492.

105. The full Arabic text of this 25-article document can be found in an appendix to Muṣṭafā al-Zuḥaylī, *Ḥuqūq al-Insān fi-l Islām*, 400–409.

106. Cf. Zuḥaylī, *Ḥuqūq al-Insān*, 303.

107. Cf. Nabhānī, *al-Niẓām al-Ijtimāʿī*, 181-183.

108. Kāsānī, *Badāʾiʿ*, v, 2247; Sibāʿī, *Takāful*, 305; Qaraḍāwī, *Mushkilat al-Faqr*, 56, 63. In the case of one's wife the unpaid *nafaqah*, also turns into a debt that the defaulting husband may be ordered to pay.

109. Muslim, *Mukhtaṣar Ṣaḥīḥ Muslim*, K. al-Birr wa'l-Ṣillah, b. fī ṣallat al-raḥim, 471, *ḥadīth* 1764.

110. Cf. Kāsānī, *Badāʾiʿ*, v.2231.

111. Kāsānī, *Badāʾiʿ*, v. 2196–97.

112. Cf. Id., v.2229.

113. Tabrīzī, *Mishkāt*, vol. 1, *ḥadīth* 3242.

114. Kāsānī, *Badāʾiʿ*, v.2246.

115. Qaraḍāwī, *Mushkilat al-Faqr*, pp. 61–62.

116. Al-Jazīrī, *al-Fiqh ʿalā al-Madhāhib al-Arbaʿah*, vol. III, *Kitāb al-Ṭalāq, Mabāḥith al-Nafaqah*; al-Zuḥaylī, *Al-Fiqh al-Islāmī*, vol. v, 527; al-Dughmī, *Naẓariyyah al-Amn*, 156ff.

117. See for details Zuḥaylī, *Al-Fiqh al-Islāmī*, vol. VII, 765ff; Qaraḍāwī, *Mushkilat al-Faqr*, 59ff.

118. Zuḥaylī, *Al-Fiqh al-Islāmī*, vol. VII, 772; Abū Zahrah, *al-Mujtamaʿ al-Insānī*, 112.

119. Tabrīzī, *Mishkāt*, vol. II, *ḥadīth* 1843; al-Ṣanʿānī, *Subul al-Salām*, vol. III, 220; al-Haythamī, *Majmaʿ al-Zawāʾid*, III. 115.

120. Al-Ṣanʿānī, *Subul al-Salām*, II, 142.

121. Kāsānī, *Badāʾiʿ*, v. 2239.

122. Qaraḍāwī, *Mushkilat al Faqr*, 88, 99.

123. Tabrīzī, *Mishkāt*, vol. II, *ḥadīth* 3346.

124. Tabrīzī, *Mishkāt*, vol. II, *ḥadīth* 1830.

125. Cf. Sibāʿī, *Takāful*, 106.

126. Cf. Abū Zahrah, *al-Mujtamaʿ al-Insānī*, 114–116; Sibāʿī, Takāful, 206.

127. For more details on *istiḥsān* see Kamali, *Equity and Fairness in Islam*. The whole of this book looks into the methodology of *istiḥsān* and its various applications. A chapter on *istiḥsān* can also be found in Kamali's *Principles of Islamic Jurisprudence*, 323–351.

128. Shahrūr's recent book, *Nahw Uṣūl Jadīdah li'l-Fiqh al-Islāmī: Fiqh al-Mar'ah*, 219ff. provides much technical detail on the issue of women's inheritance. See also a brief comment by Selim el-Awa, which appears in Essam Hassan, *Revitalisation of Political Thought*, 152–3.

129. Cf. Abū Zahrah, *al Mujtama'* , 116.

130. Cf. Sibāʿī, *Takāful*, 331.

131. Imtiazi, 'Management of Zakah,' 19; see also Afzal Peerzade, 'Expenditure tax in the Islamic Fiscal System,' 30.

132. Chapra, *Islam and the Economic Challenge*, 272.

133. Peerzade, 'Expenditure Tax in the Islamic Fiscal System,' in *J. of Islamic Economics*, vol. 11, 31.

134. A summary of their views appears in id., 31, and also in Siddiqi, 'Place for Additional Levies in Islamic Shariah,' in Syed Afzal Peerzade, ed. *Readings in Islamic Fiscal policy*, 54ff. (Delhi, Adam Publishers, 1996).

135. Abū ʿUbayd, *al-Amwāl* (Ghiffari's tr.) 514, para. 1983.

136. Id., para. 1984.

137. Id., para. 1985.

138. Al-Kāsānī, *Badā'i'*, ii, 934ff; Qaraḍāwī, *Mushkilat al Faqr*, 65; Islahi, *Economic concepts of Ibn Taymiyyah*, 209; Zarqā, 'Islamic Distributive Schemes', 177.

139. Cf. Abū ʿUbayd, *Kitāb al-Amwāl* (Ghiffari's tr.), 508, paragraphs 1951–53.

140. Cf. Islahi, *Economic concepts of Ibn Taymiyyah*, 215.

141. Ibn Qayyim, *Zād al-Maʿād*, i, 306; Qaraḍāwī, *Mushkilat al-Faqr*, 79.

142. Zaman, *Economic Functions*, 320.

143. Cf. Abū ʿUbayd, *Kitāb al Amwāl* (Ghiffari's tr.), 505, para. 1932.

144. Abū Yūsuf, *Kitāb al-Kharāj*, 126.

145. Ibn Qudāmah, *al-Mughnī*, ii, 525; Qaraḍāwī, *Mushkilat al-Faqr*, 88.

146. Abū ʿUbayd, *Kitāb al Amwāl*, 507.

147. Abū Dāwūd, *Sunan*, K. al-Buyuʿ, b. fi'l-maṭl, ḥadīth 3345; Kāsānī, *Badā'i'*, ii, 910f.

148. Cf. Munawar Iqbal, *Distributive justice*, p. 188; Siddiqi, *The Role of State*, 143.

149. Hamidullah, *Emergence of Islam*, 242.

150. Abū ʿUbayd, *al-Amwāl* (Ghiffari's, tr.) 511, para. 1971.

151. Sibāʿī, *Takāful*, 356.

152. Kāsānī, *Badā'i'*, ii, 904–908; Muḥammad Hamidullah, *Emergence of Islam*, 243; Zaman, *Economic Functions*, 319.

153. Cf. Qaraḍāwī, *Mushkilat al-Faqr*, 104; Sibāʿī, *al-Takāful al-Ijtimāʿī*, 204.

154. Id., 92–94.

155. Id., 97–79.

156. Idem, *Fiqh al-Zakāh*, 563ff; Sibāʿī, *al-Takāful*, 203; Nadwi, *Four Pillars of Islam*, 111.

157. Rayyān, *al-Riqābah al-Māliyyah*, 49.

158. See for further details, Kamali, *Principles of Islamic Jurisprudence*, 271f.; Rayyān, *al-Riqābah al-Māliyyah*, 144.

159. Dusūqī, *Ḥāshiyah al-Dusūqī*, II, 190; Yūsuf Rayyān, *al-Riqābah al-Māliyyah*, 183.

160. Ibn Qayyim, *Iʿlam*, I, 352; Kāsānī,, *Badāʾiʿ al-Ṣanāʾiʿ*, II, 35.

161. Kāsānī, *Badāʾiʿ al-Ṣanāʾiʿ*, II, 35.

162. Cf. Siddiqi, *The Role of the State*, 138ff; see also Rayyān, *Al-Riqābah al-Māliyyah*, 39.

163. Ibn Qudāmah, *al-Mughnī*, vol. II, 435ff.

164. Siddiqi, *The Role of the State*, 139.

165. Cf. Al-Dughmī, *Naẓariyyah*, 140.

166. Al-Bukhārī, *Ṣaḥīḥ al-Bukhārī*, *ḥadīth* 1407.

167. Abū ʿUbayd, *al-Amwāl*, (Ghiffari's tr.) p. 514, para. 1986.

168. Zuḥaylī, *Al-Fiqh al-Islāmī*, vol. II, p. 900ff; Qaraḍāwī, *Muskhkilat al-Faqr*, p. 66i; Sibāʿī, *Takāful*, p. 209; Siddiqi, *The Role of the State*, p. 140.

169. Abū Dāwūd, *Sunan*, *K. al-Manāsik*, *b. fī hady al-baqar*, *ḥadīth* 1750.

170. Cf. Sibāʿī, *Takāful*, 209; Zarqā, 'Islamic Distributive Schemes' in Iqbal ed., *Distributive Justice*, 179.

171. Cf. al-Sayed, *Social Ethics of Islam*, 181–182.

172. Cf. al-Zuḥaylī, *al-Fiqh al-Islāmī*, vol. II, 800.

173. Cf. Ḥasan, *al-Nuẓūm al-Islāmiyyah*, 239.

174. Cf. Mushtaq Ahmad, *Business Ethics*, 61.

175. *Cf.* Abdul Rauf, *Ummah*, 39.

176. Cf. Qaraḍāwī, *Fiqh al-Zakāh*, 434; Zarqā, 'Islamic Distributive Scheme,' 186–87.

177. Abū ʿUbayd, *al-Amwāl* (Ghiffari's tr.), 286-288, para. 258 & 265.

178. See for details Kāsānī, *Badāʾiʿ* II, 752f.

179. Ḥasan Ibrāhīm Ḥasan, *al-Nuẓūm, al-Islāmiyyah*, 239.

180. Cf. Abū Zahrah, *al-Mujtamaʿ al-Insānī*, 129; Sibāʿī, *Takāful*, 208.

181. id., 189.

182. Siddiq, *The Role of the State*, 141.

183. Tirmidhī, *Sunan*, vol. II, 85, *ḥadīth* 654; al-Dārimī, *Sunan* I, 471, *ḥadīth* 13.

184. This is a part of a longer *ḥadīth* which begins as follows: 'There are seven whom God most High shelter under His own shadows on the Day when there

will be no shadows, except His. . . and a man who gives charity but gives it such that his left hand doe not know what is expended by the right hand.' See Muslim, *Mukhtasar Sahīh Muslim*, 49, *hadīth* 937.

185. Bukhārī, *Sahīh al-Bukhārī* (Muslim Khan's trans), vol. VIII, *hadīth* 43; Qaradāwī, *Mushkilat al-Faqr*, p. 116.

186. Some details on these and other related themes can be found in Mushtaq Ahmad, *Business Ethics*, p. 60ff; al–Zarqā, 'Islamic Distributive Schemes' in Munawar Iqbal, *Distributive Justice*, 179ff; Siddiqi, *Role of* the *State in the Islamic Economy*, Chapters 1 and 5.

187. Cf. Wahbah al–Zuhaylī, *Al-Fiqh al-Islāmī*, vol. IV, 60; Qaradāwī, *Muskhkilat al-Faqr*, 132; Sibāʿī, *Takāful*, 333.

188. Shawkānī, *Nayl al-Awtār*, vol. VI, 20; see also Wahbah al–Zuhaylī, *Al-Fiqh al-Islāmī*, vol. VIII, 155.

189. Cf. Hamid Hassan, *Right to Social Security*, 33.

190. Fahmī Huwaydī, *Hattā lā Takūna Fitnah*, 155.

191. Zuhaylī, *al-Fiqh al-Islāmī wa-ʿAdillatuhu*, vol. II, 736; Siddiqi, *The Role of the State*, 147.

192. Sibāʿī, *Takāful*, 206 and 333.

193. Cf. Siddiqi, *The Role of the State*, 148.

194. Cf. Zuhaylī, *al-Fiqh al-Islāmī*, VIII, 161.

195. Hashmi, 'Management of *waqf*: Past and Present,' 26.

196. Id.

197. For further details on *waqf* and my own responses to some of the problematics of *waqf* see Kamali, *Equity and Fairness in Islam* (section on *waqf*).

198. See for detail, Islamic Fiqh Academy (India), *Important Fiqh Decisions*, 110f; also my personal conversation with my colleague Prof. Syed Khalid Rashid at the IIUM.

199. Historically the *awqāf* had been a major source of support for educational institutions and public welfare foundations before the state became the principal actor in the public education sector.

200. Māwardī, *al-Ahkām al-Sultaniyyah*, 213; Rayyān, *al-Riqābah al-Māliyyah*, 53.

201. Ghazālī, *Mustasfā*, I, 303; Māwardī, *al-Ahkām al-Sultaniyyah*, 215.

202. Cf. Rayyān, *al-Riqābah al-Māliyyah*, 37.

203. Kāsānī, *Badā'iʿ al-Sanā'iʿ*, vol. II, 959; Abū Zahrah, *al-Mujtamaʿ al-Insānī*, 187.

204. Kāsānī, ibid; Sibāʿī, *Takāful*, 210.

205. Kāsānī, *Badā'iʿ al-Sanā'iʿ*, II, 959; Sibāʿī, *Takāful*, 211.

Glossary

ʿadl: justice, uprightness.
ʿālim (pl. *ʿulamāʾ*): scholars, learned people.
ʿām: general.
ʿamal ṣāliḥ: good deed.
ʿāmilīn: employees.
ʿaql: reason or human intellect.
ʿaqliyyah: rational.
ʿarīf: commander.
ʿibādah (pl. *ʿibādāt*): devotional act, worship.
ʿilm dirāyah: transmitted knowledge.
ʿilm riwāyah: rational knowledge.
Ahl al-ḥadīth: proponents or partisans of Traditions (*ḥadīth*).
Ahl al-raʾy: partisans or proponents of opinion.
ajīr mushtarak: common employee.
ajr al-mithl: fair wage.
akhaff al-ḍararayn: the lesser of two evils.
al-ʿilm al-ḍārr: harmful knowledge.
al-ʿilm al-mafrūḍ: obligatory knowledge.
al-ʿilm al-mubāḥ: optional knowledge.
al-ʿilm al-nāfiʿ: useful knowledge.
adab: discipline.
al-ajr al-musammā: agreed wages.
al-ajr: reward, payment.
al-bazzāz: cloth merchant.
al-birr: good deeds.
ḍarūriyyāh (pl. *ḍarūriyyāt*): essentials.
al-ḍarūriyāt al-khamsah: five essentials protected and advanced in Islam, namely, life, religion, property, intellect, and family.
al-dīn: religion.
al-fahm: understanding, comprehension.

al-halāk: destruction.
al-ḥikmah: wisdom.
al-ḥirāf al-danī'ah: lowly profession.
al-ijārah: lease and hire.
al-itqān: perfection.
al-jaṣṣāṣ: painter.
al-jihād al-mafrūḍ: required *jihād*.
al-maṣāliḥ al-asāsiyyah: basic or fundamental interest of people.
al-maṣāliḥ al-mursalah: consideration of public interest.
al-najash: false bidding sale.
al-qaffāl: locksmith.
al-qaṭṭān: cotton trader.
al-ṣabr: patience.
al-ṣadaqāt: charities.
al-samᶜ: hearing.
al-ṣāniᶜ: manufacturer.
al-siyāsah al-ᶜādilah: just policy.
al-takāful al-ijtimāᶜī: social support.
al-tasᶜīr: price control.
al-yaqīn: certitude.
amānah: trust.
amīn: trustee.
aqārib: blood relatives.
asbāb al-nuzūl: occasions of revelation.
asmā' al-rijāl: *ḥadīth* transmitters.
awqāf: charitable donations.
bayᶜah: pledge for allegiance.
bayt al-māl: public treasury.
birr al-wālidayn: being good to one's parents.
ḍamān: liability for loss.
Dār al-ᶜIlm: House of Knowledge.
ḍarūriyyāh (pl. *ḍarūriyyāt*): essential interests.
ḍawā'iᶜ: unclaimed assets.
dayn: debt.
dhaw al-arḥām: distant kindred.
dhihn: psyche, mind.
dīniyyāt: theological matters.
diyyah: blood money.
faḍīlah: praiseworthy.
farḍ ᶜalā al-dawlah: obligatory upon the state.
farḍ ᶜayn: personal obligation.

farḍ kifāyah: collective duty.
fāsid: irregular or voidable.
fatwā: legal opinion.
fuqarā': the poor, the indigent.
furūʿ: branches.
ghanīmah: war booty.
gharar: excessive uncertainty.
ghārimūn: the insolvent debtors.
ghaṣib: usurper.
ghulūl: cheater, swindler.
ḥaḍānah: child custody.
hadhyān: unnecessary expatiation.
ḥājiyyah: complementary.
ḥalāl: lawful.
ḥalaqah: mosque circle.
ḥaqq al-ʿamal: right to work.
ḥaqq al-ḍamān al-ijtimāʾi: right to social security.
ḥaqq al-taʿlīm: right to education.
ḥarām: forbidden, unlawful.
hawā: whimsical desire.
ḥifẓ: memorisation.
ḥisbah: lit. computation or checking, but commonly used in reference
    to what is known as *amr al-maʿrūf wa-nahy ʿan al-munkar*, that is,
    promotion of good and prevention of evil.
ḥudūd: prescribed punishments.
ḥukm: legal ruling, value.
hurriyat al-ʿamal: freedom of choosing one's own profession or work.
hurriyah al-ra'y: freedom of opinion.
iʿtibārāt shariʿiyyah: juridical valid considerations.
iʿtiqād: belief.
ihsān: beneficence, kindness.
ihtibās: retention, exclusive dedication.
ijārah fāsidah: defective contract of hire/lease.
ijmāʿ: general consensus.
ijtihād: lit. 'exertion', and technically the effort a jurist makes in order
    to deduce the law, which is not self evident, from its sources; legal
    reasoning.
ikhitiyār al-aṣlah: the choice of the fittest.
Ikhwān al-Ṣafā: the Brethren of Purity.
infāq: spending.
iqṭāʿ: land grant.

istiḥsān: juristic preference, to deem something good.

qiyās: analogical reasoning.

jihād: holy struggle.

jizyah: poll tax.

juhd: effort.

kaffrah (pl. *kaffārāt*): expiation.

kanz: treasure trove.

kasb: acquisition or gain.

khā'in: traitor.

kharāj: land tax.

khayyāt: tailor.

khilāfah: vicegerency.

khiyānah: betrayal of trust.

khiyār al-ʿayb: option of defect.

khiyār al-taḍmīn: option of guarantee.

kidhb: lying.

maʿdan: mineral find.

maʿrifat al-aṣlaḥ; identification of the fittest.

madhhab (pl. *madhāhib*): juristic/legal or theological school.

madhmūmah: reprehensible or blameworthy.

madrasah: religious school, college.

maḥmūdah: praiseworthy.

makrūh: reprehensible.

mandūb: recommendable.

manfaʿah: usufruct.

maqāsid al-Sharīʿah: Objectives of *Sharīʿah*.

masākīn (sing. *miskīn*): the needy.

maṣāliḥ al-nāss: people's welfare.

maṣāliḥ ḍarūriyyah: essential interests.

maṣāliḥ: benefits.

mawārid al-shubh: instances of doubt.

muḥtasib: market inspector.

mukāshafah: spiritual discovery and inner illumination.

muqallid: imitator.

murū'ah: personal dignity and decorum.

mutakallim: theologian.

nafaqah: maintenance.

naqliyyah: transmitted.

naṣīḥah: advice.

nisāb: quorum.

qaṭʿī: clear and unequivocal, decisive, free of speculative content.

qīmah al-mithl: equivalent price.
qirā'ah: reading or reciting.
ra'y: opinion.
rafʿ al-ḥaraj: removal of hardship.
ribā: usury.
rikāz: mineral tax.
ṣadaqat al-fiṭr: charity given at the end of fasting month of Ramaḍān.
shahīd: martyr.
sharaf: honor.
shaykh: master.
ṣilat al-raḥīm: ties of kinship.
sulṭān: ruler.
taʿabbud: devotional act.
taʿaddī: transgression.
taʿāwun: mutual cooperation.
tadlīs: concealment, misrepresentation.
tafsīr: interpretation.
taḥsiniyyāt: embellishment.
tājir: trader.
taklīf: juridical obligation, liability.
talaqqi al-rukbān: meeting the riders before arriving at the market place.
tamyīz: age of discernment.
taqwā: God-consciousness.
tasʿīr fi al-ʿamal: pricing of labor.
taṣawwuf: mysticism.
tashrīʿ zamanī: temporary legislation.
taṭawwuʿ: supererogatory.
tawḥīd: affirmation of oneness of Allāh.
tijārah: commerce, trading.
ujrah al-mithl: equivalent wage.
ulū al-amr: persons in authority and in charge of community affairs.
ʿulūm sharʿiyyah: juridical or transmitted knowledge.
ʿurf: custom.
ʿushr: Tithe.
uṣūl al-fiqh: sources of Islamic Law.
wahy: revelation.
wājib: obligatory.
wakīl: representative.
walī: guardian.
warāthah: successorship.

waṣiyyah wājibah: obligatory bequest.
wilāyah: guardianship.
zabbāl: rubbish collector.
zakāh: legal alms.
ẓannī: speculative, doubtful.
ẓulm: injustice, oppression.

Bibliography

ʿAbd al-Hādī. *Al-Fikrah al-Idāriyyah al-Islāmiyyah*.

Abū Dāwūd, *Sunan Abū Dawūd*. Muṣṭafā Dib al-Bugha (ed.). Damascus: Dār al-ʿUlum al-Insāniyyah, 1416/1995. I have also used the Eng. Trans. of this work by Ahmad Hasan, 3 vols. Lahore: Ashraf Press, 1984.

Abū ʿUbayd, al-Qāsim b. Salam, *Kitāb al-Amwāl*. Muḥammad Ḥamid al-Fāqī (ed.). Riyadh: Maṭbaʿah Muḥammad ʿAbd al-Laṭīf Ḥijāzī, 1353. Also see Eng. trans. of this work by Noor Muammad Giffari, *The Book of Finance*. Islamabad: Pakistan Hijra Council, 1411/1991.

Abū Yūsuf, Yaʿqūb b. Ibrāhīm, *Kitāb al-Kharāj*. 5th edn. Cairo: al-Maṭbaʿah al-Salafiyyah, 1396AH.

Abū Zahrah, Muḥammad, *Al-Mujtamaʿ al-Insānī fi Ẓill al-Islām*. 2nd edn. Jeddah : al-Dār al-Sauʿdiyyah li'l-Nashr wa'l-Tawzīʿ, 1401/1981.

———*Tanẓīm al-Islām li'l-Mujtamaʿ*. Cairo: Dār al-Fikr al-ʿArabī, 1385/1965.

Al-ʿAbūdī, Muḥsin, *Al-Ḥurriyyat al-Ijtimāʿiyyah Bayn al-Nuẓum al-Muāṣirah wa'l-Fikr al-Islāmī al-Siyāsī*. Cairo: Dār al-Nahdah al-ʿArabīyyah,1410/1990.

ʿAfīfī, Muṣṭafā, *al-Ḥuqūq al-Maʿnawiyyah li'l-Insān Bayn al-Naẓariyyah wa'l-Taṭbīq: Dirāsah Muqāranah fi'l-Nuẓum al-Waḍʿiyyah wa'l-Sharīʿah al-Islāmiyyah*. Cairo: Dār al-Fikr al-ʿArabī, 1990.

Ahmad, Fu'ād ʿAbd al-Munʿim, *Uṣūl Niẓām al-Ḥukm fi'l-Islām*. Alexandria (Egypt): Mu'assasah Shabāb al-Jāmiʿah, 1991/1411.

Ahmad, Mushtaq, *Business Ethics in Islam*. Herndon, Virginia: the International Institute of Islamic Thought, 1995.

Al-Ahwanī, Ahmad Fu'ād, *al-Tarbiyah fi'l-Islām*. Cairo; Dār al-Maʿārif bi-Miṣr, 1968.

Ali, Abdullah Yusuf, *The Holy Qur'an, Text, Translation and Commentary*. Jeddah: Islamic Education Centre, n.d.

Ali, Ausaf, *Islam, Science and Islamic Social Ethics*. Occasional Paper 24, Islamabad: Islamic Research institute, 1996.

Al-Ālim, Ḥāmid Yūsuf, *Al-Maqāṣid al-ʿĀmmah li'l-Sharīʿah al-Islāmiyyah*. 2nd edn. Jeddah & Herndon, Va: al-Maʿhad al-ʿĀlamī li'l-Fikr al-Islāmī, 1415/1994.

Al-Alūsī, Shihāb al-Dīn Maḥmūd, *Rūḥ al-Maʿāni fī Tafsīr al-Qur'ān al-ʿAẓīm*. Beirut: Dār Iḥyā' al-Turāth al-ʿArabī, n.d.

Asad, Muhammad, *The Message of the Qur'ān*. Gibraltar: Dār al-Andalus, 1980.

Ashraf, Ali, *New Horizons in Muslim Education*. Cambridge: Islamic Academy, 1982.

Azmeh, Aziz al, *Arabic Thought and Islamic Societies*. London: Croom Helm, 1986.

Badawī, Ismāʿīl, *Daʿāim al-Ḥukm fi'l-Sharīʿat al-Islāmiyyah wa'l-Nuẓum al-Dusturiyyah al-Muʿāṣirah*. Cairo: Dār al-Fikr al-ʿArabī, 1980/1400.

Al-Bājī, Abū al-Walīd Sulaymān b. Khallāf, *Al-Muntaqā Sharḥ Muwaṭṭā' Mālik*. Cairo: Maṭbaʿah al-Saʿādah, 1332AH.

Al-Bannā, Jamāl, *al-Islām wa'l-Ḥarakah al-Naqabiyyah*. 3rd edn. Cairo: Dār al-Fikr al-Islāmī, 1998.

Al-Bāqi, Muḥammad Fu'ad, ʿAbd, *al-Muʿjam al-Mufahras li-Alfāẓ al-Qur'ān al-Karīm*. 2nd edn. Cairo: Dār al-Fikr li-l-Ṭabāʿah wa'l-Nashr wa'l-Tawzīʿ, 1401/1981.

Bassiuni, Cherif M. (ed.), *The Islamic Criminal Justice System*. London & New York: Oceana Publications, 1982.

Al-Bayāti, Munīr Ḥāmid. *Al-Nizām al-Siyāsi al-Islāmī Muqārinan bi'l-Dawlah al-Qānuniyyah*. N.p. Dār al-Bashir li'l-Nashr wa'l-Tawzi', n.d.

Al-Buhutī. Manṣūr b. Yūnus al-Ḥanbalī, *Kashshāf al-Qinnāʿ ʿalā Matn al-Iqnā'*. Hilāl Muṣṭafā Hilāl (ed.). Beirut: Dār al-Fikr li'l-Ṭiba ʿāh wa'l-Nashr, 1402/1982.

Bukhārī, Muḥammad b. Ismāʿīl, *Saḥīḥ al-Bukhārī*. Eng. Trans. Muhammad Muhsin Khan. 9 vols. Lahore: Qazi Publications, 1979.

Chapra, Umar, *Islam and the Economic Challenge*. Leicester, U.K; The Islamic Foundation, 1412/1992

Cranstone, Maurice, *What are Human Rights?* London: The Bodley Head, 1977.

Al-Dārimī, Abū Muḥammad ʿAbd Allāh b. ʿAbd al-Raḥmān, *Sunan al-Dārimī*. 2 vols. Beirut, n.d.

Drooger, Andre, 'Cultural Relativism and Human Rights,' in an-Na'im. *Human Rights and Religious Values.*

Al-Dughmī, Muḥammad Rakan, *Al-Naẓariyyat al-Amn al-Ghadhā'i min Manẓūr al-Islāmī.* ʿAmmān (Jordan): Yutlab min al-Mu'allif, 1408/1988.

Dusūqī, Shams al-Dīn Muḥammad ʿArafah, *Ḥāshiyat al-Dusūqī ʿal Sharḥ al-Kabīr li-Abi Barakat Sidī Aḥmad al-Dardir.* Cairo: ʿĪsā al-Bābī al-Ḥalabī, n.d.

Al-Faruqi, Ismail, 'Is the Muslim Definable in Terms of His Economic Pursuits?' in Khurshid Ahmad and Zafar Ishaq Ansari (eds.). *Islamic Perspectives, Studies in Honour of Sayyid Abu'l A'la Mawdudi.* Leicester (UK): The Islamic Foundation, 1979/1399, 183–195.

Al-Ghazālī, Abū Hāmid Muḥammad, *Iḥyā' ʿUlūm al-Dīn.* Cairo: ʿĪsā al-Bābī al-Ḥalabī, 1957, with a commentary on it by Ḥāfiz Zayn al-Dīn al-ʿIrāqī entitled *al-Mughnī ʿan Ḥaml al-Asfār fi'l-Asfār fī Takhrīj mā fi'l-Iḥyā' min al-Akhbār.*

———*al-Iqtisād fi'l-I'tiqād.* Beirut: Dār al-Amānah, 1969.

———*Al-Mustasfā min ʿIlm al-Uṣūl.* Beirut: Dār Iḥyā' Turāth al-ʿArabī. N.d.

———*al-Risālah al-Laduniyyah: al-Jawāhir al-Ghazālī min Rasā'il al-Imām al-Ghazālī.* Cairo: Matbaʿah al-Saʿādah, 1934.

Al-Ghazālī, Muḥammad, *Ḥuqūq al-Insān Bayn Taʿlīm al-Islām wa I'lān al-Umam al-Muttaḥidah.* Alexandria (Egypt): Dār al-Daʿwah li'l-Nashr wa'l-Tawzīʿ, 1413/1993.

Al-Hādī, ʿAbd Ḥamdi Amīn, *Al-Fikr al-Idāriyyah al-Islāmiyyah wa'l-Muqāranah.* Cairo: Dār al-Fikr al-ʿArabī, 1976.

Hamidullah, Muhammad, *The Emergence of Islam.* Islamabad: Islamic Research Institute, 1991.

Ḥasan, Ibrāhīm Ḥasan & ʿAlī Ibrāhīm Ḥasan, *Al-Nuẓūm al-Islāmiyyah.* Cairo: Maktabah al-Nahdah al-Miṣriyyah, n.d.

———*Tārīkh al-Islām al-Siyāsī.* Cairo: Maktabah al-Tijāriyyah, 1961.

Hashmi, Sharafat Ali, 'Management of Waqf, Past and Present.' In *Islamic Research and Training Institute. Management and Development of Awqaf Properties.* Jeddah, 1407/1987, pp.19-27.

Hassan, Essam Mohammad (ed.), *Revitalisation of Political Thought Through Democracy and Human Rights, Islamism, Marxism and Arabism.* Cairo: Cairo Institute for Human Rights Studies, 1995.

Hassan, Husayn Hamid, *Right to Social Security in Islam.* Lahore: Shah Muhammad Ashraf, 1986.

Al-Haythamī, Nūr al-Dīn ʿAlī b. Abū Bakr b. Ḥajar, *Majmaʿ al-Zawā'id wa-Manbaʿ al-Fawā'id.* Cairo: Maktabat al-Quds, 1352AH.

Hepple, B. A. and M. H. Matthews, *Tort: Cases and Materials*. London: Butterworths, 1974.

Hitti, Phillip K., *History of the Arabs*. 10th edn. Basingstoke and London: Macmillan Press Ltd, 1970.

Al-Ḥuṣarī, Muḥammad, *Al-Dawlah wa Siyāsah al-Ḥukm fi'l-Fiqh al-Islāmī.*, 2nd vol. Cairo: Maktabah al-Kulliyat al-Azhariyyah, 1408/1988.

Huwaydī, Fahmī, *Ḥattā lā Takūna Fitnah*. Cairo & Beirut: Dār al-Shurūq, 1989.

Ibn ʿAbd al-Ḥakim, *Sirāt ʿUmar Ibn ʿAbd al-ʿAzīz*. Cairo: al-Maṭbaʿah al-Raḥmaniyyah, 1927.

Ibn ʿĀbidīn, Muḥammad Amīn, *Hāshīyah al-Radd al-Mukhtār ʿalā Durr al-Mukhtār* (known as *Hashīyah Ibn ʿĀbidīn*). Cairo: Dār al-Fikr, 1399/1979; and 2nd edn. Cairo: Maṭbaʿah al-Bābī al-Ḥalabī, 1386/1966.

Ibn al-Athīr, ʿAlī b. Aḥmad b. ʿAbd al Karīm, *Al-Bidāyah wa'l-Nihāyah fi'l-Tārīkh*. Cairo: Maṭbaʿah al-Sa'ādah, 1351/1933.

———*al-Kāmil fi'l-Tārīkh*. Cairo: Maṭbaʿah al-Shaykh Aḥmad al-Bābī al-Ḥalabī, 1303AH.

———*Tafsīr al-Qur'ān al-ʿAẓīm* (also known as *Tafsīr Ibn Kathīr*). Cairo: Dār al-Sha'b, 1393/1973.

Ibn Ḥanbal, Imām Aḥmad, *Musnad*. 6 vols. Cairo: al-Maṭbaʿah al-Munayminah, n.d.

Ibn Ḥazm, Muḥammad b. ʿAlī b. Aḥmad b. Saʿīd al-Ẓāhirī, *Al-Iḥkām fī Uṣūl al-Aḥkām*. Aḥmad Muḥammad Shākir (ed.). 4 vols. Beirut: Dār al-Afāq al-Jadīdah, 1400/1980.

———*Al-Muḥallā*. Aḥmad Muḥammad Shākir (ed.). Cairo: Maṭbaʿah al-Nahdah, 1347AH. Also Beirut edn. by Dār al-Kutub al-ʿIlmiyyah, 1408/1988.

Ibn Khaldūn, ʿAbd al-Raḥmān, *The Muqaddimah: An Introduction to History*. Eng. Tr. Franz Rosenthal. New York: Pantheons Books. 3 vols, 1958.

Ibn Mājah, Muḥammad b. Yazīd al-Qazwinī, *Sunan Ibn Mājah*. Istanbul: Cagli Yayinlari, 1401/1981.

Ibn Nujaym, Zayn a-Dīn, *Al-Ashbāh wa'l-Naẓā'ir ʿAlā Madhhab Imām Abī Ḥanīfah al-Nuʿmān*. ʿAbd al-ʿAzīz al-Wakīl (ed.). Cairo: Mu'assasah al-Ḥalabī wa shurakā'uh li'l-Nashr wa'l-Tawzīʿ, 1387/1968.

Ibn Qudāmah, Muwaffaq al-Dīn Abū Muḥammad ʿAbd Allāh, *Al-Mughnī*. 12 vols. Cairo: Maṭbaʿah al-Manār, 1367AH.

Ibn Rushd Abū l-Walīd Muḥammad b. Aḥad, *Bidāyat al-Mujtahid wa Nihāyat al-Muqtaṣid*. Cairo: Muṣṭafā al-Bābī al-Ḥalabī, 1401/1981.

Ibn Saʿd, Muḥammad b. Mani', *Al-Ṭabaqāt al-Kubrā*. Beirut: Dār al-Ṣādir, 1398/1978.

Ibn Saḥnūn, Muḥammad, *Adāb al-Muʿallimīn (mimmā dawwanā Muḥammad Ibn Saḥnūn ʿan Abīhi)*. Ḥasan Ḥusnī ʿAbd al-Wahhāb (ed.). Tunis, 1348, appearing in appendices of al-Ahwānī, *al-Tarbiyyah* pp. 351-371.

Ibn Sīnā, *Risālah fī Riyādat al-Subyān*. Appears in appendix to al-Ahwānī, *al-Tarbiyyah*, p. 158f.

Ibn Taymiyyah, Tāqī al-Dīn Aḥmad, *Al-Hisbah fi'l-Islām*. Cairo: al-Maṭbaʿah al-Salafiyyah, 1387AH.

——*Majmūʿ Fatāwā Shaykh al-Islām Aḥmad Ibn Taymiyyah*. 2nd edn., Muḥammad ʿAbd al-Raḥmān b. Qāsim (ed.). Riyādh: Dār al-Buhūth al-ʿIlmiyyah, 1398AH.

——*al-Siyāsat al-Sharʿiyyah fī Iṣlāh al-Rā'ī wa'l-Ra'iyyah*. ʿAbd al-Rahman b. Qāsim (ed.). Beirut: Mu'assasah al-Risālah, 1398AH.

al-ʿĪlī, ʿAbd al-Hakim Ḥasan, *Al-Ḥurriyat al-ʿĀmmah fi'l-Fikr wa'l-Niẓām al-Siyāsī al-Islāmī*. Kuwait: Dār al-Kitāb al-Ḥadīth, 1983/1413.

Imtiazi, I. A., 'Management of Zakah' in *Modern Muslim Society*. Jeddah, Islamic Research and Training Institute, Islamic Development Bank, 1989.

Iqbal, Muḥammad, *The Reconstruction of Religious Thought in Islam*. Lahore: Shah Muhammad Ashraf. Reprint 1982.

Iqbal, Munawar, *Distributive Justice and Need Fulfilment in an Islamic Economy*. Islamabad: International Institute of Islamic Economics, n.d.

Islahi, Abdul Azim, *Economic Concepts of Ibn Taymiyya*. Leicester, UK: The Islamic Foundation, 1996/1417.

Islamic Fiqh Academy (India), *Important Fiqh Decisions*. New Delhi, 2001.

Al-Jarīshah, ʿAlī Muḥammad, *Iʿlān al-Dustūr al-Islāmī*. Al-Manṣūr (Egypt): Dār al-Wafā li'l-Ṭabāʿah wa'l-Nashr, 1405/1985.

Al-Jawziyyah, Ibn Qayyim, *I'lām al-Muwaqqiʿīn ʿan Rabb al-ʿĀlamīn*. Muḥammad Munīr al-Dimashqī (ed.). Cairo: Idārat al-Ṭibāʿah al-Muniriyyah, n.d. Also Cairo: Maktabah al-Kulliyat al-Azhariyyah, 1968.

——*Al-Ṭuruq al-Ḥukmiyyah fi'l-Siyāsat al-Sharʿiyyah*. Muḥammad Jamīl Ghāzī (ed.). Jeddah: Maṭbaʿah al-Madanī, n.d. I have also used the Cairo edn. By al-Mu'assasah al-ʿArabīyyah, 1380/1961.

——*Zād al-Maʿād fī Hudā Khayr al-ʿIbād*. Makkah: Maṭbaʿah al-Makkiyyah, n.d.

Al-Jazāʾirī, Abū Bakr, *Al-Dustūr al-Islāmī*. 2nd edn. Beirut: al-Maktab al-Islāmī, 1391AH.

Al-Jazirī, ʿAbd al-Raḥman, *Kitāb al-Fiqh ʿAlā al-Madhāhib al-Arbaʿah*. Beirut: Dār al-Fikr liʾl-Ṭabaʿah waʾl-Nashr, 1392AH.

Kamali, M. H., *The Dignity of Man: An Islamic Perspective*. Cambridge: Islamic Texts Society, 2002.

——*Equity and Fairness in Islam*. Cambridge: Islamic Texts Society, 2005.

——*Freedom of Expression in Islam*. Cambridge: Islamic Texts Society, 1997 & Kuala Lumpur: Ilmiah Publishers, 1998.

——*Islamic Law in Malaysia: Issues and Developments*. Kuala Lumpur: Ilmiah Publishers, 2000.

——ʿThe Limits of Power in an Islamic State.ʾ *Islamic Studies* 28 (1989), 323-353.

——*Principles of Islamic Jurisprudence*. Cambridge: the Islamic Texts Society, 1991; Kuala Lumpur: Ilmiah Publishers, 1998.

——*Punishment in Islamic Law: An Inquiry into the Hudud Bill of Kelantan*. Kuala Lumpur: Ilmiah Publishers, 2000.

——ʿSiyasah Sharʾiyyah or the Policies of Islamic Government.ʾ *American Journal of Islamic Social Sciences* 6 (1989), 59-81.

——ʿTasʿīr or Price Control in Islamic Law.ʾ *The American Journal of Islamic Social Sciences* 11 (1994), 25-38.

Al-Kāsānī, ʿAlā al-Dīn, *Badāʾiʿ al-Ṣanāʾiʿ fī Tartīb al-Sharāʾiʿ*. Cairo: Maṭbaʿah al-Istiqāmah, 1956.

Kubrā Zādah, Aḥmad b. Muṣṭafā Ṭāsh, *Miftāḥ al-Saʿādah wa-Miṣbāḥ al-Siyādah*, Kāmil Bakrī & ʿAbd al-Wahhāb Abū al-Nūr (eds.). Hyderabad (Dakan, India): 1968.

Mahmaṣṣānī, Ṣubḥī Rajab, *Arkān Ḥuqūq al-Insān fiʾl-Islām*. Beirut: Dār al-ʿIlm liʾl-Malāyīn, 1979.

Al-Manāwī, ʿAbd al-Raʾūf, *Fayz al-Qair Sharḥ al-Jāmiʿ al-Ṣaghīr li al-Suyūṭī*. Cairo: al-Maktabah al-Tijāriyyah al-Kubrā, 1356/1938.

Al-Māwardī, Abūʾl-Ḥasan, *Kitāb al-Aḥkām al-Sulṭāniyyah*. 2nd edn. Cairo: Muṣṭafā al-Bābī al-Ḥalabī, 1386AH.

——*Mawsūʿah al-Mafāhim al-Islāmiyyah al-ʿĀmmah*. Maḥmūd Ḥamdi Zaqzūq (ed.). Cairo: Wizārat al-Awqāf waʾl-Shuʾūn al-Islāmiyyah, 1421/2000.

Al-Mubārak, Muḥammad, *Niẓām al-Islām al-Iqtisādī: Mabādi wa Qawāʿid ʿAmmah*. Beirut: Dār al-Fikr, 1972.

Al-Mundhirī, Zakī al-Dīn ʿAbd al-ʿAẓīm, *Al-Targhīb wa'l-Tarhīb*. Cairo: Muṣṭafā al-Bābī al-Ḥalabī, 1373/1954.

Al-Muṣaylihī, Muḥammad al-Ḥusaynī, *Ḥuqūq al-Insān Bayn al-Sharīʿah al-Islāmiyyah wa'l-Qānun al-Duwalī*. Cairo: Dār al-Nahdah al-ʿArabīyyah, 1988.

Muslim, Ibn Ḥajjāj al-Nīshāpūrī, *Mukhtaṣar Ṣaḥīḥ Muslim*. Muḥammad Nāṣir al-Dīn al-Albānī (ed.). 2nd edn. Beirut: Dār al-Maktab al-Islāmī, 1404/1984.

Al-Nabhān, Muḥammad Fāruq, *Niẓām al-Ḥukm fi'l-Islām*. Kuwait: Jāmiʿat al-Kuwait, 1974.

Al-Nabhānī , Shaykh Taqī al-Dīn, *Muqaddimāt al-Dustūr*. Kuwait, n.p., 1964.

Al-Nabhānī, al-Shaykh Yūsuf, *Al-Fatḥ al-Kabīr fi Damm al-Ziyādat al-Jāmiʿ al-Ṣaghīr li al-Suyūṭī*. Cairo: Maṭbaʿah ʿĪsā al-Bābī al-Ḥalabī, 1350AH.

Al-Nasāʾī, Abū ʿAbd al-Raḥmān ibn Shuʿayb, *Sunan al-Nasāʾī*, 6 vols. Cairo, 1964.

Nasr, Seyyed Hossein, *Science and Civilisation in Islam*. Cambridge (UK), Islamic Texts Society, 1987.

Al-Nawawī, Yaḥyā b. Sharaf, *Majmūʿ Sharḥ al-Muhadhdhab*. Beirut & Damascus: Dār al-Fikr, n.d.

——*Minhāj al-Ṭālibīn wa ʿUmdat al-Muftīn*. Cairo: Dār Iḥyāʾ al-Kutub al-ʿArabiyyah, 1343AH.

——*Rawḍat al-Ṭālibīn*. Beirut: al-Maktab al-Islāmī, 1395/1975.

——*Riyāḍ al-Ṣaliḥīn*. 2nd edn. by Muḥammad Nāṣir al-Dīn al-Albānī. Beirut: Dār al-Maktab al-Islāmī, 1404/1984.

An-Naʾim, Abdullahi, Jerald Gort et al. (eds.), *Human Rights and Religious Values*. Michigan: Grand Rapids: Wm. B. Eardmans Publishing Co., 1995.

Al-Niʿmah, Ibrāhīm, *al-ʿAmāl wa'l-ʿUmmāl fi'l-Fikr al-Islāmī*. Jeddah: al-Dār al-Saʿudiyyah li'l-Nashr wa'l-Tawziʿ, 1405/1985.

Peerzade, Syed Afzal (edr.), *Readings in Islamic Fiscal Policy*. Delhi: Adam Publishers, 1996.

——'Place of an Expenditure Tax in the Islamic Fiscal System.' *Journal of Islamic Economics*. King Abdulaziz University, vol. 11 (1419/1999), 29-63.2.

Al-Qābisī, Abū 'l-Ḥasan ʿAlī, *Al-Risālah al-Mufaṣṣalah li-Aḥwāl al-Muʿallimīn wa-Aḥkām al-Muʿallimīn wa'l-Mutaʿallimīn*. Appears in appendix to al-Ahwānī, *al-Tarbiyyah*.

Qāḍīkhān al-Farghānī, *Fatāwā Qāḍī Khān*. Appears on ʿUlamāʾ of India, *al-Fatāwa al-ʿAlamgiriyyah*.

Qala‘jī, Muḥammad Rawās, *al-Ihtirāf wa-Athāruhu fi'l-Fiqh al-Islā-mī*. Jeddah: al-Markāz al-‘Alāmī li-Abhāth al-Iqtiṣād al-Islāmī, 1404/1984.

Al-Qaraḍāwi, Yūsuf, *Al-‘Aql wa'l-‘Ilm fi'l-Qur'ān al-Karīm*. Cairo: Maktabah Wahbah, 1416/1996.

——*Al-Khaṣā'is al-‘Ammah li'l-Islām*. Cairo: Maktabah Wahbah, 1409/1989.

——*Fī Fiqh al-Awlawiyyāt: Darāsah Jadīdah fī Daw' al-Qur'ān wa'l-Sunnah*. 2nd edn. Cairo: Maktabah Wahbah, 1416/1996.

——*Fiqh al-Zakāh*. 2 vols. Beirut: Dār al-Irshād, 1969.

——*Min Fiqh al-Dawlah fil-Islām*. Cairo: Dār al-Shuruq, 1417/1997.

Al-Qurshī, Muḥammad ibn Aḥmad, *Ma‘ālim al-Qurba fi Aḥkām al-Ḥisbah*. Cambridge edn., Maṭba‘ah Dār al-Funun, 1937.

Al-Qurṭubī, Abū ‘Abd Allāh Muḥammad, *Al-Jāmi‘ li-Aḥkām al-Qur'ān* (known as *Tafsīr al-Qurṭubī*). Cairo: Maṭba‘ah Dār al-Kutub, 1387/1967.

Quṭb, Muḥammad, 'Islam and the Crisis of Modern Mind.' In Khurshid Ahmad (ed.) *Islam, Its Meaning and Message*, pp. 243–259.

Quṭb, Sayyid, *Al-‘Adālat al-Ijtimā‘iyyah fi'l-Islām*. 4th edn. Cairo: ‘Isā al-Bābī al-Ḥalabī, 1373/1954.

Rabbih, Aḥmad Ibn ‘Abd, *Al-‘Aqd al-Farīd li'l-Mālik al-Sa‘īd*. Cairo, 1346/1948.

Al-Ṣadr, Muḥammad Bāqir, *Iqtisādunā*. 3rd edn. Beirut: Dār al-Ta‘āruf, 1400/1980.

Al-Ṣan‘ānī, Muḥammad b. Ismā‘īl al-Kahlanī (known as al-Amīr, d. 1182AH). *Subul as-Salām Sarḥ Bulūgh al-Marām min Jam‘ Adillat al-Aḥkām*. 4th Edn. Cairo: Muṣṭafā al-Bābī al-Ḥalabī, 1379/1960.

Al-Sarakhsī, Shams al-Dīn, *Al-Mabsūṭ*. 32 vols. Beirut: Dār al-Ma‘rifah, 1406/1986.

Al-Sayed, Abdul Malik, *Social Ethics of Islam: Classical Islamic Arabic Political Theory and Practice*. New York: Wantage Press, 1982.

Shaḥrūr, Muḥammad, *Naḥw Uṣūl Jadīdah li'l-Fiqh al-Islāmī: Fiqh al-Mar'ah*. Damascus: al-Ahāli li'l-Ṭibā‘ah wa'l-Tawzī‘ wa'l-Nashr, 2000.

Shaltūt, Maḥmūd, *Al-Islām ‘Aqīdah wa Sharī‘ah*. Kuwait: Maṭābi‘ Dār al-Qalam, c. 1965.

——'Manhaj al-Qur'ān al-Qur'ān fī Bayān al-Aḥkām,' in ed. Muḥammad Tawfiq ‘Uwaydah, *Al-Fiqh al-Islāmī Asas al-Tashri‘*. Cairo: al-Majlis al-‘Alā li al-Shu'ūn al-Islāmiyyah, 1391/1971.

——*al- Fatāwā*. Cairo: Maṭābi‘ Dār al-Qalam, n.d.

Al-Shāṭibī, Abū Isḥāq Ibrāhīm, *Al-Iʿtiṣām*. Cairo: Maṭbaʿah al-Manār, 1332/1914. Also Beirut: Dār al-Maʿrifah, 1402AH.

——*Al-Muwāfaqāt fī Uṣūl al-Sharīʿah*. Shaykh ʿAbd Allāh Dirāz (ed.). Cairo: al-Maktabah al-Tijāriyyah al-Kubrā, n.d.

Al-Shawāribī, ʿAbd al-Ḥāmid, *al-Ḥuqūq al-Siyāsiyyah li'l-Mar'ah fi'l-Islām*. Alexandria, Egypt: Mansha'ah Maʿārif, 1987.

Al-Shāwī, Tawfīq, *al-Mawsūʿah al-ʿAṣriyyah* (see under ʿAwdah).

Al-Shawkānī, Yaḥyā b. ʿAlī, *Nayl al-Awṭār Sharḥ Muntaqā al-Akhbār*. Cairo: Muṣṭafā al-Bābī al-Ḥalabī, n.d.

Al-Shaybānī, Muḥammad b. Ḥasan, *al-Iktisāb fi'l-Rizq al-Mustatab*. Muḥammad b. Sama'a (ed.). Cairo: Maktabah Nashr al-Thaqāfah al-Islāmiyyah, 1357AH.

Shīshānī, ʿAbd al-Wahhāb ʿAbd al-ʿAzīz, *Ḥuqūq al-Insān wa-Ḥurriyyatuh al-Asāsiyah fi'l-Niẓām al-Islāmī wa'l-Nuẓūm al-Mu'āsirah*. ʿAmmān: Maṭābiʿ al-Jāmʿiyyah al-Malakiyyah, 1400/1980.

Al-Sibāʿī, Muṣṭafā, *Ishtirakiyyāt al-Islām*. Damascus: al-Dār al-Qawmiyyah li'l-Ṭibāʿah wa'l-Nashr, 1379/1960.

——*al-Takāful al-Ijtimāʿī fi'l-Islām*. Beirut: al-Maktab al-Islāmī, 1419/1998.

Siddiqui, Abia Afsar, 'Abortion and Euthanasia.' In *Essays in Islam*, pp. 182–194 (cf. entry under Islam).

Siddiqui, Mazheruddin, *Modern Reformist Thought in the Muslim World*. Islamabad: Islamic Research Institute, 1402/1982.

Siddiqi, Muhammad Nijatullah, *The Role of State in the Economy: An Islamic Perspective*. Leicester (UK): The Islamic Foundation, 1996.

Soroush, Abdolkarim, *Reason, Freedom and Democracy in Islam, Essential Writing of Abdolkarim Soroush*. Tr. & ed. Mahmud Sadri & Ahmad Sadri, Oxford & New York: O.U.P., 2000.

Al-Sulamī, ʿIzz al-Dīn ʿAbd al-Salām, *Qawāʿid al-Aḥkām fī Maṣāliḥ al-Anām*. Beirut: Mu'assasah al-Rayyān li'l-Ṭibāʿah wa'l-Nashr, 1410/1990. Also Cairo: Maṭbaʿah al-Ḥusayniyyah, 1934.

Al-Suyūṭī, Jalāl al-Dīn, *Al-Jāmiʿ al-Ṣaghīr*, 4th edn. Cairo: Muṣṭafā al-Bābī al-Ḥalabī, 1954.

Al-Ṭabarī, Abū Jaʿfar Muḥammad Ibn Jarīr. *Tārīkh al-Umam wa'l-Mulūk*. Cairo: al-Maṭbaʿah al-Tijāriyyah, 1358/1939.

Al-Tabrīzī, ʿAbd Allāh al-Khatib, *Mishkāt al-Maṣābiḥ*. Muḥammad Nāṣir al-Dīn al-Albānī (ed.). 2nd ed. Beirut: al-Maktab al-Islāmī, 1399/1977.

Tirmidhī, Abū ʿĪsā Muḥammad, *Sunan al-Tirmidhī*. 3 vols. Beirut: Dār al-Fikr, 1400/1980.

Torrey, Charles, *The Commercial and Theological Terms in the Koran.* Leiden: E. J. Brill, 1982.

'Ulamā' of India, *Al-Fatāwa al-Hindiyyah* (also known as al-Fatāwā al-ʿAlamgiriyya). 6 vols. Cairo: al-Maṭbaʿah al-Munayminah, 1323AH.

Wāfī, ʿAbd al-Wāḥid, *Ḥuqūq al-Insān fi'l-Islām*, Cairo: Maṭbaʿah al-Risālah, n.d.

Yasif, Muhammad, 'al-Ḥaqq al-ʿIlmī fi'l-Islām.' in Muḥammad Yasif (edr.) *Niẓām al-Ḥuqūq fi'l-Islām.* Rabāt: al-Matbūʿat al-Akadimiyyah, 1990.

Zaman, Hasanuz S. M., *Economic Functions of an Islamic State: The Early Experience.* Leicester: The Islamic Foundation, 1991/1411.

Al-Zarqā, Anas, 'Islamic Distributive Schemes.' In Munawar Iqbal (ed.), *Distributive Justice and Need Fulfilment in an Islamic Economy.* Islamabad: International Institute of Islamic Economics, n.d.

Zuḥaylī, Muḥammad, *Ḥuqūq al-Insān fi'l-Islām: Dirāsah Muqārinah maʿ al-Iʿlān al-ʿĀlamī wa'l-Iʿlān al-Islāmī li-Ḥuqūq al-Insān.* 2nd edn. Damascus & Beirut: Dār Ibn Kathīr, 1418/1997.

Zuḥaylī, Wahbah, *Al-Fiqh al-Islāmī wa ʿAdillatuhuh.* 8 vols. 3rd edn. Damascus: Dār al-Fikr, 1409/1989.

——*al-Ḥaqq al-Ḥurriyah fi'l-ʿĀlam.* Damascus: Dār al-Fikr al-Muʿāṣir, 1421/2000.

List of Periodicals

All E R (All England Law Reports)

MLJ (Malayan Law Journal)

Index

ʿilm al-mubāḥ, see knowledge, optional

al-ʿilm al-nāfiʿ (uscful knowledge), 36

ʿilm al-riwāyah, see knowledge, transmitted

īmān, 20, 24, 96, 99

Indonesia, 86

industry: basic industries to be sustained, 114, 176

inheritance, 228ff purpose, 229; women's share, 229

Iqbal, Muhammad, 30, 76

irhāq (suffocation), 49

Islamic epistemology, 17, 82; and history, 30; and nature, 30; and sources of learning, 29; and unity, 18, 31; classification of knowledge, 35, 38, 39ff; development, 30; Ghazālī, 38; Ibn Khaldūn, 38; Iqbal on, 30; sources of learning, 29; utilitarian view of knowledge, 36

istiḥsān, 10, 69, 230, 231

iʿtibārāt sharʿiyyah, 121

iʿtiqād (belief), 32

Jews, 23, 64, 124, 234, 237, 251, 257

jihād, 33, 43, 106, 115, 123, 127, 157, 215; collective obligation, 115; *al-mafrūd*, 60; work as, 106

jizyah, 245, 257; under modern law, 246

journalism, 58

kaffārah (expiation), 14, 190, 191, 247ff; meaning, 248; pursuit of knowledge as, 26

kalam, see theology

kanz (treasure trove), 247

al-Kāsānī, ʿAlā al-Dīn, 144, 149, 157, 162, 164, 165, 215, 225, 227, 257

al-kasb (earning a living), 97, 98, 100, 101, 107

Khan, Sayyid Ahmad, 87

kharāj, 245, 246, 257

Kharijites, 27

khilāfah: Qurʾān on, 102

knowledge: and action, 38; and passion, 78; and worldly gains, 51; as light, 20, 25, 50; based on insight, 28; beneficial, 36; collective obligation, 35; destructive, 22; dichotomy, 17, 88; al-Shāṭibī, 34; dissemination of, 25, 26, 44, 59, 63, 67, 87; harmful, 37; hierarchy of, 50, 67; holistic view, 17, 33, 36, 38–40, 88; juridical and non-juridical, 38; obligatory, 31, 33, 60; of life and creation, 39; optional, 31; practical, 32; praiseworthy, 35; prejudicial, 68; pursuit of, 4, 22, 25–27, 31, 34, 36, 45, 51, 57, 58, 60, 62, 66, 67, 81, 240; as devotion, 67; by women, 60, 61, 63; in China, 60; Qurʾān-centred, 17; Qurʾānic concept, 74; rational, 28, 35, 38, 72, 74, 75, 79, 81, 85; reprehensible, 35; sacred character, 19, 20; sharing as a religious duty, 58; superior to wealth, 27; through the senses, 76; transmitted, 28, 35, 38, 77; useful, 36; *see also* science

Kubrazada, Tāsh, 45

Kufa, 65

labour market, 1, 158, 177

language, 35, 63; Arabic, 38, 41, 49, 54, 55, 65, 96; Assyrian, 27; at al-Azhar, 73; foreign, 27; national, 55; of the Prophets, 51; Qurʾānic, 4

ences among jurists, 225–228; entitlement, 226ff; Ḥanbalīs on, 225; male responsibility, 229; medical treatment, 225; students, 227

nahḍah (awakening), 86

naqliyyah sciences, *see* knowledge, transmitted

naṣīḥah, 51, 73, 135; in commerce, 136

Nasr, S. H., 83

al-Nawawī, Imām: on manual labour, 120

niṣāb, *see zakāh*, quorum

Nīshāpūr, 65

Niẓām al-Mulk, 64

Niẓāmiyyah, 64

orphans, 12, 44, 47, 124, 152, 196, 197, 222, 234, 250, 258

Ottomans, 2

parents: support, 221, 224

passion, *see hawā*

pensions: ʿĀʾishah as recipient, 206; allocated on merit, 206, 207

Pharaoh, 80

philosophy, 22, 30, 31, 38, 64, 65, 76

physics, 34, 64, 93

Plato, 30

positivism, 82, 85

poverty: defined by Nawawī, 215; eradication, 209; eradication of, 2, 40, 209, 247, 249

pragmatism, 38

price control, 159

propedeutics, 65

The Prophet, Muḥammad, 2, 19–21, 23–27, 33, 37, 38, 43, 47, 51, 52, 57, 59, 61, 62, 67, 71, 77, 79, 100, 103–105, 107, 108, 110–112, 114, 115, 117, 118, 124–126, 129–132, 134–136, 138, 139, 142, 146, 149–152, 168, 169, 171, 172, 191, 192, 195–201, 203, 205–208, 213, 215, 217, 219, 222, 224, 233, 235–237, 242, 244, 251, 252

prostitution, 118

psychology, 82, 93

public interest, *see maṣlaḥah*

public treasury: *see also bayt al-māl*

public welfare: history of in Islam, 203

punishment, *see ḥudūd*

al-Qābisī, Abu'l Ḥasan ʿAlī b. Muḥammad, 45, 46, 49, 53, 90, 146; on children's education, 46; on education, 43–45; on punishment, 46–48

al-Qaraḍāwī, Yūsuf: on welfare work, 117; on work as obligation, 107

Qarawiyīn, Fez, 65

qiyās, 69, 230

Quṭb, Muḥammad, 84

Qur'ān: and freedom of expression, 71; and gender equality, 61; and science, 70; decisive or speculative text, 69; ideal of justice, 69; interpretation, 69; on dignity, 192; on equal rights to education, 61; on marriage, 221; on natural resources, 102, 110, 147; on trading and commerce, 110; on workers, 127; orthography, 54; teaching to read, 20, 27, 29, 43–45, 49, 53–55, 86, 91, 133, 157

Quṭb, Sayyid, 216

Ramaḍān, 12, 116; and *kaffārah*, 14, 248; exemptions, 219; *ṣadaqat al-fiṭr*, 232, 242

rationality, 18, 22, 74, 84ff

ra'y, 18, 72; *see also* freedom